The Way Things Were

A Backstreet Boyhood

Denis Cassidy

FOREWORD BY
Sir Bobby Robson

SUTTON PUBLISHING

First published in 2005 by
Sutton Publishing Limited · Phoenix Mill
Thrupp · Stroud · Gloucestershire · GL5 2BU

British Library Cataloguing in Publication Data
A catalogue record for this book is available from the British Library.

ISBN 0-7509-4037-9

*This book is dedicated to
my mother
Barbara Cassidy
(née Curry), 1889–1973*

Typeset in 11/14pt Garamond.
Typesetting and origination by
Sutton Publishing Limited.
Printed and bound in England by
J.H. Haynes & Co. Ltd, Sparkford.

CONTENTS

FOREWORD

Denis and I share so much common ground. We were both born in February 1933, are both Geordies and have had a passionate love of football from an early age. His landmarks in this record of everyday life between 1933 and 1952 are much the same as mine, such as when we went to school for the first time, when we were evacuated, when the war ended and when we started work. There were some differences, though, because Denis lived in the centre of Newcastle while I lived in a small mining community in County Durham, but the place names and the surroundings are less important than the activities, the neighbours and our shared way of life that were so similar and are so well captured.

Reading this book brought back many happy memories almost as if it was my life I was revisiting. Anyone who was born before 1950 will remember the kind of games that we all played, particularly those in back lanes, back streets and in local parks. Our entertainment was homemade in those days before television, and for most boys like us falling in love with football and cricket was almost inevitable. But this is about more than childhood games. At a time when life was hard for most people it recalls the joy of important family occasions, as well as the struggles of parents bringing up a family.

This book is, as I always like to be, optimistic and somewhere in the world children less able to afford a football and the replica strips that British children take for granted today will no doubt be getting the same joy from a tennis ball, or even something simpler, just as once we did! The sheer enjoyment that people, young and old, derived in spite of often difficult lives shines throughout this book.

Howay the lads.

Sir Bobby Robson
June 2005

PROLOGUE

Although this book is written chronologically and is about the people I knew and the way we all lived in the twenty years from my birth in 1933 to the early 1950s, it is not an autobiography. The core is autobiographical because most of the events, the circumstances of my life and their context that I have described are as I saw them; yet my prime purpose is to describe not only my life, but also a way of life experienced by millions of British people during the same period. It was a way of life that had endured for over a hundred years and which appeared to be so embedded and slow to respond to pressure for change that few of those who experienced it would have believed that it could be swept away in less than a generation.

Much of that way of life was unhygienic, hazardous, unequal and uncertain. It was – as it had been, with little change, since the early nineteenth century when my great-grandfather was born – a society in which to have some modest wealth and a regular income guaranteed a disproportionately attractive way of life. To have neither of these benefits condemned most people to an uncertain life bereft of opportunity and offering little hope of ever breaking out of the cycle.

For the majority it was a world in which possessions were few and housing conditions were simple, frequently unhygienic and sometimes squalid and dangerous. For all who were employed in manual labour, conditions in the workplace were dangerous to a point where they virtually guaranteed a short life.

As I look back, our living conditions – which I knew at the time were unattractive – were the same as those endured by the majority of families; in that way, if in no other, we as a family were certainly not discriminated against. We had been born by our parents' choice and – as both their own parents before them – into a large family, supported in the traditional way principally by an income-generating husband and head of the household. It meant there would be few opportunities outside the home for collective leisure, and little or no financial scope to take advantage of them if they occurred.

I am certain that neither of my parents had illusions about the probable course of their life when they married in 1916 and began raising a large family. Throughout their lives I was at first aware of, increasingly influenced by and finally grateful, for not only the selfless way in which they devoted themselves to creating as many opportunities as they could for the enrichment of our lives, but also the pleasure they took in whatever benefits we enjoyed from their dedication. There was never any bitterness, regret or remorse that opportunities they created for us had not been available to them. Neither was there any attempt to pursue any frustrated ambitions through us.

In describing 'the way things were', there is a danger that the material framework I have re-created to describe and explain the context of the way in which we lived will dominate the narrative to the diminution of the human dimension. I hope it does not, for it was the patient creation of values which was the main bulwark of protection for the family against the harsh environment. That is the central theme I have tried to convey.

I cannot and will not argue that my parents, or the rest of my family, were unique in this dedicated pursuit of values and learning. But by observation I found that they were rare, and however financially deprived we were – and most of us were exposed to a deeper understanding of life's material inequalities when attending grammar school – we saw neither resentment nor despair, nor did we hear tirades against inequities inherited by birth into an urban, working-class community.

But much more than that, I hope that what emerges is the genuine feeling of optimism that ensured we didn't only 'get by' through thrift and discipline, but that everyday life was on the whole made fun by a positive determination to ignore, or at least not worry too much about, those things which were beyond our control.

Anyone who was born between the two great wars, particularly in a similar urban, working-class environment, will identify with some – probably most – of the circumstances I describe. All those who lived through the Second World War will know what a remarkable experience it was; but few of them would have believed that social and economic change would happen so dramatically from the mid-1950s onwards. The history of the nineteenth and twentieth centuries up to that point gave no such clue. Had not the battle-weary troops coming home after the horrors of trench life during the First World War believed that change was inevitable? That after their suffering, and with the promise that they would 'return to a land fit for heroes', their lives would improve? My mother and father, born as they were in 1889 and 1892 respectively, and married in 1916, experienced the swift restoration of the old order and the painful manifestation of global economic recession – mass unemployment and widespread poverty after 1918. Between the wars the primary objective was to hold on to whatever job you could get, particularly for a married man with a young family; the hopelessness and indignity of the unemployed men around them became a powerful incentive for most working men to make the best of what they had, however inadequate it was. It was difficult for them to believe that anything would happen to change this way of life; after all, it was simply 'the way things were'.

What would have happened had the Second World War never taken place?

Any change a decade and more after the war came too late to influence my parents' lives: certainly my father's. He died in 1958, one year after he retired, earning £10 per week and receiving the statutory clock and a small pension which ceased upon his death.

It is true that the foundations for the massive changes that followed were laid by Attlee's Labour government, which came to power in 1945 and which did then implement many of the changes promised in the Beveridge Report of 1944.

But governments don't change society as much as they would like to think they do. Today's society was shaped by more prosaic agents. In the 1950s UK households began to acquire material possessions, including television sets, so rapidly that by the end of the decade most households had at least one set. By the 1960s increasing affluence was being enjoyed by most working families, who 'had never had it so good', on a scale undreamt of when I was born in 1933. The first to exploit this new-found wealth were the 'baby boomers' of the immediate postwar years. The combination of television and increasing affluence led to a widening of horizons, encouraged and enhanced by travel abroad through package holidays; thus the three key agents for social change had been established. Put simply, they were: more money, universal television, and packaged Mediterranean holidays. Widespread, yet by no means universal, affluence had granted most people the greatest of all freedoms: choice. How we as a nation have exercised this freedom since has resulted in many casualties, principally in the decline of values which historically bonded together individuals, families and working-class communities. Meanwhile, those excluded from this new-found affluence – the unemployed, the sick, the elderly, the homeless – seem to have become more obviously marginalised than ever before.

What few people – dare I say no one? – would have predicted in 1933, as Hitler came to power, was that there would be such a widespread rejection of the social attitudes and mores that were held sacrosanct by the world into which I was born, and where I was educated and formed. Certainly had it not been for the egalitarianism and meritocracy which began emerging in the 1950s, my life would probably have been little different from my father's.

Yet it appears that the yearning, then frustrated, for freedom and greater choice, for the opportunity to enjoy leisure and the pursuit of knowledge, has been trivialised now that it has been attained. The principal means of achieving at least some measure of satisfaction was through literature and music; the former was better provided than it is today by unlimited access for all the family to the free, widely available reading rooms and lending facilities of high-quality public libraries. Nevertheless, the rapidly increasing range of wireless broadcasts and gramophone records brought serious music within reach of the many still denied attendance at opera houses and concert halls. What would those men and women have thought of today's screen-based pursuit of enjoyment through television and computer games?

My purpose in telling this true story lies in the hope that it will stimulate some thought – not in the minds of the 'great and good' who collectively seek to influence or dominate our lives, but in the minds of young parents and their children growing up in the twenty-first century, who may never know what enjoyment and enrichment can potentially be found in a very simple way of family life.

There are no publicly acknowledged heroes in this book. There are extraordinary achievements by ordinary people; but inevitably I single out one in particular – Barbara Cassidy, née Curry, my mother – whom I believe was the most remarkable and successful person, the most generous and the best organised of anyone I have ever met. For me, she was a role model *par excellence*. She had all the characteristics of a great leader: tremendous vision, an ability to create clear, simple objectives for herself and others, the skill to organise limited resources to achieve those objectives, and a highly developed capacity to communicate consistently and effectively. She was without self-interest or self-doubt. She was gentle, optimistic and resilient, yet had an iron will. But her greatest achievement was that throughout her marriage, as she struggled to make ends meet financially, she rose above problems on a daily basis and somehow managed to inject fun into all our lives. Whatever happened there was always an opportunity to smile, to be . . . just happy to be alive. Conquering adversity was not going to be made any easier by being gloomy about the causes or the prospects.

In a varied business life I have often been required to make decisions having serious, far-reaching consequences on the lives of many people. At such times I have reflected on whether or not the values implied in the final judgement would have met with her approval.

For me no better – indeed no other – imprimatur would be needed.

ACKNOWLEDGEMENTS

So many people, family and friends, have helped me in the process of writing, editing and publishing this book that it is impossible to mention them all. I hope they will accept my grateful thanks despite their anonymity.

My surviving siblings, Roma, Vincent and Rex, have contributed their memories of events to ensure accuracy, as have the many other reference sources I have used.

My wife, Ronda, has been patiently supportive throughout this long process while she and her mother, Dorothy, have been the earliest readers and most enthusiastic supporters.

Vicki, my secretary, converted the handwritten drafts into a presentable manuscript and retyped countless thousands of words in the evolving editing stages.

I found my way in the publishing world with the invaluable guidance and encouragement of John Whitney, Dr Barry Turner, Professor Peter Hennessy and Ion Trewin, and I am grateful to Sir Bobby Robson for his foreword, written when, not for the first time, he was under considerable pressure in his day job.

Finally my special thanks to Simon Fletcher, the Commissioning Editor, and all his colleagues at Sutton Publishing Ltd for their confidence and belief in *The Way Things Were*.

1

IN THE BEGINNING

This is about ordinary people, in ordinary places, living in ordinary times. Or with hindsight, perhaps they were extraordinary people, living in remarkable times, in surroundings which simply don't exist any more. So this book is as much about the context in which we lived our lives as it is about us.

It is a tale that is best started at the beginning: but since life is a continuum, where is the beginning? So I shall start at a time just before I emerged into this world.

It was 1933. Economically Great Britain, like the rest of the world, was in a deep depression. There was a Labour-led coalition government in power; over 2 million people were unemployed, of whom 50,000 had publicly protested in London at the end of January. King George V was on the throne and was reported, on 1 February, to have attended his first-ever picture show: a Movietone newsreel, a Disney cartoon and *Good Companions*. On the same day Rupert Gould, after twelve years of unpaid work, finished rebuilding John Harrison's timepieces at the Maritime Museum in Greenwich.

There was worrying unrest in Germany. Adolf Hitler had come to power on 30 January. That week the Reichstag was burned down, with Goering blaming the communists and publicly announcing they would be shot on the spot.

Newcastle United were the FA Cup holders, having beaten Arsenal in May of the previous year and . . .

That night, 1 February 1933, was wild and inhospitable. Rain fell endlessly all over the country, winds battered the British coast, and in 15 Elswick Row – the Cassidy home, heated only by a dying coal fire and lit only by gas jets – it was cold, damp and gloomy. Barbara Cassidy, at the age of forty-three, was about to go into labour for the seventh time in her sixteen-year marriage. Her husband Harry, having finished an arduous shift as a tram conductor, was in one of the local pubs he frequented, spreading his good humour around. The four surviving children (Roma aged thirteen, Alan eight, Vincent six and Rex two) were in bed – Roma in a makeshift bed in the parlour and the three boys in the front bedroom together.

Thursday 2 February was a typical winter's day, cold, wet and miserable; it was still raining heavily, still blowing a gale. Barbara, knowing that the new baby's arrival was imminent, packed Alan and Vincent off to St Mary's Boys' School and was attending to the baby, Rex, when Roma appeared, dressed in her school uniform and ready to leave for Fenham Convent, a Catholic grammar school run by nuns of the Order of the Sacred Heart. Barbara said she was feeling unwell and asked Roma to stay at home and not go to school that day, but Roma pleaded that she had some important 'tests' to take. While that wasn't entirely true, she felt that something bad was about to happen and she wasn't certain why. She suspected that it might be yet another baby – after all, they had appeared regularly – but since these matters were never talked about, she was both unsure and largely disinterested. However, she couldn't entirely block out the thought that if it was another baby, there would be further overcrowding, more chores and – horror of horrors – probably it would be another boy. She already had three brothers and she remembered, with a shudder, that she had had two other brothers, one younger than her and who had died in infancy. She quickly blocked off the unpleasant memory of tears, the tiny coffin and her mother's anxiety over her health in those early days. She rammed on her hat, picked up her school bag and hurried out into the wind and rain. Harry was already at work, and once again Barbara was left to face the birth at home without much support. It's true that her mother-in-law lived on the other side of the street, at 32 Elswick Row, and would no doubt put in an appearance; but this would be purely in a token or supervisory, doubtless highly critical role and there was precious little chance of her becoming supportively involved. In any case she was old, not very well and very high-handed.

Roma returned from school that afternoon, in the rain, surprised to find a dreary atmosphere and visible signs of a washday – always a Monday and never a Thursday. Of course it was wet, very wet, outside; but she was still puzzled by the warm, dank air, the smells of wet cloth and soap flakes, the noise of feet on bare oilcloth and the trickle of condensation on the walls. As she removed her school hat and walked up the stairs she was greeted by the formidable figure of Miss Hindmarsh, the midwife, who had come to light the gas mantle at the top of the stairs. Her heart sank; she knew her worst fears had been realised. The boys, Alan, Vincent and Rex, were playing in the corner of the kitchen which served as living room and dining room – the parlour was only for Sundays. A coal fire was burning and some clothes, principally sheets and towels, had been washed, but with the rain still falling heavily outside these were, of necessity, being dried around the fire. As usual on a washday the cloth had been removed from the table, the floor mats had been rolled up and stacked in the corner and everything was steamy, damp or, like the floor, very wet! Harry came back from an early shift wearily, and was given the news by the midwife: 'Another son; aren't you the clever one?'

The usual ceremonies were performed: a cake, which Ma had baked in readiness for the occasion, was produced from the cupboard and a bottle of port was opened. As was customary, the midwife had the first glass. The midwife said to Roma, 'Would you like to see your new little brother?' 'Not particularly,' Roma thought, but replied 'Yes' unenthusiastically. 'Don't be silly; he's lovely. Your grandma was over earlier and she said he's the loveliest baby she has ever seen.' Reluctantly Roma went in, saw her mother and saw the baby, which she thought looked much the same as any other baby – pretty horrible, really.

There was a loud knock at the front door. Harry went down to answer it, puffed his way back up the stairs and asked Roma to take the rent book down to be marked up by the landlady, Miss Temperley, the first Thursday in the month being the usual day for calling. Miss Temperley smiled at the pretty, dark-haired girl in her school uniform, always neat and unfailingly polite. If she had had a daughter, she would have wanted her to be like this little girl. But her 'intended' had died, like so many others, on the Somme, about the time the Cassidys were married, in fact; her hopes had died with him and she knew she would remain a spinster for ever. As she marked up the book she heard the new baby cry and her face stiffened. 'A sister for you, dear?' she asked, feigning interest. 'No, another brother.' 'Dear Lord,' she thought, 'these Catholics – and he's Irish! – breed like . . . When does it finish? She's not exactly in the first flush of youth, either!!' She handed back the rent book, turned up her coat collar, opened the silk-covered umbrella and stepped from the damp, cramped space that masqueraded as a hall out into the wind and rain.

Roma trailed up the stairs to be met by Pop. 'Would you go to the corner shop and get two gas mantles? – AND BE CAREFUL!'

Roma returned with the tiny, delicate, ceramic spheres and began to clear a space from the wet clothing that had been washed and was piled on the corner of the table, when Pop asked if she was going to get his tea ready. She sighed, put down the homework which she was going to do and set about making his tea. She heard the new baby, whose name she did not yet know, begin to cry. Alan punched Vincent, which was a very frequent occurrence; Rex stumbled out of the way and in so doing fell over the clothes-horse, pulled some wet sheets onto the floor and began to cry. Pop shouted at the boys to stop, Alan punched Vincent again, the baby cried louder and the midwife left. Pop lit the gas jets and as there was no wireless to listen to, because the accumulator battery was dry and needed recharging, silent gloom descended with the darkness on the damp household. This was an unpromising start to my life yet, in a sense typically, worse was to follow.

Ma, as we always knew Barbara, and Pop had been consulting about names. The priest had suggested that Simeon would be appropriate, which my mother rejected with her customary disapproving snort. Grandma Cassidy was a formidable lady, clinging tenaciously to the fading, middle-class status inherited via the long-gone wealth of her father-in-law, Patrick; he had made his money in rather doubtful circumstances in India, where he served as a private in the 43rd Light Infantry Regiment. Given that her husband was also a 'Patrick', she insisted that the baby's name should be Patrick – but that was similarly avoided, diplomatically. My mother had determined on 'Denis' and added 'Patrick' as a conciliatory gesture. However, there was an important refinement, as 'Denis' had to be spelled as in Saint Denis, the patron saint of Paris. She believed it to be the Catholic way of spelling 'Denis', as opposed to the Protestant variations of 'Dennis' or 'Denys'.

When the birth was registered, a week or so later, Harry was having his 'day off'. His 'day off', which was determined by a moving rota system, usually meant that he met his cronies and had a serious day's leisure, broadly equivalent to an all-day drinking session. Inevitably this was the day appointed by Ma for the registration of the birth. Harry was always immaculately turned out, but particularly high standards were required for Sunday Mass or days off – which was no coincidence, since both would end, and very often also begin, in a pub. The best suit would be worn with a sparkling white shirt with a clean, starched collar, carefully chosen tie, gold monogrammed cufflinks – a wedding gift from Barbara – and black shoes gleaming so brightly that he saw himself reflected in the toecaps. This was in marked contrast to his 'off duty' appearance around the house – a round-necked vest or shirt worn with long-john underwear covered, in the main, by suit trousers held up by braces, one of which was always worn off the shoulder. The trousers would also be buttoned at the waist, but he had an alarming tendency to overlook the fly-button fastening. Hardly a fashion plate, yet he still showed the underlying, dark good looks of his younger days, although his figure was now visibly spreading.

As always on days off, he left home in good humour and with the best of good intentions but unfortunately, some 200 yards from the house, he passed the first of the pubs – 'Adrian's Head', or in local parlance 'The Blue Man', because the pub sign showed the head as a blue, Wedgwood-like relief. Even more unfortunately, he met up with one of his acquaintances outside the pub and inevitably there was pressure to 'wet the baby's head'. Certainly by the time he got to the office of the Registrar of Marriages, Births and Deaths he had passed, or rather more accurately visited, at least eight licensed premises, and in each had been obliged to extend his celebrations to include any of his friends or acquaintances who were about.

His memory of the actual process of registering the birth was somewhat hazy, which is strange since he'd been through it six times before; but he certainly advised the Registrar of the name of the baby, and he pocketed a birth certificate for which he paid the due fee. He retraced his steps, literally, visiting even more pubs on the way back, and was beyond coherent conversation when he got home – happy nonetheless, with warm memories of his day off.

The following day, not unusually on these occasions, he was in what might euphemistically be described as a very prickly mood first thing in the morning, muttering darkly and provoked to shows of irritation by any minor mishap, imagined or real. He was asked by Barbara if the birth had been registered, which he dismissed with: 'Of course it has; where do you think I was all day?' – which really was an unanswerable question, or at least one that did not require an answer.

There were other important rituals to be completed, the first and most important of which was to have me baptised 'into the faith' and recorded as a member of the 'Church on Earth'. This ensured I would not be sent into limbo if I died prematurely. The second ritual, insuring my life, was to provide funds for a decent burial if the good Lord exercised this option early. Both were achieved before February was ended. The insurance, with the Royal London, was limited by law to a maximum premium of a penny per week, with an ascending scale of benefit, if death occurred, from one pound ten shillings up to three pounds after one month, and progressively up to fourteen pounds at ten years of age. Infanticide and high infant mortality rates made both parties ultra-cautious and aware of the risks.

At some stage the birth certificate was deposited – along with the other important documents such as the rent book, insurance policies, marriage certificate, birth and baptismal certificates – in the family chest, a handsome box fashioned as a wedding present by one of Ma's two brothers, who were skilled cabinet-makers. It was highly polished, with a replica conch shell inlaid on the lid, and a small brass key was usually protruding from the lock. Such lax security seemed inconsistent with Harry's use of it as a savings bank, as he had developed a habit over the years of interleaving ten-shilling notes with the documents, providing a useful reserve in times of need.

But before depositing the certificate Harry had read it, probably to negotiate with Barbara a refund of at least some portion of the fee to replenish, if only in part, his empty pockets. What he read was not pleasant and no doubt added to his bad humour! However, he kept his counsel, buried the certificate, and there it remained, simply being waved at Barbara when she asked for confirmation that the birth had been registered. I lived for at least sixteen years happy in the knowledge that my name was the chosen 'Denis'. However, either Harry had not read the certificate, or was incapable of reading it by the time he was given a copy of it, because my birth certificate recorded *'Dennis* Patrick', with two ns – and so it remained a secret.

Our poverty didn't lessen and was unlikely to with Harry's job. He started work on the trams in October 1919 and worked for the

Corporation continuously until he retired in 1957. Unemployment didn't improve, the general economic situation didn't improve, the political situation didn't improve and Hitler's march to greater power carried on unchecked. The football scene deteriorated as Newcastle United were knocked out of the FA Cup and began their slide down the First Division league table, soon to be relegated to the Second Division. But the King kept on going to the pictures, which didn't show any reference to Rupert Gould's amazing feat any more than they did to my birth. Happily I was blissfully unaware of all this, and so far as I can remember remained blissful for the next two years or so. I did enjoy very temporary special status as the youngest in the family, but I was too young to know, let alone to enjoy it – and even that was too good to last.

In April 1935 Sydney was born, his birth certificate properly completed as 'Sydney Bede', and my short reign as a visible member of this particular clan ended abruptly as I receded into anonymous childhood. Happily that coincided with my first faltering steps into, and exploration of, the outside world.

For Roma it was even more traumatic. Ma told her that she was now fifteen, rising sixteen, and the time had arrived for her to leave the convent and take her first steps into the adult world. Neither her tears, nor pleading from teachers, nor a letter from the bishop offering to pay her fees, was of any avail. Cries of a 'promising academic career', a 'recruit for the church', a 'properly educated young woman who could aspire to a good marriage' all fell on deaf ears. The household with so many mouths to feed was seriously short of income and there was literally no alternative – Roma's talents were to be devoted to 'earning her keep'.

The Easter of 1935 was indeed a watershed for the family and in particular for Barbara, Roma and me. For Barbara it was the end of child-bearing, after giving birth to eight children in nineteen years of marriage. Marriage began on a low income when Pop was a barman and about to be enlisted in the greatest of great wars; and now with him still on a low income, living in seriously overcrowded conditions, the marriage was about to enter its second phase in the shadow of another great conflict.

The happenings involving the Cassidy family in 1935 were a microcosm of what was happening in the wider world. New figures were emerging, others were strengthening their position; some were enjoying temporary glory before they fell from grace to join the ranks of the many who had never enjoyed even temporary glory. Only days before I arrived in the world on 2 February 1933, Hitler had achieved his first major step up the ladder leading to the assumption of ultimate power by being appointed Chancellor of Germany; by the time Sydney was born in 1935 and my star was pushed into decline, so Hitler was busy exercising his recently acquired total power.

As if deliberately setting the scene for a long, dark period ahead, Hitler had announced a series of decrees which progressively diminished the status, role and security of all Jews in Germany. At the same time, in the Far East, the less-well-known Mao Tse Tung was busy completing his 1,000-mile march – another precursor of a wider tyranny to come.

As the King was celebrating his Silver Jubilee in May 1935, it was clear that there would be a change of prime minister, given Ramsay MacDonald's failing health, and in June Stanley Baldwin duly became head of a continuing coalition national government. Mussolini then marched into Abyssinia, and by the end of that Jubilee year King George V was nearing his death, which occurred in January 1936.

Away from the monarchy, international diplomacy and political manoeuvring, speed in all its forms was a national preoccupation. On the one hand it was being celebrated and its achievers feted. The fastest-ever train journey was made by the topically named 'Silver Jubilee' on the Newcastle to London rail route; Malcolm Campbell set a new world land-speed record in excess of 300mph; the new Spitfire fighter, the fastest aeroplane in the world, went on show; and foreseeing the expansion of air travel, a new airport was due to be opened at Gatwick to replace the old one at Croydon.

To enable everyone – well, nearly everyone – to participate in this latest craze a new car, the SS Jaguar, capable of almost 100mph, went on sale for less than £400. That just happened to be equivalent to the cost of a new detached house in a desirable district, or several years' pay for my father.

On the other hand, to offset the obsession with speed and in keeping with the pace of change over the previous 100 years, a 30mph speed limit came into force in an attempt to reduce the number of road deaths and injuries caused by the rapidly multiplying motorcar. Since legislation to abolish the 'red flag man', required by law to walk in front of a motorcar, had occurred only in 1896 when my parents were children, it suggested parliamentary reaction was lagging behind the march of progress.

News of other dramatic, technological innovations were released which to most people were incomprehensible, ranging from a government commitment to broadcast a public television service during the year, to the announcement that a new radio-based detection device, later to be known as radar, had been invented to improve national security.

In the sleepy calm of rural England a wealthy eccentric, aided principally by his new, young, soprano wife and two talented Jewish refugees from Nazi Europe, had embarked on a visionary cultural journey to build in the garden of their country manor an opera house, in which to mount an artistically impeccable music festival. It was for the operatic aficionado and the wealthy, at £2 per seat – a week's wages on which my parents were supporting a family of eight. Even with a dozen eggs or a pound of butter costing one shilling and a pound of tea even less at only tenpence, there was nothing left for entertainment within our limited household budget.

It was indeed simultaneously the best of times and the worst of times.

2

LIFE IN THE BACK LANE

The back lane was a T-shaped strip of ridged concrete that ran, as its name implied, between the backs of the houses of three streets. To the south, the bar of the 'T' standing on its head, were the rears of even-numbered houses in Havelock Street, with a cul-de-sac on its west side and an opening to the front street of Elswick Row on the east. From Elswick Row you could just see the tips of the shipyard cranes on the banks of the Tyne, and the steep slopes of the Tyne valley rising to the south.

The main stretch of the back lane ran from south to north, dividing on its east side the smaller houses of Elswick Row — all constructed as upstairs or downstairs two- or three-bedroom flats — from the bigger, more expensive, three-storey terraced houses that faced west onto Campbell Street. The lane had been cobbled once, but more recently had been covered by a layer of ridged concrete. The east side of Elswick Row also comprised large, terraced houses, which meant that those like us in the flats on the west side were sandwiched between bigger and once much grander houses. All these houses had been built during the mid-nineteenth century as Newcastle expanded rapidly to house the workers — who included numerous immigrants — for the new industries centred on the Tyne, many of which had developed from historic trades such as shipbuilding, shipping and fishing.

Whether large houses or smaller flats each home had its own front door, with a paved front path inside a miniature railed garden on the front street; and all had a separate back yard divided by yet another high brick wall leading to the back lane. Collectively the back-yard walls of all the houses presented a uniform and overpowering mass of common red bricks, a colour which changed with the weather from deep burgundy when wet with rain to blood red in bright sunshine. They were high walls, which in many cases had been topped roughly with a layer of cement studded with broken glass bottles – all lethal, jagged edges. This did not signify the presence of great wealth in the houses which lay behind the walls, but rather that the inhabitants, many of whom were old, were fiercely protective of their limited space. The razor-sharp glass barrier was intended to deter intrusion by animals – or boys. Boys, rarely girls, had an insatiable appetite for climbing over walls to retrieve a ball, to just gaze on the inhabitants, or in many cases simply to walk the wall in a display of simulated high-wire acrobatic bravado. The activity often resulted in deep gash wounds after errors of judgement; when healed these became tribal virility symbols. Because the lane rose steeply from its southern end to its northern end, the back-yard walls were stepped; the only break in this monotony of red brick was from the different-coloured back doors – a rare display of individuality, but also a useful form of identification for those who couldn't read. House numbers were usually painted on the door or, less likely, indicated by individual metal numbers which could be purchased from Woolworths. An even more esoteric aid to recognition, loved by younger children, would be a broken or missing door handle, and occasionally the back door itself was missing altogether. A further territorial subdivision had been created by the random placing of the all-important gas street lamps at irregular intervals on either side of the lane; they were given names, just as bus stops were.

For adults all of this probably presented a rather dreary environment, but for children nothing could be further from the truth. The 'back lane' for us was a large playground, familiar and secure. It is true that on many occasions it was no more than a simple thoroughfare, since the back doors of the houses and the back lane were used by most people for everyday activity rather than the front doors, which were usually reserved for special visitors. The latter opened onto a miniscule garden, flanked by a tiled path and surrounded by railings into which a wrought-iron gate had been set as an approach to the front street. The fronts of houses – doorstep, path and pavement – had by convention to be kept pristine, and were assessed by neighbours as a mark of the comparative care that the inhabitants, who were never the owners, lavished upon their modest property. Every housewife's daily priority after husband and children had left for work and school was to sweep and 'swill' with water the front path and their own area of pavement, before 'stoning' the front doorstep with 'donkey' or 'brown stone'. Door handles and furniture would be polished before she retired indoors to begin the unending schedule of cleaning, cooking, mending, patching, washing and ironing. Throughout this she would have watched, and been watched by, neighbouring wives completing identical routines and wearing identical garments, with the certainty that it would be expected as much tomorrow as it had been yesterday irrespective of the fact that no one had crossed the threshold.

Neither was the front street for tradesmen – they, too, were part of the rich tapestry of everyday life in the back lane. Back yards and the back lane were different from the front street. They had the throb of real, everyday activity, where the heartbeat of the community could be felt. There was constant movement to and fro of the people who lived there – to work, from work, to school, from school, to shops, from the shops – but much more than that. On Mondays, after the children had gone off to school and husbands or sons had long since departed to the factories or other workplaces and if the weather was fine or at least dry, the lane was transformed, as is an ocean by sails, when bed linen was pegged in a series of envelopes on lines stretched across the lane from east to west. Although this required cooperation and shared use with the occupiers on the other side, which couldn't be taken for granted, there was rarely a problem. Frequently a zigzag of washing lines used principally to dry sheets ran virtually the whole length of the lane. It was unlikely that many women would be prepared to reveal, even to their closest neighbours, the limitations of their family wardrobe of underwear, outerwear or even towels, but sheets could only dry satisfactorily if hung in the lane before the workers returned home at the end of the day. What a picture they presented on a fiercely windy, bright, sunny day! Yet perversely, as always happened in working-class back lanes such as ours, Monday was also the day favoured by the coalman to deliver. The coal lorry was a simple vehicle with a drop-sided platform which housed a set of scales at the rear, complete with large, black, cast-iron weights to make up hundredweight and half-hundredweight deliveries. A pile of filthy, coal-blackened sacks were always stacked in one corner and the lorry carried a mountain of coal and coal dust. Unsurprisingly, the coalmen themselves were filthy. They were dressed not unlike the miners, who had extracted the coal in the first place. They wore large, hobnailed boots, and thick socks into which trouser-legs had been tucked, with string tied across the leg below the knee to stop the invasion of all-pervading coal dust further up the trouser leg to what could have been equally grimy underpants, in the unlikely event they wore any. A large, leather apron, a cap, a nondescript ragged 'ganzy', an old suit jacket and a shirt that clearly looked its part – as if it had been trampled in coal dust to give it an air of respectability before the coalman put it on – completed their outfit. The lorry would appear with a cloud of coal dust billowing from the back and accompanied by yells of 'COAAAL', which was a rather unnecessary piece of pre-publicity for the self-evident activity. Nevertheless, these cries brought frenetic activity as hordes of housewives, usually wearing outsize overalls or multicoloured pinnies, short-legged wellingtons and a turban round the head to cover the 'rollers', would appear en masse and begin to roll up the sheets on the line before lifting the clothes props – the large, cleft sticks that held the clothes-lines – high in the air, like oarsmen at a regatta, to allow the lorry to pass. Of course, because everyone needed coal the lorry had to stop between lines of washing, creating a temporary disturbance with insults and banter freely exchanged. If the washerwomen did not immediately scurry out to roll the sheets around the line and then lift them, the coalmen would oblige by doing it themselves, usually leaving a gratuitous set of extremely black fingermarks on the sheets. On these not-infrequent occasions they were – to put it mildly – unpopular and were subjected to a volley of colourful language and an interesting stream of expletives. Thus began my further education in my mother tongue.

Why did the coalman have to deliver on a Monday? At the time I didn't care, but I suppose only because someone had to receive coal on a Monday. Since washday was a mandatory Monday activity whatever the status of the household or the district, then it was inevitable that the poorest, the least important households, should be the dubious beneficiaries of a Monday delivery.

The dependency on coal, and its high cost, meant that it had to be stored securely. A coalhouse or shed was set into the outside back-yard wall to the back lane, into which a small door some two feet square for the delivery had been set. It could be opened only from the inside by withdrawing a bolt. The family had access to it through a full-sized door opening into the back yard, and the relative affluence of a family could often be gauged by the number of wooden planks placed horizontally inside the door from floor level upwards – to prevent the coal inside from spilling out when the door was opened! This was never a problem in our house. But our planks had a secondary security benefit – they deterred some family pets from going in, as those that did so were in mortal danger from a coal delivery. It was generally unannounced – for pets, anyway. The coalman would open the outside hatch and with a tilt of the shoulder and two hands carefully positioned on the sack, would fire the contents at, and hopefully through, the opening. If he missed, accidentally or deliberately, there would be a quick scurry of activity to retrieve the spilled coal before the coalman or some vulturous neighbours could claim it. Since our cats, ever-present residents, enjoyed using the coal dust and the dark of the coalhouse for their ablutions, it always had an instantly recognisable air. But our cats were streetwise and were never buried under a well-aimed, swift delivery – not that either quality characterised normal deliveries – whereas 'Chocolate Drop', a young brown-and-white pet rabbit, vanished under an avalanche and was never seen again. One winter's night, with a steeply banked fire burning cheerfully, there was a hint of . . . could it be roast rabbit? I don't know who named the rabbit 'Chocolate Drop', but it was a strangely prophetic curse. 'Chocolate Drops' was the name of a popular Cadbury's children's chocolate product, and was also acquired as a nickname by a boy who went to St Mary's – probably because he too was brown in colour and diminutive in stature. One day he was doing nothing more hazardous than walking down the street when a gas stove exploded in a house he was passing. It blew out a section of wall and he was killed instantly by flying debris, which not only put an end to calling anyone or anything 'Chocolate Drop', but also didn't do much to encourage sales of the product in the area.

But there were other interesting tradesmen who plied their trade in the back lane, such as the fishmonger who was always a Friday visitor, and while he did not unleash a cloud of coal dust he certainly left a pungent vapour trail of old fish. Little wonder that so many children grew up with a strong aversion to eating fish, even if it was allegedly good for the brain on any day, and for the soul also on Friday. He too dealt from the back of a cart, but a horse-drawn one: much smaller, although with similar drop-down sides. He sold from boxes in which various kinds of fish were stored: herring, cod, haddock and sometimes mackerel, though the latter was regarded as inedible and usually thrown back into the sea by fishermen. If available, it was 'very good value' for money. A purchase of fish, usually whole and sometimes still alive, involved the fish man throwing the fish with great dexterity from a considerable distance onto the once-shining brass pan on the scales at the rear of the cart, where it would land with a satisfying, smelly 'plop' in a shower of silvery fish scales before skidding to rest. He never missed.

Just as the coalman always appeared on Monday, so the fish man always appeared on Friday. The coalman was always known as just that, even though the firm's name was written on the tailboard of the vehicle, and the fish man was known similarly. He always appeared on Fridays because, as in so many working-class districts, Catholic families were among his most regular customers and for Catholics the fish was obligatory – it was regarded as a sin to eat meat on Fridays. For non-Catholics it was a welcome opportunity to buy low-cost food which undoubtedly fish was, particularly varieties such as herring and mackerel.

Our fish man never carried the more expensive fish or other seafood, even though it was abundant, freely available and of a very high quality. He always wore a flat cap, a neckerchief tied at the throat, a shirt and jacket over which hung a leather apron smeared in fish blood, innards and scales, with his trousers tucked in to wellington boots, and he had a well-developed habit of wiping his hands on the seat of his trousers before accepting money and giving change from his satchel. Cats from several blocks away would gather and mournfully follow the progress of the fish man, which perhaps provided part of my fascination with him, although it didn't override the unpleasant vapour trail of this 'pied piper'-like character.

He could also appear frighteningly aggressive, reacting with swiftness and ferocity if a cat, unable to resist the appeal of the fish, leapt onto his cart. The fish man and coalman were the most predictably regular of the tradesmen since they called weekly on a fixed day, but they didn't have the appeal of some others.

The stick lady was a curiously Dickensian character who at first sight seemed extremely stout, but that was almost entirely due to the layers of clothes she wore. On her head she wore a flat cap, banded round with a shawl or scarf knotted under the chin, while over the voluminous, multilayered clothes and around her waist she wore a grubby pinafore, tied in a bow at the back and with a large pouch at the front holding coins, which she jangled loudly as she called 'STICKS' in a piercing voice.

On her feet she wore thick woollen socks covered by a variety of footwear according to the season: sometimes flat, open sandals, sometimes clogs, sometimes men's boots with an array of sharp studs which scratched the concrete surface and showered sparks in every direction.

The sticks she sold were in small bundles tied by string or wire, carefully stacked in a handcart made from an old fruit-packing crate with panels from another crate nailed roughly to the sides of the body to form handles. A set of wheels taken from a pram, sometimes the whole four-wheel bogie, completed this quaint yet inexpensively efficient vehicle. Her sticks had been roughly chopped into pieces, about an inch square, of equal length and tied loosely with a piece of wire or string at the middle. They were, of course, a vital household commodity and sold by her at a discount from the price charged in the local corner shop, where we could also buy similar bundles. Saturday was her regular day.

Coal was the most vital commodity in any household, because it was our only means of providing heat; consequently fire-lighting with sticks and newspaper was an everyday activity, as were cleaning out the fire grate and removing the ashes afterwards. Both were central to everyday life, requiring everyone to acquire at a very early age the skills necessary to do it effectively; these began by carefully rolling old, dry newspaper into twists with one end left flared to facilitate lighting. On top of the tightly rolled criss-cross of paper twists went a similar pattern of sticks, followed by carefully selected, small pieces of coal, with larger pieces ready to build up the fire as the base took hold. To help, a metal plate was positioned over the grate and a double sheet of newspaper held over it; when done expertly this would cause a great sucking of air through the bottom of the grate and a roar as it 'bleazed' the fire and drew the flames up the chimney. There were a number of golden rules to be observed, such as: don't waste too much paper or too many sticks in the relighting process, and don't allow the double sheet of newspaper in the bleazing process to catch fire. The first was financially imprudent; the second potentially disastrous, but very exciting!

Inevitably fireplaces themselves were central to our lives and inspired another activity – cleaning, by black leading, the grate and kitchen range. Pop – for it was always his task – would spread newspapers on the hearth and surrounding floor, open the tin of liquid black lead, dip in an old shoe brush and smear the grate generously. When that had dried he would buff vigorously with another old brush and then finish with a vigorous rub using an old shoe cloth! Exhausting work and very unhygienic, but satisfactorily producing an almost new kitchen range after two hours' hard work.

Another tradesman was the knife grinder, a regular if infrequent visitor who, rather like the stick lady, created showers of sparks, but his flew from his grinding wheel as he pedalled furiously to rotate the grinding stone while he ran a knife blade across it. He too wore distinctive clothes: a thick, brown leather apron and always a cap, but never goggles. He looked, but wasn't always, a serious professional – knives of every size and description, axes and scissors were sharpened apparently with great care.

All of these trading transactions, whether with the coalman, the stick lady, the fish man, the ice-cream man, or the knife grinder, were for cash. Since that was never freely available, there was always much debate and deliberation about price before any purchase was made. Everyone had a deep, well-founded suspicion that everybody else would try to take advantage of them. The coalman had been known to put stones in the coal, thereby depriving you of your true weight. Worse still he could, with a neat sleight of foot, prop one foot against the scale, depressing it to make it look as though the required weight had been shovelled into the sack, when you were actually substantially short. Easiest of all, if you were 'out' but had pre-ordered coal as a regular delivery, you could be short-delivered – one and a half sacks while paying for two, or receiving the due weight made up to include a disproportionate amount of dust or 'slack'.

The fish man had the same habit, of course. He would lean carefully with one hand on the corner of the scale while putting weights on and pressing down, then remove the weights with another dextrous flick of the wrist before you could see if balance had been achieved. His mental arithmetic was also often eccentric!

The stick lady was not immune from this 'short change' disease, but in a more obvious and probably unintentional way, either by selling green wood which would not light easily or bundles that were not of the required size.

Inflexible, often insecure income and never-ending demands which outstripped their weekly allowance combined to make most women walking calculating machines, with highly developed negotiating skills. Buying from local tradesmen was therefore an art form for the experienced wife and mother, who doubled as a sharp-eyed security officer and relentless, tough purchaser. These were not activities to be delegated to children and the reality was that since there were few alternative suppliers available, a fine balance had to be struck between being satisfied she had her 'pound of flesh', and being so difficult as to cause the seller to look for further opportunities to defeat her sharp eye or wit.

The most welcome visitor to the lane, though, so far as I was concerned, was a man who sold nothing, and although he was not overtly begging he nevertheless hoped he would be offered the odd small coin. He would appear, always on a Saturday morning, at the top end of the lane. Irrespective of the season he would be wearing a bright ginger cap, a dark blue Burberry raincoat belted carefully at the waist, well-worn but neatly pressed, smart, brown trousers, gleaming brown shoes reflecting the light – and to match his gleaming shoes was the wonderfully polished wood of the violin he carried. He looked an old man, but he was probably no more than forty-five. He played serious music, not the frivolous music-hall songs of the time or the popular dance-band tunes that were heard on the wireless, but music which made me aware, even as a boy, that there was something deeper and more powerful, more moving in it, in spite of the fact I had no idea why or what it was.

He walked slowly down the lane, pausing occasionally, lifting the handkerchief from the violin under his chin, wiping his brow with it, replacing it underneath his chin and resuming his playing. He must have been a very advanced student once, or a professional musician, to have had such a repertoire, but like so many others he had fallen on hard times. A tangible trail of sadness followed him, a combination of his mournful looks and wistful melodies.

The back lane was, however, more than an open market hall for the purchase of goods, a playground for children, or a highway; for adults it was a forum, a showground, a council chamber, and sometimes a battleground – a coliseum in which Catholics, Protestants, Jews, 'Eye-ties' or 'Chinkies' were occasionally the protagonists. Yet as in all neighbourhoods, the commonest causes of dispute were fractured relationships between the sexes, unruly children, drunken husbands, neighbours at war over noise or territorial transgressions, or simply a personal but public railing at the inequities of life, poverty and the despair of unemployment.

Even to me as a child the presence of the unemployed was so obvious. They gathered in knots on street corners, near bus stops, outside premises where work might be available unexpectedly, at the Labour Exchange, in their constant search for jobs or to queue silently for the modest unemployment benefit they received. Frequently tired of being the object of disapproving stares they gathered in the back lanes, for although no back lane was ever a private place, the people who used them constantly were their own kind, who knew them and sympathised with them. Their dress was uniformly drab, preserving their best clothes – if they had any – for occasions which demanded them. They had old boots, trousers, a jacket worn over a collarless shirt because the unemployed could not afford starched collars from the Chinese laundry – and yet to cover its absence there would be a white silk scarf knotted at the neck, and almost invariably a cap. They would squat on their 'hunkers', share bad-luck stories, converse about politics, football, religion and pets, but seldom about family affairs. They would roll their own flimsy, loosely packed cigarettes and pass one around, and although they smoked in public they never drank in the lane.

In the main these were neighbours, not 'dropouts', defeated temporarily by lack of work and opportunity and anchored by family responsibilities. There were some who had given up entirely and become tramps, of course, but tramps invariably were passing figures constantly on the march, not people who squatted in doorways or on street corners. Frequently, when conversation had dried and showing off their dogs to each other had palled, they would indulge in simple gambling games for small stakes, a cigarette, a halfpenny, a box of matches. This was usually 'pitch and toss', a version of 'two up', possibly taught to them by Australians during the 1914–18 war; it was simple, quick, required no skill, and was absolutely unpredictable. A variation of it was to use the same coins and throw them against a wall to see who could get nearest to it, which determined the winner. Like the envied employed they husbanded their miniscule resources extremely carefully, but men, whether employed or not, would always retain some cash from whatever payments they received or, in very rare cases, had been allocated to them by a wife who held the purse strings. Some of the employed were frequently generous to their less fortunate neighbours, which was demonstrated usually when they gathered before walking to a local pub.

There were two other visitors to the lane, whose activities were intertwined. There was the bookie's runner, whom I remember as a small man with a long, belted raincoat and the mandatory scarf and cap; he was as identifiable as if he had carried a promotional banner on the back of his raincoat. He carried a rolled-up newspaper in which he kept a foolscap sheet of paper, on which he wrote details of the bets that were placed with him before he handed the slip back to the gambler and accepted the stake money. This caused another gathering of the unemployed or temporarily inactive at the paper shop when the late afternoon newspapers arrived carrying the racing results, for which the 'Stop Press' columns were scanned frenziedly. The bookie's runner, having taken the bets, would appear the next day to pay out the winners and hopefully take more bets, which were always laid in extremely small sums.

The other equally regular visitor tried very hard to anticipate the movements of the first. He was the policeman or 'pollis', for whom the handed-down criteria for the maintenance of law and order included arresting the bookie's runner if he was spotted. In practice this usually meant a physical scuffle, some threats and occasionally a wager by the policeman on the winner of the yet-to-be-run 3 o'clock race at Newmarket. The appearance of the pollis did more than have the bookie's runner sprinting away as fast as he could; it also usually caused the unemployed gathering to stand up, disperse and slouch off in different directions, just as it caused children climbing walls or lamp-posts to get down quickly and make themselves scarce.

Policemen were uniformly large men. They were big in every sense, tall, broad-shouldered and with big feet. Their height was exaggerated by the helmet with an 'uhlan'-type spike on the top, and increased further by the thick soles of their gleaming boots. Their florid faces glowed from the benefit of good food and constant fresh air. We all knew they were keepers of law and order, yet somehow they always exuded an air of potential menace, not entirely due to the fact that they wore a holster in which a long, threatening truncheon was housed on a belt around their tunics. It was some of this menace that imparted itself to the unemployed and discomforted them. Harmless though they might have been, deprived of work, income and plentiful food, they by contrast seemed at the very least stoic and at other times much more optimistic about life in general and their fellow citizens, particularly the children, who played around the clusters of unemployed men quite happily without the one interfering with the other. In truth it seemed as though policemen regarded the unemployed as inveterate troublemakers and lawbreakers, rather more than the random casualties of economic malaise. Of course there had been open warfare between these two groups, reaching its peak in the protests and demonstrations surrounding the 1926 General Strike, but that had occurred several years ago; yet now, even if there were sporadic outbursts of domestic violence, neighbours would have resisted calling the police to intervene.

But the event which would cause most concern was a serious dispute between the men, when fists might fly, bad language would be used and very quickly Ma, like most other mothers in the street, would call the children indoors or at least into the back yard, where the door would be bolted firmly. While disputes seldom lasted very long, they were often the visible expression of tragedies, a heaping of unhappiness on people barely able to cope with the problems they already had, and there was a desperate longing to return to normality as soon as possible.

From the very earliest age I became unavoidably aware of this cycle of life in the back lane: quiet very early in the morning, whether in the calm of sunny spring or summer mornings, in the foggy gloom of late autumn or in the hush of a lane covered in snow on winter mornings; gathering pace through intense bursts of activity during the day; then returning to quietness as night fell slowly on the long, summer evenings or rapidly as the winter darkness closed in. There would be few people in the lane when it was lit only by the handful of gas lamps turned on by the itinerant gas lighter, using his long pole to click open the lamp window, unhook the gas tap and light the internal mantle.

The back lane was the stage for a way of life that was at once both simple and complex, and like a stage it seldom changed, while the dramas played out on it did change, with infinite variations every day. It was for me, as for most people, their first experience of life outside the home, and usually their last before death claimed them.

3

THE CORNER SHOP

The corner shop was at the exit of the back lane, marking the last stop before the lane opened into the wider world via Elswick Row. It looked so inviting and yet so strange, so mysterious and, at first, intimidating. It was only 50 yards or so from our back door, and even closer to our front door.

The shop door, off the back lane, was glass-panelled, painted green and had a large brass handle and 'sneck'. It was set between a display window on the left and a brick pier on the right, which formed the corner of the building and its 'return' on Elswick Row, into which was inset another display window.

As you entered you were faced with the side counter, on which were a variety of machines and ancillary equipment. These ranged from a high-tech (for those days), automated weighing and slicing machine to a Heath Robinson cheese cutter. The weighing/slicing machine was emblazoned with the name Berkel, in white letters on a brilliant red surround, and the scale platform was silver, as was the electrically operated, circular blade which whirred and flashed as it sliced meats which fell gracefully and obligingly onto a sheet of greaseproof paper.

But that was in marked contrast to the simplicity of cutting cheese. A gently sweating block of Cheddar – there never was any other kind of cheese – was placed on a large wooden board and a long piece of piano wire, attached at one end to the corner of the cutting board and with a wooden toggle on the other end, was stretched taut and drawn swiftly across and down through the cheese. The skill was in the judgement of what size piece was likely to be close to the required weight, or more relevantly the customer's cost ceiling!

Both these pieces of essential food preparation equipment were a favourite snoozing place for the ageing black-and-white cat which was kept to eliminate the ever-present menace of mice. That it was singularly ineffective could be readily gauged by the amount of mice droppings which had to be removed before serving from the sugar sack that stood on the floor below the counter. The shopkeeper, Reg Gerry, would studiously take a small, stiff, blue paper bag, blow it open with a heavy puff – only mildly unhygienic – take a scoop, plunge it into the sugar, pick out the droppings, empty the scoop into the bag and laboriously return to weigh it. Next to the sugar was another sack, this one containing soap flakes, which presented endless opportunities for frothing tea and other diversions because the same scoop was used to dispense both. However, the elementary precaution was usually taken of wiping the scoop on the seat of the trousers or running the forefinger across it, often preceded by a generous application of spit and another wipe on the trousers.

Between the sacks and the return counter, which was the main serving area, were the eye-catching, tiered, glass-fronted cases holding tins of biscuits. The standard display was achieved by inserting a square tin of biscuits, without the lid, angled to give the prospective purchaser a view of the contents in the glass-fronted compartment. There were nine different tins on view, yet the one that always captured my attention was that reserved for broken biscuits. While it was filled with the broken remnants from a variety of tins, the effect was hypnotic: a miscellany of ragged-shaped pieces of biscuits – chocolate, bourbon, ginger, digestive, shortbread, assorted creams. The shopkeeper always tilted the balance in his financial favour by including a disproportionate quantity of tasteless, shattered water biscuits; yet the appeal of low cost on a tight budget never dimmed for housewives! No one buying biscuits would expect to be given a single broken or cracked biscuit when paying full price, and therefore any even suspected of being cracked were removed at once and thrown into the designated broken-biscuit tin. Biscuits were never pre-packed unless you bought a whole 7lb tin, which was unimaginable even at Christmas; and few other foods were pre-packed either – not even flour, sugar, soap flakes or cheese. Wrapping was usually an inner sheet of greaseproof paper, itself then further wrapped in an outer sheet of newspaper. In this way packaging was an environmentally friendly and unsophisticated process.

To the right of the shop door was the window facing onto Elswick Row. It was this window that provided the 'objects' for our childhood guessing games, since it was a display window of sorts. It usually contained the latest, or at least different, Guinness adverts with the unchanging slogan 'Guinness is good for you!' We soon became familiar with scenes of cheerful, archetypal working men nonchalantly carrying steel girders on one shoulder, or the friendly toucan, or both. Inside, beneath the window display shelf, was a useful space to stack bundles of sticks and fire lighters, which added a strong smell of paraffin to those of bacon, cheese, bread and tobacco.

Reg, the owner, always wore a brown dustcoat and his 'wife', Gertie Whitfield, wore a floral 'pinny' – as normal in their dress as they were abnormal in their assumed marital status, for it was very unusual in those days to be cohabiting in such a public role. That provided rich material for 'out of earshot' local gossip. Reg always positioned himself behind the main counter to the left of the shop door, which when opened rang a simple brass bell hanging from a leather strap, causing anyone already in the shop – and I can never, ever recall it being empty – to swivel their head to confront or greet the newcomer, be they child or adult. A necessary precaution sometimes, given the frequent need to arrange credit – 'Will you put it in "the book" until Friday, Reg?' – which even for the most regular users of the facility was an extremely private, sometimes embarrassing, matter.

The 'tick' book in question was a red-backed, alphabetically indexed credit ledger, the spine of which was bound in black tape, and each of the regular customers would be allocated a page under the appropriate alphabetic index. It also had a pencil stub topped by a blackened eraser, attached by a piece of string and serving as a bookmark; into this grubby, grease-stained ledger, Reg or Gertie entered the date and the value of goods which were not paid for at the time. Some families used it constantly and only reduced the debt each week, without ever clearing the arrears; others used it only *in extremis*; and a lucky, proud, or embarrassed few never used it at all. It was also used to record payments made to the Christmas Club account, a facility which was advertised heavily by means of a foolscap-sized, overprinted holly card, and displayed above the cash register from October onwards. In truth the 'club' method of saving was used throughout the year, for Easter or for weddings, and though the amounts saved were small, usually a few pence at a time, it provided a useful cash reserve in times of need. After all, few wives could guarantee their men would even be working, let alone prepared to hand over a predetermined housekeeping allowance, if there was one. Because of its frequency of use the book was always kept on the main counter, but it was obscured from general view by the tall, glass jars holding a variety of sweets and was exposed only when sweets were sold – but the secrets within its covers were never revealed.

Liquorice of all shapes and sizes dominated the choice of sweets and was my first introduction to the shopkeeper encouraging impulse buying. There were 'pomfret' cakes, as we called Pontefract cakes, which resembled a black, embossed wax seal made of liquorice. There were liquorice all-sorts, liquorice torpedoes, and a selection of liquorice sticks, twists and 'pipes', as well as other very highly flavoured sweets such as aniseed balls, toffee balls, jelly babies, fruit pastilles, dolly mixtures and sweet hearts. Nothing was ever subtle in flavour, size, style or colour, but they provided endless temptation for children.

In addition to the temptations of the sweet jars and the broken-biscuit tin, there was a children's 'lucky dip' strategically placed on the counter above the biscuits display, visible immediately to anyone who entered the shop. The 'lucky dip' consisted of a board about 18 inches square covered in silver foil, beneath which were more than a hundred small pigeon-holes each containing a strip of paper on which was written a message. For a small fee – 'two goes for a halfpenny' – you pushed the progger attached to the board through the foil cover and withdrew a message from one of the holes beneath. The message might tell you that you had won threepence, or a large gobstopper sweet, a balloon or a badge, but in most cases the message was 'Bad luck; try again.' It took a long time to exhaust all the squares covered by foil, but a much shorter period for mothers to refuse further requests for a halfpenny 'lucky dip', as the gambling instinct became implanted at a very early age. And it was not uncommon for Reg to plunge his hand into a sweet jar and give a child – usually hanging onto the marble-topped counter – a sweet, in an early, low-cost version of the loyalty bonus.

Since his normal serving station was the main counter, there was clear counter space – the only one in the shop – between the sweet jars and the large, brass cash register, which stood next to another set of brass scales with assorted weights nearby. On the shelf behind the shopkeeper would be his 'tools of the trade': tongs and scoops, knives and bags, which were always large white for flour and small blue for sugar, although there was never any chance that bread, for example, would be placed in a bag. Above this were shelves of canned goods; nothing was refrigerated.

The cash register used to fascinate me. It was large, brass, ornately figured with scrolls and flowers and had a visual display panel; when the shopkeeper pressed large, round keys – not unlike a giant typewriter keyboard – with a heavy downward pressure, a bell would ring loudly, the levers would crash noisily and a set of price signs would pop up in the panel. If, however, it was simply to give change, the pressing of the keys would produce a red 'no sale' sign. There was no such thing as a till roll or receipt, and there was something compellingly attractive about the register's appearance and sound, the clash of the keys, the simultaneous ringing of the bell which announced the transaction and the rattle as the cash drawer sprang open and jingled the coins inside. Notes were seldom used, as purchases tended to be restricted to shillings and pence, although once a £5 note was offered, which had to be signed on the reverse side by the tenderer – indicating how unusual this was, being double a working man's average weekly wage.

The floor of the shop in front of the L-shaped counter was about the size of a smallish room in a nearby house and was covered with thick, well-worn, brown lino. Since everyone had to mount two steps from back-lane level to enter by the front door, even I had a good view of the interior before I actually pushed open the door. My first view of the shop was from an eye level that was substantially below the level of the counter, and was further handicapped by having one hand firmly in Ma's hand while she did the shopping. Subsequently I made visits with one of my brothers, who almost always had a piece of paper, which was the shopping list, wrapped round the exact amount of money required, until finally I was allowed to do this 'message' myself.

Shopping there was never a frenetic activity. It was taken at an extremely leisurely pace; since everything had to be cut, spooned, sliced, wrapped, bagged, weighed, priced and totalled, it hardly encouraged speed. The skill of the shopkeeper in working-class neighbourhoods like ours was to stock everything that might be required. This presented a challenge to shopkeeper and customer alike, as the search for the article – 'I know I've got it here somewhere' – frequently involved stepladders and hunts through labelled drawers, usually ending with a triumphant yell: 'Got it!' There were times when the proceedings resembled a pantomime, with the housewife shouting 'Up a bit, left a bit; no, too far – right a bit', and it was unwise after one of these searches to tell Reg that what he had located wasn't really what you wanted.

Just as men would find in pubs, there was seemingly endless conversation between the shopkeeper and the customers – who were always women or children, never men; between women waiting to be served; and sometimes among the whole shop collectively. The atmosphere of the corner shop was one of neutrality, neither hostile nor welcoming, and children were always given priority and dealt with promptly. No one appeared to have any difficulty in allowing the small child with the outstretched hand clutching the paper and accompanying money to be given precedence, even if they themselves had been waiting for some time. Sometimes, of course, the child would be discussed – as I found – by the other people in a rather open way: 'Yes, that's the youngest Cassidy', and sometimes we were the subject of less flattering comments, even if these were not meant to be serious.

The corner shop was the hub of everyday activity, and although as far as I know we never sought credit, or 'tick' as it was known, the vast majority of our neighbours did, as the tick book's regular use testified. The food stocked was seriously overpriced and of damagingly poor hygiene: yet the shop was probably scrupulously fair as far as weights and measures were concerned. It was a prized part of local life, existing only through the continued patronage of its customers, who often seemed to be in equal partnership with Reg and Gertie rather than served by them. The corner shop seemed to have a permanency to rival the Church or the state. Only occasionally did tensions surface there, usually when someone was driven by financial necessity to ask for credit which Reg felt he could not extend any further; in such circumstances, embarrassed silence followed by an occasional noisy departure, to avoid the inevitable scene, was the usual outcome. In an attempt to forestall this – although it wasn't entirely true – the shop displayed a bold sign which read, 'Don't ask for credit as refusal may offend.'

There was great sadness when Reg and Gertie sold up, lock, stock and barrel, and great anxiety about the unknown new owners. But we need not have worried as Matt Brown, who was a tall Canadian and Randolph Scott lookalike, brought with his wife and brother-in-law a continuity of style with a whiff of glamour, if only because of their North American drawl and high-heeled cowboy boots.

As usual such uncertainties played no part in children's considerations. Our main interest was principally in the exterior of the shop, rather than its interior activity, because its side display window which looked out onto Elswick Row provided us with a large, ready-made 'prop' for one of our standard outdoor games as young children. The corner-shop window was of ideal height, very low, and perfectly situated, since it overlooked an open space equivalent in size to two small gardens bordered by the back lane, the pavement and railings to neighbouring gardens. To complete the ideal stage for young children's games, there was a street gas lamp set in the pavement near the kerb and central to the window. This served both to illuminate the play area and to mark the course for the game.

The game began as a version of 'I Spy', by someone choosing and declaring the first letter of the name of an object in the window, but it was then blended with 'tig', as we called it, or 'tag'. Whoever successfully nominated the object had to 'tig', or touch the back of, the nominating player before he could run round the lamppost and touch the base, which was the windowsill of the shop. It was a game in which speed of thought, physical speed and anticipation were paramount. Apart from that it allowed endless opportunities for people to cheat and claim the game, conditions which were at their best in winter darkness when there was a gap between the penumbra of the gaslight illumination and that of the shop window.

4

WATCHING, WAITING AND LEARNING

There was a reciprocally strong desire for parents to allow their children out of the house and into the back yard, and in my case that soon created a powerful ambition to go independently into the back lane and join the wider society there at will. I understood that the boundaries of the territory I would have access to would be the lane north as far as Wilson's Lamp, and south-east as far as the corner shop. Of course these thresholds had been crossed by me many times, but always as a captive of Ma, Pop or one of the older siblings. Before independence could be achieved, though, the dangerously steep back stairs from the scullery to the back door of 15 Elswick Row had first to be negotiated. Until that journey could be accomplished safely on my own, further ambitions were pointless. It was a swift, although sometimes painful learning curve, first attempting the journey head first; then by shuffling on my bottom one stair at a time – which must have done some early damage to the spinal column – and finally by walking, however unsteadily, with my right hand fixed firmly on the handrail. Soon I was able to reach and open the latch on the back door and get out into this large and still strange world, with continuous coaching on how to behave with other groups of people exercised from the open scullery window under Ma's ever-vigilant eye. However curious, pleased, surprised or daunted I was, I became aware that others had similar feelings about me.

On their part, there was first curiosity and some interest, which quickly gave way to disinterest, followed by boredom, followed by irritation and disownment. I know what it was like! I can still feel it sharply and imagine with my inner eye those eager little eyes, the overriding urge to run on still-wobbly legs to join in. And the confusion when I was, at first gently but later increasingly roughly, pushed out of the way and – worst of all – ignored.

But none of this prevented me from hanging around on the fringes. Occasionally there was a shout from Ma looking out of the scullery window, 'Vincent, Rex, let Denis play.' Then their pretence of welcoming me: 'Come on, then', quickly followed by 'He's no use.' Neither was I, nor any other child, spared the scathing criticism because my undeveloped legs couldn't move fast enough, my grasp of what was being attempted was nil and my coordination of hand and eye was pathetic. But I, like every other child, persevered. Ma would appear periodically at the back door: 'Are you enjoying this, are they letting you play?' All eyes would be fixed on me, weak smiles would be worn and I would nod or clap. Ma would turn her back and go off to the corner shop or return to resume her housework. She would sometimes stop, turn and say, 'Would you like to come with me?' and on a bad day I would accept quickly and run to her, for the weak smiles hadn't fooled her. She had seen it countless times before.

Yet gradually I was included, as older boys grew out of that particular group and graduated to different games, spending an increasing amount of time outside the lane, or doing things well outside my range, racing old bikes at furious speed around the block for instance and – oddly, I thought later – spending more time on mixed games with the girls. More importantly, other young children emerged from the local production line and replaced me as the eager-to-be-involved 'baby', one of the most unwelcome names any child can be called. There were very few overbearing or overanxious parents to plead for their offspring to be included, although there was the exceptional 'only-child household' where the probationary period was more extended. Since I was for a short period the youngest of a sizeable brood this was, exceptionally, rather helpful. My older brothers were a point of contact, often to their embarrassment. But I, like everyone else, learned by observation, by mimicking, by practice, aided by a developing physical strength – never a selling point with any of the Cassidys, as underfed, weedy and ragged a lot as you would be likely to see. The jeers and the mockery at my first attempts only strengthened my desire to be included. Not that there was any real alternative; certainly tears and tantrums were useless, a lesson already well learned within the house.

For children, above all, the back lane was infinitely variable in its uses. For the older boys it could be a cricket or football pitch, it could be a racetrack, it could of course be a boxing ring, and it was frequently the training ground for all forms of sporting activity, since it provided an arena for tug-of-war, for leapfrog, or for short- to long-distance races.

For these games an endless variety of sporting equipment was created or acquired. A cricket bat could be anything broadly proximate to the shape and size of a cricket bat, but might be simply a panel from a wooden crate, with a roughly shaped handle bound with string. Sometimes, rarely, it was the genuine article – old and battered, acquired in some junk shop for a pittance; although on one glorious occasion a brand-new bat appeared. No one dared to ask how that was acquired! The ball could be anything from a light, soft sponge ball to, most often, a tennis ball – even more frequently, an extremely old, worn tennis ball. It was never a leather cricket ball; even back-street boys' carefree spirits realised what damage that could inflict, not on them but on property, with dire consequences. Sometimes a ball of some composite mix which replicated the hardness of a cricket ball and its ability to inflict personal injury was produced. Part of the fun of this was the pain that was meted out to others through the hands and arms, even if the batsman middled the ball. Most satisfying of all to the bowler and fielder was when the hard ball removed part or most of the home-made bat: a resounding crack and a splintered bat – a great triumph, even if the game was over until a replacement was found! Over a back-yard wall was always 'six and out', not only defying cricket laws but imposing a serious penalty, since the offender had to retrieve the 'lost' ball irrespective of broken-glass-topped walls, savage dogs or raging neighbours.

Sponge balls and tennis balls were also used most commonly for the games of football, and yet on rare occasions a real leather ball, a 'caser', would emerge. The major problem with a 'case' ball was not only that its life was exceedingly short, since the concrete of the lane was an unforgiving surface on which to play, but inevitably the protective, broken-glass, anti-scaling devices on top of the walls inflicted serious and immediate damage. It was one thing to lose a tennis ball, quite another to write off entirely a real football.

Girls' games seldom converged with boys' games, although the common use of a tennis ball meant rather frequent raiding of their possessions. Chivalry was non-existent and no amount of pleading, irritation or anger from girls wrongfully deprived of a ball for their game could detract from the joy of a game of doubles headers. But there were some games of common interest and appeal, and unsurprisingly the common interest seemed to accelerate as the boys got older and the games required more physical contact. Creativity caused the emergence of new games, frequently requiring the use of chalks to mark 'go' and 'no go' areas, while the other source of creativity required was in the provision of equipment for whatever the contest was, be it a bat, a ball, a bicycle or some form of cart. The cannibalisation of old prams, the use of any loose timber, of rope and string, of balls and chalk, made the acquisition of these key raw materials a precondition to enjoyment and yet its ownership precarious. Boys' games were frequently accompanied by loud shouts of disparagement or encouragement; the girls' usually by songs, chants and rhymes which in some mythical, mystical way formed an essential part of their game.

It was always so obvious that girls' games were very different from ours. They were overtly collegiate games in which collective participation seemed much more important than anyone winning, which was seen by me as a vice rather than a virtue. They were certainly highly active, rather than passive games, requiring much hopping, skipping and throwing which seemed to permit narrower margins of error, and required greater dexterity with better balance than boys' games demanded. Much less equipment was involved, most of which played no part in boys' games, such as skipping ropes, spinning tops and jacks, with the only common element being a ball or some coloured chalks. It nevertheless puzzled me why most of these games required them to tuck their dresses into their knickers, while the continuous chants of mumbo-jumbo made me curious; it all seemed very strange indeed.

It was inevitable that cliques, sub-groups and 'gangs' emerged, formed on the one hand of those who might be the most successful players of the game, or the big, fast, tough kids, and on the other by those creating an alternative form of activity after having been rejected by the more successful or competitive group. In every case there were hangers-on, often potential providers of equipment, the softies, the clumsy or the pampered, who were tolerated but never warmly welcomed.

My first encounters with these games brought overwhelming joy. I would stand transfixed; I am told, with eyes shining and hands clapping. Frequently I jumped and shouted and clapped and laughed so hard it should have brought on a swift run inside to the lavatory but . . . accidents do happen! But as I grew older and bolder and persistently sought to join in new games, I would again be ushered away. I learned that to plead, sometimes in tearful frustration, was of no avail; but I had also learned to play at the edges, often running after a stray ball, and even if often pushed roughly out of the way, eventually I got my chance. But the real test was to come! – how to survive in the game on your own merit. So this natural process of being perpetually on the fringe of older children's games was a learning carrot forever moving away from me.

Consequently the most interesting time was at weekends, when older children did not have to go to school, and it was on Saturday also that the violin man and the stick lady always appeared. The memory of a sunlit back lane, part sunshine, part shadow, the first distant and then approaching sound of the violin singing its tunes, seemed as predictable and unchanging as the seasonal pattern. It probably was always sunny when he came, because he surely didn't risk his violin in pouring rain, or his fingers on freezing cold days. Then Ma's voice would call me back from my apparent trance and I would be given a coin to hand to the violinist. The music must have moved my mother for her to have given a precious coin so regularly, no matter how small the value. He would pass on, to be followed by the shuffling, bellowing, spark-producing trudge of the heavily rugged 'stick lady', come hail or come shine, with her bumping, rattling stick barrow and her piercing cries of 'Sticks – bundles four a penny.'

Weekdays in the lane were quieter with the absence of the older boys and girls, who were either at school or at work, and children's games were displaced by more adult activity. There were heavy jobs to be done, some indoors, some outdoors, such as washing, ironing, carpet beating, and there were the itinerant tradesmen to be dealt with. The noisiest and dirtiest, the coalmen; the quietest, the 'Frenchies', with their strings of onions; the smelliest, the fish man; the most exciting, the knife grinder; the most threatening, the gypsies and tinkers, always ready to bestow a curse if you had nothing for them; the funniest, the organ grinder and his monkey; the most welcome, the muffin man; the jolliest, the Italian ice-cream man, pedalling his tricycle with the ice-cream tub in the box front of the bike, singing his Neapolitan songs – badly.

The noise from all this activity swirled around and echoed from the endless brick walls to the accompaniment of supervisory cries from the scullery window: 'Come out of the way, Denis, until the coalman has gone', or 'Come in and close the door properly' when the gypsies loomed into view. Of course all the children returned home from school for dinner, although what they received would not accord with the Trades Description Act's definition of dinner. Then they would be gone again for the walk back to school, always accompanied by explicit instructions such as, 'Hold his hand', 'Don't dawdle', 'Hurry home after school', 'Don't lose him' and so on.

Silence never lasted long. There was no peace for Ma, and soon Pop would be back for his mid-shift or end-of-shift meal. It was then that culinary creativity and economy were merged to produce sustaining, sometimes appealing, low-cost meals. Pig's head or trotters, sheep's head or brains or heart, rabbit pie, ham and pea soup, smoked haddock and poached egg, tripe, liver, soused herrings, ribs and lap, brisket and shoulder, any cut of any meat that was cheap. But my stomach turned at the sight of a sheep's alabaster-white skull bubbling in an open pan of water on the fire, gently cooking the brains which my father spooned directly from the grinning, eyeless head.

If it was a mid-shift break, and particularly if I couldn't be sent out to play because of the weather, Ma would empty Pop's tram-conductor's black leather money satchel, take out the small blue bags marked with various coin denominations ('copper' – farthings, halfpennies or pennies, and 'silver' – threepenny bits, sixpenny pieces and the larger shillings, florins and half-crowns) and teach me to sort the coins by denomination, then stack them, count them and put them in the correct bag. First sitting on her knee while Pop ate; then on a chair by myself, by which time she was nursing Sydney; then showing me how to write the numbers and denominations; and finally, after a long apprenticeship, teaching me to add them up. Pop, wiping his mouth and plate usually with the same piece of bread, would check his remaining ticket numbers, deduct from them the opening ticket numbers and strike a balance. If there was a difference he would trace it, correct it and usually offer me a word of encouragement or correction. If he was tired or overdue for a visit to the pub, those words could be mildly sarcastic. Ma never appeared to be subject to such human frailties – right or wrong, my counting would be assessed, patiently explained and always concluded by a quiet 'Good boy.' Pop would depart, the table would be cleared and the pots washed, and it seemed that in no time the others would return from school.

In the evenings there was an equally simple meal – bread and jam or similar; sometimes, if we were lucky, melted cheese on toast: the cheese grated, a pan with a little butter placed on the fire hob, some milk added to stretch out the quantity, all vigorously stirred while we held pieces of bread on a toasting fork close to the fire.

As the days shortened and the temperature fell, the coal fire had to be prepared, with paper twists topped by sticks and small pieces of coal, lit and 'bleazed' with a metal plate and a double sheet of newspaper which made the fire roar up the chimney until it had 'taken hold'. The gas mantles, wretched, delicate, expensive little ceramic burners for the gas jets, would be lit and the tap adjusted. Curtains, such as they were, would be drawn. Until the younger children went to bed the wireless, which was powered by an accumulator resembling a motorcar battery but made of glass, would seldom be switched on. Roma and Alan would be encouraged to read, sometimes aloud to the others, or we would play games, more often of Ma's own making rather than manufactured games like ludo, snakes and ladders, tiddlywinks or dominoes. Her games were more difficult and more fun, but since they were based on knowledge I was at a disadvantage initially, as was Sydney after me, until Ma introduced her own handicapping system. If it was a spelling 'bee' the words were chosen to match the degree of difficulty to our individual ages. The same happened with lines of poetry, proverbs, similes, capital cities, rivers, dates in history, kings and queens, and so on. And as we all grew up, more complexity and higher degrees of difficulty were injected by us, and these became a characteristic of our games.

Above all I was conscious of how much I wanted to answer correctly, how I longed to win and, improbable though it was, beat everybody else. Naturally the urge to cheat – 'I didn't say that', or 'But that's what

I said', was stronger in some than others. Usually Ma kept that in check with a sharp word or two, but she never allowed me or anyone else to 'win' just to keep the peace. The best you could hope for would be a 'replay'. But if she wasn't playing or controlling proceedings, sharp exchanges were sometimes followed by scuffles or blows and an ill-tempered breakdown of law and order – 'Rat', 'Spoilsport', 'Cheat', 'Pig', 'Brat', 'Idiot', 'Moron' – followed by more scuffles. The table would be scattered, chairs pushed until Ma, the voice of authority, would say with unmistakable intent, 'STOP THAT AT ONCE! Roma, go to bed', or more frequently, 'Alan, why do you always have to cause trouble?' or 'Leave him alone, he's only little.' And so the fire died and we all went to bed, Roma in the seclusion of her own room, even if without a proper bed; the rest of us to one large bed in another room, in a variety of formations which gave some clue to the underlying state of hostilities. The gas mantles would be turned down and we would often hear the wireless playing as we drifted off to sleep. Ma would most often wait up until Pop came in, usually having stopped off for a pint or three somewhere, unless of course he was working late shift, when the house would be still and in darkness apart from the glow from the fire's dying embers as he returned.

5

WIDENING HORIZONS

Slowly, almost imperceptibly, my dictionary of names and atlas of places grew, and day by day it went on increasing. There was no formal structure for this inexorable process; it just happened and went on happening! Daily life for Ma was an endlessly repetitive process of cooking meals, cleaning, replenishing and organising. It was the replenishment activity, which could be anything from food to clothing, which contributed most directly to my learning cycle. Food shopping, where I was taken along by necessity, at first centred on the corner shop but gradually extended to the butcher's, the baker's, the fruiterer's and many others. But it was the expeditions to acquire clothing and footwear that dramatically widened my horizons and began my introduction to a whole new – or should it be second-hand? – world. Ma's life was always dominated by cost considerations and her fertile imagination produced many unlikely solutions, preceded sometimes by rather unsuccessful attempts to meet stringent spending limitations.

One of these memorable early calls was to a Mrs Curry, memorable because that was Ma's maiden name, although this woman was unrelated. She dealt only in second-hand clothes from her house, which was as small and unprepossessing as our own. She had a sorrowful and rather furtive air about her but she was honest, which was not always the case with dealers in any second-hand goods; she had regular 'suppliers' and a reputation for quality and cleanliness. I was taken only because I couldn't be left at home, but the principal purpose of my first visit was to provide a new wardrobe for Vincent – probably because he was about to go to grammar school. After what seemed like endless viewing of row after row of assorted clothes in a multitude of sizes, shapes and styles, Ma pronounced herself satisfied and the deal was concluded, not without some haggling. Vincent seemed less than satisfied on the grounds that the baggy white shorts, 'ideal for both football and PE', were 'hairy' and playing havoc with his 'private parts', while the starched, detached collars were too large. Ma dismissed these minor complaints by pointing out the name tag on all the articles – 'Lord Swinley'. None of this made any sense to me at the time, but subsequently I wondered whether Lord Swinley was a weedy dwarf or a recently deceased aristocratic schoolboy. If he hadn't died tragically, why were the clothes not handed down within his own family as they were in mint condition? Yet Vincent, with a developing interest in the novels of Dickens, might have asked, 'How did Mrs Curry know Lord or Lady Swinley, or in what mysterious circumstances did these nearly new clothes pass from such noble hands to a back-street second-hand dealer?' – a question that was never resolved.

But we weren't finished, neither was Vincent's rerobing complete, for the most bizarre was yet to come. We walked further until we arrived at another seedy, terraced building where a bang on the door caused an old, round-faced lady, wearing an equally old, well-worn coat, to appear. Ma had obviously been here many times before because we were immediately asked to enter the upstairs flat, where she quickly outlined her requirements, frequently tugging Vincent in various directions – first in profile, then full face, then lifting his leg and showing the sole of his boot, rather as a blacksmith handles a horse when shoeing it. Throughout this command performance Vincent looked a picture of misery, long-faced and forlorn, in which art he was well practised. The old lady, whom Ma addressed as Mrs Cowans, turned swiftly, disappearing for a while until a temporary silence was replaced by knockings and bangings; then the footsteps could be heard returning. These were followed by her breathless reappearance carrying an armful of assorted boots and shoes in an amazing variety of sizes and even more varied styles. But Ma was not satisfied and we were asked to follow Mrs Cowans to a large room, empty except for the huge mound of shoes on the floor. Not a stick of furniture anywhere, no floor covering, not a picture to be seen. Little wonder that in this sea of bareness the slightest movement caused a deafening sound. Vincent groaned, affected to want to visit the lavatory and was quickly admonished by a look – *the* look – from Ma, and the pantomime resumed. Happily most of the shoes didn't fit 'by a mile', but two pairs did, more or less, and we were treated to Ma's critical appraisal and Mrs Cowans' sales pitch simultaneously. Vincent plucked up enough courage, a commodity in rather short supply in his otherwise attractive personality, to show interest in acquiring the well-worn sandshoes, 'useful to wear' with the newly acquired hairy, privates-chafing white shorts; but he was adamant that the almost new, pointed-toed, black patent-leather dancing pumps would only be worn 'over his dead body'. It very nearly came to that before weariness at Vincent's lack of enthusiasm for this shopping expedition brought it to a premature end, at least for that day.

Ma was indefatigable, drawing on a seemingly inexhaustible pool of energy, since this typical shopping trip was both preceded and succeeded by a formidable sequence of those repetitive household chores.

So it was on another day I set off with her on another footwear-based trip, but this time to arrange some repairs or cobbling. Yet again this was not to any formal shoe-repair shop – 'far too expensive' – but to Mr Atwell's house. As we approached the house, another nondescript, brick-terraced house divided into an upstairs and a downstairs flat, a faint noise of hammering could be heard which grew louder and ever louder.

The front door was open because these were business premises, after all, and a little girl was sitting on a lower step, humming gently to herself while the hammering continued incessantly. Ma gently interrupted her reverie by asking to see Mr Atwell. The little girl, who had a mane of curly hair and saggy stockings pouched round her ankles over her little black boots, rose, ran up the stairs and disappeared along a corridor. The hammering stopped; more footsteps and an old man, wearing a cap, spectacles on a grizzled face and a long, bib-style, grey apron, came down the stairs. He took the shoes, examined them carefully, asked a few questions: 'Soled and heeled? Segs?' and quoted a price. Ma had bridled visibly at the mention of 'segs', a small, shamrock-shaped metal stud hammered into the soles of new or resoled shoes to extend the life of the shoe or boot. These were 'common' and were a visible sign of 'low' – which in this case was equated with 'tasteless' – people! How could he make such an error?

Of course it was much later when I realised that while Ma alone could do the bargaining over the cost of repairs, collection was always delegated, although it was a long time before I would be entrusted with that task unaccompanied. Over many visits and many years, I took a part in the same little cameo countless times. 'Are our shoes ready?' 'What's the name?' 'Cassidy.' 'Daaaaad, are Cassidy's shoes ready yet?' There were typically two possible responses to the question – that is, if he had heard it in the first place: 'No, come back next week', or 'Coming', followed by the scraping of a chair, the clump of feet and the later appearance of the old man at the top of the stairs. Frequently he was removing small nails from his mouth as he held up the shoes to show, with some pride in his workmanship, the new leather soles. While his appointment as 'cobbler to the Cassidy family' was no doubt a financially prudent choice, it must have had a long-lasting effect on the health of our feet, because he invariably used leather of a thickness reminiscent of a battleship's steel plating and equally lacking in flexibility, as a result of which we all developed a tendency towards walking flat footed. It was also rumoured that he had once added leather soles to repair a pair of sandshoes.

Mr Atwell was an amateur cobbler whose availability, like so many other amateur tradesmen, was caused by the lack of 'proper' employment, and so they took to doing essential tasks for themselves. If they were reasonably proficient, that was extended to a service for others which provided some income as a means of survival; it was the beginnings of

'DIY man'. The attraction for them was that they gained not only income but some independence and self-respect, and they provided for their customers – such as the Cassidys regularly were – some essential goods or services at a much lower cost than would be the case in a normal retail environment. Essentially, they provided things we could not have afforded otherwise. The hazard, of course, was that the quality of the work was rather 'hit and miss', but since there were very few protections afforded by the law even if goods purchased in a normal shop failed prematurely, this was hardly a serious risk!

In the particular case of shoe repairing, virtually every household owned a cobbler's last, which could be bought in F. W. Woolworth's. They were usually black, cast-iron, three-legged affairs, with one of the legs sporting a plate that would take an average size man's shoe. On one of the other legs was a standard woman's shoe size and on the third, a child's shoe size. In the no doubt zealous, ambitious days of early married life, Pop had invested in such a cobbler's last. I am afraid that his talents were best displayed in the saloon bar, in conversation and good 'crack' there or at home with his friends, but not in undertaking manual tasks. Our cobbler's last was soon relegated to what was in his view its proper role – acting as a doorstop. In fairness most families only attempted emergency repairs, but even this was beyond Pop's skill threshold. Someone before me drew the line when an emergency sole fixing, completed with some pride, drew blood. The shoe inner resembled an Indian fakir's nail bed. We all resorted to cardboard or newspaper stuffed in the shoe to keep our feet reasonably dry, until replacements or a visit to Mr Atwell could be afforded. Mr Atwell had clearly proved rather more dexterous or tenacious than Pop in the pursuit of a new skill and I often wondered if he ever saw the light of day or stopped his hammering, for as you left, with or without the shoes, it would resume, fading only as you walked further and further away from his house.

Pop's lack of interest in most manual tasks was the last stage on his sliding scale, as he tended first to lose patience, then his temper and finally any interest in most manual activities. Surprisingly, however, he was always more than diligent with tasks that he decided he wanted to do, whether it was going to work, where he was punctilious in being on time and well dressed, or at home doing a dirty unhygienic task like black-leading the grate. No pain was spared in such cases, while a task such as knocking a nail into a wall on which to hang the rare picture or mirror, or undertaking a minor repair to a chair leg, was literally beyond his patience and therefore skill. As a result we had fewer tools than other houses seemed to possess. However, we did possess a claw hammer, useful for extracting nails that had been badly knocked in in the first place, and a pair of large, black, cast-iron pincers, which looked as if they could have extracted the incisors from a tiger but were usually required to extract nails from our shoes. But we had no screwdriver, saw, plane, oil can, nails or screws.

If a simple repair job was necessary, most families could and would do it themselves. As in our case, that was driven more by financial necessity than by desire, because if they couldn't do it themselves it was left undone. We tended to choose the latter route. Frequently, if the 'man of the house' knew how to do a job but equally frequently did not have the tools with which to do it, he would first seek to borrow his needs from a better-equipped neighbour. Such requests were not always granted, even reluctantly, no doubt because tools were precious and whether by accident or design were not always returned. An informal dossier was compiled mentally by most families as to who was reliable and who was not, from whom you could borrow tools or, indeed, to whom you could lend tools if you could reciprocally trade.

Inevitably such precious implements were a frequent source of conflict and recrimination if a tool was broken, lost or never returned. Unsurprisingly too, given the nature of the neighbourhood, the jobs to be done were endless – doors to be lifted on their hinges, handles to be replaced or refixed, leaking enamel dishes, pails or baths to be repaired, door locks adjusted or oiled and, more preciously, lavatory cisterns or chains to be replaced. During winter, given the primitive nature of heating arrangements and the near universality of outside toilets, there were pipes to be unfrozen or, when burst, to be repaired.

Pop, having given up formal repairs following his lack of interest in the acquisition of tools, adopted an approach that would have done Heath Robinson proud, and he became as inventive in these Heath Robinson repairs as Ma was in her search for value. Unfortunately perhaps his were less permanent and less successful. Inevitably a broken caster on the one armchair we had, or in later years a chaise longue, was replaced by a book of the required thickness, after a search for a book of no literary value since books were never in short supply in the household. A burst downpipe in the toilet in the middle of winter was rather more problematic, but a tight binding with a set of rags resulted in a stemming of the loss of water and a rather attractive Niagara Falls-like ice stream building up on the pipe.

Apart from the endless search for cheaper goods or services when those were beyond available means or skills, there was an everyday need for materials that resulted in everybody saving everything. If a household was lucky enough to be able to purchase some new goods, they would be presented in most shops carefully wrapped in sheets of stiff brown paper, wonderfully smooth on one side and coarse on the other, beautifully bundled, wrapped and tied with string and with a string-formed handle. It was simply unknown for people to use a knife or scissors to cut the string, which was carefully untied and rolled in a ball to be preserved for when it had to be used next for whatever purpose, perhaps a replacement for a metal link in the lavatory chain if it broke.

The brown wrapping paper was also carefully removed, never torn, straightened and the creases eradicated frequently by ironing with a damp cloth. Everyone treasured the empty biscuit tins which on a good day you might be given at a local corner shop; or fruit boxes from the fruiterers, when the claw hammer and the black pincers came in useful to break the box down to separate pieces of wood, removing as carefully as possible all the nails and straightening those which had been bent to preserve them for use at a later date.

The daily newspapers had endless uses, including being a wonderful material for polishing off windows which had been cleaned with a wash-leather, and an absolute essential to provide toilet paper. Newspapers were kept, refolded, slit with a kitchen knife, a hole punched in a corner using a meat skewer then tied with a piece of string and hung on an appropriate hook in the lavatory. In all my schooldays I can never recall seeing toilet paper on sale in any of the shops that we used, let alone seeing it in our lavatory. On occasions when it was known you were going to replace the linoleum, or oilcloth as it was generally known, newspapers would be retained over several weeks to act as an underlay. Of course in later years when the lino was removed they provided an amazing source of nostalgic information.

Many mothers were adept at sewing and darning, but it was a rare household that had a manually operated sewing machine, and ours was not one of them. Mat and rug making was much more popular and making a traditional 'clippy', 'hooky' or 'proggy' mat became a regular winter family leisure activity. It had several advantages, prime of which was that everybody could join in and the resulting rug was a useful addition to the household inventory, particularly for Christmas. Although we didn't own the required rug-making equipment – an adjustable, rectangular wooden frame was required – we were able to borrow one, and the only other implement needed was a screwdriver-type instrument with a hook instead of a chisel end, hence the name 'hooky' mat. Hessian was used as the base material and strips of old rags of any fabric or colour formed the pile of the rug. These were inserted with a stabbing or progging action – hence the alternative name of 'proggy' – and then withdrawn to form a loop. This action was repeated until the strip of cloth had been used, when the process was repeated with another strip until the whole surface had been covered. The rug was then finished unless a cut pile was preferred to the loop pile, in which case the loops were cut or clipped – hence 'clippy'.

We always made 'hooky' rugs in a random, harlequin pattern, while more gifted neighbours used to produce complex designs such as animal portraits or landscapes, and some would make these of any design to order. Such levels of artistic excellence were beyond us, but at least everyone could 'have a turn', and with the age and skills range we represented it was probably more realistic to harbour limited ambitions.

On a regular basis we were gathered together as a troupe – Vincent, Rex, myself and later Sydney – and taken by Ma to yet another house in Phillip Street within easy walking distance of ours. Here we would be ushered into another typically bare room, this one in a downstairs flat, in which there was a settee with old, worn, black hessian covering a horsehair filling, which had a nasty habit of escaping and playing havoc with delicate skins. There was a bare, unshaded light in the middle of the ceiling under which was a large, brown leather chair, making the whole scene reminiscent of a death cell in an American penal institution. This was our monthly visit to the hairdresser's or the barber's, as it was always known.

He had created his own promotional slogan, displayed prominently on a placard near the barber's chair. It read:

Our haircuts are	A1
If you are not a customer why not	B1
To judge our haircuts just	C1

The barber's name was Mr Dixon, although to us he was, as usual, known simply as 'the barber'. Like Mr Atwell and many others, he was a self-taught amateur. Since newspapers and magazines regularly advertised manual, scissor-type hair clippers, haircutting was just another expensive need the willing amateur could fulfil for his family or do for others – but wisely Pop eschewed this also.

We were processed in descending order of age, with Vincent first and Sydney last, but apart from his careful 'sizing up' of the head we had his unvarying standard cut. Since the chair height could not be adjusted as it had no mechanical means of moving up or down, we were perched on boxes of varying heights placed on the seat to lift us approximately to his optimum cutting height.

He combed the hair down all round the head, usually remarking to Ma that we had lovely round heads, and then with a large pair of scissors he would trim horizontally around the head from a point midway between the eyebrows and the hairline. He would then produce enormous, scissor-action sheep shears, which were hand operated with a tendency to drag, and with a downward motion he would shave the head from below the new hairline. He would finish his task by sharpening an open razor on a large, black leather strap, with quick movements to and fro, and then whisk some soapy water on an old shaving brush before quickly 'sloshing it' around the back of the neck. There would be a sharp intake of his tobacco-laden breath, a firm warning not to move so much as an eyelid as he scraped away the remaining stubble from the lower neck. When we entered there was a pile of hair clippings around the chair's pedestal; when we left there was an even bigger pile. Presumably these were cleared away at some stage, but I never saw it done and some said it was to be used for theatrical wig making, others that it was used to stuff upholstered furniture.

There were no niceties, no mirror in which you could observe your own changing appearance, and so when we left we were all uncertain about how we looked. However, the obligatory visit to the barber every few weeks was not intended to be a fashion statement or to improve your appearance; it was simply a task which now and again had to be done, rather like cutting the lawn that we didn't have. I regarded it as an unwelcome and uncomfortable chore, with loose hairs inside my shirt and a neck that felt red raw, while Ma saw it as a regrettable, cost-incurring activity: but there were standards to be maintained, albeit those standards were not based on aesthetics, as well demonstrated by the four more or less identical haircuts and four shaven necks. Since

Mr Dixon's attempts to prevent hair trimmings from finding their way down the inside of the collar were superficial in the extreme, the walk back home was usually accompanied by constant scratching down the back of the shirt. No doubt with this in mind, much as we disliked Saturday night 'bath night' it was preferable to visit the barber on a Friday afternoon, as close as possible to the weekly routine of the zinc bath in front of the fire.

A visit to the barber on a Saturday was out of the question, as the more rewarding job of cutting men's hair took precedence, and we had already concluded that it was a mistake to be waiting to have a haircut at any time if an adult appeared. They always took priority, irrespective of how long the boys had been waiting or how many times they were queue-jumped; yet it was an experience that was repeated endlessly. Adults knew that their seniority entitled them to impose themselves on children without rights, as indeed they had been imposed upon during their own childhood — except of course when, in those early days, Ma was with us. To have queue-jumped her tribe would have required a whole Zulu regiment, and they would still have been routed.

Pop could still surprise us with his attempts to master new cost-saving techniques, as he demonstrated when he purchased a Rizla 'roll your own' cigarette machine, cigarette papers and loose tobacco. It was said to be foolproof, he had seen others do it: but alas, an hour-long struggle with these three simple components, plus liberal helpings of saliva, produced five cigarettes. These ranged in size from a thread-like, tobacco-free, soggy paper to a loose, oversized, cigar-like tube that came apart when it was handled, let alone lit. Like so many innovations before, it was discarded neither to our surprise nor our disfavour; indeed, to our benefit later when we surreptitiously joined the smoking fraternity. At least we would go on receiving welcome cigarette cards from Pop's daily dose of the weed.

Most men smoked regularly, although it was very rare to see a woman smoking even in private, and never in public. It seemed that smoking, like going to the pub, was a male preserve. There was no stigma, either economic or cultural, attached to smoking, and being in male company in a fug of cigarette smoke while drinking beer was the working man's right – an all-too-brief escape from everyday pressures. The route between pub and the home was littered with cigarette butts, variously known as 'tab ends', 'dumps' or 'nippers'.

It was a combination of these elements, the 'dumps' and the discarded Rizla machine, that persuaded me and some of my friends to try to be 'manly' prematurely. The lead was given to us by an unemployed man nicknamed the 'nipper king', who walked up and down the street in a curiously lopsided manner collecting 'nippers' with amazing speed from the gutter, where they had been swept by housewives during their morning front path- and pavement-sweeping routine. Having collected a pocketful of these he would stop, squat on the kerb, pull out a large handful of nippers, peel off the remaining paper stub, discard these while holding the residual tobacco, produce a Rizla cigarette paper and in one swift motion single-handedly roll a cigarette, lick the paper, roll it again, stick it in his mouth, produce a match from his pocket, with a flick of the finger light up his 'fag', lie back and with a blissful look on his face puff out a cloud of blue smoke. He would then immediately spring back into action, lurching lopsidedly, with one foot on the pavement and one in the gutter, a trail of wispy smoke following him.

There were two 'rag shops' – O'Donnell's and Landau's – both near the junction of Heber Street and Barrack Road, which provided a very different kind of shopping experience: one which took you back to a previous century in a few footsteps, without requiring any imagination to achieve this journey in time. Both the rag shops were in similar, decaying old premises in an enclosed, congested yard in which every conceivable item of scrap metal was lying randomly about or formed part of a miscellaneous pile that included old baths, bedsteads, wheels, mangles, pots and dishes.

Indeed it was to one of these that Alan and Vincent had trundled the old mangle which had so nearly cost Vincent his fingers – after which Ma had decided on principle to dispose of it, but to deny its potential value to the rag-and-bone merchants who made regular trips to the back lane to acquire old clothing or scrap metal by fair means or, more often, foul. Unfortunately both rag shops refused to buy it, on the grounds that 'We don't buy scrap metal from children under sixteen.' The brothers were both so exhausted after pushing, pulling and steering this heavy, dangerously unstable machine through lanes and streets for over a mile that they abandoned it outside Landau's premises rather than attempt the even more difficult journey back to Elswick Row, only this time up the steep streets they had negotiated earlier with so much difficulty.

But it was usually to sell old woollens that we made our trips to the rag shop. Then we would cross the cluttered, scrap-metal-littered yard to climb a dirty staircase by a set of creaking, dusty stairs that opened into a large, barn-like loft with a few grimy windows through which some light penetrated, to be supplemented by randomly placed light bulbs hanging on long flexes from the cross-beams. The air was heavy with dust, regularly recirculated in clouds by the actions of an army of old women pulling apart garment seams, unpicking coarse-knit clothing and finally throwing the torn remnants to the floor while differentiating those which were being kept from those to be discarded. One of the women nearest the door would temporarily stop what she was doing to attend to us as she went through a silent sorting process, throwing onto a set of platform scales those garments they intended to purchase while discarding others on the floor at her feet, generating yet another cloud of dust. After that she would set the weights before calculating a bid price for the rags. She would mumble this at us, with lowered eyes, 'Tenpence', which would be the only words she uttered until she fixed you with an unblinking stare; if there was even a moment's hesitation she would begin to gather them up to return them, which was always enough to secure a reluctant 'OK then.' She would go to a wooden box, fish out a handful of coins, push them into your hand and immediately gather up all the rags, including the discards, and dump them near one of the workers. As I left after these stressful negotiations in which I was only an attendant, I was always grateful for the fresh air, heavy with the smell of malted hops from the brewery, after the overpowering stench of old clothes, perspiring old bodies and clouds of dust. We usually left with some cash, which was reassuring however small it was in value, but feeling somehow unclean after the visit.

6

THE ENDING OF INFANCY

Whether the Cullercoats holiday was taken because war was imminent, or because there would be no more children – Ma was after all forty-nine at the time – or because family finances were temporarily eased because Roma and Alan were at work and contributing a major slice of their meagre wages to the household budget, I will never know, and didn't even consider at the time. What did emerge later was that both Ma and Pop knew at the time that she was displaying signs of a serious, potentially terminal illness, and the urgent need for some 'fresh air' and rest had probably been stressed by Dr Taylor.

It may even have been inspired by the euphoria that followed the coronation of George VI in May 1937, after the national gloom upon the death of George V in January 1936 and Edward's abdication in December of the same year. I was four when the coronation took place and was about to become a loyal subject of my third king in my first four years. Some going. I am told I had already experienced the pageantry of George V's Silver Jubilee standing, or rather being held by my mother, in an enthusiastically huge crowd on Barrack Road. Ma at least recognised that the car which carried them was large and black as they sped past, and given Ma's lack of inches I wouldn't have seen much anyway, even if I had been able to stand on her shoulders.

But soon George V was dead and buried and Edward was embarrassingly addicted to 'the American Divorcee': both good reasons to dislike her on Tyneside. For weeks children throughout Newcastle, and doubtless elsewhere, chanted 'Who's that coming down the street? Mrs Simpson and her sweaty feet.' So much for the establishment's belief that the affair was secret or that common people didn't much care; you couldn't get much more common than Elswick Row. We did know and we, or rather our parents, disapproved; but suddenly he and she were gone.

There were no tears at home and we quickly learned more about George VI, his unfortunate stammer – was it right for a king to have a stammer? – his 'sensible' queen and their two attractive daughters, Elizabeth and Margaret Rose. Everyone, however poor, bought souvenirs before the great day; the most popular, which usually equated to the least expensive, was a Rington's tea caddy, with an individual portrait of the four royals, one on each of the four sides. Rington was the local tea merchant. And as usual, and particularly after the shame, scandal and upset of Edward's 'goings on', a 'grand' street party was to be held. More excitement, what organisation and what problems! – even though it was a rerun of the King's father's jubilee street party two years earlier. An impromptu committee with 'Judge' Wood prominent formulated the events timetable; everyone brought their own chairs and tables, which were then all linked in long rows with some family groups, such as ours, staying obstinately together. Catering was a sharing of everything everyone had brought, but with the usual complaints – Mrs Dodds' cakes were indigestible, Mrs Wood's sandwiches were all filled with cheap fish paste, Mrs Birkett's tea was too strong, Mrs Goundry was supposed to provide milk, Mrs Wilson had no teacups, and so on! Many of the women wore Christmas-style party hats, an odd combination for those wearing pinnies and slippers as they all hurried backwards and forwards to their kitchens, filling and refilling huge, brown metal teapots.

The back lane looked festive and was properly dressed for such an important party, with home-made paper chains replacing the usual washing lines zigzagging across it. Mr Wood had framed and displayed a portrait of the new king and queen, using the front page of the

Daily Express glued onto a plywood panel from a tea chest, and the children ran races and were given prizes.

As the day ended a dispute erupted as usual, of which unfortunately – if unusually – we were the epicentre, or rather Ma was. She had collected money for a raffle, mandatory on these occasions, handing out numbered cloakroom tickets she had purchased; with the cash collected she had bought a de luxe souvenir tea caddy, complete with the finest tea, and with the surplus cash she had purchased a large tin of biscuits for the party. The cloakroom tickets had been folded and placed in an upturned hat, and when the raffle was drawn it was Ma's own ticket which was the first out of the hat. Mutterings were heard, cries of 'redraw' followed, but Ma, the most scrupulously honest person in the world, would have none of it. It was fair, she had won on the luck of the draw and that was that. Let the crowd bay, and shame on them for suspecting foul play. It was a marginally unhappy ending to a day when I heard Mr Wood, known as 'the Judge', proclaim passionately, from the chair he was precariously standing on, the benefits of being English (not British) and of being honest (presumably meaning not like foreigners), and why the map of the world was largely coloured pink – a reference I didn't understand at the time, any more than I understood his obvious dislike of foreigners 'across the Channel'.

A spontaneous, if disharmonious, massed choir of adults and children broke into 'God Save the King', and afterwards everyone started to reclaim their chairs, tables and crockery and slowly return indoors. As gas jets were lit indoors, small clusters of men slouched off to their favourite pub – of which there was a surfeit of choice, if not of cash to spend in them – leaving the lane to a few younger men and women, some fumbling embarrassedly with each other. As the lamplighter made his way up the lane lighting the street lamps, they threw downward a narrow cone of yellow light in which the remaining partygoers were fleetingly illuminated and then lost, with only the squeaks, the fading laughter and the departing footsteps as quietness returned. Fires were lit indoors, chimney smoke made the lane more eerily foggy, and it would be some time before the pub-goers returned to disturb the silence.

Hardly had the street party for the coronation been relegated to history, which never did take very long whatever the event, when we became aware that we were to go on holiday. Of course we weren't faced one morning with an announcement that we were going on holiday – things didn't work like that in our house; but it slowly filtered down, passed on by word of mouth after overheard conversations. For me this was quite puzzling, because I didn't know what a holiday was; I certainly hadn't been on one before, but then neither had Rex, Vincent or Alan. As this dramatic new event was shaped by more information about where, with whom, when and for how long we might be going, speculation gave way to excited anticipation. We were going to the seaside, indeed to Cullercoats, where we were to live in a house in Beverley Terrace not far from the seafront – even though anywhere in Cullercoats is close to the seafront, and the accommodation was being provided, no doubt at a heavily discounted rate, by a relation of one of Pop's colleagues on 'the trams', none other than Geordie Fleming.

Cullercoats is only about 7 miles from Newcastle, but it is on the seafront and it was at the time still a largely unspoiled fishing village lying between the more commercialised Whitley Bay, with its brash modern 'Spanish City' fun park, and the larger, more important and historic Tynemouth on the north bank of the Tyne, with the Old Priory ruins at the cliffs' edge. Cullercoats had an attractive, horseshoe-shaped bay with a long breakwater, an aquarium and an operational lifeboat, housed in its own Royal National Lifeboat Institute station on a steep ramp sloping down to the cold waters of the North Sea. Cullercoats village sat on a clifftop and the way down to the beach was either by a ramp which ran close to the lifeboat station, or by some very steep stairs with a metal handrail. Its sands were fine and silver, the water was clear, and the rocks, particularly at low tide, were both safe and accessible. They offered endless opportunities to indulge in simple fishing or crab catching, while above on the cliff frontage were rows of old cottages outside which old 'fishwives' sat all day with a table displaying trays of cooked local crabs, whelks and cockles. The old ladies were dressed in layers of old scarves, shawls or outsize pinnies; I only ever saw them seated, with their heavy clogs poking out from under the tables, with never so much as an ankle visible between pinny and clog. They never rose to sell the seafood; they just rolled around on their chairs, dipping, bending, reaching, wrapping, with hands disguised in fingerless mittens.

Even the journey to Cullercoats was going to be special, because Newcastle had a modern, electrified-loop railway-line system, the first of its kind in Britain, which ran in both clockwise and anticlockwise directions – a concept I found hard to grasp at that age, making me frequently wonder how there were no collisions. We hoped whenever we went to Newcastle Central Station that a great adventure lay ahead for us, because its impressive presence and unique atmosphere created the thought that such an outcome was almost inevitable. Its massive iron and glass barrel roof, the huge stone portico, the rows of busy platforms, the 'hissing' of steam, the blast of whistles, the clashing of carriage doors, the noisy thrust of pistons, the clank of giant wheels and the endless variety of other shouts and noises which accompanied the great steam trains through the station, en route either north to Scotland or south to London, were far better than any model train set. The electric trains were more like domestic pets compared to the wild animals of roaring steam engines, but they were new, comfortable, relatively inexpensive, accessible and took you to the seaside.

I had been to the station many times before since it was very close to St Mary's Cathedral, directly opposite the south aspect behind the high altar, and we caught glimpses of it every Sunday morning. We would often go there after Mass as a less tiring alternative to the Quayside and sometimes were allowed to use the label maker, a red pedestal machine in the concourse with which you could print your own name, on a flimsy narrow tin label, by moving a big brass pointer to the letter or number required, setting it for capital or lower case and pulling a lever to emboss the tin strip. When you had finished you pulled a different lever which cut the label and there, for the price of a halfpenny, you had your own name or address printed on a label with a nail or screw hole at either end ready to be affixed to some important object. Of course if a mistake was made then that was that; there was no going back to start again and there would certainly be no other opportunity to get another halfpenny to produce another label that day, which would have made the whole process tediously lengthy for Pop, Roma or whoever else was our guardian. But this time it wasn't simply going to be a visit to the label machine and it wasn't just going to be to look over the platform railings to see the trains; we were going to travel on one.

On a sunny, fine day we set off with a large suitcase, dressed in our Sunday best and with Sydney, then about three, decked out in a white blouse with large polka dots and brown velvet shorts with bib and braces. His jet-black hair was combed rigidly downwards all round, making him look like a cross between a member of the Hitler Youth and one of the Three Stooges. I can't remember what I wore, but Rex was wearing a short-sleeved, multicoloured Fair Isle sweater over his shirt, with blue shorts and a pair of sandshoes. His hair, which was equally distinctive, being fair and a mass of curls, made him look rather like one of the Marx Brothers. I am sure that whatever anyone else thought, Ma was proud to be shepherding her tribe down Elswick Row to the tram stop outside Beysen's patisserie.

We travelled by tram to Collingwood Street, only a short walk away from the Central Station, and it is eminently possible that one of my father's colleagues might have somehow forgotten to take our fare. We queued in a rather orderly way – although it was carefully designed to shield Vincent from view – as child's fares were requested at the ticket window in the railway station. Small, green, stiff cardboard rail tickets were dispensed and much as I clamoured for one, there was absolutely no possibility that such valuable documents could be entrusted to me or anyone else. Vincent was ordered to go through the barrier with another large family group, since no ticket had been bought for him for economy's sake. Then we were hurrying to the platform to board the train; away we went and very quickly Ma had us all engaged in one of her 'guessy' games. What would be the next station, what would be on the first poster on the platform at the next station, would there be a bridge over the line at this station and if so would it be at the end of the platform we approached or in the middle or at the far end? Pop was taking us down to Cullercoats and staying with us, while Roma had been designated to look after Alan until our long holiday – all of one week – was over.

It was a week of endless pleasure and sunshine, of hours on the sands, of pleading – occasionally successfully – to be taken with Vincent on crabbing expeditions, or to watch as fishing lines were baited with whelk and cast from the end of the pier. He took us to see an immense variety of marine life in huge green tanks in the aquarium, an experience matched by the sight of starfish, blenny, sprats, dogfish and shoals of mackerel beyond the breakwater at twilight. Best of all, however, was to go with him on appointed days to the lifeboat station, to walk on the gantries around the huge, dark blue, red-trimmed hull and the white deck, to gape in awe at the yellow-oilskin-clad crew who manned it.

The lifeboat station visit was free of charge although voluntary donations were encouraged, if not expected. A quick turning out of our trouser pockets enabled us to leave with a clear conscience, as all the other beach pleasures were free and available from sunrise to twilight, when we were herded back to the holiday home. I longed for a trip out to sea on a fishing boat, but that was beyond family finances and therefore defined as being 'too dangerous'. But the pleasures of the week were so intense, so continuous and varied, that it hardly mattered.

However, holidays – even one as pleasurable as this, my first – must be marred by the occasional problem. Periodically one or more of us became lost, but this was only an inconvenience, for although the beach was always crowded the custom had been formed, by some informal, unspoken consensus of adults who found children wandering – frequently crying, occasionally throwing tantrums because they were lost – of taking them to the foot of the nearest set of steps and bellowing that a lost child had been parked there. This was an infinitely more effective and satisfactory solution for the temporary guardians than wandering through the sprawling mass of bodies looking for the matching families.

It was an extremely quiet, formal, civilised beach crowd with most men wearing a cap, or even a bowler hat, over a suit complete with a collar and tie, although the occasional dashing, younger figure would be wearing a Fair Isle jumper, rather like Rex's, over an open-necked, soft-collared shirt, slacks and a pair of carefully 'blancoed' white sandshoes. Women, too, frequently wore a hat. For those who could afford them deck chairs were available, but for most it was some form of rug or blanket on the sand on which to spread either their body or, more commonly, the food. I observed how blankets had a magnet-like attraction for sand and anything left on these makeshift picnic tables would soon be smothered in it, the commonest cause being children chasing each other between rows of people. Reality suggested that food was best eaten immediately it had been taken from its wrapping, and attempts at over-formality by setting it out were usually doomed to failure. Since few families possessed 'thermos' flasks they brought their own teapots, as well as cups, to the beach; hot water was sold in jugs from a trestle-tabled stall at the foot of the cliff steps.

An accident-free holiday with so many children was statistically highly improbable. My accident, which occurred towards the end of the holiday, was to fall on the steep concrete ramp near the lifeboat station, when a combination of sand and ridged concrete played havoc with the skin on my kneecaps. Vincent's accident was of a more predictable nature. He had an addiction to liquorice sticks and one day had seriously overindulged himself. Where he got the money from I am not quite certain, but overindulge he certainly did. Everyone knew that liquorice, taken in these quantities, had a strongly laxative quality and the net result was an accident which found him in favour neither with we who shared a bed with him, nor with my mother who had to repair the damage, nor with the lady of the house. Vincent, as usual, was contrite, but it merely served to underline his hard-earned reputation for being accident prone. He was in the process of consolidating the reputation he had earned in his earlier days, when he had managed to get all the fingers of one hand in a mangle, with serious consequences.

All too soon the sand, the breakwater, the rocks, the fishing expedition, the lifeboat, the aquarium, the fishwives and their cottages, were left behind. We were back on the train, dashing to get window seats, and what awaited me on my return was the next stage in my growing up. Infancy was most certainly at an end once children began going to school. Well, almost at an end, because we did have another unexpected seaside holiday, although this one was more like 'the norm' and lasted just one day!

It was, in fact, a free outing organised by a charitable organisation called the Poor Children's Holiday Association, or the PCHA. As far as I know we certainly met the criteria by which poor children were defined, but on this occasion our inclusion on the trip was due to an invitation from old Mrs Dodds, an octogenarian who lived beyond Wilson's Lamp. She was small, stooped, extremely wrinkled, always well turned out, but friendly; she was well aware of the circumstances of all the people in the neighbourhood, no doubt feeling that nominating us for a day out was a worthwhile 'good deed'. She was also a local councillor, which gave her the power to ordain the selection of some children to be included. Sydney was too young to be entrusted to other adults, and I was allowed to go only because both Rex and Vincent were going as well. The journey was by buses carrying large banner signs proclaiming that this was a PCHA trip, but fortunately for us – because I suspect otherwise we would not have been allowed to go – the buses were to depart from Worswick Street bus station in the centre of town, to which we could travel on the tram.

Our appearance was supervised by Ma, who insisted we made the obligatory visit to the lavatory first, just as she made sure we had a clean handkerchief before we left – with a very clear instruction, meant as much for us as it was for anybody to whom we had to impart the information, that we were going on the trip and had been included not because we were poor, but because our family was friendly with Mrs Dodds. Ma's objective, to protect our collective and individual self-esteem, demanded that she be as innovative as ever.

Three buses packed with children left the city centre for South Shields, which gave the added spice of crossing the Tyne Bridge, a journey I had not made before. While no one could suggest we were better dressed than the other children, we were certainly better behaved; there was much raucousness, jostling and some unseemly words from both boys and girls before eventually we arrived at a church hall not far from the seafront at South Shields. We all sat down at long, bench-like tables, where a variety of sandwiches and drinks were provided which we viewed with great suspicion, as we had been taught to do because of Ma's entrenched view that the rest of the world cooked and served food in a less hygienic way than that to which we were accustomed. Unlikely though such a proposition was, she required unquestioning belief, as though it were a Papal Bull.

The noise was reaching storm proportions because the city-based children were very anxious to get down to the beach, when eventually, after a few feeble attempts to control the noise, a minister of some non-conformist sect stood up in a pulpit, implored the boys particularly to be quiet and to join him in a prayer of collective thanks for the charity that was being granted to us, for the food and drink we were consuming, and for the generosity of those who had contributed to such a splendid day. What followed took us totally by surprise.

A group of boys in reasonable proximity to the speaker picked up their square-shaped raisin cakes, colloquially known as 'fly pies', and hurled them at him, scoring more 'hits' than 'misses'. Such encouragement was unlikely to be resisted by many others and the net result was that a huge volley of 'fly pies' hurtled through the air and peppered not only the speaker, but also many of the other adults who were supervising the occasion. The ringleaders then left their seats, dashed up the gangway to the back of the hall and seeing that their escape via the main door was barred by some adults, opened the windows, leapt out and made off to the beach.

For what seemed a long time we sat transfixed, but in the end we decided that discretion was the better part of valour and that it was unlikely anybody would have been able to determine we were innocent of any crime; the evidence was non-existent because we had eaten our 'fly pies', which were one of the few things we really enjoyed. Vincent ushered us to the back of the hall and put his foot on the window sill with the intention of helping me out, when hands grabbed us by the scruff of our necks and pulled us back. We were to assume collective responsibility for the sins of others, along with a handful of other children who had been even more cowed than us and hadn't moved; we had to clear up the hall before we could be allowed to go to the beach. There was nothing else for it.

Ultimately we were allowed out and joined a number of people on the beach. Mrs Dodds very quickly took us in her care and advanced my anatomical knowledge substantially in the next twenty minutes. She began, as carefully as possible, to disrobe and put on a swimsuit. This was not only an unusual practice for anyone on pre-war beaches, but for an octogenarian it was both brave and outrageous almost to the point of being scandalous. Until then I hadn't believed that human skin could fade and wither as hers had done. It was not the prettiest of sights but, having changed, old Mrs Dodds was yet braver and exposed this translucent, parchment-like skin and what lay underneath it to the cold waters of the North Sea, before returning to prop herself up in the pose more reminiscent of the 'pin-up' film stars I was used to seeing on the cover of Roma's favourite magazine *Picturegoer*, than seemed appropriate either for South Shields beach or for an old lady.

Nothing that happened in the summer of 1938 could diminish the happiness of our seaside holidays, not even the humiliation of being punished for others' misdeeds on the PCHA trip.

I left 1938 behind in a haze of happiness, knowing but not caring that I would be taking some very big new steps the following year, when for the first time I would be expected to act as an individual and not under someone else's direction. That summer did indeed signal the end of my infancy.

7

FAITH, HOPE – AND NOT A LOT OF CHARITY

Weekends were marked not only by the increased noise of the children playing with, fighting and teasing each other in the back lane, but also by Sunday's special nature, since everything about a Sunday was different.

We were all clean and at our peak of freshness until the same time next week; we always had a cooked breakfast of sausage, bacon, egg, white pudding, black pudding and fried bread, before or after which we all went to Mass at St Mary's Cathedral, though seldom all together. We always had the best meal of the week, usually a simple roast of beef, lamb or pork, roast potatoes, vegetables and wonderful, large, golden Yorkshire puddings, all accompanied by a soft drink, Tizer or lemonade, instead of the usual tap water or tea. Sunday was special in every conceivable way.

Pop always prepared meticulously for Sunday Mass. Carefully shaved, dressed in his best suit, white shirt, gleaming shoes, and a carefully brushed hat, he pocketed his rosary beads, carrying his missal with its red, black and gold silk marker ribbons as he left the house, usually for the longer, sung, 'High' Mass at 11.30, after we had returned from earlier Masses, which were 'Low' and therefore shorter. In my younger days I mistook this for religious fervour, although later I realised it was sound strategic planning to ensure that he was unaccompanied and meant that he arrived simultaneously with his boozing companions at the Café Royal, from which he seldom returned until shortly after

2 o'clock. 'Where have you been all this time?' 'I just happened to bump into Geordie Fleming and he wanted me to go for a pint, and well . . . I couldn't say no, could I?'

It hadn't always been like that. In his younger days, still new to his parental role, he used to take Roma and Alan to the Quayside after an early Mass to see all the entertainments and activities. There was stall after stall selling crockery and objets d'art, linens, clothes or cutlery, all accompanied by raucous shouts and improbable offers. Plates were thrown high in the air and deftly caught, or a whole set of dinner plates were shuffled like a pack of cards. There were ice-cream sellers and sarsaparilla makers, whose water supply appeared to be drawn from the 'coaly' Tyne. No wonder it looked so black and smelled of tar.

There were wrestlers and boxers, big, pale skinned, pimpled and scratched: hairy, ugly men, stripped to the waist summer or winter, snarling at and threatening each other to the jeers or cheers of the crowd who threw coins in appreciation at the end of each bout. There was the 'chain man', naked except for what looked like 'long johns', who sought out any compliant member of the audience to bind him in ropes and heavy metal chains, put him in a sack, tie that with more ropes and chains and throw him to the ground. You would hear grunts, snarls, whimpers, choking, tears . . . yet he always emerged free and untied.

And most impressive of all was the 'ostrich man', who swallowed a sharp sword, a string of razor blades, a watch on a chain, and who chewed broken glass and clay pipes. All these items, except the clay pipes and broken glass which presumably were swallowed, were retrieved, often with bloody saliva dripping from them. Horrible but fascinating, and all these activities were carried on amid a huge, bustling throng of people on the temporarily inactive, cobbled Quayside wharves.

There was also the attraction of the river traffic. Merchant ships disgorging cargoes of grain from the prairies, sugar from the Indies and fruits from South America, colliers taking on coal for Europe, iron rails and wooden sleepers for the empire. And of course there were always warships being built or repaired, massive ships with batteries of fearsome, gleaming, long-range guns. There were the bridges to be explored, with the excitement of being on the swing bridge as it moved through 90 degrees to let ships pass, or very occasionally of being taken on the internal lift, which cost a penny for an adult, from the Quayside to the street level of the Tyne Bridge. Or just standing, watching trains puff their way across the Redheugh Bridge with its double-decker system. All this excitement and free, live theatre prepared you – if you still had some energy left – for a climb up the almost vertical steps of the Dog Leap stairs to the brooding, gloomy majesty of the Old Castle Keep and Black Gate Museum, perched high above the river.

Pop would start his long walk home with the children by avoiding the near-vertical steps, but still tackling very steep streets. The only direct route from the Quayside without taking the alternative sets of stairs was to walk up Dean Street to its junction with Moseley Street and Grey Street; this was marginally less demanding than the stairs. Its name was embedded in local folklore, because any unrealisable yet expressed hope, ambition, wish or dream was likely to be met with the response that it would be fulfilled or granted 'when the big ship comes up Dean Street'. The attraction for Pop was that the Turks Head, one of his favourite watering holes, was on Grey Street. It was like an oasis in the desert as he struggled with the children up the steep street from the Quayside. Such exertion demanded that he caringly stopped and bought the children lemonade which, because they were not allowed into pubs, they consumed in the doorway – while quite naturally Pop had time to refresh himself, more than once, inside the pub.

By the time I was old enough to be introduced to the unchanging pleasures of the Quayside after Mass, his reasons for the prolonged journey home had worn a little thin, the children were bored with spending endless hours in pub doorways, and in any case the cost of bribing increasing numbers of us into patient silence had become excessive. First Roma, now working, and then Vincent assumed Pop's mantle as the supervising guide for our post-Mass, Sunday morning expeditions. So it was that Pop had taken to combining the spiritual uplift of sung High Mass with the transient temporal pleasures of draught Bass, always in a straight half-pint glass, in the upmarket, leather-armchaired, gentlemen's club-like comfort of the Café Royal.

Pubs closed at 2p.m. on Sundays and the family had usually finished their dinner when he returned smiling, full of Bass and bonhomie, disgorged his religious artefacts and had his lunch alone. He would then usually retire with his *Sunday Express*, not Ma's *News of the World*, to the bedroom, and the loud snores and mutterings would tell us how well he was absorbing news of international, political and economic events!

For us there were games, inside or out, usually Alan with Roma, Vincent with Rex, and me – not by choice – left with Sydney. Ma, the special nature of Sunday reflected in her food, continued with the making and cooking of plain scones, fruit scones, potato cakes, and my own favourite cheese-and-potato cakes or cheese straws.

And in an appropriate final act to his Sunday of spiritual refreshment, Pop would re-emerge from the bedroom about 7p.m., bleary-eyed, yawning in his familiar state of 'dishabille', one brace off the shoulder, trouser flies half done up, vest and long johns showing, usually in a very prickly and irritable mood. Yet there began a swift metamorphosis, and less than an hour later he would be shaved, groomed, impeccably dressed, before announcing he was off to the 'Blue Man' 'for a swift half and a game of dominoes'. While that was a serious underestimate of the time and the quantity to be consumed, it wasn't quite as bad as one friend's father, who made a similar announcement in similar circumstances and only reappeared twenty-six years later!

Within two weeks of my birth I had of course been baptised into the 'faith of my fathers', and godparents chosen on my behalf renounced 'the Devil and all his works and pomps'. While I am told that I behaved impeccably when holy water was poured over my unsuspecting brow, I knew nothing of this, or what the baptism meant, but throughout my pre-school days I was soon and increasingly aware of the rituals of the Catholic faith.

There was always Sunday Mass, usually early – 7a.m. or 8a.m. – if one went with Ma, which was rare for me in my pre-school days. There was a children's Mass at the cathedral at 9.30a.m. to which Vincent, Rex and frequently Roma went, and while that was slightly longer than the 7a.m. or 8a.m. versions because of the hymns, it was a more enjoyable occasion for children. The 9.30a.m. Mass was succeeded by the last Low Mass at 10.30 and finally the sung High Mass at 11.30a.m.

Apart from the mandatory attendance at Mass, which was the principal external worship in which I took part, there were the constant reminders at home. These took the form of holy artefacts: the crucifix, the palms from the previous year's Palm Sunday, the statue of 'Our Lady of Victories' on the sideboard – usually adorned with my father's and sometimes my mother's rosary beads, or 'holy' medals which everybody was given by those relatives, such as Auntie Minnie, who were wealthy and devoted enough to travel overseas before the war to places of worship and pilgrimage. Adults' conversation, particularly after a pilgrimage, often included references to Lourdes or, more rarely, to Rome, and then more artefacts would appear in their own homes.

One of Auntie Minnie's prize exhibits in her own home was Our Lady standing on a rock in a glass dome which, when shaken, magically showered snow on the holy person. Auntie Minnie was always pleased to show it to us without allowing us to play with it, as she had a well-founded suspicion of the destructive habits of boys and a total ignorance of what pleased or displeased them.

We were all sure by the time we started school that we were Catholics. We knew we were not Protestants; we were certainly not Jews and certainly not foreigners, but in a working-class environment each family's faith was an important distinguishing characteristic. While some people may have scorned others' religion, I can't remember there being any particular dislike of others, although nevertheless everyone held a trenchant belief that their own faith was the 'only' faith. There were few publicly professed atheists or agnostics, probably on the basis that if you were poor and working class, why should you risk alienating higher authority?

As soon as I started school I was introduced to the obligatory purchase of the red-backed 'penny catechism', that guide to faith by which all Catholic schoolchildren are taught and which is intended to be a lifelong guide to understanding the important elements and articles of faith. There could be no saving here for the family by handing a used copy down from an older child, for this was meant to be your own personal catechism, your guide through life. We painstakingly learned the contents by rote, just as we did numbers, multiplication tables, words and phrases, by a teacher asking the questions and children either individually or collectively repeating the answer. And so, shortly before the might of the German Army was unleashed in a blitzkrieg of the Low Countries, I attained the 'age of reason' and was prepared for my next major step, that of my first Holy Communion, through which I would become a fully active member of the faith.

Everyone's first Holy Communion was to be preceded by their first confession, for which there was ample preparation followed by a slow march down from the school to the cathedral, a distribution of the children around the various confessional boxes, and the lottery of which priest heard your confession. The process had been drilled into us – entering the darkened cubicle, kneeling before a black-curtained grille, hearing the rustle of the priest's garments or the muffled cough or yawn, and then with faltering voice, 'Pray Father, give me your blessing for I have sinned . . .', followed by a recital of sins in which you had been coached at school – after which I had asked a few rather curious questions of my mother. The concept of sin for a seven-year-old is quite difficult to understand, but soon confession was over and each child was given his or her penance to fulfil – understandably rather uniform at that stage – before we were ready, in a state of grace, for the great day.

Our first Holy Communion was due to take place on Easter Sunday, when we were all dressed in our Sunday best – rather better than best, really – with clean white shirts, wearing a sash given by the school, brushed up and wheeled into church. Since it was Easter Sunday there was colour in the vestments and excitement in the congregation, after the dark purple vestments and sadness of Passion Week; there was singing and there were young girls dressed as brides with white veils, walking in procession and strewing flowers in a choreographed ballet down the aisle, preceding the return of the Blessed Sacrament to the high altar. It was heady, emotional stuff and afterwards there was a communion breakfast to celebrate this important act of faith, further marked by the issuing of illustrated parchment scrolls on which our own name was beautifully written with the date of the communion; and finally we were given another holy medal to treasure.

Whatever the uncertainties of life, of which there were many, this faith in Catholicism was to be our central pillar from then on and it gave Ma further opportunities to keep on educating us by implanting values. 'Blessed are the poor . . .', 'Blessed are the peacemakers . . .'. But she wasn't too keen on 'Blessed are the meek . . .' or on 'turning the other cheek'. It wasn't that she was selective in what she believed; it was just that some beatitudes had a more obvious practical application in her real world than others. But she who had adopted the faith in order to marry Pop with his Irish Catholic background – it couldn't have been the reverse – was as fervent in her beliefs as any missionary; yet her common sense caused her to scorn excessive shows of religious zeal as 'showing off', or excessive devotion to priests as 'toadying'. Her faith was deeply rooted in her belief in the existence of God, and not in any priest or his interpretation of His will.

Mrs Brown, a devout old lady whom Ma dismissed curtly as 'crackers', was different. She would enter the church through the main door, never the side doors, and after sloshing an unseemly amount of holy water all over herself, rather like a blackbird bathing in the early morning, she would cross herself with extravagant gestures, prostrate herself with a groan and then raising herself to her knees proceed down the aisle on them, gaspingly chanting the rosary as she went. This was not an occasional command performance, but a regular weekly event. It was rumoured that she wore hessian bags of sawdust under her voluminous garments as a constant penance.

The sidesmen who took the offertory collections were also always subject to Ma's suspicious probing glare and sometimes to her open hostility. If they proffered the velvet-lined plate or long-handled wooden box for her to submit her offerings, she would prise their fingers from it, deposit her coins quietly and pass it on. There was no hope of its being returned directly for them to inspect for this, as always, was a matter between her and her Maker. She reserved her greatest scorn for those who made blatantly transparent gifts of notes or large coins, often with a great flourish or a noisy shake if it was into the box; 'the widow's mite' was always close to Ma's heart.

While as a boy I often harboured a latent wish to be a Salvationist, if only to bang a drum or shake a tambourine – or better still to be a member of the Boys' Brigade, for whom drums were accompanied by a smart black and white uniform – it was patiently explained that these were Protestant rituals and not for us. There was even a feeling, probably driven more by curiosity than anything else, that I could accompany one of our back-lane pals to Sunday School, from which they often returned with books or with some curious but decidedly un-Catholic 'holy picture'. However, we were again dissuaded from this – gently, yet with the very firm view that while this was 'all right for them', it was not the same as worship in the true faith.

But we as Catholics had our public displays, particularly on holy days such as Whit Sunday. Then it was common for a large procession to move round the cathedral, led by priests in their vestments, followed by choirboys carrying candles and banners and then the other clergy in cassock and surplice, followed in turn by as many of the congregation as could muster the enthusiasm for such a public display. They were always good-tempered occasions which didn't cause offence; there was never any conflict and there was a certain joy in this public demonstration of faith.

In much the same way everyone was conscious in our street, or in the back lane, of the presence of the Catholic priests. The curates were usually Irish, fresh from a seminary in their native land and most at home in the back streets, where it took very little encouragement to have them playing a game of football. They loved visiting the houses, which they were required to do as part of their 'guardians of the flock' role, and ours must have been a particular favourite because of the number of noisy boys in the household, who must have been the most powerful reminder for many of them of what they had left behind. In the main they were good-humoured, cheerful, simple souls and it was difficult to imagine them sitting in the dark calm of the confessional listening to the litany of human failings poured out by their parishioners – most of whose voices they no doubt recognised – or to the chanted, implanted failings of the children.

My own favourite throughout this period was Father Cahill, principally because at one stage, having lofted the ball following a goal-line clearance it lodged in one of the few trees in the street, and rather than escaping with dignity he prevailed upon a neighbour to lend him a clothes prop. By great skill he managed to dislodge the ball before donning his jacket again and going about his parochial duties, with a wink to us as he left.

Religion wasn't only for Sundays; it was part of everybody's daily life one way or another.

8

NOT-SO-DEAR OCTOPUS

The most frequent visitors to the house were members of the two families, the Cassidys or the Currys. The Cassidys tended to visit us more frequently than the Currys did, and I suspect that was because the Currys as a family were looked down upon by my father's family – quite wrongly – as being of a lower social status. It was quite clear that the Cassidy family's former wealth, acquired by great-grandfather's exploits in the middle of the nineteenth century and short-lived though it was, had given rise to ideas about their own station which by the 1930s were seriously misplaced.

Great-grandfather had been born into an Irish peasant family, so this certainly was not a case of the Cassidys being Irish landowners and passing down their wealth to their son Pat, who had no inheritance whatsoever and had escaped the hungry years in Ireland only by joining the British Army's 43rd Light Infantry Regiment. Patrick enlisted in Fermanagh on 26 January 1843 at the age of nineteen years and six months, and according to his army account book he was '5 feet 7½ inches tall with a pale complexion, dark grey eyes and brown hair'. He enlisted for a bounty of three pounds, seventeen shillings and sixpence, of which he received three shillings and sixpence in cash, while his 'necessaries' – jackets, trousers, shirts, boots, caps, haversack and others – accounted for the balance of the bounty and a bit more, since they came to four pounds, one shilling and ten pence halfpenny. He was already in debt to Her Majesty.

1988 Private Cassidy served throughout his twenty years in the British Army as a private soldier in the infantry. Midway through his twenty years' service, when he and his regiment left Africa and their campaigns behind for the East Indies, no savings were recorded in his army pay book. Yet after serving throughout the Indian Mutiny in some of the more troublesome spots, for which he won further medals, he had accumulated quite rapidly a sum of nearly £600 in his savings account. Family mythology later seemed designed to protect the probity with which such great wealth had been accrued, the most popular version being that he had won the Bangalore Sweepstake; but history suggests that it was probably attributable to the common practice of distributing booty among serving regiments when cities were sacked following the opposition's defeat. Whatever the truth, such a sum would have enabled Patrick to adopt the lifestyle of a country gentleman when he retired in 1863, and that appears to be what he did. However, two generations later the money had gone, or rather it had been redistributed extremely unequally. The wealth had either been cornered by successive eldest sons, or dissipated by more feckless members of the clan. Since my Grandpa Cassidy, who had been born in Madras when his mother was 'with the regiment', died in 1916 long before I was born, and Grandma died later in the same year that I was born, the members of the Cassidy family we saw tended to be my father's brothers, interspersed with frequent visits from his only surviving sister, Minnie.

Auntie Minnie's visits were different from those of my uncles. It was clear that while she wanted to see Pop, who was four years older than her, she also wanted to see the family as a whole. Auntie Minnie appeared to have another, albeit secondary, reason for her regular visits: her visible attraction to my dimple-cheeked, curly-haired older brother Rex, who not only looked different from most of us but also behaved more sedately. Both he and Sydney exercised an obvious appeal to the maternal instincts of childless women, Sydney by his cap of jet-black hair above his coal-black eyes, and Rex by his mass of Shirley Temple-blonde curls above his dimpled cheeks, hands and knees. It was a physical attractiveness that neither Vincent nor I could muster, while Alan's frequently glowering manner had not inspired such affection in his earlier days. Sydney was drawn to and accompanied Roma on every possible occasion, while Rex was adopted for short visits by Auntie Minnie. She matched perfectly the caricature of a maiden aunt, being rather 'flutter tut' in her manner and given to excitable giggles, while she was as impractical and 'airy fairy' as Ma was practical and down to earth. She had an unfortunate habit of being, perhaps unintentionally, patronising by giving Ma – often with great ceremony – some of her cast-off clothing: which because of their extreme physical disparity would never have fitted Ma anyway. On occasion the second-hand clothes were of a more intimate nature, such as her voluminous 'grabbed at the knee' green bloomers, which Ma wouldn't have contemplated wearing, but in order to keep the peace she accepted these and other things which either ended up as dusters or were consigned to the bag destined ultimately for the rag shop. In good times the money received from the cast-offs would be shared among us for treats, such as going to the pictures, but more often it was needed for food.

Pop's brothers were more regular in their visits, which on the whole tended to be of a shorter duration, at least in the time they spent in our house, because the prime purpose was to have a male conversation in male surroundings with Pop – in short, over a beer in a pub. They all had their own broods at home and there was no reason to believe that they found time spent with their brother's brood in similarly cramped conditions any more attractive than their own homes.

However, both the youngest and the eldest brothers were different and less predictable in their habits. The youngest son, Alan, was a drifter by nature and one of only two of the brothers who had migrated from Newcastle. The other was the eldest son, John Patrick, who was always known as JP. Uncle JP had been privileged, having been given a good education partly at the recently opened St Cuthbert's, and as the eldest he had inherited serious wealth at the age of twenty-five following his father's death in 1916. He now lived in the wealthy London suburb of Swiss Cottage and ran his part-owned chemist shop in Great Portland

Street, W1. JP's visits seemed intended more to emphasise his wealth and success than to share it with his brothers and in-laws. Uncle Alan, by contrast, was forever on the move and there was always an underlying suspicion that there were good, if unknown, reasons for that being constantly so. He was unmarried and whenever he appeared in our house he would be delighted to accept the offer of one of Ma's meals, while also ensuring that he and Pop spent some time outside together, when he would 'borrow' some money before vanishing again for months or sometimes for a year or two. In these long periods of absence it was often rumoured that he 'was on the run', but it was probably from cuckolded husbands or irate members of his own family rather than from the law.

One of Pop's other brothers had a similar propensity for seeking money whenever he appeared, not that he was financially worse off than Pop, but because it was just in his nature. Visits from Uncle Bertie usually resulted in Pop lending him sums of money which, although small, were large in relation to his disposable income. On occasions I overheard Pop subsequently referring to this as, for example, 'Uncle Bertie borrowed ten shillings from me', which would be greeted by Ma's familiar snort of disbelief. She knew that if it was a loan it was one on which the only interest would be whether or not it would ever be repaid. More frequently, however, the visit would be to obtain money by the more direct participatory route of persuading Pop to accompany one or more of them to a pub where he could be the provider. Not that he needed much persuasion, but having exhausted his spending money on his brothers and returned home somewhat the worse for wear, he recognised often that he had been generous to the point of being extremely careless – which usually resulted in a serious attack of retrospective remorse and made him irritable and introspective.

With Uncle JP and Alan living away from Tyneside and with the natural affinity shared by brothers closest to each other in age, it was Uncles Bertie and Vincent whom Pop saw most often. Neither was remotely like Pop, either in looks or temperament. Vincent was thin, tight-lipped and mean, both in looks and in habits, and being affected by deafness from an early age he was an unwelcome visitor as far as we children were concerned.

Bertie, on the other hand, although he had some of Pop's cheerful gregariousness, tended to talk about himself incessantly, and since he was employed as a dental mechanic making false teeth he had developed a disconcerting, stomach-churning habit of pulling out his own false teeth to show you how beautifully they were made. It was not something that appealed to Ma and certainly had us children running for cover. He had striking, pale blue eyes which bulged from his head and watered incessantly, requiring rapid, frequent mopping with his handkerchief. Since he was also given to endless religious invocations, often accompanied by nostalgic references to departed friends and family – 'God rest them' – it was difficult to tell whether the watering eyes were tears of sadness, some genetic fault or simply chronic alcoholic overindulgence. It was hardly a surprise that soon after he arrived Ma would be only too glad to see the back of him, even if it meant Pop was going to be absent for a prolonged period and would return home in less than the best of spirits.

Uncle Laurie was a rare visitor who had been born partially deformed, with a pigeon chest and a hunchback, while Uncle Syd was an even rarer visitor, largely because he lived in Jarrow with his family, making it that much more difficult and expensive for him to visit regularly. The seven or eight miles seemed such a long way to travel; in relative terms it was, since as many family visits as possible were undertaken on foot.

In spite of the Cassidy family's collective disapproval of the Currys' pedigree it was clear that Pop's brothers and their wives looked upon Ma with respect, if not affection. She was demonstrably a good manager in modest financial circumstances, and courteous even when courtesy required the patience of a saint; but there were occasions when she spoke sharply to one or other, usually with the consequence that there was a short break before the regular visits resumed. In addition she had been an attentive daily nurse and carer for their mother, Grandma Cassidy, as she declined in health in the years immediately preceding my birth. Ma had for some years cooked and carried meals across the road to No. 32, where Pop's family had lived since 1914. The even-numbered houses in Elswick Row were larger terraced houses, none of which was divided into two flats as were the odd-numbered houses opposite, including ours, No. 15. In addition the larger, even-numbered houses had bigger front gardens, usually neatly kept with a border of flowers inside the spear-headed iron-railing fence.

Minnie lived in No. 32 with Grandma until her death in 1933, but was incapable temperamentally of providing the increasing care which Ma undertook; if Ma had been unwilling to do so, though, Minnie would have been obliged to give up her well-paid work at Vickers Armstrong. Of course we lived the closest to Pop's parents, in the same street from 1928, but Ma probably had the heaviest domestic workload, given the size of our family. As always she shrugged this off and despite the superior, patronising air adopted by some of her in-laws towards her, she let this wash over her as she did with so many other provocations. When Grandma died in October 1933 she left her entire estate to Auntie Minnie, so that whatever was left after Uncle JP was financed to set up in his London pharmacy now passed to the only daughter, my spinster aunt. If my parents had any illusions about an inheritance to ease their financial situation – which I feel sure they didn't – they were extinguished during my first year. Auntie Minnie then moved to her own flat in Strickland Street, the principal reason for, and benefit of, this relocation being that she was closer to her work at Vickers Armstrong.

There were many differences between the two families, although they also shared much in common. Ma's family, in marked contrast to Pop's, was dominated by girls. In addition her father, John Curry, was a skilled saddler and harness maker and her mother had been born to country stock near Berwick-on-Tweed. I knew neither, since both had died before I was born, and of the eight children six were girls. The two boys Robert and Samuel, Uncles Bob and Sam, both became skilled carpenters, cabinetmakers and polishers. Barbara, my mother, was the youngest in the family and there was a seventeen-year gap between her and the eldest, Anne. While the Cassidys were Irish Catholics, the Currys were English Protestants.

Auntie Anne married John Pendriegh, a near neighbour, and in 1908 settled in New Zealand. Lydia, who was six years older than Ma, married and emigrated to Canada in 1912 narrowly missing, because of oversubscription, the disastrous maiden voyage of the *Titanic*. These were distant, rather romantic figures whose regular if infrequent letters from far-flung parts of the empire caused a great stir when they arrived and gave my mother so much pleasure. Bob and Sam usually visited us when we required some manual jobs to be done, but their visits became less frequent in inverse proportion to the increasing number of outstanding repairs. Ma was extremely fond of Sam, who was eight years older than her but five years younger than his brother Bob, and she saw her other three sisters regularly, usually by visiting them. They had many shared characteristics, principally those of being warm, gentle and fond of laughter; but all were much quieter and less forceful than my mother, as were the brothers Bob and Sam. Ma seemed to exude determination, energy and purpose, yet in the process never lost her family inheritance of a gentle spirit and generosity.

As her own family increased in size, it clearly became increasingly difficult for my mother to visit as often as she had done previously and would have liked to continue doing. Elizabeth, who was always known as Auntie Tis, lived in Byker; from my earliest recollections she was a semi-invalid sitting in a wooden-armed easy chair, wrapped in a shawl. She had been badly affected by a serious stroke, from which she never fully recovered, and in the years that I knew her she subsided into a long, slow decline. But she never lost her twinkling 'Curry eyes', and she was helped by having two attractive daughters who were always fun to have around.

I never cared much about our visits to other members of either family because of the long preparations, long walks and occasional tram rides, but this one was different because both Dora and Barbara were always such warm hosts. Family visits were much looked forward to by, and very special for, my mother but I, as most young boys did, found them rather boring. These visits were usually made at weekends, generally in the afternoon when tea would be provided which, if it could be afforded, included tinned fruit such as pineapple chunks or sliced peaches with 'Carnation' cream, accompanied by buttered brown bread and scones. As far as I was concerned the food was an inadequate compensation for lost playtime, and the gloom of patient conversations with an ill, ageing aunt weighed heavily against electing to accompany Ma on these visits.

However, there was some enjoyment in the tram ride if we were lucky enough to go by tram. Wherever possible we would rush to the upper deck, and if the weather permitted to the open-ended front or back of the tram, where we could sit on the brightly polished, slatted wooden seats, watching the buildings go backwards while the tramcar rattled noisily and swayed violently from side to side. The noise of the tram accelerating or braking became a familiar sound, and I envied the driver moving the gleaming brass handle with gauntleted hands to control the rattling monster.

My father's family were uniformly Cassidys, since the only girl remained a spinster throughout her life, whereas Ma's family had only two surviving Currys, the brothers Bob and Sam. All the girls married and adopted their husbands' names – Cassidy of course for Ma, the youngest, but Grey, Hills, Peddie, Pendriegh and Scott for the others. The Curry family were shy, retiring, soft, gentle and very feminine with Barbara, the youngest, being as gentle as the rest but also as tough as teak. The Cassidys were male, aggressive, vociferous and inclined to be vaguely superior, whereas Pop, the third youngest, was much more gentle, with a hint of romanticism, but just as blustery as the rest.

The two family cultures were so different that it was inevitable that their courtship would be at best questioned and at worst threatened. They met when Barbara was a shop assistant in a corner grocery shop on Scotswood Road, close both to the River Tyne and the industrial heart of Tyneside. She would walk two miles from home to open the shop, and twelve hours or more later would retrace her steps to Wellington Street.

One evening one of the other shop girls was frightened by a large rat in the stockroom, and while Barbara kept the rat under surveillance the other girl was sent to bring male assistance from the pub next door.

Harry Cassidy was a darkly handsome and extrovert young man, who quickly despatched the rodent but in the process was smitten by Barbara. He took to looking out for her and if he saw her, trailing unseen behind her going either to or from work. Taking his courage in both hands he sent to the shop a postcard addressed to 'Miss Barbara . . .', entitled 'Fair exchange is no robbery', featuring a baby sucking a dachshund's tail while the dog sucked on the baby's milk bottle.

This was a rather unorthodox way to open relations, but the romance blossomed and Harry soon revealed to his parents that he wanted their blessing before he sought her parents' approval to marry her. It was 1915 and the threat of conscription for Harry was self-evident in the face of mounting casualties in France. His mother's reaction was to walk to the shop, unannounced, to tell Barbara that she couldn't possibly marry her son because she was not of the Catholic faith. Barbara, who was a 26-year-old managing a shop and with the experience of growing up in a large family in difficult circumstances, replied that she understood that so well that she had already started to 'take instruction' in the faith. If Grandma Cassidy's strategy was to focus on what she thought was Barbara's Achilles heel, rather than her undesirability as a daughter-in-law because of her poor background, she had badly misjudged matters. Barbara, not for the last time, had carried the day.

They were married in St Mary's Cathedral in November the following year and throughout their marriage she proved to be a good wife, mother, daughter-in-law, and – not least in Cassidy eyes – a devoted convert to the faith.

Henry Edward Cassidy and Barbara Curry made a very complementary pair, and because of this there was seldom a scarcity of people seeking to visit the simple homes they created and share in the happiness of those who lived there.

9

PREPARING FOR SCHOOL

Days succeeded one another in the same relentless way. For all of us, whether adults or children, it started with a brisk wash in the kitchen in cold running water or a kettleful of hot water boiled for the occasion. The boys' clothes were changed on a weekly basis, to follow the Saturday-night bath in a large, zinc tub placed in the hearth. Nobody had a toothbrush, and we never had underpants to change until we were at the long-trouser stage of adolescence, but we always had very long vests to compensate for this absence. Queuing for the use of limited facilities was therefore short and transformation from bed wear to play-, school- or workwear extremely swift and simple.

Seven is generally regarded as a lucky number, but I was relegated to number five in the surviving family and soon my temporary status as the pampered youngest vanished when Sydney was born in April 1935, to become number six – the 'baby' – as well as the seventh son of one of seven sons. But in many senses that was welcome, for while the scrutiny attached to being the 'baby' may have been pleasant I remember very little of it. The subsequent anonymity of being in 'no man's land' was helpful, while most people thought I enjoyed very obvious benefits because I could look up to older brothers and a sister. It was true that some of the dangers and difficulties of growing up, moving into new territories, visiting new places, meeting new people, playing new games, doing new things, were mitigated, at least theoretically, by the fact that you had an older brother to help you through this social minefield.

Inevitably my questioning and curiosity were channelled initially by their knowledge, pride or prejudice. Younger children always want to play with older children, while older children themselves suffer the reverse problem and don't want to be associated with younger ones; but given the organisational stranglehold that Ma had over our household such philosophical issues were seldom left to personal inclination. If one of the children was going somewhere, any other one could be attached to him or her. Thus it could be 'Vincent, you've got to take Denis along too', or 'Alan, don't forget Vincent and Rex are here as well'; such a request was seldom questioned and was definitely not to be argued with. But there were penalties in consequence and not infrequently I was abandoned somewhere, quietly parked as a dog is tied to a railing, told to sit, stand or do anything, provided that I would 'Shut up and don't get in the way.' Initially I suppose I was tempted to complain tearfully. If I tried that tactic, and I think I must have done to have learned the lesson so quickly, their own resulting chastisement was likely to be followed by swift retribution. The solution was obvious: if I was lucky enough to be taken anywhere, whether reluctantly or not, I had to make the best of it and if necessary plead with my brothers, rather than complain later.

I suppose it was the lesson that my great-grandfather learned in the hungry years of approaching famine in Ireland, during the Kaffir wars in South Africa, and in India during the mutiny. My grandfather must have learned similar lessons in the process of growing up in the second half of the nineteenth century, having been born in Madras 'on the march'; and my father had learned them in the harsh final years of the nineteenth century. Apart from great-grandfather's experience on hot veldt or dusty plains, which was at least rewarded by medals and booty, not a lot had changed in England since, for things looked, and society behaved, much as they had done in the days of Dickens. Children still worked in dangerous factories or other hazardous occupations when both my parents left school in the first few years of the twentieth century, but they at least were at school until the age of fourteen and loved it. Ma became a shop girl and remained so until she married Pop in 1916, while his first job was as a van delivery boy at the Woodbine Laundry, collecting and delivering by horse-drawn cart to the great and good of the time. This was followed, inevitably for him, by a stint as a barman before he took a job as a conductor on the city's Corporation Transport after his marriage.

I had been well indoctrinated: attendance at school and the opportunity to learn was a privilege, not a duty, and a gift, not a right, so going to school for the first time was not going to be a problem for me or my parents. I was ready for new adventures. Vincent and Rex were already at St Mary's and Ma would accompany me, as she had done for all my siblings, for my registration at the school. That was duly accomplished with very little excitement and I found myself in what was a normal-sized class of about thirty-six children in a well-worn schoolroom, with well-worn, ink-stained desks and teachers to match. For most of that year's intake learning would be about to start, but for me, as it had been for my brothers and sister before me, the basic skills of reading, writing and a rudimentary knowledge of words, phrases and numbers had already been acquired.

Yet this process, achieved by informal lessons such as counting the coins from Pop's conductor's satchel, or writing on any scrap of paper that could be found, was so advanced that my first year at school was a disappointment. I, together with one or two others, was held back and consequently became bored.

The elementary school to which all the Cassidy boys went was St Mary's Boys' School, a unique school building in my experience because the playground was on the roof, with high, inward-pointing, curved, cast-iron railings to prevent pupils from falling, jumping or escaping over the parapet. But even more bizarrely it had its lavatories on the roof too, which proved an irresistible challenge for some boys. If they weren't allowed to climb through or over the railings they could certainly pee over (more flashy) or through them (more satisfying), and many a passer-by must have wondered why it was drizzling when the sun shone brightly overhead. The school was situated in the quaintly named Oystershell Lane, adjacent to the main local brewery, the Tyne Brewery Company, of which the brewhouse pumped out steam and the smell of malted hops while our young brains were fermenting with the input of further information and knowledge. We were under the watchful eye and tutelage of Miss Timoney – in a time when women teachers were nearly always 'Miss', irrespective of their marital status – or the headmaster, Fred Kelly (everyone knew the headmaster's Christian name), or Mr O'Donnell, or 'Fatty' Abbott – aka Mr Rabbit, since many teachers had derogatory nicknames. There were two other women teachers, Miss Corr and Mrs Lumsden. The males all wore suits, with waistcoats and watch chains, while their jackets and trousers always had a film of white chalk dust covering them. Indeed, classrooms had a permanent cloud of these fine, white particles filling the air, generated by the large, wooden-handled dusters used to clean the blackboards. Little wonder that there were regular outbreaks of coughing and throat clearing. The women always wore thick tweed skirts, thick lisle stockings and flat shoes, from which I couldn't help noticing how big Miss Timoney's feet were; later on in the war we likened them to landing barges.

It was at primary school that I probably benefited most from being among the lower orders of the Cassidy family, simply because most, if not all, who had gone before had distinguished themselves as bright, studious, reasonably well-behaved children. Alan was an exception to every rule, but since the gap between him and me was nine years his record had been more than adequately compensated for by the earnest endeavours of Vincent and Rex; and I have little doubt that I, for my part, smoothed the way later for Sydney, whether or not he agreed.

Life always extracts a price for these favours, however, and I was expected to outperform all the other children in the class. Happily this was no great problem with classmates, and neighbours, like Reggie

Wood. Reggie, if asked a question of even the simplest kind, such as, 'Why not write your name and class number at the top of the exam paper to start with?' would gaze skywards, thoughtfully stroke his chin, bury his head in his hands, rub his brow furiously, look heavenwards with imploring eyes, seeking at the very least divine inspiration and, when that was not forthcoming, bang on his temple with the knuckles of his left hand. Reggie was undeniably not a natural scholar.

There were others who never gave you the opportunity to determine their level of intelligence, simply because they were seldom present. Joe Horsfall, for instance, whose family were gypsies, on returning to school after an absence of a month said without apology that he had been 'selling horses'. His parents had been to the Appleby Horse Fair, which gypsies had been doing for centuries, where Joe was doing what he did best – riding ponies bareback and racing them to establish their pedigree and selling value. Happily there were some others who were brighter, more diligent, and who provided both companionship and competition.

Prime among these was Alan Thornton, who by definition must have been bright because his mother's maiden name was Cassidy; there was some tenuous link between the two families although quite a while back, presumably in the hungry Irish years of the 1840s. When I met him at St Mary's it began a friendship which lasted through school years and beyond; he was a much bigger boy than I was, but then who wasn't? He was rather like his father, naturally inclined to a spreading figure with a rather broad, slack backside and a shuffling gait partly caused by his extremely large boots with, I assumed, large feet within them. He also had a curiously turned-up nose, as though in his earliest days he had run into a wall and perhaps as a result had some difficulties in breathing normally through his nose, as is necessary on some occasions such as when eating or talking. This gave rise to some interesting, sometimes exciting, sometimes strange snorting noises, but as a boy I found this all rather normal and somewhat amusing. We became inseparable, and with him I enjoyed some of the companionship

I couldn't expect from my older brothers, who had more or less 'paired off'. He was of a more appropriate age than my younger brother, for whom nevertheless I felt, and was required by Ma to feel, a deep sense of commitment and a need to exercise protection; given my physical stature this was not always a realistic ambition. Alan Thornton, though, while neither the nimblest nor the fleetest, was one of the biggest boys in the class and could be relied upon to remove most of the threats of physical aggression from others.

He and I formed, at first unconsciously and effortlessly, a mutual security pact. We enjoyed being together and I welcomed the increased sense of security, which I had never felt from my older brothers who gravitated towards each other. It enabled me to exercise a mild benevolence towards Sydney when he started attending St Mary's because I could now offer protection by proxy, which given my rather slender physical resources would have been undeliverable otherwise.

Because we were so advanced Alan and I became 'monitors' and were entrusted with tasks such as handing out pencils and books. We, but few others, were allowed to use pen and ink and to fill our own inkwells. Yet these were small compensations for the enforced idleness and loss of freedom, as we sat and suffered the stumbling attempts of Joe, Reggie and others to conquer 'the cat sat on the mat' or multiplication tables '1 times 2 is 2, 2 times 2 is ?'.

The summer holidays came and, although lacking in the heady excitement of 1938 with its blissful week at Cullercoats, went in a blur of sunshine and games in the back lane. As September approached, and with it the end of the holidays, private anxieties were growing. For my parents it was the dread of war and the fear that their older children would be destroyed by it, as so many of their contemporaries had been in the 1914–18 conflict which, after all, had not proved to be the 'war to end all wars'.

For me it was the potential disappointment of another tedious year at school – that which I had looked forward to so much the previous year and which had proved such a frustrating experience. That was not a criticism of the teachers; they had to find a common base and once that basic level had been achieved for all, then the brighter children were encouraged as obviously as the duffers were openly mocked.

Two things had rescued me from mutiny or the temptation of truancy. The first was Ma's frequently delivered warning about truancy: that the dreaded 'school board man' would come hunting for us, would certainly find us, bind us with ropes and transport us in a large wheelbarrow back to school. There we would be shamed before the whole school, and if that wasn't enough to deter me – although it was – then the second event, coming just as school was to reopen, changed life for everyone, and for the better as far as I was concerned. Hitler invaded Poland on 1 September 1939, confirming Ma and Pop's worst fears.

And so began the second phase of growing up.

10

ADOLF HITLER'S PUBLIC APPEARANCE

Although the storm clouds of war were gathering swiftly, life went on much as it always had and no doubt always will. On the one hand younger men in pubs talked enthusiastically about the prospect of war and older ones talked reluctantly about the horror of the Great War. On the other hand, while great political divisions grew within the country other, more mundane, issues preoccupied most men and their families at home, manifesting deeply held fears and prejudices.

In this strange, twilight world, suspended between war and peace, it was to sport and gambling that, as usual, most working men turned for relief. Littlewoods Football Pools had been launched nationally at about the time of my birth, and in some quarters were being condemned as 'immoral'. For example, butchers in Worthing collectively and publicly pronounced, with high moral indignation, that some customers were buying cheap foreign meat instead of their more expensive British product – which implied the latter was also better, of course – simply so they could afford the addictive weekly gamble on 'the pools'. In the real world of football, Bryn Jones was transferred from Wolves to Arsenal for an astronomical £13,000, while a young Yorkshire cricketer called Leonard Hutton scored a record 364 runs for England against Australia at The Oval – the highest individual Test score ever recorded at the time. In athletics Sidney Wooderson, physically more like a Cassidy than an international sporting hero, set a new world mile record.

Yet in spite of these distractions there was little doubt that war was imminent, and that prospect hung like a black cloud over everyday life and plans. For my parents and so many like them, there was the recurring nightmare of what they had suffered personally during their courtship and marriage less than twenty-five years before and which was now going to be revisited on them. Adolf Hitler, whose name we heard increasingly frequently after the minor reoccupation of the Rhineland, the aggressively blatant reacquisition of Sudetenland and the *Anschluss* of Austria, was clearly now focused on all-out war. Most working men agreed with Winston Churchill – not one of their favourite politicians – who was the most vocal public figure denouncing Herr Hitler and his evil intent, but Mr Chamberlain and his government did not, instead seeking 'peace with honour'.

To my parents, as for most working-class families throughout the land but particularly in areas such as Tyneside, with its dominant activities of coalmining, shipbuilding, ordnance manufacture and heavy engineering, the signs by 1938 were unmistakable, yet not without some benefit. For the first time since the armistice of 1919, employment had increased. The knot of anxious, unemployed men on street corners had first diminished and then disappeared. Even my nineteen-year-old sister was aware that something very strange was happening when she was paid a substantial bonus for her part in the increased output of the Vickers Armstrong munitions factory, where she was working as a clerk.

When in 1935 the birth of Sydney caused the family, or rather our own Chancellor of the Exchequer – Ma – to reappraise its delicately poised financial situation, a new economic regime was introduced which required Roma to leave school in order to work for her, or rather our, living, thus abruptly ending a promising academic career. Perhaps it was preordained that she would work at Vickers Armstrong. After all Grandpa, in one of his many jobs, had worked there as a foreman. As such his employers required him to wear a suit and convention decreed he wore a bowler hat as a symbol of authority. Family history demanded that he displayed its, if not his, wealth – although even that was now more illusory than real – in the form of a gold, half-hunter pocket watch, worn on a heavy gold chain draped across his waistcoat and housed safely in the left-hand lower pocket. Auntie Minnie, Pop's only sister, was also working at Vickers as a departmental supervisor, having been there since leaving school. As a spinster now over forty, everyone recognised she was 'on the shelf' and that was unlikely to change. It may well have influenced the relationship she had with her attractive, intelligent and popular niece, although not necessarily for the better. Yet 'blood is thicker than water', and she played a prominent role in securing her niece a modest clerical job at the Scotswood works.

While Roma's employment at Vickers was something of an 'arranged marriage', it was probably as good a job as she could have obtained, and it was likely that without the family influence she would not have achieved even that in 1935. At the beginning her contribution to the family economy was eight shillings a week. Her gross pay was eight shillings and sixpence per week of which threepence was deducted for the 'government stamp', leaving her a net eight shillings and threepence. Ma gave her threepence a week back as pocket money, although with four journeys a day to and from work – of course she had to come home for dinner, as finances wouldn't stretch to an alternative – she had to decide which journeys she would make on foot to stay within her financial limits.

But one day in early 1939 the Office Manager, outside whose office she sat, approached her with a handful of envelopes. He took one from the pile, looked at it carefully and then gave it to her. Her heart missed a beat. Was this her 'notice' and if it was, what would Ma say; what had she done to be 'laid off', and what would the family do? She hardly heard the manager say, as he turned and left her desk, that 'the directors of the company were very pleased' with her work. She sat for a long time, hardly breathing, looking at the envelope, and then eventually plucked up enough courage to open it. She was in quick succession relieved and then ecstatic to find that inside was a large, white, carefully folded £5 note together with one shilling and sixpence in three small, silver coins. This was a sum she had neither seen nor handled before. What she didn't know was that it was substantially more than Pop earned: indeed, in excess of two weeks' pay for him.

Having gazed at the money for some time she stowed it carefully in her handbag, regularly checking to make sure it was still there, and when the finishing bell went, hurried home to 15 Elswick Row as fast as she could. While her face must have betrayed some of her inner excitement, she said nothing to Ma, but simply handed over the envelope. Ma opened it, looked at the contents, said 'Well, that's very nice', smiled and gave Roma back one of the three silver sixpences.

When Roma reappeared at work the next morning the 'girls', as the mature women with whom she worked were always known and who were very fond of Roma and must have known of the modest financial circumstances of the Cassidy household, asked what her mother had said when she took the envelope home. Roma told them exactly what had happened; her mother had been very pleased and had said so. 'How much did she give you?' they asked. 'Sixpence,' said Roma, and was immediately embarrassed by the hilarity with which they received the news. While she didn't fully understand it, she knew it emphasised that she was still very much a child in an adult world. For a long time after that she was troubled by the question of why the bonus was so large – much more than she was about why the girls had greeted her story with such hilarity.

The school-leaving age was still fourteen and Alan, having failed his scholarship exam, had completed his education at St Aloysius' Technical School rather than at St Cuthbert's Grammar School, for which a scholarship was necessary. He had now left school and was also in his first year, working on the shop floor at Vickers Armstrong as an apprentice turner and fitter. Both Roma and Alan demonstrated the depressing, almost inevitable social trap for working-class families – that economic circumstances usually forced them as children into an endlessly repetitive cycle of life identical to that of their parents, their parents before them and their parents before that. Without completing a grammar-school education, no one was likely to escape manual work. A successful grammar-school education wouldn't guarantee it, but it should lead, particularly if succeeded by university or more probably by further education at night classes while working by day, to earnings of about £500 a year, and thus to the financial security and physical well-being which derived from being badged 'middle class'.

On Sunday 3 September Rex and I were in the back yard talking while planning a game with two back-lane pals, Teddy Birkett and Sidney Dansky – all of us within three years of each other in age – as Ma opened the scullery window and said, 'Be quiet, I want to listen to the broadcast.' The wireless was turned up and something, some tension, some increased awareness, made us go quiet as the sunlight played on the brick walls of the back yard, a mixture of sun and shadow on the ground, as we heard the hesitant, slightly whining voice of Neville Chamberlain and the concluding words '. . . and that consequently, this country is at war with Germany.' It meant little to us at the time, except perhaps that we could imagine another game, another adversary; hardly noticing that the house had gone quiet, strangely quiet on that Sunday morning. We were told to go and play.

By the middle of the following week we were embarked on our first of many wartime adventures, as it had been decided to evacuate all school-age children from the city – a reasonable decision given that Newcastle was built along the River Tyne, was the hub of the north-eastern armaments and munitions industry and, being as critical to the nation's survival as any city in England, was certain to be a high-profile target.

At the outbreak of war one-quarter of the world's shipping tonnage was built on Tyneside, and the factories of Vickers Armstrong produced shells, bullets, guns, tanks and other armoured vehicles; predictably a battleship was being fitted out on the Tyne, along with submarines, destroyers and merchant vessels. The hinterland of Tyneside produced coal and steel, the national food supply chain was fed by fish from the North Sea; the area was vulnerable to attacks by German bombers, the risk of invasion had to be considered and, based on the experience of the Great War, the use of poison gas was widely predicted. Voluntary recruitment and territorial conscriptions accelerated and most children were to be moved to the safety of the west coast.

And so on Tuesday 5 September the four younger boys gathered and unusually, if not uniquely, with Ma to accompany us we prepared to leave home for a strange town, with strange people, for an indefinite period. Ma had decided that Roma could now take the next step in preparation for her preordained role in life, that of housewife and mother, as in addition to being a major contributor to the household finances she was also to become the housekeeper. It was clear to Ma that her duty was to be with those least able to defend themselves – Vincent, now aged twelve, Rex, nine, me, six, and Sydney, four, whom she was going to accompany to the safety of the countryside 'for the duration'. Roma, without consultation or consent, meanwhile could work and keep house for Pop and Alan, since all three of them were required to stay and work in their reserved occupations.

Vincent should not have been going with us anyway, since he had passed his scholarship examination and was due to start at St Cuthbert's, but unfortunately on 1 September St Cuthbert's had been evacuated to Cockermouth, while St Aloysius', a possible temporary alternative, had gone to Workington. So Vincent, the archetypal 'victim of circumstances beyond control', was readmitted temporarily to the junior ranks he had notionally and very recently left, although physically, academically and emotionally he had outgrown St Mary's, but . . . war plays strange tricks on many people.

The evacuees were required to pack clothes – never an onerous or lengthy task in the Cassidy household – and when assembled we were each issued with a brown-paper carrier bag containing our survival rations for the journey. These consisted of a sandwich, a piece of fruit, in my case an orange, a bar of 'Aero' chocolate, and a tin of 'Fray Bentos' corned beef, which could have presented an interesting puzzle of how to open it had it been required en route. Around our necks we had to wear the cardboard box containing our gas mask, which had been fitted a few weeks previously, and like any consignment of luggage we all wore a large, manila label round our necks. We were ready for the journey and we were ready for war.

We assembled at the school where we were counted off, following which we marched in a ragged formation to the Central Station. where we were blessed by the priest and boarded onto an old, corridorless train – itself rather a hazard given the hyperactive bowels and bladders of any large group of schoolchildren. Some of us were allocated teachers, some went in classroom groups; Ma elected to travel with me and Sydney, who had not yet started school, and Miss Timoney, one of my schoolmistresses, for company in our carriage which seemed to be another mark of affection and respect for the Cassidy family. We falteringly sang old songs from the Great War – 'Keep right on to the end of the road', 'It's a long way to Tipperary' and 'Keep the home fires burning' – to lift our spirits as our train steamed out of Newcastle accompanied by much hankie waving, tears and warning shouts at those unruly or stupid enough to lean out of the windows.

The journey was long and tedious as the smoke, the noise and the heat took some of the edge off the enjoyment of my first steam-train journey, my only other journey having been on the electric train to Cullercoats and the coast. In addition I didn't like the sandwich, which I found extremely disagreeable since I was unaccustomed to having mustard spread heavily on ham; it made me very thirsty, a condition for which my survival kit did not provide.

Several hours later a tired and bedraggled lot disembarked from the train, struggled over the iron bridge straddling the railway line and lined up for the inhabitants of Aspatria to consider. I am sure my mother's unspoken thoughts would have been unprintable, for it was clear she thought precious little of the inhabitants of Aspatria marching up and down as they inspected us to select, as if at a slave auction, who they would be prepared to billet. Everybody wanted Sydney, 'the l'il laddie' in their – to us – curious Cumbrian accent; but Ma insisted Sydney and I were a pair as inseparable as any Siamese twins and since she was determined to accompany us, effectively we were a package of three. Whether it was my relative unattractiveness or the prospect of having to billet the formidable Ma I have no idea, but enthusiasm for this package was scarce. Vincent and Rex were not faring much better and would have been separated had not Ma again intervened, leaving us to dash across to the respective class groups like a lioness guarding her cubs and insisting that Vincent and Rex went together. She had long accepted that all five of us couldn't be housed together, but beyond that limit she was not prepared to go.

Ultimately we were all settled. A long, arduous, tedious and humiliating process ended as we marched off in the dying light to our various abodes, happily all in the same street, St Mungo's Park. Ma, Sydney, and I were to be housed on the poorer side of the street with a rather odd, elderly, childless couple, and Vincent and Rex with a well-off family in a larger house almost opposite. Their wealth and culture were exhibited as they arrived home by their son playing the violin, while posing in a rather extravagant fashion before the window of a candlelit front room. They went to the McKees and we went to the Tunstalls.

The Tunstalls had no children and it soon became apparent that the wife, to put it generously, was somewhat neurotic. Mrs Tunstall had an unfortunate habit of carrying permanently in her hand a yellow duster and when a hand rested upon a door handle, even if only to enter or leave the room, she immediately rushed after the offender and polished the handle vigorously. It was clear that this was not going to be a lasting tenancy for us. Nevertheless, the old man was pleasant, he liked children and wanted to take us on walks, but there was a problem even with this simple activity. He could do so only if, as Ma ordained, she accompanied us, and Mrs Tunstall wasn't too keen on that.

On the first Sunday after our arrival Ma, having debriefed Rex and Vincent to satisfy herself about their living conditions, sent all four of us out together to explore the area, where we soon met up with some other evacuees from St Mary's School.

While the older boys were exchanging stories about the strange world into which we had landed, a large local youth walked up to Vincent and belligerently asked him if he was the leader of the group, since he was visibly the biggest of the evacuees. Vincent said he was, to which the local youth asked even more aggressively, 'Do you box?' Vincent, rather foolishly and precipitately said 'Yes' – clearly without much forethought, because he did have an ill-disguised tendency to cowardice in the face of physical threat and was certainly not trying to be belligerent or provocative. Unfortunately this positive response backfired, since the next thing he knew he was lying on his back, having been punched unfairly yet squarely in the mouth by the large youth, who then demanded that Vincent get up and continue to fight. Vincent, whose capacity for rapid thinking had gone on improving ahead of his physical development, but whose naivety about the consequences of being quick-witted was probably at its peak, then replied, 'I am better at wrestling.' Before he knew where he was the youth's knees had landed on his chest and his hands were about Vincent's ears, engaging him in a rather painful, possibly terminally injurious headlock. 'Come on, then,' said the youth, 'let's wrestle.' Vincent's inbuilt sense of fear now drove his well-rehearsed survival instincts, as he said, 'I never box or wrestle on Sundays.' Whether or not this would have had any mollifying effect on the belligerent youth, who had indiscreetly announced he was Tom Metcalfe, was never tested, because at that stage the formidable Ma reappeared – fortuitously – to send the youth packing and to deliver a well-earned lecture to Vincent on the need for caution and for more appropriate responses when attacked.

Later that day we all went, as appointed, to the local church hall where, unusually, an evening Mass was to be said. Unfortunately when we assembled there, and it was virtually the whole school that did – children, teachers and those mothers who had accompanied us – we found to our consternation, and contrary to prior written agreement, that the church doors had been locked and barred securely from the inside, while a handwritten notice was displayed outside advising that we would not be allowed to use the hall for religious purposes. There were cries of 'Break the door down' from the more impetuous members of the parish, but the arrival of the priest from a neighbouring parish – since unsurprisingly there was no Catholic parish in Aspatria, a solidly Protestant community – prevented a serious civil disturbance by suggesting that we should be Christian and turn the other cheek while a solution was sought for future weeks. Although this seemed a deeply disappointing and humiliating experience for the adults, who were prepared to take on the Aspatrians as if they were Prussians, with cries of 'Let's get at them, Father', we children thought this was an immensely wise and practical decision which bestowed certain very obvious benefits on us – principally that we could escape the confines of a strange church hall for more play and exploration. Aspatria was a very small, simple village set in rolling countryside which pressed in on us on every side, with meadows and soft hills, copses, pastures, paddocks with thick hedges, streams in which silvery fish swam and swamps lying alongside. There were horses, sheep, cows and fearsome, snorting bulls all within a few yards of the village streets; much to explore, with endless material for new games of make-believe – why should we bother about being locked out of their dingy church hall, which was nothing like the cathedral we had left behind anyway?

It wasn't long before the absurd habits of Mrs Tunstall drove my mother to search for alternative accommodation, but not before the old man, on our many walks, had introduced Sydney and me to the countryside, pointing out and naming the hedgerows, trees, flowers, animals and birds. He was full of knowledge, simple and dexterous, with a countryman's knack of harnessing nature in the most surprising ways. He could suddenly take out a pocket-knife, deftly cut a branch from a bush, trim it, hollow it, shape it and there, in minutes, was a miniature flute on which he could produce a respectable tune with his quick fingering, and he would then give both Sydney and me an instrument each. I loved our walks, but Mr Tunstall loved them even more. Perhaps he was making amends for his wife's strange behaviour, or perhaps both his and hers were related to a frustrated desire to be parents? It was probably the latter, because I subsequently learned that they had asked Ma if they could adopt me, a question which no doubt sealed their fate and simply increased Ma's determination to move on as quickly as possible.

Rex and Vincent meanwhile, being billeted with people whose means were substantially greater than the Cassidys, were learning some rather curious lessons about the eating habits of the middle classes. It's true their food was better, but they were often faced with the bizarre sight of Mr McKee getting down on his hands and knees if he spotted crumbs on the floor and pecking at them, while clucking like a chicken or crowing like a rooster; this was apparently intended to encourage rather tidier eating habits. Indeed, good table manners were rewarded by the presentation of a badge after every meal to the tidiest eater; but throughout their stay there was a form of apartheid in the household with the parents and Malcolm, the violin-playing son, treating Vincent and Rex very much as the 'boarders' that indeed they were, and never seeking to integrate them with the family. Whereas we looked for every opportunity to escape the Tunstalls, Vincent and Rex had very little choice in the matter and we collectively set out, irrespective of the weather, to return only at mealtimes. The son kept up his violin-playing habits, striking the most unlikely poses at the front window, and although no prodigy he behaved as if he were an international concert artist in the making.

Yet just as Mr Tunstall befriended Sydney and me, Mr McKee did Vincent a great service. Vincent developed a badly infected wound on his leg which became steadily worse, until one night he was feverish and delirious. Mr McKee came to his room, took one look at the leg, bathed it, burst the offending boil and diligently sucked all of the poison from the leg, cleaning his mouth several times in the process, until the wound was perfectly clean. He then bandaged it, after which Vincent recovered swiftly. Unorthodox as the treatment may have been, effective it certainly was, displaying a generosity and simple goodness that was at odds with the family's general attitude.

And then by a minor miracle Ma stumbled upon, or was directed towards, an old widower living on his own in a small farm cottage in Whinnbarrow Lane. His name was Bob Stoddart and Ma negotiated an eminently satisfactory deal with him to bring the whole family in, overcrowding the cottage admittedly, but nevertheless bringing life and warmth and above all creature comforts in the shape of lit fires, a clean house and cooked food for the widower. Bob Stoddart was a simple farm labourer, almost inarticulate, but for a few brief weeks he was transported, or perhaps returned, to a state of almost perfect happiness. His contentment was visible and we resumed life with all the fun that was associated with our days in Elswick Row – the collective games at night, the quizzes, the questions, the spelling bees, the competitions, the arguments and the laughter.

From Mr Stoddart I learned yet another practical lesson about the countryside, which was how to deal with rats – although I practised it neither then nor subsequently. It was inevitable, living in a cottage near the farm, that rats and mice would be a constant nuisance and to combat this Mr Stoddart had set rat traps at strategic points around the property; we soon developed the habit of inspecting them to see whether rats were in the trap before excitedly telling him. If they weren't already dead he would spring the trap, holding the rat by the tail, and then club the life out of it with an old horseshoe. I used to watch with admiration, tinged with fear rather than distaste, as the rat would jiggle and wriggle until eventually it hung lifeless with blood dripping slowly from its nose, when Bob would discard it over a hedge, rinse his hands under the outside tap, reset the trap and go back in to finish his meal.

But the days dragged. There was an unhealthy tension between the urban strangers and the rural inhabitants, and after a stay of a few weeks my mother decided, following a weekend visit from my father, that the prospect of invading Germans held no more terrors and anyway they were unlikely to be as un-Christian and unfriendly as the inhabitants of Aspatria. None of us shed any tears as we packed up and left, but we were all conscious of the distraught widower standing at his cottage door with tears streaming down his face as we went. His brief period of domestic bliss came, sadly for him, to a premature end; the Tunstalls lost their prospective adopted son; and Malcolm McKee returned to playing the violin without his unwilling, unappreciative young audience.

What none of us knew at the time was that our reception was mirrored by hundreds of thousands of others who were evacuated, and by the following spring more than half of all the children who had been evacuated had, like us, already returned to their homes. But this was the period of the phoney war and it was to be some time yet before the grip of real war began to affect us. Temporary evacuation was merely a prologue to the main event.

There was little to mar the joy of the whole family, individually and collectively, at being reunited. After all, Pop had Ma back again to cook his meals; gallantly though Roma had tried, it hadn't been quite the same. Roma was particularly relieved to be spared the unforeseen burden of keeping Alan under control, who had developed a tendency to absent himself from work. Ma was delighted to be going back to familiar surroundings where she could control and care for the whole family without exception, even if it meant increased physical risk.

For my brothers and me it was a chance to reunite with the other boys in the back lane and swap stories of our adventures, while Ma had some additional worries to occupy her fertile mind. Vincent now had to be enrolled at grammar school, and there was the question to be resolved of whether he should be re-evacuated to join St Cuthbert's, still temporarily in Cockermouth. More importantly, the separation of the family through the evacuation process had made every one of us even more conscious of the overcrowded conditions in Elswick Row to which we had now returned; Ma therefore had to face the question of how long they could be tolerated once the initial pleasure of being together in familiar surroundings had worn off.

For me the war had started promisingly, and I guessed rightly that better things were to come.

11

HAVELOCK STREET

In May 1940, just when the 'phoney war' which had lasted since 3 September 1939 was about to give way to the real thing as the Nazi Blitzkrieg in Europe began, and after we had returned to brave the expected air raids on Tyneside rather than struggle to achieve compatibility with the citizens of Aspatria, we moved to a larger house. Ma had decided to act on the decision she had reached even before our return from evacuation: that we had at last outgrown our flat in Elswick Row. That decision was hardly surprising, as apart from herself and Pop it was accommodating a girl of twenty and five boys aged between fifteen and five, and if such overcrowding wasn't insufferable, illegal or unusual, it was certainly extremely uncomfortable.

The principal criteria to be satisfied were that the next house should be in the same area, larger and yet no more expensive, and soon a much larger, three-storey, Victorian terraced house less than 100 yards away from our home became available. It was No. 5 Havelock Street, a street which ran at right angles off Elswick Row, some of the even-numbered houses of which shared our old back lane there. It would provide the extra space we needed, but at a modestly increased cost that we could afford only because Pop's income was supplemented by contributions from Roma and Alan, who were both working. The potentially short-term nature of that supplement had to be weighed against the fact that the new house provided us immediately with the much-needed extra space, and it was perfectly located to enable us to maintain domestic, school and work commitments without adjustment or interruption.

There were three floors and every one of the rooms was larger, with higher ceilings, than those in Elswick Row. It also had the benefit of electric light, but it still suffered from some of the other deficiencies which we would have liked to correct. There was again no heating other than by open-grate coal fires; yet again the kitchen was fitted with a range, which allowed supplementary cooking although there was no hot-water system and no bath, let alone a bathroom; and since no gain is achieved without pain, we were to substitute a better-ventilated outside lavatory for our previous inside one.

There were two large windows and an entrance door on the ground floor fronting Havelock Street, looking out over a modest front garden, yet substantially larger than that of 15 Elswick Row. In common with all the neighbouring houses the ornamental railings which had once given it an appearance of respectability had been hacked down recently to provide scrap iron for the war effort, resulting in an external appearance not unlike a toothless old man. Since this scrap metal was never used, it must rank as one of the worst cases of bureaucratically inspired vandalism anyone has ever known, arising from crass and uncoordinated central planning.

As you entered through the front door there was a small, tiled outer hall about 6 feet by 6 and a glazed inner door, with a white ceramic door knob and coloured glass panes, leading to the front hall – or as we preferred to call it, more accurately and less ostentatiously, the front passage. On the right of this passage was the common wall to the property next door and on the left was a large front room immediately designated as 'the parlour', which was to become the receiving and entertaining room for the infrequent family events and celebrations. At the end of the front passage was a staircase leading to a landing, which then led to a reverse staircase to the larger landing and the three bedrooms. At the foot of the staircase on the left was the door to the kitchen, as the passage continued between the kitchen and the staircase to a back door from which a flight of stone steps led down to the back yard. There was a row of coat hooks on the outer kitchen wall to what was known, without a hint of irony, as our back passage; that also housed the door to a large cupboard under the stairs, later to become our air-raid shelter.

The large kitchen was the main family living area, with a fireplace and range on the left-hand side facing the door to the passage and a high, rectangular, shuttered window looking out over the back yard. Between them was a doorless entrance with a step down to the small, narrow, cramped, stone-floored scullery. The scullery doubled as the primary cooking kitchen because it contained an ageing gas stove, but since it also had a large, stone sink and a cold-water tap it served also as the family bathroom. When hot water was required it had to be boiled either in a kettle on the gas stove or on the open fire, or as was more often the case in an enamelled pail. In these surroundings privacy could not be guaranteed.

On the first-floor level there were three bedrooms. Three windows, two in the one large, double bedroom and one in the single bedroom next door, looked out on Havelock Street. The third bedroom overlooked the back yard. Above, on the third level, there was a large attic with a dormer window set into the roof at the rear. Of the three bedrooms on the first floor, the largest with the two windows to the front was to be shared by all five boys until Alan joined the RAF in 1943. The smallest on the front was Roma's room until she married in August 1943; and the back bedroom with a window looking out over the back yard was Ma and Pop's room until we were requisitioned later in 1943 to billet sailors attending a training course, after Roma and Alan had fled the nest.

The physical move from Elswick Row to Havelock Street was happily over a very short distance and as ever cost-effective solutions were sought and found, while we benefited also from having so few household effects to move – although those we did possess were as prized by us as any rare antique. A hand-barrow was rented for a few pence and Ma's favourite brother Sam, whom for whatever reason the wider Cassidy family tended to look down on, and a slightly – indeed more than slightly – backward cousin were persuaded to undertake the task. No doubt Uncle Sam had been engaged because he was a skilled carpenter, and it was impossible to remove the bigger pieces of furniture from Elswick Row without a substantial amount of dismantling and subsequent reassembly on the new site. Since that was well beyond Pop's extremely limited range of skills, Sam's selection was as automatic as his readiness to undertake it.

He was a slight, balding, bow-legged man but had a heart like a lion and he, with Septimus, the backward cousin who could neither read nor write, worked long and hard through a hot day in May 1940 carrying furniture down the steep, narrow stairs from the flat, loading it onto the handcart, wheeling it round the corner to Havelock Street, unloading it and putting it in the required position before reassembly. Sam, at least, looked what he was: the professional, with a carpenter's large, long, white, bib-fronted overall tied with a broad tape at the back, together with a cap which he frequently lifted with one hand while simultaneously scratching his bald head with other fingers of the same hand. He was as energetic and amiable as everybody in Ma's family, so it was no surprise that there were no dramas, no breakages and the new home base was soon laid for us.

Ma then began what she no doubt saw as an ambitious refurbishment programme. Some of Ma's nieces joined Roma to redecorate most rooms in the house, and for the first time in my experience we acquired some new furniture. There was a piano, which cost £1 at the salerooms and which a cousin tuned more or less satisfactorily; for a further £1 we gained an elegant, inlaid, oval table with a central tripod of carved legs on brass claw feet; and these items were accompanied by a large, rectangular, Indian carpet. We had of course brought our wind-up gramophone from Elswick Row, and our modest but well-used collection of 78rpm records – including Charles Penrose as 'The Laughing Policeman', the Band of the Welsh Guards playing at the Trooping of the Colour, Gracie Fields singing 'The Biggest Aspidistra in the World', and a number of John MacCormack recordings always calculated to have Pop in a tearfully nostalgic mood – provided, of course, it had been preceded by the usual visit to 'The Blue Man'.

Most of our furniture from Elswick Row fitted well into our new, larger kitchen, particularly the sideboard, dresser and table. We acquired a new electric wireless to which we could now listen at will, without the tedious need to have accumulator batteries recharged; more beds; and a large chest of drawers for the boys' bedroom with at least one large drawer allocated to each individual.

It was clear that Ma's ambitions to refurbish the house had been scaled down, as they were rather more expansive than Pop deemed wise, since he shunned totally the risk of a modest investment in the recently adopted habit of acquisition by 'hire purchase'. Thus it was that all these acquisitions were made in second-hand shops and salerooms where, on the whole, Ma demonstrated the same negotiating skill as she had done elsewhere.

There were two other major benefits arising from the move to Havelock Street. First, we were invited to share the washhouse facilities with the family next door at No. 3; this arrangement for the first time diminished the domestic disruption and the work load and improved the safety of this major weekly chore. Second, Havelock Street provided us with further space, both in the large attic, the potential use of which exercised us for a long time, and in the large back yard with a covered shed area outside the coalhouse, which gave us the opportunity to keep additional pets. Since the effects of war were just beginning to bite, this enabled us to keep chickens and ducks, most of which typically, if rather unhelpfully, had to be reared initially in the warmth of the kitchen.

On the day following the move we had a visit from Mrs Pattinson, our new neighbour in No. 3, and it was this visit that led ultimately to the shared use of their washhouse. She was a woman of average height but with a huge spread. She was never seen around the house, inside or out, without a pinny, always with her large, flabby, mottled, bare arms exposed below a sweat-lined face as she hauled her enormous bulk around the house and energetically through various major household tasks. She had jet-black, stringy hair, streaked now with grey, and a formidable, very obvious black moustache. She was given to great roars of laughter, and to ensure that whoever she was talking to enjoyed 'the joke' she had a disconcerting habit of jabbing them in the ribs with her elbow to reinforce the point of any story. Apart from her husband, Mr Pattinson, there were three boys, Willie, Gordon and Raymond, and a daughter, Rosie. On the far side of the Pattinsons, at No. 1, were the Misses Waller, who kept a calculated distance from everybody else since they had once been both wealthy and influential in the earlier days, now long gone, when that had been the norm for residents of Havelock Street, rather than the exception as it now was.

On our other side at No. 7 was a more mysterious house which remained a puzzle to me for many years, until I learned it was a brothel: but since I wouldn't have understood the meaning of the word even if I had heard it, it provided yet another opportunity for Ma to indulge in her undoubted skill as a presenter of facts in whichever way she deemed to be most appropriate to the listener. She was a masterly spin doctor long before the term had been invented, and if pressed described it dismissively as 'a common lodging house'.

Havelock Street was to be our last family home as our numbers gradually diminished – some to be temporarily exiled in the armed forces, some more permanently later after marriage.

As if signalling that some of the family were no longer children, or perhaps simply as a consequence of our improved circumstances following our move to Havelock Street, we discarded some of the long-established habits of our life in Elswick Row. The most obvious one was that there we had seldom used the front door, except for a few, very formal activities, and in keeping with the practice of most of our neighbours we had used the back door for all day-to-day purposes. Yet immediately and unselfconsciously, after the move to Havelock Street we adopted the practice of always using the front door, and we only rarely used the back one except for those activities which centred on washing day or tending to our animals – not forgetting, of course, the frequent

visits to the lavatory, outside the house in the back yard. This may have
been a more pragmatic choice than it was philosophical, but it was
curious nevertheless, because the two houses had some striking
similarities. Neither front door had a Yale lock, but both had a large
mortice deadlock. Since the key to that lock was similar in size and
weight to those which had been used in medieval castles, it could not be
regarded as portable, and so questions as to whether or not adults in the
family should have their own key were redundant even for the head of the
household.

Neither back door had a lock at all, both being secured by a large bolt
– of similar vintage to the mortice lock on the front door – which was
withdrawn in the morning at Elswick Row and bolted nightly only when
everyone was safely indoors. Of course security had been much easier to
manage in Elswick Row where, although the back door was open all day,
anyone entering the house had to climb a flight of stairs to reach the
living area; Havelock Street was potentially less secure, as the house
could be entered unseen through the back passage which bypassed the
kitchen, always the hub of domestic activity in both houses. It was this
that probably led to the decision to concentrate our comings and goings
on the front door of Havelock Street and in a reversal of practice it was
left open all day, although the inner glass door was closed but unlocked.

The front door was left open until Ma and Pop retired at night, when
it was closed and locked; since we had no doorbell, this was as effective as
any curfew in ensuring that respectable hours were kept. Perhaps because
the front door of Havelock Street looked out onto those houses which
bordered Elswick Row's back lane, we continued our close association
with it and it remained the centre of our social activity and our principal
playground throughout the 1940s.

And so with more space to read, play and do homework, a reduction in
the number per bed to a more acceptable maximum of two, no great
change in our neighbours or companions, and notionally greater security
from enemy air attack, the future in 1940 seemed reasonably promising.

12

AT SCHOOL ON THE ROOF

Although disrupting our lives in many ways, it was on our schooling that evacuation had the most serious impact. Classes during the short period in Aspatria became larger, embracing a wider age range, with shared use of a local junior school allowing lessons in the afternoon only, and in consequence the amount of learning was minimal. It appeared from the very beginning to be an interim arrangement and as soon as the ill-fated evacuation came to an end, which for the Cassidys was after only six weeks, we returned home and were able to resume normal school routine at St Mary's Boys' School. Happily it became a much more exciting place. The pace of teaching and the scope of what we were expected to learn increased with the added interest of, and in many cases with our involvement in, the school preparing itself for a new supplementary role as an emergency relief centre when the 'imminently expected, devastating air raids' began on all major cities.

Thus the school found itself being provided with piles of blankets, wound dressings, water and sand buckets, and stirrup pumps – items needed both to preserve the building and to comfort the afflicted in case of attack. Emergency rations were brought in and stored and 'blackout' materials were provided to ensure that standard air-raid precautions could still be satisfied in the event of the school being used in its new role over extended hours.

The introduction of all-year-round British summertime helped to avoid curtailment of school hours or infringement of air-raid precautions, just as it did in many offices and factories, while most teachers assumed additional roles as air-raid wardens and firewatchers as the impact of war remorselessly increased throughout 1940. Air raids began later in the year and even if they never reached the intensity from which London suffered, they were frequently deadly, damaging and disruptive.

From May onwards, after the fall of Dunkirk, the fear of invasion and of Fifth Columnists – 'walls have ears' – was stimulated by the experience of France and the Low Countries. Neutrality was not going to save Denmark or Norway either. Propaganda from the Ministry of Information created a febrile awareness, bordering on neurosis, about strangers and visitors. Everyone was on the lookout for quislings, named after the eponymous Norwegian traitor who had played such a destabilising role in the collapse of Continental opposition to German invaders; the tension of preparation for, and expectation of, an imminent invasion increased, while the manpower available to resource and resist it steadily decreased.

In this process, model pupils who required little instruction or supervision, like Alan Thornton and me, were allotted the task of helping to store the emergency supplies with which the school had been provided, and it was during this process that we made a remarkable discovery. By chance, while looking for cartons to store safely for the duration some holy statues, we came upon all the props from a pre-war school production of *Treasure Island*. Since Robert Louis Stephenson's book was on every school's reading list these were instantly recognisable, but the discovery of the props – eye patches, swords, striped jerseys and hats adorned with skull and crossbones – was miraculous: surely something to do with the care we were taking of holy artefacts. Of course at that age, seven rising eight, we were unable to resist the temptation to make full use of such a find and after carefully checking all the exits, we donned the hats, swords and eye patches and engaged in an unrehearsed but very realistic sword fight. During the furious, hand-to-hand exchange that was being fought as a matter of life and death, we crashed into one of our holy statues – a large, blue-gowned version of the Blessed Virgin Mary standing on a rock; over went the statue and, worse still, the tall, fragile glass dome, which protected the blessed image from earthly dust, shattered. For a few moments we were stunned and then with the same resourcefulness which had earned us our privileges – and I must admit also driven by the fear that as pirates we might be hanged for this offence – we retrieved the statue and packed it respectfully with the other statues we were storing in a safe place. We then collected and buried carefully the remnants of the glass dome on the bottom layer of one of the boxes holding blankets, placed a series of folded blankets on top, jumped up and down on the blankets until the glass beneath was well and truly crushed, placed more blankets in, fastened the box, marked the outside as we were required to do and stored it carefully behind some others. It was as thorough as Billy Bones' burial of Captain Flint's treasure near Spyglass Hill.

Shortly after all visible traces of the awful deed had been removed, and while we were still recovering from shock and the fear of celestial or earthly retribution, the teacher in charge came into the hall, assessed the progress we had made and commended us for our diligence and care. In spite of the fact that we were further staining our immortal souls, we took an instinctive and mutual decision not to reveal the misdeed at that point. Thereafter no good purpose would have been served by so doing – or so we argued.

Happily none of the devastation visited on Newcastle – and at times it did come close to the school's catchment area – caused our misdeeds to be revealed while we were still at the school. Better still, the instant commendation that we'd had for our diligence and care reinforced the view of the teaching staff that we were two extremely bright pupils who were also among the neatest handwriters in the school, ahead of many of our seniors, and as a result we should be added to the select team of children who were to prepare ration books for the population.

The thirty or so children of varying ages who were engaged on this essential war work were assembled in the school hall, seated at desks as they were for the scholarship examination, and worked under the supervision of a teacher sitting on a raised dais. Another teacher moved through the groups ensuring there was maximum concentration and minimum distraction. The front cover of the books had to be completed with the name of the family written in bold capitals, with Christian names, date of birth and national identity number, the details of which were provided on handwritten sheets from which we copied accurately before they were collected for checking by the supervising teacher.

This work was rewarded with yet more praise – how hard we had worked, how well we wrote; but when we returned to the classroom little had changed. Reggie went on banging his temples and seeking divine inspiration somewhere beyond the ceiling of the classroom; Joe and his family now went on an almost permanent 'walkabout'; but sadly all the Italian boys who were in the school vanished. It was not until much later that I found out that they, with their parents, had been interned as enemy aliens – potential quislings – for the duration.

But that was soon forgotten as more excitement followed. We learned to follow the progress of the war on a map pinned up on the classroom wall, using coloured flags to indicate battlefields and the movements of the Allied and the Axis forces. By the end of 1940 the map was dominated by a series of black swastikas on red circles facing a cluster of Union Jacks. In North Africa there were red, green and white Italian tricolour flags, but with imperialist disdain Australian, New Zealand, South African, Indian, Canadian and other forces from the empire were also represented by the Union Jack – whether they liked it or not. Newspapers and comics carried special inserts showing British, German and Italian aeroplanes in silhouette from different angles so that everybody could recognise 'friend' or 'foe'; boys of all ages gained rather more than their parents from these, because if a silhouette was recognised as an enemy aeroplane it was usually in such close proximity as to make evasive action rather difficult.

In those early days of the war we were all on perpetual alert. Church bells were silenced, as were those normally rung at dusk in parks; by government decree they would thereafter be rung only if enemy parachutists were seen descending or seaborne troops were seen landing. In this way a relay of bells across the land would sound a clear warning bringing an immediate armed response, probably by the LDV or, as they were renamed, the Home Guard. No doubt the German High Command was terrified at the prospect, but then they hadn't witnessed the LDV in action as we had. Their early exercises had disrupted Mass in the cathedral and Sunday dinner at home, as an Indian file of badly dressed, embarrassed-looking, uniformed men carrying a variety of weapons – some real but old, others no more than pieces of wood – trudged among us. At home some barged through the front door, opened the back door and took prone firing positions as firecrackers exploded in the garden behind them and the yard in front of them, while Roger the dog alternately barked or licked their faces. Beaches were cordoned off with barbed wire and some were mined, or at least said to be. Cullercoats and Whitley Bay, our favourite seaside spots, were out of bounds and had barbed wire festooned over and around the promenade railings. Anti-tank barriers were erected on Westgate Road and other main roads to the city, while concrete gun emplacements and 'pill boxes' were hurriedly constructed on some beaches. Anti-glider posts were erected on the Town Moor to prevent airborne troops from using it as a landing ground and assembly area. Farcically, all street names and road signposts were removed, further confusing an already bemused population trying to cope with the war and its consequences. Street lamps were extinguished 'for the duration', a term which entered everyday language, and posters appeared urging almost everything from 'Mind out, there's a spy about' and 'Walls have ears' – usually incorporating grotesque figures with a Himmler-like appearance and steel-rimmed glasses – to the more positive 'Save for victory' or 'Dig for victory'. Everyone, whatever their age, was caught up with the momentum of war except those ridiculed as 'conshies', who applied for exemption from armed service because of 'conscientious objections'; they, like the two middle-aged brothers who kept a bicycle shop on Wingrove Road, became objects of derision and they and their businesses were shunned. Others were anxious to have it widely known that they had volunteered for active service but been rejected as 'unfit'. When this was expanded, the reasons for rejection were claimed to be as varied as 'flat feet' or 'a hump', a Rigoletto-like deformity. The stoic sufferer with the latter was said to have been dismissed by the recruiting sergeant-major with the words, 'We want soldiers for France, not camels for Egypt.'

Mothers took jobs in factories and on Tyneside there was no shortage of war work for them to do, while older boys were recruited as firewatchers if they were below conscription age. Fathers in reserved occupations were encouraged, sometimes required, to work as ARP wardens or even to join the Home Guard. The streets changed in appearance. The iron railings which bounded each property and gave even modest houses such as ours an air of respectability were cut down, coarsely and savagely. And then the one last pretence that Elswick Row had to attractiveness, its generous width as it swept up to meet Arthur's Hill, was removed by the building of ugly, red-brick, concrete-topped, communal air-raid shelters in the middle of the road. Wealthier areas could have individual shelters provided for erection in their own gardens, but there was insufficient garden space in any of the Elswick Row homes to allow the installation of individual Anderson shelters. So those final remnants of a bygone attractiveness and respectability went, never to return, causing much more damage and distress in most areas of Newcastle than bombing ever did.

Yet still the demands increased as 'they' — it was always 'they' and 'them' when authorities of any kind were involved — sought to anticipate the next problem of resource shortage. There was a plea for everyone to donate old pots and pans; when this was discussed at home Ma simply looked at our small stock of aged, blackened cooking utensils, shook her head, snorted and gave a hollow laugh.

But Ma and Pop collectively and without much debate decided that there was no material difference between being subject to a direct hit from an enemy bomb in our house or in one of the communal air-raid shelters. Given Ma's frequently declared principles it was clear that if we were destined to die, it would be better to do so together, with the guidance of the 'Sacred Heart' hanging on the kitchen wall and the 'Blessed Virgin Mary, our Lady of Victories', who benevolently oversaw us from the sideboard, rather than in the company of strangers. The fact that the best protection we would get within the house was by sheltering in a cupboard under the stairs demonstrated her fatalism, optimism and courage as much as her undoubted faith. When air raids occurred we sheltered initially in the cupboard, but later gave this up as being neither safer than nor as comfortable as sitting under the kitchen table, where there was at least some light.

But Pop was rather more cavalier. We had after all just acquired Havelock Street, and we had an attic with a window which looked out to the sky above the Tyne, over the Numol warehouse building opposite. If he was home and an air-raid warning sounded, he would puff his way up the four half-flights of stairs to the attic, and there he would gaze out of the window at the night sky. It wasn't long before we escaped to join him, although there were occasions when even he believed that was too dangerous. The drone of Junkers 88 bombers, Heinkel 111s with a buzzing fighter escort, the searchlights punching their way through the night sky, the crash of heavy anti-aircraft guns, the tracer stream from lighter guns and aeroplanes captured in the searchlights – all made these very dramatic nights. Then suddenly the searchlights would cut out, the guns would be silenced and we would see Hurricane fighters from Northumberland airfields diving among the enemy aircraft and more tracer streams, sometimes a spurt of flame, a mid-air explosion and then alarmingly that peculiar whistle and crump of high-explosive bombs landing, or the white, sprouting flames from magnesium incendiary bombs. Sometimes they seemed, and indeed were, extremely close; when that happened Pop would abandon his watch and retire to the notional safety of the cupboard, which at least he preferred to being with Sydney and me under the kitchen table.

Reverse followed defeat, while setbacks followed disappointments in Europe and in Africa, compensated for on the Home Front only by a seemingly endless summer of warm days, blue skies and long twilights. Just as luck seemed to desert British armies in the field, even nature was preparing to turn against those of us at home, with the onset of a hard, snow-laden, icy winter to complicate a life already strewn with the rationing of clothes, fuel and food – to say nothing of the increasing frequency of German bombing raids.

13

MRS REED'S CHRISTMAS

Whatever the trials and tribulations of the war years, and however restrictive they were even to children's activities, as usual we did our best to circumnavigate them and nothing could diminish our growing excitement as Christmas approached. There was the making of a Christmas pudding and the cake with ingredients saved over a period of months, which served to emphasise, like an extended Advent, the approach of Christmas. There was the ritual mixing of the cake, the pouring of Guinness into the cake and pudding mixtures, with everybody being allowed a turn to stir the mixture and mimic Ma's actions by dipping a finger in and tasting the mix with exaggerated relish. There were decorations to be recovered from the back of a cupboard shelf, there was the cardboard Santa Claus to be dusted off and put on display and, although we never had a Christmas tree, there was enough evidence that this was a special time of year.

The decorations were concertina-like sections of coloured crepe paper cut into Christmas-tree shapes between two cardboard ends which could be pinned to a door frame or wall, each one extending to a length of about 4 feet; these could be draped and positioned artistically. We supplemented them for the occasion by creating our own looped chains of coloured tissue or crepe paper, the sheets of which were cut into sections about 3 inches by 9 inches, the ends glued with a paste of starch and water and further loops added and glued. We tailor-made multicoloured chains for the kitchen and parlour, to which Roma added mistletoe and holly gathered at Riding Mill, where Vickers Armstrong's office had been relocated.

Our 2-foot-high Santa Claus was also a pre-war purchase from Woolworths and while he was noticeably two-dimensional, being formed from pressed cardboard, he had swelling red cheeks and nose and a scarlet-jacketed, black-belted, round tummy over long, black boots, to give him the archetypal Santa look.

The making of the Christmas cake and pudding, the paper-chain decorations and Christmas cards, followed by the placing of Santa with the decorations all made Advent pass very quickly.

By the Christmas of 1942 our long-standing inability to afford toys converged with the inability of shops to offer many, but we knew there would be something in our stocking and we spent many days writing out 'wish lists' on pieces of paper which were then carefully folded and thrown up the chimney. If they didn't immediately fall down again onto the open fire, it demonstrated to us that Santa Claus really was already in the chimney, carefully catching and storing the messages to see whether he could meet our demands.

And then one day Mrs Reed called, and asked my mother whether she could take Sydney to Fenwick's to see Santa Claus and the toy grotto. Charlotte Reed was tall and thin, always dressed in a black dress, shoes, hat and coat. She had an unmistakable, busy walk when she was in the street, covering ground faster than anybody else I ever knew, and she seemed to have boundless energy, with everything done 'at the double'. Because of this her body always seemed to be leaning forward at a 45-degree angle to the ground. She attended the Co-op Ladies' Guild, as did my mother on her occasional visits – her only social outing apart from an evening visit with Pop to 'The Blue Man' or some other pub. Mrs Reed was a distant relation to a remote cousin of ours through whom Roma, taking Sydney with her of course, had had a holiday in the country near the Scottish border in the Forest of Kielder. At the time she had taken Sydney with her because Sydney and Roma were inseparable, on his part because he was the 'baby' so he expected the attention, and Ma encouraged Roma to take him with her as a form of reverse chaperoning; on her part because she used him as a good substitute for a hot-water bottle on cold winter nights. Somehow, through these tenuous links, Mrs Reed had decided that she would do a good deed and, no doubt in that warm, sentimental wrap that people adopt in the run-up to Christmas, Sydney was a perfect vehicle for her nostalgia about lost childhood. It was also known, at least to Ma, that she desperately wanted a baby and at the age of forty-two was now almost certainly too old to conceive for the first time.

Ma considered the request cautiously, as she had an inbuilt screening system to ensure there was no catch, no unforeseen consequences; Fenwick's was simply not the kind of place at which we shopped. It was the 'crème de la crème', the latest, the most fashionable, the most expensive of the three department stores Fenwick's, Bainbridge's and Binn's. It had been rebuilt immediately before the war and furnished in the latest style, and was a genuine competitor for even the finest London department store. Its new logo was 'very thirties', its sales assistants were the most polished of ladies, its carpets were the deepest and its haute couture salon, 'Fenwick's French', was 'it'. In addition, Ma was concerned that the invitation was for only Sydney to accompany Mrs Reed, whereas I was also in the house when the invitation was issued. Clearly at nine I was, in Mrs Reed's view, perhaps a little old for the grotto and Rex, at twelve, was clearly well over the age limit. Readily, or otherwise, Mrs Reed agreed to take me as well and off we set.

Fenwick's was a revelation. I simply didn't know what to expect, but I had never been in a shop like it before. Certainly British Home Stores, Woolworths and Marks & Spencer, with their bare wooden floors and dark brown block counters, were nothing like this. Neither did Fenwick's have the familiar smell of creosote, candles and wax polish of the other shops but, in their absence, it had perfumed air. Decorous ladies in hats floated by, and throughout there was the plaintive, lingering voice of Vera Lynn singing over and over again, interspersed with the occasional Christmas melody, 'We'll meet again, don't know where, don't know when, but I know we'll meet again some sunny day'. We met the large, bearded Santa Claus who greeted us affably, and as we returned from our visit after sitting beside him on his chair, Mrs Reed's face betrayed the fact that she was as excited as we were. Then she took Sydney by the hand, I held his other hand and we walked off towards counters full of toys.

Our eyes first lit upon the country scene – there was a farmyard, a large, green board with walls and a barred gate with pigsties and horseboxes. There were black and white cows, pink pigs, and a brown shire horse in harness pulling a cart with red-spoked wheels. There was a farmer dressed in a cap, shirt and cords, wearing a big buckled belt and with the sleeves of his shirt rolled up; a milkmaid with removable milk churns on a pole across her shoulders, with a bucket of milk on each end; and a farmer's wife with rosy cheeks, a checked dress and a plain apron. Both Sydney and I were amazed and delighted at being allowed to handle and move the animals and the farmer. Mrs Reed smilingly asked Sydney, 'Do you like it?' What a daft question; his flushed cheeks conveyed his boundless delight. What else would he say but 'Yes', and so she instructed the staff to pack it and in no time there it was, boxed, packaged and wrapped. I couldn't believe our luck – but we weren't finished. From there we went on to the counter of lead soldiers, endless regiments of them, and then to the Dinky cars – fleets of them, with removable tyres. Then to a large, tin motorcycle with a policeman mounted on it with big, white gloves and black leggings. When I pushed the tin motorcycle sparks came from the exhaust, while the policeman sat with a fixed grin dimpling his highly coloured pink cheeks. Finally there was a drum. All these things were bought and wrapped and with each package she said pointedly, but only to Sydney, 'Do you like that?' And when it was all packed Sydney struggled to carry the pile of boxes and bags. He didn't want to be helped, but the mountain of parcels was too much for him and Mrs Reed happily carried most of them.

I thought it was curious at the time that I wasn't asked to carry a package and Sydney, unsurprisingly, didn't want to lose possession for a minute. More than that: I was puzzled, and I wondered several times when my turn would come – and if it wasn't to be in Fenwick's then it certainly would be somewhere else; but where? As we left through the swing doors I heard Vera Lynn still singing 'We'll meet again' before we returned in the gathering gloom, by trolleybus, to Elswick Road.

Mrs Reed deposited us at home, said how much we had all enjoyed it, and Ma was surprised to the point of being disconcerted at her generosity, so obvious from the stack of parcels and green Fenwick's bags. Sydney started ripping parcels open to show Ma what he had, but then she looked at my no doubt crestfallen face and, allied to Syd's glee, it told her without any further explanation being sought or required exactly what had happened. She immediately said, gently yet firmly, 'The toys are for Christmas', swept them up and removed them. After an initial bout of tantrums Sydney was mollified by the thought that with Christmas close, Santa Claus would soon be returning, and ultimately his anxieties calmed.

Christmas morning arrived and it was clear that Santa Claus had been. On the sideboard next to the statue of the Virgin Mary our pressed-cardboard Santa had been smoking, as was his habit at Christmas, and we had the smouldering 'dump' of a Capstan cigarette impaled on a pin beneath his moustache, above his white beard. It was clear he had come down the chimney, as the sooty finger marks all over the white linen sideboard runner testified – much too realistic for Ma, as was the greeting 'Happy Christmas' from Santa scrawled, in soap, on the mirror. Individual stockings were hanging by the fire and I had an apple, some liquorice all-sorts and a walking stick-shaped pencil, as indeed had Sydney. The pile of Mrs Reed's toys was strategically and centrally placed in a 'no man's land' between all our Christmas stockings. Not another word was said about ownership, although Sydney was not in doubt about it and Ma, who had been deeply embarrassed by Mrs Reed's generosity and lack of sensitivity, never mentioned the matter again.

But another miracle had occurred, as Ma soon found out. Charlotte was pregnant – had been so when the memorable Christmas shopping expedition had taken place. Ma instantly forgave her for any insensitivity; after all, women 'do strange things at times like that'.

14

DELIVERING THE NEWS

I suppose the idea of being a newspaper boy was just another case of learning by example from an older brother. Alan had delivered papers for a local newsagent's shop for three years or so before he started full-time work at Vickers Armstrong in 1938. Both Vincent and Rex had tried it briefly, but perhaps felt it was beneath their grammar-school status: or perhaps they didn't like having to get up at 6a.m. on cold, dark, wet winter days to complete their morning round before school – or perhaps they lacked the commitment required to, worse still, deliver the evening newspapers late on a summer's afternoon after school, when the prospect of staying out through the long, wartime summer evenings was such a compelling counterattraction. Since nearly every household had its *Evening Chronicle* delivered, as well as a variety of morning newspapers and magazines, both were lengthy rounds.

Yet the incentive to deliver papers was strong. Alan had been a good paperboy and had been rewarded by being allowed to keep some of his weekly pay to buy a new Halford's bicycle on the recently introduced 'hire purchase' scheme. Ma had supervised the process of arranging the staged payment scheme for Alan at a local cycle shop and ensured that whatever else he did, he paid this off on a weekly basis as required. Appealing though this new concept was it was never extended to household purchases, largely because Pop was firmly set against it – 'Neither a borrower nor a lender be . . .'.

Of course it could have been that my opportunity arose because Pop was approached by Mr Hannah, who owned and ran a newspaper and tobacconist's shop on Arthur's Hill, which was across Westgate Road near the north end of Elswick Row. Given that Hannah's were looking for a boy to fill a vacancy, it would have been reasonable for Mr Hannah to ask Pop if any of his sons were interested, and such an opportunity would not have required any more diligent research than to wait, probably not for too long, at the bar of one of the local pubs at which Pop made his usual homebound appearance for an evening drink. Virtually everyone had their newspapers delivered and in consequence there was an employment opportunity for younger boys. After all, most of those over the age of fourteen were working full time, many in reserved occupations. Those over seventeen were probably doing some form of national service, and older men were working as members of the Home Guard, as Air Raid Wardens or as Firewatchers. Mr Hannah probably had Vincent, who was then fifteen, or Rex, then twelve, in mind; but somehow I suspect I was volunteered by Ma after Vincent and Rex had declined.

Even allowing for the slimmed-down, wartime versions of newspapers and magazines, the job still required stamina if not great strength; but above all it needed a commitment always to turn up on time and to complete the rounds before most men left for work in the morning and before they returned home in the evening for their 'tea'. That I was the possessor of such stamina and commitment would not have been immediately obvious from my appearance, although my pedigree – Ma's own energy allied to the family's intelligence – was by then well recognised in the neighbourhood.

Newspapers to be delivered were carried in a large, white canvas bag on a broad canvas strap, which caused consternation to me and entertainment for those customers in the shop on my first day. There had been no prior interview, no selection process since I was the only candidate, and no negotiation over terms and conditions. It was two shillings and sixpence per week for a 6½-day week, since there were no evening papers on Sunday – with the bonus of a few days off annually as there were no papers at all on Christmas Day, Boxing Day, New Year's Day, Good Friday and Easter Monday. No training was given and there was no 'fitting' for the newspaper delivery bag. A list of street names was shown to me and each paper, or magazine, was marked with a house number in a thick, wax pencil in the top right-hand corner. The first delivery in any street also had an abbreviated street name next to the house number, and thereafter the sequence of numbers indicated the route planned by the newspaper shop owner. Sometimes this would be down the odd-numbered side of the street and then up the even-numbered side; in some other cases it would mean alternating between odd and even numbers by crossing the street repeatedly.

This post-recruitment briefing occupied a full five minutes after which, though with some difficulty, I lifted the very heavy bag, placed the strap around my neck – and the bag hit the floor, bending my neck happily only slightly, if sharply. I had not expected the weight to be so great or the strap to be so long. When the mirth had settled, Miss Hannah, the very kindly, slight, elderly spinster sister of Mr Hannah the owner, adjusted the strap and then tied the excess in a large knot.

She sent me off, climbing the few steps out of the basement approach to the shop, with an encouraging pat and the cheerful, if rather obvious, comment that the load would get lighter as I progressed through the delivery round. It was more difficult physically than intellectually, and I puzzled as to how the delivery sequence had been determined because, even at my age of nine, it seemed ill thought out.

But in my first week I suppressed those instincts as I became much more familiar with local street names, most of which I had known only slightly. I slowly got to know the characteristics of individual houses, their occupiers and other important facts – such as which families kept dogs that barked or jumped up at me. At the end of that first week I received my two shillings and sixpence, and I proudly carried it home and showed it to Ma. Well, I did rather more than that: I handed it to her and she took it with great calmness but such self-evident gratitude.

I knew without any words being spoken how important it was. I didn't expect anything back for myself on that occasion, which was just as well because I didn't get any. My knowledge of the round kept improving; my times – the first element of self-motivation that I subconsciously attempted – got progressively quicker. I learned how to shield the papers when it was raining by pinching the top of the bag, and by the end of week three I was being rewarded additionally by being given a daily newspaper, sometimes two, for Ma, which she loved. Within another couple of weeks I was being given a magazine or two for Ma, and above all – perhaps because of being able to pass on these treats – I grew to love the job, whatever the weather. I enjoyed getting up early; I got a great thrill from knowing the individual houses so intimately as to know whether to fold the newspapers to push them through the letterbox, or tuck them behind an open front door in the hall or lobby; and on summer days I could throw a folded newspaper through an open door for it to unfold itself in a narrow hallway or passage.

By autumn I could have completed the round blindfolded and I needed another challenge. Once again self-motivation came to the fore and without discussing the matter with either Mr or Miss Hannah I redesigned the route, memorising it rather than remembering by physically reshuffling the newspapers. What suited the old man or perhaps other paperboys certainly didn't suit me, and I realised I would have to ensure that if anybody was waiting for the newspaper – because some people timed me, rather like a bus route – I would have to compensate for any delay I might have created by the route change. And so I used my elementary but steadily growing knowledge of mathematics to assist me, and the net result was that I finished the round even more quickly. I created time to read some of the papers as I walked, and during this period I soaked up any news about the war. Of course the national morning papers were far more informative than the one-paced local evening paper – evening deliveries consisted of only the *Newcastle Evening Chronicle* or, less importantly, some late deliveries of magazines.

By the end of that year I had acquired an encyclopaedic knowledge of wars, sectors and battlefields, of generals and armies during what was, although we didn't know it at the time, the darkest period of the war, when defeat followed defeat and when a reversal was often succeeded by disaster. Singapore had fallen early in the year, not long after my ninth birthday, and the Japanese were overrunning the Far East – in spite of the might of America being in the war 'on our side' – and they were threatening to invade Australia. Rommel was dominant in the desert and his Afrika Corps looked at this stage to be invincible. General Von Paulus had Stalingrad encircled and the Russians appeared close to collapse. The assassination by Czech special agents parachuted into Czechoslovakia of Reinhardt Heydrich, the protector of Bohemia, triggered a savage reprisal in Lidice, followed by much soul-searching at home about the naivety of the Allied tactics.

While bombing raids on Newcastle were no longer increasing, they nevertheless still occurred spasmodically, but in this my natural curiosity saw adventure, excitement and some, albeit modest, exposure to danger. Some boys were prevented by their parents from delivering newspapers because of the risk, not only of air raids but of finding, in the early morning particularly, unexploded bombs or incendiary devices, or even of becoming victims of buildings made dangerous from the previous night's bombing raids.

And the pride and pleasure of earning some money for Ma, rather than the household, was matched by the pleasure I got from the newspapers I read – newspapers of which I hadn't even dreamt. I made deliveries of the *Jewish Chronicle* and the *Catholic Herald*, as well as the more obvious *The Times, Daily Telegraph, Manchester Guardian, News Chronicle, Daily Herald, Daily Mirror, Daily Sketch* and *Daily Graphic*. I even delivered *Hansard*, published weekly during the war, to one household and for the first time read some parliamentary debates. There were also the *John Bull, Lilliput, Picture Post* and *Illustrated* magazines, which I scanned, although I didn't waste much time on *Woman's Weekly, Red Letter* or *Peg's Paper*!

Apart from the fun, the benefit I got from this was my improved status – or so I thought – with my older brothers because they, having scorned newspaper delivery, were not as well read about current affairs as I was. While Ma's informal lessons never slackened, always something daily, always in the evening, almost always beginning as soon as we had heard the last of Uncle Mac and *Children's Hour* – Denis the Dachshund, Mr Grouser the Grocer and Larry the Lamb – there would be other things to do as well. Cards or dominoes or quizzes to which we began to add our own questions about the war – names and shapes of planes, the regimental flashes and cap badges, the names of generals in various sectors of the war, the names of recent battles, of shipping losses, and throughout this now I had my own private world – that of newspapers and streets and of the people to whom I delivered.

And so the summer and autumn of 1942 passed and as the days shortened, in spite of the permanent double summer time, and cold, rain or snow replaced fresh sunny mornings, I needed another injection of self-motivation. There was a great deal already. I loved the job and I knew that Ma was thrilled by the extra cash and the newspapers she received regularly now and which enhanced her enjoyment of her all-too-limited spare time. She also derived great satisfaction from the obvious enjoyment that I took from doing the job well, while I was rewarded by being given some money almost every week out of my earnings. I was encouraged to invest it in the purchase of a new bicycle, just as Alan had done many years earlier.

And then Christmas of 1942 dawned – Mrs Reed's Christmas, as I will always remember it. Alan had already told me that I would enjoy this time of year particularly, because many people were in the habit of giving a 'Christmas box' – provided, of course, that they believed you had done a good job during the year. This tipping was usually compressed into the two or three days before Christmas, some giving this gift as late as Christmas Eve; yet as Christmas approached and each of the days on which I received some money succeeded another, I became more and more amazed. Two old ladies gave me two shillings and sixpence, a whole week's pay, with a smile, and yet later, on New Year's Day, they invited me into their house to be their 'first foot', to carry in a piece of coal and put it on the fire before giving me a glass of ginger wine and a piece of cake to have with them. When on that Christmas Eve I went home having delivered the last of the evening newspapers, I didn't hand over to Ma a half-crown: I simply laughed, turned out my pockets and let all the money I had been given in tips spill onto the table. We counted it together and there was over £5. She was ecstatic and I basked in her pleasure, which did much to remove some of the questions and confusion that had surrounded Mrs Reed and the trip to Fenwick's. Ma gave me half a crown to spend and I lost no time in running round to a local shop, where I 'blew the lot' on a new sledge with metal runners that I had seen in their window. After Christmas was over my own anxiety to thank the people who had given so generously to me, in the only tangible way I knew, meant that I coped easily with the really bad winter days of January and February 1943.

At that time, like most other people, we were constantly looking for legal ways to supplement our food rations, and although we kept rabbits at home they were pets and there was no way we or anyone else was going to eat our rabbits. However, that wasn't a problem, since the butcher usually had rabbits for sale; just as well for our pets, since rabbit soon formed part of our and most other households' staple wartime diet. We also kept ducks and chickens which we bought, as economically as possible, as chicks in the Pet Market and reared them fairly successfully in the kitchen, housing them initially in one of the ovens to keep them constantly warm. When they were deemed to be old enough to survive outside they were transferred to the back yard, where we had a securely netted-off covered area; yet later, when we created more space to enable them to move freely, it enhanced egg production and the single surviving duck, misnamed Donald, together with the more numerous surviving hens, laid prolifically. Those which proved to be poor layers were discreetly earmarked for the menu for some appropriate celebration. Donald, in particular, had an annoying habit of laying an egg at the top of our steeply sloping concrete back yard instead of on the bed of straw provided in safe accommodation; this had the unfortunate yet entirely predictable consequence of a cracked egg having to be retrieved from the back-yard drain. The main problem with our livestock was how to obtain sufficient feed at an affordable cost; as a result I used to avidly collect chicken weed from gardens on my paper round, and collectively we were in the habit of searching Denton Burn or Jesmond Dene for small frogs, which we believed were an essential part of the duck's ideal diet.

It was with this in mind that one day, when I was delivering to a basement flat not far from Hannah's the newsagents, I saw a large, green frog sitting, croaking loudly, halfway down the flight of stone stairs. I made my approach stealthily, grabbed it with both hands and popped it in the middle of my paper bag. But it wasn't my frog and we would have taken a very dim view if somebody had pocketed one of our rabbits, chickens, ducks, cats or even the dog for that matter, so I didn't simply deliver the newspaper that day but knocked loudly on the front door. A rather irritable-looking woman, no doubt in the midst of preparing breakfast, asked me rather sharply what I wanted, to which I said as clearly as I could, that I wondered whether she wanted her frog any longer. I got the kind of look that tells you without a word being spoken that she believes you are mad, but hasn't yet worked out what brought on this sudden bout of insanity. It certainly wasn't hot enough for sunstroke, so she asked me again, even more irritably, what I wanted. I repeated my question and since she still seemed baffled, could see no evidence to support my request and was about to slam the door in the face of this rambling, ill-dressed child, I plunged my hand into the paper bag and pulled out an overweight frog with bulging eyes – whereupon she screamed at the top of her voice, shouting 'Go away!' and slammed the door.

Regrettably Donald the duck didn't care for the frog either, for after several vain attempts to swallow it, she gave up when the frog almost impaled itself on her beak before it leapt off. Try as she might, Donald couldn't quite shovel the frog, which was at least as big as her, back in again. However, it served to provide a useful lesson that the size of frogs, as well as their quality, was quite important to the duck.

Some years later I decided, in the impulsive way that young boys do, that a new paper round somewhere else would be a good thing. Whether or not that was driven by the fact that Sydney was now delivering newspapers and was extremely happy where he was, I have no idea, but I decided to seek a new challenge by transferring my talents to the same newsagent employing him, which was on Elswick Road. There was also a modest increase in pay, but that was not a significant factor. I enquired whether a job would be available, was told 'yes', and armed with that I advised Miss Hannah that I would be leaving. She asked 'Why?', to which I simply and truthfully told her it was to work for another shop and she expressed herself as being very sorry.

Two or three days later Pop asked me why I had decided to leave Hannah's and I told him with the same vagueness I felt that it just seemed like 'a good idea'. He then told me, with a barely suppressed smile on his face, that he had been stopped by Mr Hannah, the architect of my recruitment, in exactly the same place as the original recruitment opportunity was discussed, and had been asked why I was leaving. Pop had told him quite honestly that he didn't even know I was leaving, but added that what I did was my affair. He was embarrassed then to find that Mr Hannah broke down in tears in the pub. He pleaded for Pop to interfere, because I was not only 'the best paperboy he had ever had', but in the years I had been working for them I 'hadn't made a single mistake and there had never been a complaint of any kind' about me – apparently the woman from whom I took the frog was more relieved than disgruntled. Pop relayed this to me and I expressed my great surprise, although it was really puzzlement: the same degree of confusion that

I had experienced over Mrs Reed's Christmas shopping trip! On this occasion, why should anybody become upset because I was leaving? — there were going to be other boys who could do the job, after all! I was now determined to leave because I was too ashamed to go back. It was not until I was sixteen years of age and starting work in earnest that the significance of what Mr Hannah had felt began to dawn on me. It gave me some insight into the self-esteem and self-confidence some other, better-off boys had exhibited during my grammar-school years. But come what may, and in spite of Mr Hannah's sadness, I left and resumed happily delivering similar newspapers in adjacent streets for somebody else — heartless creature that I was.

15

BE PREPARED

In wartime everyone is surrounded by uniforms, everybody admires uniforms and everyone, young or old, soon becomes aware of the role that people in specific uniforms play. Of course it didn't need a war to introduce us to uniforms, because uniforms abounded before the war anyway. The postman wore a uniform; even the telegraph boy on his bicycle wore a dark blue uniform with piped red edging, pillbox hat and black leather belt and pouch. Commissionaires at posh shops, hotels and the best cinemas wore them. Railway workers wore uniforms. I suppose, in a sense, butchers wore uniforms because whichever establishment they worked in they all wore a blue apron with narrow white stripes. Bakers and shopkeepers wore them – bakers' were white, shopkeepers usually wore a khaki dustcoat, which was also the standard dress for storekeepers. Tram conductors and drivers wore them and, as I knew from my father, great importance was attached to the uniform not only being worn, but worn with pride and kept in pristine condition. Hence his button stick, with which I so often watched him assiduously gather the brass buttons together to clean them with 'Meppo' before using a clean duster to polish them vigorously. This was one of his regular 'day off' duties, along with black-leading the grate of the kitchen range before he left for his day out. As the momentum and impact of war gathered pace, so the number of civilians in uniform increased, serving in the LDV or Home Guard as air-raid wardens, special constables, or in the auxiliary fire service.

As a younger child in peacetime I had often cast an envious eye myself over Boys' Brigade uniforms and displayed an interest in, if less enviously, Salvation Army outfits. It may have been the accompanying opportunity to play drums, pipes and tambourines as much as the uniform itself that attracted me. But during the war the possibility of a uniform of my own arose unexpectedly, when one of my back-lane pals suggested that I should join him in his new role as a Boy Scout. It wasn't that the Cubs had had no appeal earlier – simply I had never heard of them or seen a Cub in uniform. I had seen Girl Guides in their blue uniforms, of course, but they were just that, girls, and as yet I had precious little interest in them or their uniforms; but to become a Boy Scout – that was different. I had already heard of and read about Lord Baden-Powell and the origins of the Scout movement in the Boer War, and in that innocent yet clear-sighted way in which young boys' imaginations operate, I linked uniforms with heroism and death with triumph and glory – because after all that was what the map coloured pink, the 'thin red line' and the British Empire were all about.

By now I was deep into, and in truth very knowledgeable about, the Second World War. I had, with my father's encouragement, exploited my membership of the local library to read extensively about the earlier Great War, as it was always known, so that I knew about the great battles on the Somme and at Verdun. I knew immense detail about emotive place names such as Ypres, the Marne, Hill 60, Passchendaele and hundreds of others, as I also knew about trench warfare and firing lines, different howitzers, machine guns and rifles and the introduction of the tank at Cambrai. I knew about the scale of the Great War but I understood nothing about its sadness and tragedy, which were absent from the historical records then available. It was all about *Dulce et decorum est, pro patria mori* . . . Sir Henry Newbold, and Rudyard Kipling-style jingoism – but not about disease, shellshock, lost limbs, poisoned lungs, fear, cruelty and the rawness of death.

And so it was hardly surprising that an invitation to join the Boy Scouts and acquire my own uniform, and somehow to be part of a quasi-militaristic organisation – for that is how I thought of it – seemed another good idea. There were, of course, the usual potential financial pitfalls to be negotiated. A uniform cost money, and since no one else in the family had been a Boy Scout before me, there was no clothing or kit to be handed down to me. We were hardly a camping family, and even if I could overcome these hurdles there was the ever-present concern to be satisfied as I was not joining a non-Catholic organisation – like the Boys' Brigade or Salvation Army – which ultimately might undermine, however unwittingly, my faith.

With the usual balance of optimism and realism I was persuaded by Ma to go along and seek to enrol before I started purchasing a uniform, if only to see whether this splendid specimen of boyhood actually fitted the specification for a Boy Scout. I returned home with excellent news. First, I had enjoyed the experience, and although there was some mumbo-jumbo which I didn't understand but still loved, it was neither anti-Catholic nor endangering my faith, because it was the 55th Bishop's Own troop of scouts. Second, the meetings were held in a church hall and were supervised; and third, they included, apart from the usual rather rumbustious physical exercises such as 'British Bulldog' – broadly a thinly veiled excuse to have a scrum with as many boys as could be persuaded to form a line to stop the rest trying to get from one side of the hall to the other – some serious and rather appropriate educational exercises. We could gain swift recognition for our skills by learning and then submitting to tests. There were tests on fieldcraft – not one of my strong points, since apart from that learned under Mr Tunstall's tuition in Aspatria, I had little experience of the open countryside and we didn't exactly live in the middle of parkland; on first aid, about which I knew a great deal from Ma's encyclopaedia of home-made remedies, although this did not include how to bandage wounds properly or how to tie those bandages perfectly; on how to tie knots, at which I soon became adept, even if I had never heard of most of them before and probably would never use them again, like the bow line, sheepshank and half reef; and there was a test on my own special forte – observation. The observation test was intriguing and much more fun than playing 'fish', a card game which we engaged in incessantly and competitively at home. A table full of objects was laid out before us, and we had three minutes to memorise them before it was removed; we were required to list as many of those objects as we could remember. I was apparently quite rare in that I memorised 100 per cent of the articles in the exact order in which they appeared, and was rewarded with a badge even before I had a shirt on which to sew it.

The third bit of good news, which perhaps by then I should have expected, was that in the 55th Bishop's Own troop, a Catholic group in a working-class district, the highest standards of uniform were not rigidly applied. Those who were already enrolled wore a variety of shirts, shorts and socks, although with a near-universal adoption of the regulation stocking flash, neckerchief and toggle, whistle, scout's belt and hat. Perhaps that was because those items constituted a 'uniform' for most boys. Consequently it was easier to buy these items cheaply, certainly the stocking flashes and toggles, in the Scout shop or in a second-hand shop or from a market stall, when older boys grew out of the scouting habit. A few diligent enquiries with neighbours and relatives, some discreet shopping in second-hand shops in which most members of the family helped, in arcades and in the market soon had me provided with a shirt broadly conforming to the required colour and enough accessories to feel adequately equipped as a proper Boy Scout.

This was just as well, because shortly afterwards we were told with great gravity that the troop was to go on its first major exercise for some years – to Lord Armstrong's estate at Cragside, near Rothbury, where camping facilities were extended to Boy Scouts from all over the county. Lord Armstrong lived in a huge mansion set on the gloriously wooded slopes of Northumberland above the village of Rothbury, through which the River Coquet flowed on its way to the North Sea at Amble. It was not only a beautiful part of the county, as I was to find out, but this was the baronial home of the Lord Armstrong, the founder of Armstrong's

Munition Works, the restorer of Bamburgh Castle and probably the original landlord of both 15 Elswick Row and 5 Havelock Street.

However, in the late summer of 1943, two weeks before we were due to leave on the trip, I was given a list of equipment, clothing and victuals which for a period threatened to be a terminal blow to my aspirations of joining the Boy Scouts at camp. The list contained necessary utensils and provisions – pots, pans, knives, forks, spoons, dishes, bread, flour, milk, butter, jam – together with various other articles, bedding, an alarm clock, as well as appropriate pocket money I would require for a trip which was to last approximately one week. Finally there was the plea that *everyone* should be prepared to provide a tent. Although it was clear that tents could be shared with other boys, no one should assume that 'space in someone else's tent' would be available. For me a tent was 'out of the question', as was an alarm clock – how could I be provided with an alarm clock when we had only one to serve our whole house, and that operated only if laid on its side on a metal plate? Food provision was possible in part – such as a loaf of my mother's home-baked stottie cake, some butter and perhaps a small portion of dried egg – together with some kitchen utensils such as the metal plate (God knows what was going to happen to the alarm-clock system in the household), a knife, a fork and a spoon: but pots, pans and other kitchen utensils were definitely out.

A recently acquired surplus army blanket was the best I was going to be able to muster by way of bedding, but the emblazoned US Army Star lent a degree of military appropriateness to offset its shabbiness; while the family would simply have to pool its resources to see if we could unearth a rucksack to carry my kit. Yet nothing could be guaranteed other than that the bus fare would be available; pocket money was deleted from the list.

With this heavily edited version of what was possible, I returned to the Scouts meeting the following week only to find I was by no means an exception and, although no one in charge bothered to aggregate the committed resources, at least we were all assigned to owners of tents as we prepared for the great day. I had been allocated to share the tent owned by a lanky, blond-haired youth called Billy Gibson who was somewhat older than me and whom I had not met before, although I had seen him at some previous Scouts' gathering; he not only had a tent, but looked every inch a Boy Scout. Somewhat daunted by this I nevertheless reassured myself that I would learn much from his experience and would be a much better Boy Scout myself as a result.

We gathered, and on what passed in the 55th for a brisk military march went from the church hall on Elswick Road down Westmoreland Road, along Grainger Street and on to the Haymarket. We set off with the Scout troop leader and two patrol leaders encouraging us, singing – as any British fighting troops would have been – stirring battle songs. The best we could muster, however, was the troop's own song: 'We are some of the 55th. We are some of the boys. We watch all our manners. We save all our tanners. We are respected wherever we go. When we march down the street, down the street, all the doors and windows open wide, open wide. All the boys and girls come out. All the people there they shout, "Here come the old 55th".'

Sometime later that day, on one of the many long, warm, twilight evenings of the wartime summers of double British summertime, we disembarked from the battered, red 'United' bus, marched for what seemed like an hour and found either our designated camping site on the estate or something judged by our leader to be equally suitable. It was a field in unspoiled countryside, hedged round by tree-sized wild rhododendron bushes of purple and pink, glowing in the soft twilight. The sounds of the countryside made the whole atmosphere strangely ethereal to the gang of back-street children, most of whom, like me, had neither seen nor imagined this kind of remoteness and calm – not even in Aspatria.

We were instructed by the Scout leader to prepare our tents, to set them out on the ground so he could satisfy himself that we were all within reasonable proximity yet not too close to each other, and after a few minor adjustments had been made we were instructed to erect them as quickly as possible.

Then came the first shattering blow to my illusions. Billy Gibson may have looked the archetypal Boy Scout, but he was now revealed as a very inexperienced camper because he had never erected a tent before, and moreover he had probably not seen this particular tent before it was acquired, borrowed or stolen – all serious possibilities given the knowledge I acquired later of Billy. Nevertheless, with the seasoned skill of a natural conman he told me what I should be doing; I set about it, he did similarly and after half an hour's fumbling he told me we were 'there'. We tightened the guy ropes and the whole tent, along with our optimism, collapsed. Furtively and shamefully I looked round and happily there were one or two others in a similar state of disarray, although the majority of tents were now looking very good and sadly most were bigger, looked extremely comfortable and certainly much more appropriate than ours. We got some help from a patrol leader, a much older boy with an authoritative air who certainly did know his business, and before too long we had the tent erected. We set out our meagre contents on the floor before we gathered around a campfire for a supper of shared food, which turned out to be a pan of baked beans with chunks of corned beef added.

We then began to discover the deficiencies in our combined resources. We could not muster one watch among us, let alone an alarm clock; many had the prescribed water bottle but there was no water; we knew broadly where we were but nobody had a map; and the aggregate cash pool of the troop was about six shillings, which was supposed to last us for a week. It was decided that if anyone was thirsty they would have to remain so until the following morning, because although it was still light it was clearly time to go to bed. We were all exhausted and although some doubts and setbacks had been experienced on our first day, we were nevertheless exhilarated.

Tomorrow's programme, being a Sunday, was to begin with Mass in Rothbury's Catholic church. Obviously no one knew where it was located, nobody had any idea what time the Masses were, and it was probably only assumed that there was a Catholic church there in the first place. It was then that the problem of no one possessing a clock or watch emerged, since we didn't know what time it was as we went to bed, we had no idea of the times of Masses, and we had to estimate how long it would take us to get to Rothbury and to find a church whose existence and whereabouts were unknown to us. The Scout leader, with masterly incisive decision taking, decreed that the first Scout to wake should wake everybody else; we would then find a stream, wash, fill the water bottles, dress, breakfast – probably on baked beans again – and march in formation to the church.

I remember I slept uneasily because of rustlings in the bushes, and on one occasion I was disturbed by a noise outside which I believed was probably a snake – Rothbury being one of the few places in the British Isles where poisonous snakes are occasionally found. The adder may be rare, but it is deadly. Ultimately, like everybody else I drifted off to sleep, more anxious than relaxed. It seemed only a matter of minutes before a pan was being rattled and we were told it was time to get up. It was true the sun ·wasn't up, but then of course daylight always precedes sight of the risen sun.

We got up, found some water in which to wash and have a drink, we breakfasted and set off for our march to Rothbury. It must have taken us well over an hour before we sighted the village, having followed some signposts – happily now re-erected after the early enthusiasm for enemy parachutist-defeating tactics early in the war, which had resulted in all signposts being taken down – and we marched into the centre of Rothbury. We rounded a corner and found ourselves in the village square, when two amazing things happened.

First, the clock struck 3.30 – in the morning! We had probably been asleep for about forty minutes by my reckoning, and the light we were seeing was not the pre-sunrise but the post-sunset twilight of those balmy, endless, summer evenings. That was a shattering blow to our confidence in the organisational skills of our hierarchy, but was soon forgotten in the thrill of the second revelation. We saw a huge, armoured, camouflaged tank, the like of which we had never seen before. It was a large tank, with a huge howitzer mounted on its turret, but on the front of the tank was a curious bar with chains dangling from it. The vehicle was mounted on a tank transporter, but the crew had taken off the netting wraps in order to do some cleaning and maintenance and were shocked to the point of charging at us and telling us to go away, while hurriedly replacing the wraps. Their agitation made us all the more interested, their behaviour all the more eccentric, and it wasn't until the following year and D-Day that we learned this was indeed a secret weapon – the flail tank, being developed to precede troops onto the beaches to explode minefields. It must have been undergoing a field trial, or troops were undergoing a familiarisation process, when we stumbled upon it. Whatever the truth, we were forced by armed soldiers to march away from the spot as though we were the Hitler Youth, the tank wraps were restored, the tank transporters left and we returned to sit nonchalantly in the village square until we could muster enough strength to look for the Catholic church. Eventually a raiding party was sent out, the church was located, and in a further blow to our morale we learned that the first Mass would be said at 10a.m. By 10a.m. I was faint with a combination of tiredness, hunger and thirst – obviously I didn't have a water bottle – but boldly we marched off and into church. Mass began, the incense was burned, the faintness didn't disappear and it was all too much. I fainted and was carried out into the fresh air.

That established the pattern and the tone of our camping expedition. After a week of aimless marching about the tops of Rothbury, compensated only by the excitement of catching and killing an adder and the wonder of the glorious wooded grounds with rampant rhododendrons, we exhausted our provisions. We struggled through a week of ghastly meals, about which nobody complained yet which left much to be desired even in wartime, until finally our meagre funds ran out. There was nothing else for it; we marched in as tidy a formation as we could muster and returned with our tails between our legs three days earlier than planned, on Thursday afternoon. Only the weather had been glorious. I recounted some of our adventures, but my mother immediately noticed that I was scratching my head. Out came the tin plate from my rucksack, out came the small toothcomb, out came the kettle of boiling water and the de-infestation programme began. Billy Gibson had not taught me a lot about scouting, nothing at all about tents; but he had left me with a very irritating memento of our time together – head lice.

16

MUSIC HATH CHARMS

The old Burberry-clad violin man with the polished shoes had made a huge impression on me from my first sight of him. I would watch out for him and when allowed would gravitate up the back lane towards him as he moved slowly down, occasionally stopping – whether for breath or in hope of a coin – while constantly playing his gleaming wooden instrument and producing fascinating music. I didn't know why I was fascinated, but I knew I was. And while that musical experience made the deepest, most lasting impression on my pre-school and early schooldays before the outbreak of war, childhood was punctuated by hearing lots of other different music.

There was always music at home on the wireless. My father, in his better moods, would frequently sing snatches from old-time music-hall songs, some of which clearly had a particular significance for Ma and him such as 'Hold your hand out, naughty boy'. We had a varied, if limited, collection of gramophone records which were played carefully ('adults only, please') on the wind-up gramophone with the stubby, short-life steel needles replaced after every other 'play' in the heavy, cumbersome swivel head. Perhaps for other children the mechanics of the process might have seemed more interesting: lifting the lid, winding the handle, lifting and turning the swivel head on the needle holder, placing the record carefully on the base, switching on and, as the record rotated to the correct speed, gently – otherwise it was fatal for the record – lowering the heavy needle head onto the record; and then magically the sounds would come out, blurred and scratchy maybe, but nevertheless music.

The family taste was, like its religious inclination, catholic and as I heard our limited repertoire over and over again, my own favourites changed over time. First 'The Laughing Policeman' by Charles Penrose, with a continual laugh that all children loved, through the Massed Bands of the Household Cavalry playing a whole series of rousing marches at the Trooping of the Colour, to John McCormack with his lyrical tenor voice singing popular Irish songs, operatic arias or quasi-sacred hymns, Enrico Caruso's two arias from *Rigoletto*, and even popular music-hall artistes of the day like Gracie Fields, singing 'The Biggest Aspidistra in the World'.

And good though all that was, it was never as much fun as the impromptu concerts that were held, usually early on a Sunday evening, in the school assembly hall. Frequently these were linked, both in timing and content, to religious feast days and unsurprisingly, given the nature of our community, a date around 17 March would produce a crop of John McCormack 'sound alikes' singing poignant songs with nasal tenor voices reminiscent of Dublin and their native land, usually about the women and the places they had left behind. Occasionally the Sunday evening concert was hijacked by a visiting missionary fresh from Africa who would show his home-made movies of the jungle; these would be preceded and usually succeeded by a selection of hymns and an inevitable cash collection, even though the musical content was much less inspiring than that of other concerts. I enjoyed few things as much as an Irish labourer dressed in his Sunday best, with his neck bulging out of a tightly fastened celluloid collar, straining to reach the soulful high notes McCormack achieved in 'I hear you calling me'.

But like so many other simple pleasures, they came to an abrupt end as the war began and the school hall was required to be on permanent standby as an emergency reception centre. The war's effect was total – no space, no men to sing: not even missionaries to bring back tales of recent conversions from darkest Africa. Worse still, because the substantial Italian community was swiftly and unceremoniously interned, church choirs as well as the concerts lost their Italian tenors, and their Irish counterparts.

Perhaps because of this I was persuaded by Alan Thornton – whose older brother, John, had a good tenor voice and who already sang in the cathedral choir – to accompany him to an audition as a cathedral chorister. It seemed interesting enough, and on the grounds that choristers were usually up in the organ loft looking down on the congregation, Ma's principal objection that my dress and appearance might not be worthy of the Lord – equating broadly to 'not fit to be seen in public' – was redundant anyway. We had an exhaustive audition, singing various notes and short passages, were pronounced fit and summoned to attend choir practice two nights each week, with immediate effect. Before very long we were installed, with a surplice to cover our normal outer clothes – some of which could be left on our own named, personal peg in the vestry – standing in the organ loft singing increasingly familiar hymns such as 'Panis Angelicus', and parts of a sung Mass such as the 'Kyrie eleison', the 'Gloria' and the 'Sanctus'. In addition if we sang at the children's Mass on Sundays, which we didn't usually, that would include some more recent popular hymns; our principal appearances, though, were singing at the 11.30a.m. High Mass and at Benediction later in the afternoon, when we excelled with a moving version of 'Tantum Ergo Sacramentum'.

There was one major drawback to being a member of the cathedral choir, and that was the choirmaster. He was an old tyrant whose surname was Harriett – well, that would have been a very funny name as a Christian name, we used to joke – and to whom we always referred as 'Mr Harriett' or 'Sir'. He had a huge mane of white hair and a white moustache, making him appear a hybrid of Einstein and Barbirolli. He was a brutal martinet. He alternated between facing us to conduct both the choir and the organist, and turning his back on us to follow the Mass. On those occasions when a lower-grade school choir joined in the singing below us, he would also periodically turn his back on us to conduct their singing as well. But whichever way he was facing, if he heard or thought he heard a false note, or even if he felt someone had omitted to sing a note, he would spin on his heels, rather impressively for his age, and without breaking his conducting rhythm, would crack the culprit across the face and continue with his movements. I suppose a Joe Louis uppercut might have been more painful, but it was difficult to believe that at the time. I don't believe it encouraged a greater contribution during the rest of the Mass from the individual who had been struck.

The younger boys in the choir sat in the front row – and during a sung High Mass there were significant periods of sitting down. Harriett would turn his back on us, watch the priest and follow the progress of the Mass intently. We determined to wreak our revenge; since it was wartime we did so by chalking a swastika as heavily as we could on the soles of our shoes, which we did quickly while Harriet's back was turned, and then gently although firmly enough to make an impression, imprinting a white chalk swastika somewhere near his striped-trousered bottom. Frequently we got away with it, at the time that is; but sometimes he either caught us involuntarily while spinning on his heel or our touch was less than delicate on his buttocks, and retribution of a more direct nature followed swiftly. It was a contest for supremacy which lasted as long as I was a cathedral chorister. Overall there are few experiences that so embed music in your soul as being in a dimly lit cathedral with the smell of candle wax, the heavy scent of incense, the swell and crescendo of the organ and the singing, however imperfect, by you and the choir of great music – all against a backdrop of priests in their rich vestments while the emotional ritual binds the entire congregation together.

But Ma wasn't satisfied – yet. There was to be another attempt to broaden our musical education. Early in the war years, soon after our move to Havelock Street, she had acquired a piano at a saleroom for one pound, a substantial sum in itself, for us at least. Uncle Sam – Ma's brother, not the American one – once again came to the fore with a hired barrow and the piano was transported to the house and installed successfully in the parlour. Another distant relative who tuned pianos as a part-time activity came along, did a reasonable job on the piano and, in

Ma's view at least, we had taken a step forward in our neighbourhood status, in our pursuit of education, and in our demonstration – even if only internally – of our cultural intent. As yet that was the job only half done. What was needed now was to encourage the four children at home, Vincent, Rex, Sydney and myself, to take 'pianoforte' lessons. Inevitably a low-cost solution was needed, which materialised in the form of a neighbour several doors further along Havelock Street – a Mrs Creighton.

The Creightons were 'different' in many ways, one of them being that they were a smaller family – five in number. The father's name was Benbow and put simply, as everyone did in those days, he was a 'loony'. The wife was called Winifred, a pianoforte teacher who had descended from much better things to the modest circumstances of Havelock Street. The elder son, Cecil, was an overweight, pompous, rather sweaty individual with a nose like the prow of a boat. There was one daughter, Emma, while the younger son, who would have been in his late twenties or early thirties, was Wilfred; having been born 'one sandwich short of a picnic', he was doing his best to follow in his father's footsteps. Sadly Benbow had been involved in some industrial accident, the details of which were unknown; he was now unable to work and was given to indulge in the most eccentric behaviour. Obviously his misfortunes had caused the decline in the financial and social status of the family. All the children knew Wilfred well, because he would arrive to watch their games and often plead to be allowed to play with children twenty years his junior. He was always well dressed in a suit, with shirt, collar and tie and carefully polished shoes. Frequently it was a three-piece suit with a gold watch on a chain draped across the two lower pockets of his waistcoat. He always had money, obvious because he had a convulsive, jerky habit and to control or disguise this he would put his right hand in his pocket, with the result that the coins there were jangled incessantly. He often drooled as he laughed, but he was utterly harmless. Occasionally he made us nervous when he would grab hold of one of us and rub his rough, whiskered face against our soft cheeks, but he was never physically aggressive; while we saw him as an object of derision, as children sadly will, all our parents regarded him as an object for sympathy, often marked by the spoken 'There but for the grace of God . . .'.

This, then, was to be the household in which we would begin our serious musical studies. Vincent, once again for reasons which were never offered but could probably be assumed, declined firmly. Rex, Sydney and I were volunteered and began to attend weekly lessons, usually one after the other on the same afternoon with each lasting approximately forty minutes. There is little doubt that in spite of my deep, instinctive love of music I was probably the least diligent and the least successful at learning anything about it from Winifred's teachings. I regarded this not as a criticism of her teaching style, but of my own readiness to be distracted by what were undoubtedly strange goings-on in the house; whether or not Sydney and Rex suffered to the same degree from similar problems I never knew, but presumably these events were not kept as showpieces just for me.

On one occasion, shortly after I had rung the doorbell to be admitted by Mrs Creighton – beautifully groomed in long skirt and an abundance of flowing white lace, clothes more suited to the turn of the century than the early war years – I was shown into the front room where her piano stood. The piece selected for today's practice was already on the music stand when she shouted downstairs to the kitchen, as it was a larger house than ours, to her husband Benbow to instruct him to put some coal on the kitchen fire. His mumbled assent could be heard as we went into the parlour, the door was firmly closed and I began crashing away with tonic sol-fas and various other exercises, finishing with a hesitant rendition of the 'Snowdrop Waltz'. As we got up to go I was asked to accompany Mrs Creighton to the kitchen downstairs, where she would mark up my book and take the payment from me for the lesson. Then, as we descended the stairs, I heard the distinctive sound of coal being shovelled. Since this was some forty minutes after the instruction had been given to Benbow, either he had started his task very late or . . . ; it was the latter. When we entered the kitchen the coal was piled on the fireplace at least 4 feet high, in a pyramid disappearing up the chimney. The fire, of course, had by then been obliterated, and in order to keep on putting coal on the fire Benbow was employing a garden rake, an implement unfamiliar to me as it was not included in our household's limited inventory of tools and in truth would have been of very little use, since we didn't have much of a garden either. But Benbow was ensuring he made a very good job of stacking the coal right to the top, even if in the process there was a fair amount of coal and a great deal of dust on the kitchen floor. Temporarily I was forgotten, as Mrs Creighton gently remonstrated with Benbow. She told him that was enough, and was beginning the lengthy process of removing the excess coal, which no doubt would occupy her for a considerable time, when she remembered me, dealt with the payment and I was sent off, leaving her in a state of some confusion.

On another occasion, as I was leaving, Benbow was standing in the hall, where the Creightons kept a very elegant hallstand with an inset mirror around which hung clothes and hairbrushes and I had to negotiate my exit around Benbow, who was combing his hair in the mirror. In saying goodbye to Mr Creighton as well as his wife I had to suppress a laugh, because the implement chosen for this grooming was neither the brush nor the comb placed on the table above the drawer of the hallstand, but a large, white candle from the candelabra on it.

It must have been a particularly difficult life for Mrs Creighton. She was summoned once by a knock on the front door in the middle of the night because Benbow had been found by the police wandering in the centre of Newcastle, dressed only in his nightshirt and carrying a suitcase. The contents of the case had caused the police to wonder about his intent, since it contained a hammer and one nail – nothing else. Apart from Benbow she also had the constant worry about Wilfred – poor old Wilfie, or 'step and fetch it' as we dubbed him because of his skipping-style walk. The high point of his life no doubt came in the summer of 1939 in the days preceding the outbreak of war, when he was seen at the bus stop outside Beysen's cake shop on Elswick Road dressed in a Territorial Army officer's uniform; rather incongruously this was being worn with white sandshoes, which even we knew was hardly the appropriate kit for an officer of the line. It may be an apocryphal tale but we believe he had actually presented himself at the Territorial Army recruitment base and had at first been accepted, as there was a desperate need for volunteers after all; but within a day he had been returned home with a form stamped 'unfit for duty'. In those days the fear of madness was a very obvious, everyday thought; mentally ill people were openly called lunatics, or loonies, and were kept in special 'hospitals'. Our local one was St Nicholas's on Salters Road, Gosforth – a huge, gloomy, stone building in large grounds surrounded by a high, blackened stone wall with locked gates. It was known to all children as the 'loony bin', and the threat of imprisonment there was used often as a warning by exasperated parents or neighbours to those who misbehaved seriously.

Just what effect these events had on my lack of enthusiasm for the pianoforte, or whether it was the repetitive tonic sol-fas or the laboured sounds I produced I have no recollection, but after a relatively short time – certainly less than a year – I had made it clear that I saw no point in pursuing this course; I reverted to, and continued with, my choral singing. Surprisingly Ma had few objections at my defection, no doubt because it brought some welcome reduction in family expenditure levels, underpinned as a by-product by the fact that Rex at least, and Sydney to a lesser degree, were showing some promise.

Her ambition, later partially fulfilled, was for the family to be gathered under her and Pop's wings in the parlour, with one of us playing the piano and the rest singing in some rather touching re-enactment of the classic, happy Victorian family's evening at home. Achieving that rosily romantic state was akin to Pop's winning the Grand National Irish sweepstake – highly unlikely, statistically extremely improbable, but no less desirable.

17

THE WEDDING

The spring of 1943 brought more than its usual ration of optimism. As I knew from my avid reading of all the newspapers I delivered daily, the tide of the war was turning inexorably in favour of the Allies. As early as January the Russians had broken the siege of Leningrad, and by the end of the month the German armies surrounding Stalingrad had surrendered, marking the end of probably the greatest battle of the Second World War and the pivotal one. After the victory at El Alamein late the previous year, the Eighth Army was mopping up German resistance in North Africa, while in the Far East American troops were retaking Guadalcanal. The RAF was regularly bombing deep into Germany, with frequent raids on Berlin, and in May came the dramatic bombing of the Möhne and two other dams, flooding the industrialised Ruhr. Nevertheless there were still periodic major setbacks, although they were beginning to diminish in frequency. The U-boat war was still causing heavy monthly loss of merchant ships, thus prolonging the severe shortage of food and other imports; in Warsaw the Germans were busy exterminating the Jewish population after an uprising in the Warsaw Ghetto; but the trend was unmistakable. To bolster the optimism of the nation, although denying mischievous boys as we were the opportunity to cause some occasional alarm verging on panic, Winston Churchill, the prime minister, announced that since the danger of invasion was over, church bells could be rung once again for their more normal celebratory and religious purposes. This was a pity, because on more than one occasion we had removed the constraining straps on the Nuns Moor Park bell and rung it loudly, waiting only long enough to hear the warning taken up by the other bells before fleeing to safety. On reaching home Teddy Birkett had a well-practised routine of changing his jumper – as an only child he had more clothes than most of us – and wearing his mother's spare set of false teeth. It was intended to be an uncrackable disguise.

In peace or in war, April and May every year brought the need for an intensive 'spring clean' in every house, once the days began to lengthen and the weather became warmer and drier. Doors and windows could be thrown open and every carpet, rug, mat and heavy curtain would be taken outside for beating. This was a physically demanding outdoor activity in which the whole family would happily participate. Many families used a purpose-made cane carpet beater rather like a shamrock-headed squash racquet – if we had known at the time what a squash racquet looked like, which we didn't – to beat vigorously the accumulated winter dust out of every furnishing. Simultaneously the bare floors of the house would be swept before being scrubbed, and every surface from window surrounds and ledges to furniture tops would be wiped and polished. This was not an optional chore, neither did it indicate particular house-proudness; it was simply a necessity, since houses became a health hazard, particularly for those of a delicate nature and inclined to be 'chesty'. Coal and coke were the only fuels used for heating and in many cases for cooking also, and consequently open coal fires burned day and night throughout the winter.

We had open fireplaces in the kitchen, parlour and all three bedrooms. However, the bedroom fires were never lit because they constituted another hazard – that of the house going up in flames. The parlour fire was lit probably once or twice a year and then on Christmas and Boxing days, emphasising the special nature of the celebration and a temporary relaxation from spending constraints. But for most of the time the kitchen fire was the fulcrum around which family activity moved.

The kitchen range had ovens on either side and a small boiler to heat water for cooking and washing. Unfortunately the boiler had sprung a leak before we moved in, was irreparable and we couldn't afford – neither would the landlord countenance – a full-scale replacement. Thereafter our cats found this an attractive winter residence and maternity home. The hobs of the fire permanently housed a kettle of constantly boiling water; the ovens baked bread after the hearth had encouraged the dough to rise; scones and potato cakes were griddled over it; and flat irons were heated on it.

The onset of winter was unmistakable. In the cold, damp nights of November the constant output from thousands of domestic coal fires and hundreds of factory chimneys produced annually a thick, greyish-green fog so dense that it was impossible to find your way to and from the corner shop without difficulty. When in January the fogs gave way to ice and snow, whatever extra clothes we possessed, sweaters, scarves, gloves and overcoats, were worn indoors and outdoors; when removed at bedtime they were needed to provide extra bedding. Hot-water bottles and bedsocks were necessary to make ice-cold, damp bedrooms habitable, and it was essential, if at times revealing, to change in front of the kitchen fire before catapulting up the stairs at speed to leap into a bed which felt rather like diving into an unheated swimming pool – even though we had never experienced public swimming baths.

The kitchen range and fire were the centre of our universe on the long winter nights when the family clustered around it, pressing ever closer with freezing cold backs and lightly toasting fronts. There were frequent disputes when some other family member entered from outside. Yells of 'Close the door!' rang out as the warm fug was disturbed by a blast of cold air, before the jockeying for a privileged space began sparking off more disgruntlement: 'Why should I be the one who has to move?' At times like this everyone read in silence, but periodically we all stared at the dwindling fire, knowing that sooner rather than later, someone – poor unfortunate – would have to go outside and collect a shovelful of coal from the coal house, negotiating a freezing temperature and icy surfaces down the steps to the back yard and down its steep slope to the coal house. Permanently burning fires meant emptying ashes daily into the dustbin. Removing ashes from the house to the dustbin was always a hazardous activity and on windy days was sometimes counterproductive, dirty and dangerous.

If it was possible spring was the time to have the chimney cleaned, and while this was done as regularly as was affordable it was seldom achievable in wartime. Smoke would often fill the room when there were strong winds, exacerbated if the chimney was dirty from falls of soot which, if heavy, resulted in an avalanche of black, smoking, lung-choking, burning filth landing in the hearth, like the slopes of Vesuvius during an eruption.

The chimney sweep wasn't a particularly clean or tidy worker; he simply produced a controlled avalanche. He was as black with soot as a Kentucky minstrel, with white eyes staring from a blackened face. His cap, clothes and boots shed a trail of soot, as did his protective floor coverings and chimney-breast sheets, and as also did his brushes and the canes which he used to build up a lengthening handle, until the huge circular brush on the end of it poked clear of the chimneypot on the roof. His assistant, usually an equally grimy, under-age boy, would run into the house to advise him that the brush handle was long enough, after which the sweep began vigorously pushing it up and down until he released the cascade of thick, black soot. While he took the bulk of this away in his sheets, there was still a formidable clearing-up task to face, sweeping up the remains with a soft brush before washing down the surfaces with soapy water. Meanwhile, the 'sweep' loaded his baggage of soot, cloths, brushes and canes in the trailer behind his bicycle and rode off, with the grimy little boy perched on the back.

Few houses, and certainly not ours, had a mechanical carpet sweeper. No one in the neighbourhood had a newfangled 'Hoover' cleaner, and the only method available for cleaning in winter was the dustpan and brush.

This had a tendency to redistribute the dust rather than remove it, and therefore unsurprisingly the annual 'spring clean' was as much a collective celebration that winter had passed as anything else.

Cricket bats, walking sticks, and the occasional shamrock-like, cane carpet beater – the most effective but still an expensive rarity – were all employed. The activity was so productive, judged by the amount of dust it removed, that it became a health hazard in itself, and early in the war those who were inclined to be 'chesty' took to wearing their gas masks to enable them to take part. Everything that could be moved and beaten in this fashion, was. For those wealthy enough to possess one, even the stair carpet – normally held in place by stair rods, lightly tacked at the top and bottom to give it the additional benefit of being movable within a limited range to disguise worn parts – was hauled out, coiled over a clothes line and thrashed. Curtains too delicate or worn to be beaten safely were washed.

Although open fires were relit and maintained through the summer for cooking purposes, to heat the flatirons and to boil water, they would burn less intensively, never remain lit overnight and could be cleaned more easily. With substantially reduced coal dust and ash residue, and the benefit of fresh air circulating through open doors and windows, the air in houses would remain tolerable until late winter.

In the spring of 1943, apart from the wave of national optimism, the annual cleaning was carried out even more intensively and enthusiastically than it had ever been done before. Roma and Walter Harnan, after careful consideration and close consultation with Ma and Pop, had announced that they were going to marry in the summer; they were preparing to have the banns read at the cathedral for their marriage on Saturday 7 August. The manner and timing of the decision were a surprise, even if an engagement was not!

Roma often met servicemen when travelling by train to work: hardly uncommon when the area was full of men from all three services. On one of these journeys she had met, and continued corresponding with, what she described as a particularly 'dishy soldier'. It was, at least on paper, quite intense, as wartime romances usually were. Then Walter, who was ten years or so older than Roma and exempt from military service, appeared on the scene and she took to meeting him in the park on evenings after he had completed his obligatory Home Guard stint.

After one apparently pleasant evening in a local park they returned to Havelock Street to find a sealed letter waiting for Roma. Ma darkly suggested she didn't open it.

'It's my letter; of course I'll open it,' Roma replied.

'I wouldn't if I were you,' said Ma, as if she knew the contents.

'I am going to,' Roma insisted.

'I won't tolerate other men writing to my future wife,' said Walter.

'Don't open it,' said Ma.

'What do you mean "your future wife"?' said Roma. 'You haven't even asked me to marry you yet.'

'I can't do that until I've asked your father's permission,' replied Walter.

'Well, you'd better do that now,' sighed Roma.

'I don't know where he is,' said the exasperated Walter.

'In here,' said Pop cheerfully, emerging from the scullery in his usual state of unbuttoned flies, vest and braces. 'Hang on a minute till I get dressed, and we'll talk about it over a half in the "Blue Man".'

Walter was a teacher at St Aloysius's, the secondary school that Alan had attended until 1938, but he had aspirations to acquire a position on the teaching staff at the grammar school. He was one of two sons of the widower Walter Harnan senior, a Northern Irish Catholic who, like Pop, worked for the Corporation Transport. He too was employed by now on trolleybuses. Pop had known 'old man Harnan', as he always referred to him, for many years, and as a former tramcar colleague he had inevitably socialised with him after shifts. While he was not one of Pop's closest friends they had shared some interesting evenings together, and surprisingly not only in the Westfield Club or some other pub; indeed,

Walter senior was with Pop and his old friend Paddy Conlon at a protest meeting in the Bigg Market during the 1926 General Strike, when mounted police had dispersed the crowd. There were repeated, baton-wielding charges to scatter the crowd, resulting in many casualties, but with the inherited skill that had been demonstrated by his grandfather in Africa and India nearly a century before, Pop and his colleagues had escaped injury – by sheltering in a pub doorway!

Although the wedding, being in wartime, was going to be a small affair, it still required careful planning and preparation over a long period. What would have caused additional financial stress in peacetime had the added complication of requiring goods and services to be sourced that were in extremely short supply, if available at all, as well as sparse rations to be sacrificed and clothing coupons to be saved.

The downstairs areas of the house – hall, parlour, kitchen and scullery – were to be redecorated and the obvious time to do this was coincidental with the 'spring clean'. Wallpaper was unobtainable, as was oil-based paint, and we were obliged to use the only available alternative, a water-based material called 'distemper' which had the disadvantage that when it had dried it tended to powder and fade. To create a pattern you could make or buy a stencil or, as became common practice, roll a rag across a still-wet surface to achieve a random, 'stippled' pattern. When the redecoration had been completed it gave 5 Havelock Street as fresh and attractive an appearance as it was ever likely to have, at least at ground-floor level.

Suitable clothes were going to be particularly difficult, in terms of both cost and coupons, and an early decision was made – although not communicated to us at the time – that Rex, Sydney and I would not be in attendance at the wedding ceremony. Vincent qualified because his school uniform was judged to be appropriate for such an important occasion. That certainly would have been true in his first year at St Cuthbert's but was no longer applicable, as his blazer suggested that he had created a new fashion of wearing a short-sleeved jacket; because of his now rapid growth, it matched his 'half-mast' grey flannel trousers. But it was wartime.

Pop's colleagues on the buses who doubled as his drinking companions came to the fore with style and generosity. Tommy Johnson, a trolleybus driver – who after a drinks interval between shifts had once sheared a telephone box from its concrete plinth; fortunately there was no one in it at the time – volunteered his wife, who was a skilled dressmaker, to make Roma's outfit. Roma happily accepted and bought the material as soon as she could, exhausting all her available clothing coupons in the process.

The bridal-bouquet problem and the provision of buttonholes for the wedding party were solved by an unlikely combination. Vickers Armstrong's administrative staff, including Roma, had been relocated for safety far away from the ordnance factories and shipyards on the Tyne to a lovely old country house at Riding Mill. The head gardener promised Roma he would provide her bouquet, but since the wedding was to be in August she couldn't have the 'Lily of the Valley' spray she had set her heart on. Instead he made a beautiful arrangement of sweet peas and carnations, and provided a large bunch of roses for the buttonholes. 'Tiger' Smith, another driver not known for dexterity, civility or sobriety, then sat in our kitchen on the eve of the wedding patiently making the required number of elegant buttonholes by wrapping each stem with silver paper from cigarette packets.

Food was a much bigger problem because even if it could be obtained, it meant cumulative saving by reducing the normal, meagre weekly rations, by no means generous in the first place. There wasn't a lot to be saved from the personal allowances of two ounces of bacon/ham, one ounce of cheese, four ounces of butter, two ounces of margarine and two ounces of jam. But Ma's long training in, and genius for, managing scarce resources came to the fore. Meat was rationed by value rather than weight and so cheap cuts, for example a raw ox tongue, could be obtained by careful negotiation. Readiness to take unrationed tinned meats such as ham and Spam helped, as did her ability to barter our sugar rations for more necessary components. Cracked eggs from the Byker egg factory provided a good reward for tiresome queuing and allowed home-made cakes and savouries to be planned. By starting the stock building early some tinned products such as the ham and spam were bought and stored, while arrangements were made with Billy the butcher for the fresh ox tongue to be provided nearer the wedding day. It would then be cooked at home over the fire, pressed using the heaviest flatiron, normally used to complete the weekly ironing routine, and stored in the larder. It wasn't the most attractive piece of raw meat I had ever seen and I felt sorry for the animal which had had its tongue ripped out, but when it was ultimately served it was delicious.

The wedding cake would have proved difficult, because there was a need on this occasion for a professional finish. Even though both Roma and Ma were excellent cake makers they had seldom attempted icing, decoration and presentation of the standard required, neither had they produced a three-tiered cake. Indeed, we didn't have enough cake tins to achieve that and in any case wartime restrictions prohibited the icing of cakes, presumably as a wasteful use of a scarce material, sugar. However, the local network proved more than adequate once again. Alan was leaving his reserved work to join the RAF less than a month after the wedding, together with his pal Johnny Walker, and coincidentally this provided the ideal solution. Johnny's father, a small, serious Scotsman, was a master baker, who agreed not only to make and decorate the cake but to make a gift of many of the ingredients. However, he swore everyone to secrecy because of the illegal nature of his work. He must have known or guessed extremely accurately that what was a celebration for Roma and Walter was also going to be a farewell party for Alan, and by extension his own son Johnny, as they went off to war. Happily he could not have known that it was a war from which Johnny would not return.

Drink presented the greatest problem of all. Notwithstanding that there would be some time during the celebration when the male members of the party would go to a local pub and, subject to previously negotiated availability, have a pint or two there in the evening after the 'formal' party was over, there was still a ritual to be observed of providing and enjoying drinks in the house with the whole wedding party present. Pop's assiduous development of pub contacts over the years was of great assistance. The fact that he had also been a barman early in his working life helped, as did Roma's part-time activity, primarily to help her save for her wedding, as a barmaid at the Westfield Club, which Pop used regularly. This was where she had met Walter, with his father, in the first place. At least the booze had the associated benefit that if it could be located and afforded, it could be stored safely and both the cost and the accumulation spread over a period. Unlike food there would be no temptation to attack it prematurely, simply because it was not Pop's normal habit to drink in the house – if only because he'd usually had his fill outside before he returned home. Home consumption was left for times of celebration such as Christmas, when pubs were closed anyway, and now the forthcoming wedding.

The invitations were prepared, the cathedral confirmed that the wedding could take place there in a Nuptial Mass at 9.30a.m. and the final arrangements were made, which Pop decided must include the hire from Coxon's Garage of a Rolls-Royce decked in white ribbons. Once Sydney and I knew that a Rolls-Royce was going to be involved we began to plan where we would sit in it, and it was this debate that caused the bombshell to be dropped, when we were told that we would not be going to the wedding ceremony at all. In Ma's usual style the plausible explanation was that we were required to look after the house, making sure that cats, dogs, chickens, ducks, rabbits and mice would not get in the kitchen while everyone else was at the wedding. We were 'too young to go' anyway: yet another reminder of the disadvantage of being younger. The fact that Sydney and I had nothing resembling a blazer or jacket did not form part of Ma's rationale, neither was it relevant to Rex's omission. To be denied our first ride in a motorcar was a grievous blow but worse was to follow, because it was during the preparations for the wedding that Ma became seriously ill for the first time.

There were tears of anguish from Roma, who had seen the symptoms developing over several years and whose first thoughts were that she couldn't possibly leave Ma in these circumstances. They were rebutted by Ma's calm protest that really it was nothing and that the arrangements were to go ahead as normal; but it was a cloud that hung over the celebration and one which was to persist for two or three years afterwards.

On the eve of her wedding Roma went to confession at St Mary's, a necessary precursor to communion at her Nuptial Mass early the following day. As she was about to enter the confessional Father Cahill, one of the back-lane, football-playing curates, greeted her cheerfully and affectionately, telling her that the bishop was delighted at hearing the news of this 'match' for which he was providing his own special blessing to be read out publicly at Mass the following morning. Although this wasn't quite the same as the papal blessing she'd hoped for, it was free of charge and the Italians were on the German side anyway – or so I reasoned at the time.

The great day arrived. Wartime restrictions meant that only one car could be hired, the Rolls-Royce for two shillings and sixpence, and it was allowed to make a maximum of only two journeys. Alan, as best man, and Vincent left for the cathedral on foot, after which Ma, Roma, Nellie (a cousin in the WAAF who was the bridesmaid) and Pop followed in the Rolls. The same car had already collected Walter, his father, and their 'cleaner' Mrs Maguire, who more or less lived in, and deposited them at the cathedral earlier. The inner glass door closed and the house was quiet. Rex immediately left for the attic, slamming the door behind him, while Sydney and I decided to explore.

The kitchen looked extremely festive, decorated as it was with additional flowers provided by Mr and Mrs Rose, who had an allotment on Rye Hill from which we often bought a few flowers and salad vegetables on a summer Sunday. The wedding cake looked impressively inviting in the centre of the table and there were countless plates, knives, forks, cups, saucers and an unusually large number of chairs round the table. The green wooden bench seat, always referred to as 'the form' and which sat three children or two adults, had been moved from its customary place at one side of the large, rectangular table that dominated the kitchen and relocated at the foot of the stairs. It was to be used as a bar by Pop who, in addition to performing his functions as 'father of the bride', both at the church and in the speechifying afterwards, was intent on fulfilling his role as barman with panache. At some stage in our survey Sydney remarked gloomily that we should have been allowed to go in the Rolls-Royce. This omission was a particularly grievous blow for Sydney because he had always gone wherever Roma went, and the fact that Roma was going on honeymoon after the wedding, even if it was only to 'The George' pub at Warwick Bridge on the way to Carlisle, had itself led to his being somewhat put out when he learned he was not to accompany her there either. Hence his reflections on our absence from the ceremony were resentful, while I just felt it was inevitable.

Unwittingly I provoked Sydney further by pointing out that the really serious omission was that of not being present at the 'hoy oot'. The 'hoy oot' was Geordie-speak for 'throw out'; the 'hoy oot' followed the scattering of confetti on the bride and groom and was usually done when the main party – bride, groom, bridesmaid and best man – were about to get into the wedding cars. They would respond to the orchestrated chant of 'Hoy oot, hoy oot', repeated over and over again, by throwing handfuls of small coins onto the road, where an assembled horde of small boys, and a few not-so-small but greedy ones, would dive, scrabble and grab for as much as they could. The coins were usually the smallest value, farthings and ha'pennies, but always included one or two small silver coins: threepenny bits or even a sixpence. If it was a really posh wedding there would be several handfuls and more silver. It was always exciting and potentially rewarding, but with an element of serious danger if the wedding cars moved off before all the coins had been gathered. With St Paul's Church of England church being in our street we had become regular wedding attendees, and very expert in the 'hoy oot' stakes. It was a long-standing tradition and one which accounted for the wider appeal of weddings. Of course neighbours would always stop and watch a wedding and young girls were always fascinated, but for small boys Saturdays offered a serious opportunity for financial gain. For the wedding party it was visible evidence of their means and an expression of their happiness.

The genetic seeds of the Cassidy family were deeply embedded in Sydney and he did what Pop would have done in similar circumstances given these three consecutive blows: exclusion from the wedding car, exclusion from the honeymoon, and now a reminder that he was not going to be able to participate in the 'hoy oot' – at which he was surprisingly good, quick to spot a silver coin and even quicker to pounce on it. He resorted to drink!

We went into the parlour, opened the cupboard where the prized bottles were stored awaiting Pop's return, and Sydney decided to open the bottle of Lamb's Navy rum. He drank a good mouthful from the bottle and although his face suggested he didn't like it, he offered it to me to try, which I did: then we proceeded to the next bottle, which was 'Black and White' whisky. We tried the sherry, and enjoyed the port most of all. Unsurprisingly, when the happy party returned later there were obvious signs that the bottles had been opened although only tiny amounts had been consumed; but it was apparent from our behaviour what the sequence of events had been. We both felt slightly dizzy, unsteady on our feet and in very good humour. Pop busied himself efficiently behind his temporary bar and unlike in his earlier professional life as a barman, indulged in an exchange of drinks on a one-for-one basis with everybody he served. He was soon displaying signs not unlike Sydney and me, and for much the same reason.

When the wedding party was called in from the noisily happy parlour for the wedding breakfast, Sydney and I were already sitting at the head of the table with napkins tucked into our shirts and a knife and fork in our hands. We were dealt with swiftly by Ma, who simply lifted us up, pushed us outside the door with the words 'This is only for grown-ups', gave us a firm smack on the bottom: and the jollifications continued behind closed doors. Sydney was indeed the seventh Cassidy son of a seventh Cassidy son, and the sight of the now-open bottles on the form standing at the foot of the stairs in the front passage was too much. He simply sat down, had another few swigs, and minutes later, for the first time that day, was contentedly snoring at the foot of the stairs.

For a wartime wedding it was probably as successful and as well provided for as it could have been, with one notable exception. There was no photographer, and in consequence no pictorial record for the newlyweds or their guests to look forward to seeing on their return from honeymoon. This was the one ingredient that the collective funds, coupons, skills and energies had been unable to provide, beg or borrow. Photographers were scarce in wartime. The taking of photographs was discouraged and photographic materials were more difficult to get than vintage champagne or Havana cigars; in our house that meant 'unobtainable'.

The happiness of the day was predictably succeeded by other, less happy events. Roma and Walter left for their honeymoon. Roma knew that on her return she would be moving in with and caring for the two Walters in an upstairs flat in Farndale Road, not dissimilar to 15 Elswick Row, out of walking distance and out of the cathedral parish, but otherwise reasonably close to home. Mrs Maguire was to be displaced, her role redundant and her reign terminated.

Four weeks later Alan left as the air war over Germany intensified, and optimistic though the day's events had been, Alan's departure guaranteed that the family finances again nosedived, with the combined loss of two contributing wage earners at the same time and when needs of the remaining members of the family continued to increase as the younger boys grew up. Ma's illness worsened. Vincent became 'carer-in-chief', regularly supplemented by visits from Roma, who by autumn was pregnant. Economically we were not going to be able to survive and as winter approached and fires were relit, Ma and Pop knew that something was going to have to be done about it. It was 1935 all over again and while Ma was contemplating how she could achieve another financial Houdini act, fate provided an answer. It was fortuitous that Petty Officer Jack Harrison, Mrs Hetherington's 'fancy man', called and offered an irresistible solution.

18

ROCKFIST ROGAN, ALAN AND OTHER HEROES

Before I began delivering newspapers, I read a new comic called *The Champion*. It wasn't a picture comic, because it was targeted at older boys, and it contained principally prose accompanied by action drawings to illustrate some of the stories. It was very much in the format of, and seen as a successor to, the old *Magnet* which had launched Billy Bunter and Greyfriars, but which was now regarded as old-fashioned and was out of favour with the potential readership. *The Champion*, by now very popular, ranked alongside other relatively new titles such as *The Wizard*, *The Adventure* and *The Rover*, all of which had their stars; but the hero who captured my imagination in every weekly issue of *The Champion* was Rockfist Rogan. Rex preferred Wilson of *The Wizard*, a scarecrow of an athlete who ran in a black, one-piece, long-legged bathing suit and who trained for the Olympics by running backwards up Mount Everest. Vincent preferred the Wolf of Kabul, fighting alongside the British on the North West Frontier and crushing Pathan rebels with his favourite weapon 'Clickyba', a cricket bat bound with wire. With this he crushed skulls, deflected spears or lobbed pinless grenades 80 yards with great precision into rebel-held strongholds. Rockfist, however, was much more topical and therefore seemed more real.

Rockfist was a pilot officer in the RAF flying Spitfires (of course) with great dash and daring from an airfield in the south of England – a barely disguised Biggin Hill; single-handedly he must have shot down about one-third of the entire Luftwaffe during the Battle of Britain. Apart from his daring, his courage and his skill in the air, he was, equally obviously, a gentleman to the core who in war and peace lived by the strictest of moral codes. In addition, unsurprisingly, he was also a fine athlete and his squadron's boxing champion at any fighting weight. He was as fleet of foot in the boxing ring as his Spitfire was acrobatic and swift in the air, and as deadly with his left jab and right uppercut as he was with the Browning 0.303-inch machine guns with which his Spitfire was armed.

When I began to deliver newspapers I read each episode immediately on publication – much better than having to wait for a swap with a friend or a discard from someone at school, or even an old, torn, dog-eared copy while waiting my turn at the barber's – and I never felt less than elated by Flying Oficer Rogan's deeds. Here was a true hero, and while great warships like the *Ark Royal*, the *Hood*, the *Prince of Wales* or the *Repulse* were disastrously sunk by the enemy and our armies foundered on the battlefields of Europe, North Africa and the Far East, the RAF had defeated the Luftwaffe in British skies after having protected the evacuating army from Dunkirk. They then launched their steadily intensifying bombing raids over Germany, deeper and deeper into the heart of the Third Reich, and delivered secret agents into France. Meanwhile, Rockfist Rogan took the unusual and unlikely step, even for him, of flying his Spitfire, unauthorised, by night to a Luftwaffe base in northern France in order to challenge the German ace fighter pilot – who also was the boxing champion of his Messerschmitt squadron – to personal combat in the boxing ring. Of course Rockfist won with a knockout, although not before defeating some dirty tricks by the German ground crew; and this episode culminated in a display of gentlemanly courtesies, which one could expect only among airmen, when he was allowed to fly home escorted to the coast by a wing of Messerschmitt 109s.

Fact in my mind was entwined with fiction and it was inevitable to me that the 'real' RAF – although I couldn't distinguish the difference –

would mount something almost as audacious as Rockfist's exploits. Imagine, therefore, hearing along with the rest of the nation on the early morning news, and reading later in the newspaper, of the dash and daring of the Lancaster bombers of 617 squadron on 16/17 May 1943, defying massed German defences to breach successfully the Möhne and Eder dams, thus flooding the Ruhr and 'devastating the German armament machine'. The Sorpe dam was also attacked but was only damaged, not breached.

Perhaps it inspired my eldest brother Alan even more than it did me, since I knew that he read *The Champion* secretly, usually in the lavatory, whenever a copy was lying around the house, and he had joined the air cadet training corps early in the war. He and his pal Johnny Walker, the son of the Scottish master baker who had helped with the wedding and who lived nearby on Elswick Road, decided to volunteer for service together, joining the RAF in September 1943 – not long after the famous Dambuster raid and just before their nineteenth birthdays. Alan became 1596039 Aircraftman Cassidy, A.J.; after travelling to London he underwent his initial medical, inoculations and kitting out at Lord's cricket ground and was billeted for his initial training at Stockleigh Court on Prince Albert Road. He had never been to London before, but being addicted to sport he was bowled over by his enlistment venue and process – fancy being at Lord's, of all places. The streets of St John's Wood and Swiss Cottage were at least familiar-sounding names because the only wealthy member of Pop's family, his oldest brother, JP as he was known, lived just north of Lord's in Eton Avenue, Swiss Cottage, while owning and running his pharmacy in Great Portland Street. But my mind centred not on the seldom-seen, severe-looking JP with his 'batty wife', who ultimately spent most of their sizeable fortune on a retirement home for their cats, but on the hero we had acquired overnight in the family. More was expected and in due course it was to come.

Aircraftman Cassidy, A.J. became Flight Sergeant Cassidy and he was assigned – delirious joy both for him and me – to an operational

Lancaster bomber squadron. If my mother and father were concerned, they didn't show it. Perhaps like me they were unaware of the deadly statistic that it was unlikely that any operational crew would complete a full 'tour' of twenty-eight missions. Perhaps it was that they bore the news like everything else in their lives, with a fatalism underpinned by a deep belief in God and the knowledge that what was to be would be. Neither, after all, had led a very sheltered existence; neither had been spared crushing blows in their life together.

There were occasional bursts of huge family joy and celebration when the prodigal son came home on leave, looking every inch a hero in his uniform with his air gunner's half-wing badge, bearing gifts of precious cigarettes – always packed in 50s, in round tins sealed with foil – for my father, and any available cash he had for my mother. The celebrations that we had on his first leave were at least equal to those that we'd had for Roma's wedding the month before Alan joined up. But because his leave was unannounced there wasn't the time, the ability or the money to do as we had done with Roma's wedding and save precious food and drink for weeks. It was a matter of making the most of what we had.

The first and most obvious way to mark the occasion was to bring to the dinner table one of the weaker members of our chicken flock. On this happy occasion Alan elected also to demonstrate his destructive urge, which had already been unleashed on the German enemy, by strangling the bird himself instead of using our normal routine, which was to call on Mr Pattinson from next door who for a modest sum would do the dirty deed. We were all too squeamish to do it. Moreover, it was to be done in the knowledge that whoever strangled the victim, Mrs Pattinson would be required to 'draw' the bird, because there was no way that Ma was going to start pulling the innards from one of her pet flock, even if it was now dead.

On this memorable afternoon the fatted calf, or rather the reasonably plump chicken, was ultimately cornered by the uniformed Alan after a hectic chase, with much squawking and feathers flying, only minutes before all the boys were due to go off together, with Alan paying, to a football match at St James' Park. The chicken was held under his striped and badged arm in the regulation fashion while its neck was stretched and twisted. After the corpse was triumphantly held aloft it was tied by its feet to the clothesline and collectively we began the process of plucking it quickly. However, when the task was almost finished and the yard was covered in feathers, as were most of us, with Alan's uniform looking less than ready for immediate inspection, the chicken, having been merely rendered unconscious, decided to return to life albeit in a rather naked state. Alan's lack of progress in the art of silent killing was also sadly evident, because if he had throttled it successfully his second action should have been to slit its throat to allow the blood to drain away. We were forced as a result to endure the unedifyingly comic spectacle of all of us fleeing in terror as this naked chicken, mad with anger, shrieked and flapped until it disentangled its tied feet from its undignified, upside-down position on the clothesline and began madly racing round the limited space of the back yard, intent on inflicting serious bodily harm on its would-be assassin and his assistants. This was only a temporary dent in Alan's heroic status. Ma despatched us to the football match with hot jacket potatoes in our pockets, both to keep us warm and provide some half-time sustenance, while Mr Pattinson was summoned to complete the execution so that we could enjoy a feast the following day.

Alan returned to his unit to be allocated to 620 Squadron as replacement aircrew in what was a Royal Australian Air Force squadron. Where would my delight stop? Some names from pre-war cricket which I had now read about, some of whom were to take leading roles in the Victory Test series of 1946, made their appearance – Workman, Carmody and Sismey; but above all Alan's pilot, Alan 'Pompey' Elliott, was an Australian from New South Wales, his navigator Neville Osborne was from Queensland, and yet his rear gunner was from Byker, an even poorer district of Newcastle than our own Elswick. It was not for me to question the process that led to these mixtures, but surely it was unarguable that the war, now being waged more successfully, had at last been set on an unstoppable course for victory, with the talents of the Cassidy family harnessed to those of Australian cricketers. Aspirations lead to prayers, and prayers can lead to miraculous responses.

One day Alan arrived home on leave, this time accompanied by the aforementioned members of his Australian crew – Alan Elliott and Neville Osborne. How we managed to find accommodation for them in our overcrowded, under-resourced household I have no idea. Whether or not the natural hardiness and famed capacity for roughing it with a smile that Australians have enabled them to cope with it, I don't know; but these tall, handsome young men dressed in the most elegant uniforms, which made Alan's RAF serge look a bit tacky, were a joy. They laughed, smoked and swapped stories with Pop, they let us try on their caps, they gave us spare badges and from a smoke-filled room in Havelock Street they departed for a night of celebration in Pop's drinking club 'The Westfield', near the bus depot where he worked. Some hours later, as I was being ushered reluctantly to bed, there was a loud banging on the front door; my mother looked mildly irritated because she was absorbed in a radio programme, and asked if I would go to see who it was. Clearly it must be a stranger, because as usual the front door was open and only the inner glass door was closed but unlocked. When I opened the glass door and pulled the front door wide, I was greeted by the sight of Pop propped up against the wall, grinning inanely, with a Royal Australian Air Force officer's cap perched at a rakish angle on his head, wearing an unfastened, flying officer's jacket, and a pair of trousers which were unbuttoned and showing from the waist a wide V of 'long john' fronts. There was no sign of anybody else. He was visibly incapable of swift movement, so I sought Ma's assistance. She muttered something under her breath, looked outside and there hiding in the garden were Alan, Neville and 'Pompey', the latter in his underclothes, carrying Pop's suit jacket and trousers over his arm. In my view, this out-Roganed Rockfist.

What happened to Alan in the RAF was a miracle, as he made a remarkable transformation. As a child he was the only one who was seriously difficult, being given sometimes to very black moods and an increasing inclination as he got older to punch his younger brethren rather forcibly if they didn't immediately leap to obey his commands. For a period after he had started work he clearly fancied himself as a boxer or nightclub bouncer, and would invite Vincent to box with him for sixpence. Vincent, who had no ambitions to become a professional boxer, declined regularly but since he was punched as regularly for having refused, he took to accepting the money before refusing to fight, which I always thought was a rather smart piece of business. However, things changed rapidly when he realised he had grown taller than Alan, and the very next time Alan protested at his lack of participation and ran at him, Vincent, with what must have been accidentally acquired or inherited martial arts skills, flipped Alan over his shoulders and sent him sprawling along the front passage. This phase of seeking pugilistic confrontation with Vincent ended abruptly. There were some well-documented previous incidents in childhood when he had become uncontrollably unruly. During the most famous, having almost but not quite physically attacked Ma during one of his black moods, she had restrained him by the simple method of hitting him firmly but not fatally on the head with a milk bottle. He was never as aggressive to her after that, although he continued to be 'a problem' occasionally.

In other endeavours he had fluffed his crucial scholarship examination, in spite of his natural brightness, and had paid a heavy penalty for that. With general good humour, at least when the black moods were not upon him, he had drifted into the working-class trap of taking up hard, manual work in a local factory, without any serious prospect of improvement and advancement. But his readiness to absent himself and his reluctance to rise early, as required by his work, were ample evidence of his inner frustration and discontent.

Had it not been for the war and his friendship with Johnny Walker, it is highly unlikely he would have joined the armed services, it is highly improbable he would have met up with his young, extrovert Australian mates, and his life would undoubtedly have been blighted. As it was, the war transformed him. He loved the dangerous and uncertain life. He exulted in the admiration and he never flinched from the dangers inherent in the daily life of the bomber crew. His natural generosity meant that he now had more to give than ever before and give he did, willingly and regularly.

But above all, for me and the younger members of the family he provided a real, live, wartime hero in our midst. Although I had learned to dread the sight of the telegraph boy pedalling round the corner and stopping at our house with a hand already opening the black leather pouch, happily the only telegrams that we had from Alan's operational base were to tell us that he was coming on leave, with an estimated time of arrival. Mr Walker, the quiet gentle Scotsman, was not so lucky and came to tell us tearfully one morning that the telegram delivered to him that day was from the Air Ministry, coldly informing him that Johnny, Alan's joining-up mate in September 1943, had been 'posted as missing, presumed dead, after an operational mission' in the Far East. His parents didn't even know he was overseas.

My mother Barbara, directly above the only man in this photograph, with her neighbours, 1915.

The Cassidy children, 1934. From the top clockwise: Alan, Vincent, Rex, Roma and the author, Denis.

An expensive, rare pleasure – boating in one of the many public parks, 1936. *(By permission of* Newcastle Evening Chronicle & Journal *Ltd)*

Opposite: Free entertainment always draws a crowd, 1938. *(By permission of* Newcastle Evening Chronicle & Journal *Ltd)*

Preparing for war – the delivery of an Andersen home air-raid shelter for the well-off, 1939. *(By permission of* Newcastle Evening Chronicle & Journal *Ltd)*

Winter and war – snow and bombs fell, 1941. *(By permission of* Newcastle Evening Chronicle & Journal *Ltd)*

Previous page: The perfect adventure playground – deserted and decaying houses, 1950. *(By permission of* Newcastle Evening Chronicle & Journal *Ltd)*

A street party for the Queen's coronation, 1953, as it would have been to celebrate VE day in 1945 and the Queen's grandfather's jubilee in 1935. *(By permission of* Newcastle Evening Chronicle & Journal *Ltd)*

Coronation preparations – local pride demands a clean street, 1953. (*By permission of* Newcastle Evening Chronicle & Journal *Ltd*)

19

FOOD, GLORIOUS FOOD

For us as for most neighbouring families, by which I mean those existing on only one income – and that on or just below the national average wage – the war didn't affect our food supply or eating habits substantially. It may well be true that it had a significant adverse impact on the well-off, the middle classes – whoever they were – and those who were seriously wealthy and in the habit of eating out regularly, but not on us. While war had been declared in September 1939 and ration books had been issued early in 1940, it wasn't until the middle of 1940 that hostilities began to have any serious effect, requiring a government response, on the food supply chain.

The most obvious sign wasn't in what we ate, simply because the basics of bread, butter, margarine, meat, bacon and cheese were guaranteed to be provided in quantities which at worst were consistent with what working-class families could afford. The big difference was that products which weren't rationed – fish, fruit and eggs – were in such short supply that this caused a new phenomenon: the growth of the 'bush telegraph', preceding the forming of endless queues. Registration with a ration book at a food shop – grocer or butcher – would guarantee the family the quantity it was due, as and when it was available; but it was the capacity to hear the 'jungle drums' which would let us know when there was going to be a fruit delivery at Cavanagh's, or a fish delivery at Thompson's before most other people knew. The wider spread of the knowledge immediately caused enormous crowds to gather. Most people were courteous, patient and disciplined as they formed orderly queues, without guidance, ropes, rails or instructions, sometimes in hot sunshine, sometimes in wind, snow and rain. If available we, in common with most other children, were despatched to a shop as soon as any rumour was heard by my mother, and told to wait until she arrived. There was no instruction as to what to do if she didn't arrive, but with Ma that was never a problem; you simply stood and kept her place. Frequently the rumour was no more than that, and ultimately the shopkeeper would tell the patient queue that no supplies would arrive and then everybody would go disconsolately home; but in most cases limited supplies arrived, although frequently in extremely small quantities. Agonisingly you would follow the progress of those at the front of the queue who were allocated a limited amount, either by cash or weight, as the distribution of unrationed goods was susceptible to the interpretation, whims or fancies of the shopkeeper. You simply hoped, and frequently prayed, that there would be enough left for you when your turn came, which in our case was expressed silently by the plea, 'Please God, let Ma arrive before I am put in the position of being in the front of the queue without an order, without money and without purpose.'

Food queues weren't the only ones either, for I was bribed, very handsomely I thought at the time, by Roma to stand in a queue at Etam's in Northumberland Street whenever the rumour was abroad that silk stockings would be available, usually on a Saturday morning. Although Roma generally worked on Saturday mornings she longed for her treasured 'lie in', and when it was in prospect she was prepared to pay for the privilege of protecting it. Unlike a transaction with Alan it was never accompanied by an implicit or explicit threat of violence in the absence of ready cooperation.

Faced with the changed circumstances of wartime shopping Ma soon transferred our allegiance from the local corner shop to the local Co-operative Society in Buckingham Street, which was on my route to school, and I began a long acquaintance with her Co-op dividend number of 40800. This was an important, albeit secondary reason for choosing the Co-op. She had become a member of the movement before the war and was therefore technically a shareholder. She earned a dividend based on the profit made by the local branch of the Co-op and she was further entitled to become a member of the Co-op Women's Guild, which she did. It became a treasured, rare, social activity for her.

For those fresh meats which weren't rationed but were allocated, she retained her long-standing allegiance to Billy Bell, the butcher, whose supplies were supplemented through some contacts of Pop's. Through this we were often allowed as customers to queue on Saturday mornings at another butcher's, Kaufman's at the foot of Bath Lane, for pork sausages, white pudding and black pudding, which became the staple contents of our once-a-week 'super' breakfast on Sunday mornings.

Since meat was rationed by value rather than by weight, our pre-war diet of cheap cuts continued to be available more readily. Billy the butcher had, as I now know, a standard patter like any butcher the world over and for some reason had taken an apparent liking to my mother, to whom he frequently referred as 'the Little Wonder'. On one of my early, unaccompanied expeditions I was sent along with a simple note, with adequate money for the purchase wrapped in it. When I arrived the sawdusted floor of the shop was covered by the feet of the countless women queuing there, but on seeing me Billy called 'young Cassidy' to the front and said, with mock gravity, to the assembled women, 'I'm sure you won't mind while I just read this.' He then read out his version of Ma's note in a loud voice, rolling his protruding eyes as he did so, 'Dear Billy, my husband is working late shift tonight and I will see you at The Big Lamp at seven.' Great hilarity all round; confusion on my face as I could understand neither the message nor the meaning; and certainly I had no inkling that it was a spoof on his part. He then read out, 'Billy, don't forget you promised me 2lb of best fillet steak.' More hilarity and shrieks from the women; Billy disappeared into the back shop, came out with something, wrapped it in paper, gave it to me and said, with a saucy wink and a broad grin, 'Tell your mother I'll be there at seven.' It was, of

course, typical butcher's patter and when Ma unwrapped the parcel I saw
we had as usual a piece of cheap, 'good value' mutton lap – the fatty
piece of shoulder which made excellent stew. When I told her he had said
something like he would meet her at seven, she laughed, said 'Stupid
man', and that was that.

We were despatched regularly to the egg factory – a curious title for
an egg-packing station. Although eggs were rationed, the egg factory
used to sell those eggs which had been cracked in transit or packing
and would allocate a varying quantity to clear them out, determined by
how many were available, how old the eggs were, and how many people
were queuing. We had to be diligent, because it was not unknown for
eggs that were 'off' to be sold to unquestioning children. Eggs were
invaluable, but as far as I was concerned were never as good as the pre-
packed dried egg that increasingly became part of our basic wartime
diet. Even Boy Scouts could make a decent omelette with dried egg,
and it made wonderful fried-egg bread when mixed with a little milk
and water.

The Women's Land Army had been created to make good the shortfall
in male farm labour; but that in itself was inadequate and every
household was also encouraged to grow its own vegetables – an objective,
desirable though it was, beyond our attainment. We hardly had enough
garden to grow a weed, let alone a sufficient quantity of vegetables to
supplement our purchases, and most neighbouring families had the same
frustration, although some had access nearby to highly productive
communal allotments. Ma had made a conscious effort to assist the war
effort by keeping rabbits, ducks and chickens but most of them became
pets, which limited our contribution although it ensured that most of
them lived a long, healthy, pampered life – unlike us.

Children weren't exempt from the need to contribute to food
production at home. As a result, because of the increasingly effective
U-boat blockade around the UK in the later stages of the war, just as 'the
tide was turning', we were encouraged to spend some of our half-term

holiday on a farm at Milkup – part of Blagden Hall Estate, one of Northumberland's many stately homes – to pick the late crop of potatoes. This was hard work for children, requiring us to follow a tractor as it ploughed the potato furrows, pick the potatoes, shake them free of soil, and place them in a bucket; when it was full we emptied it into a trailer which crawled slowly behind us. We were bussed there in the morning to start work at 9.30a.m. and we were due to be bussed home at about 5p.m. – a long day by any standards, particularly for urban children unused to this particular form of labour. We were told to take with us a sandwich and something to drink and we were to be paid a pittance for this work of 'national importance', but some reward nevertheless.

Vincent, Rex and I were all recruited for this task and we set off with others on a bus from the Haymarket to Blagden Hall, where we were deposited at the estate gates; after a march of a mile or so to Milkup we were in the fields, working hard in pleasant surroundings, on the back-breaking potato picking, although our young bodies were flexible enough to cope. Being in the countryside in the late sunshine was a welcome change, as was listening to the barely understandable, rich Northumbrian accents of the local farm people.

Later in the morning we were joined by a large group of German and Italian prisoners of war, in uniforms stripped of insignia with a large, white patch sewn on the back of their jackets; although some of them were very friendly, we were all extremely nervous of being left near them. It was a strange and uncomfortable gathering, and I have no doubt that their lack of enthusiasm for the task and our fear of them caused productivity to drop sharply. There was a break from our labours at midday when people ate their sandwiches sitting on grassy mounds, among bushes, chatting in the warm autumn sunshine, while the prisoners of war were gathered together and guarded by two disinterested-looking, elderly soldiers armed with rifles with fixed bayonets.

We resumed and continued picking through the afternoon until there was a very strange incident, when several unmarked aeroplanes flew noisily and relatively low overhead. As was common in wartime everyone looked up, trying to identify them, when suddenly the aeroplanes disgorged a stream of figures and parachutes fluttered open. The prisoners of war looked in disbelief at each other and then began to jump and shout, hug each other and dance around in the ploughed field. There was no doubt in their mind, and there was precious little in ours, that the parachutists were a crack German airborne division, because no other army had used parachute troops at that stage of the war. I suspect I was as disappointed as the POWs when it became clear that these parachutists, landing only a mile or so away from us near 'the big house', were in fact soldiers from the Parachute Regiment who, unbeknown to us, were practising in readiness for D-Day and what lay beyond. This excitement took some time to subside: only to be followed by another minor crisis.

As the sun began to cool and the light faded, we were told that the bus due to take us back to Newcastle that night would not be coming; reasons were seldom given for anything in wartime. We were to be allocated to various local households where we would spend the night, and would now work through the following day and be taken home in the afternoon, when it was guaranteed that a bus would arrive. Whether or not this was a prearranged ploy we never knew, but the three of us were lodged in a very simple cottage on the estate with the family of a farm labourer; they had three children, two boys and a girl, and the mother was an extremely kindly young woman. When we were ushered into the cottage there was a fire burning in the grate of a sparsely furnished room which acted as sitting room, dining room and kitchen, and a large dog was sleeping in the hearth as we settled down with the other children to some tea, bread, margarine and jam. Wartime it may have been, but we did not eat margarine at home; Ma used that only for the cooking, and so to be required to eat it, poor as we were, was not welcome. Worse still, the tea was served in recently washed jam jars, because the host family, not unreasonably, required the few cups that they owned for their own use.

As the sparse, not particularly attractive or even well-presented meal was ending, a tall, thickset young man made a noisy entrance to the house. He was the archetypal farm labourer, from his muddy boots and thick, buckled belt to his muddy fingernails and ruddy complexion. With a perfunctory nod to his wife and some sharp questions about the additional strange children, asked in a dialect we couldn't fully understand, he washed himself briefly at the kitchen sink before taking his place at the table. While he was doing this the mother 'shooed' all of us away from the table to the side of the room and he sat down. The dog got up reluctantly from the hearth and, wagging its tail slowly, sat beside him; he fondled it and talked to it with a warmth that he certainly hadn't exhibited to his wife or his children. His wife produced from the oven a large piece of cooked bacon, which smelled delicious, and a board on which were several slices of fresh bread. All his children, as well as the three Cassidys, drooled at the smell. He ate it quickly and noisily, occasionally cutting off a piece big enough to have fed one of us and throwing it to the dog. When after several mugs of tea his meal was finished he stretched, scratched himself, belched several times and then went out noisily with the dog, telling his wife in passing that he would be back later.

The farmer's wife lit an oil lamp, the only lighting in the house, and placed it in the centre of the kitchen table to light part of the room, the rest of which was now extremely dim and lit only by the flickering fire. We went out with candles to an outside midden – unlike Havelock Street they didn't even have a flushing toilet – and when we returned the three of us huddled together on a settee and passed a cold, restless night. The farmer returned sometime in the night, again banging the door noisily, went to bed and when we got up next morning to wash in cold water before going to work on the farm, he had already left. During our brief overnight stay he had neither spoken to nor looked directly at us, and it was with great relief that we went home late the following afternoon on the bus after another day's hard labour. We learned later that simple though our lodgings had been, they were infinitely superior to those most others had experienced; our good fortune was because this was one of Mrs Reed's many country cousins.

Children throughout Britain made another – though involuntary – contribution to the war effort by forgoing sweets and other sugar-based products. We were all hit hard by the shortage of sweets; because of sugar rationing they soon became very difficult to find on shop shelves and so prized that if we managed to obtain some they were shared out very carefully by Ma. Well-known, popular brands like Rowntree's Fruit Gums were almost impossible to get, as were Cadbury's chocolate bars, particularly the fruit-and-nut variety. Some locally made substitutes did gradually appear, of which a dark chocolate called Mayvan was the most easily obtained – hardly surprising, because it tasted as though it contained sand instead of sugar and paraffin instead of butter. Its immediate effect on our bowels after eating it suggested its proper role was as a laxative rather than a sweet. However, some local substitutes were excellent, particularly the boiled toffee sweets produced by Buchanan's, who made their own sweets on the premises as permitted by the supply of sugar.

Since Pop had given up sugar in favour of tinned, sweetened, condensed milk for his tea and the rest of us had also given it up, Ma had sufficient sugar to barter in exchange for other essential foods while reserving some to make her own toffee brittle. Fruits, other than home-grown varieties like apples, pears, plums and the usual soft fruits such as strawberries and raspberries, were quite simply never seen. Bananas, peaches and pineapples disappeared completely, and by the end of the war I and many others had forgotten what they tasted like, even when we were shown colour photographs of them. Yet it wasn't only food shortages that brought a real sense of deprivation.

My father's generation was probably the first generation of serial cigarette smokers and most likely the hardship that people like him suffered most acutely during the war was not a shortage of food or drink – though neither was in plentiful supply – but the shortage of cigarettes. Happily no one else in the family smoked until Alan joined the RAF in 1943, and thereafter whatever supplies became available were for Pop's exclusive use. I had become familiar with purchasing cigarettes before the war, being sent frequently to acquire, perfectly legally, Pop's standard pack of Wills' Gold Flake at the Co-op; while familiarity with people who smoked meant that I, like every other boy, tried it at some time. If you had a halfpenny it wasn't difficult to find a long, rectangular slot machine with a knurled, silvered knob identical to a chewing-gum machine, which enabled you to purchase a small paper packet containing two 'Wills' Woodbine' cigarettes and two matches. Yet during the war it was clear and unarguable that those who had priority were the armed forces, and as supply shortages became more acute the plight of smokers became much worse and tensions grew.

A growing number of women began to smoke in public during the war, and that simply increased the demand on an already limited supply. Cigarettes, like many other items, were not subject to rationing; they were simply unavailable. It was left to shopkeepers to allocate the random, occasional delivery as fairly as possible to those who hadn't yet given up and who enquired whether any were available. Shoppers who bore with equanimity the disappointments of goods they wanted badly being unavailable railed against the lack of cigarettes, and irritation occasionally turned to an angry confrontation when a shopper was denied a supply while another customer was sold a pack of precious cigarettes from 'under the counter'. Many more now took to rolling their own, as the purchase of a small Rizla cigarette machine, a pack of cigarette papers and a bag of loose tobacco – which was equally scarce – enabled smokers to roll smaller or thinner cigarettes to stretch out the useful life of the tobacco.

Unfortunately, as in so many other things, this was not an option available to Pop, whose previous pre-war attempts to roll cigarettes we saw as funnier than Charlie Chaplin at his best. We often saw his attempts to move the rollers together and rotate them quickly to get the cigarette to take shape, end with the rollers springing open and a cascade of loose tobacco showering him and the kitchen table at which he was working, while the rollers jammed with a soggy piece of cigarette paper. However, we took to this quite well, and although we found it impossible to purchase loose tobacco in a shop we became as adept as that local, itinerant fag-end collector the 'Nipper King' at searching the streets and gutters for discarded cigarette ends; we would carefully dry them out, tear off what remained of the paper to release the tobacco and, with some new cigarette papers, roll our own. At times like this the provision of the unwanted air-raid shelters provided a perfect opportunity to disguise this activity from the prying eyes of parents as we enjoyed – or at least pretended to – this grown-up pleasure.

We graduated rapidly from retrieved cigarette 'dumps', through sticks of cinnamon, which when smoked produced the most amazing fragrant, pale blue smoke, to cigars. Our foray into cigars was abruptly terminated not only by the expense and the rarity of cigars, but because during one mammoth, collective event in our chosen air-raid shelter, a neighbour observed the smoke coming from the air bricks set high in the walls of the shelters and called the fire brigade. I have little doubt they could tell from the outside what the source of the smoke was, but they literally dampened our enthusiasm by turning on a high-pressure hose through the air bricks, flushing out some rather soggy and shamefaced boys.

The shortage of cigarettes also meant a consequent shortage of cigarette cards; these were highly prized collectables as children sought to complete sets, usually of fifty cards. They were the subject of barter in playgrounds, or a prize for which we competed against each other in a variety of games. Most of the cards in circulation were pre-war issues which had been passed down to the children, some kept in albums, some in neat bundles held by a precious elastic band. Competition for these was keen and we developed a version of 'two up' to play for them. Two cards were held between thumb and index finger and then quickly flicked into the air, as if imparting backspin to a ball, when they would rotate as they descended. The winner called their final position as they fluttered down to the ground – would it be 'Heads' (the two pictures), 'Tails' (the two descriptive backs) or 'Head and Tail'?

Inevitably, however, collections sometimes changed hands because you were attacked when playing and the cards stolen. What a grievous blow to lose a complete or near-complete set of footballers, cricketers, national flags, wild flowers, trees, army uniforms, film stars, steam locomotives, racing cars, kings and queens or any of the many other sets.

20

DIRTY CONSEQUENCES

Although most of the early games that we played required no props, pieces, boards or space since they were created either by Ma's imagination in her unrelenting pursuit of our education and mental development, or they were driven by financial constraints and sometimes by our cramped living conditions, yet there were still occasions when we acquired more formal games. Sometimes they were bought in a jumble sale for a copper or two; sometimes they were handed down from neighbours or relatives.

Games that had been around for generations because of their ageless appeal, such as ludo, snakes and ladders and 'housey-housey', were all favourites although each suffered from the same fundamental flaw. They required the use of dice, coloured bone counters or other pieces such as the numbered wooden discs required for housey-housey. In households such as ours, with a large number of children and little room for secure storage, where the competitive element was as high as ours and where disputes often erupted very suddenly, there was inevitably a tendency for the board and the pieces to be scattered in a temporary outbreak of violence. That it was usually quelled very quickly didn't alter the fact that occasionally the fracas resulted in pieces being lost for ever. Unless they could be replaced, which was usually difficult or financially prohibitive, the game frequently became pointless because home-made replacement pieces visibly signalled a number or value, leading to even more dispute. This also explained why jigsaw puzzles had very little appeal; yet occasionally new games appeared for one of our birthdays or as a collective Christmas 'box'. They were rare and therefore very special.

There were also the more formal pastimes in which, as children, we were allowed to share the adult world, increasingly the case as we grew older. Predominantly these were cards, dominoes and draughts. We learned to play all these from an early age, often encouraged by an element of gambling even if it was only for matchsticks. The importance of gambling was, and I have no doubt remains, that its introduction – playing for stakes instead of purely for the love of the game – contributed to, if it didn't initially inspire, a heightened sense of competition. Yet by exposing us to the added excitement induced by gambling, any sense of it being a 'forbidden fruit' to be explored in the company of others was removed.

One Christmas morning we woke up to find a rectangular, flimsy, yet unopened cardboard box on which appeared an extraordinarily misleading but seemingly authentic, full-colour drawing of a happy family – Mum, Dad, boy, girl – gently holding long, coloured tubes above what was a replica of a football pitch with strange-looking players. The box was emblazoned in bold letters 'Blow Football – a game for all the family'. For a long time that became a source of excited enjoyment, as well as one of continuous conflict, and it injected a heightening of competitive, intra-family tensions.

'Blow Football' was simple in concept, in that the players held a small, coloured, papier-mâché tube through which they blew at a miniature ping-pong, or table-tennis, ball to move it around a tabletop towards a miniature, replica football goal. The football players were the participants blowing through the tubes; the only concession to a miniature football team was that behind each little goal was a wire stalk with a cardboard cutout of a goalkeeper-like figure attached to one end of it. The real intention, as suggested by the happy family on the box cover, was for two teams of two players to compete against each other, one player defending by manipulating the goalkeeper on the stalk while the second player attacked, trying to score goals by blowing through the tube to propel the small ball past the opposing goalkeeper. However, to get maximum excitement and managerial control we invariably operated with one player per side, with the left hand holding the goalkeeper and the right hand holding the tube; this imposed certain limitations on the pitch length! As one player blew the ball towards the goal, the other player sought to blow it back on the counterattack, holding his static goalkeeper in reserve.

Throughout most of my 'Blow Football'-playing career I suffered inevitably from the fact that I was smaller and therefore had a shorter reach and less 'puff' than my elders; these were significant disadvantages. However, they weren't terminal, because various ploys could be employed. One, developed by Rex and readily copied by me, was to suck the ball suddenly instead of blowing it, and while holding it on the end of the tube by a continuous sucking action, to move quickly to the other goal and then propel it with a fierce blow which had an impact equivalent to a cannonball. Rex had learned his skills well with a metal peashooter, armed with rock-hard, dried peas fired at passers-by from our scullery window. Of course such actions inevitably led to a recodification of the simple rules which had been designed around the ideal 'happy family', but they were not for the likes of us anyway. However, by the time the informal 'Rules Committee' had met, Rex had won the league, and some new dubious tactic could be developed for the next season.

Occasionally Pop, in one of his more euphoric moments – usually after a lengthy visit to 'The Blue Man' or at the end of his day off – would decide to join in, presumably in the belief that he would enjoy it and that his skills would be a match for ours. However, his habit of smoking 'Gold Flake' cigarettes regularly, usually from a box of fifty bought by Ma from her weekly housekeeping allowance, meant that he very quickly became almost apoplectic, frequently dissolved into a coughing fit and gifted some extremely simple goal-scoring opportunities to his opponent. There was seldom any enthusiasm from us to use his blowpipe afterwards. In addition, while his reach was greater than ours his mobility was not, and his 46-inch waist frequently hampered his reach across the pitch.

Our games frequently ended in a dispute, pipes, balls and goals were scattered and the miniature ball could be trodden on in the resulting mêlée before the voice of authority would insist once again that the game was terminated for the moment, that the table was required in any case for tea or some other meal and peace would resume. Most of us noticed a tendency to have extremely serious dizzy spells after a ten-minute game blowing and counter-blowing, and in any case the ends of the blowpipes, being made of papier-mâché, resembled the soggy stub of a well-chewed cigar and needed time to dry out. I suspect, although we only thought about it when Pop had played, that they were probably also a haven for germs and no doubt contributed to the rapid recycling of infections whenever one of us was affected by the usual childhood ailments. Infrequent though Pop's playing appearances were, they led us once again to follow Rex's lead by adopting the more durable, effective and hygienic metal peashooter as the standard 'Blow Football' equipment.

The blow-football kit was for a time a particularly appropriate entertainment on winter evenings, when there was very little chance of playing outdoors. However, if there was a substantial fall of snow, and particularly if the snow was followed by a period of freezing temperatures – both of which happened regularly – most boys played a game which was a poor man's version of skating, skiing or bobsleighing. When snow had fallen we would designate a piece of ground – it could be a section of the pavement, back lane or road –where the snow could be quickly trampled and then made glassy smooth by sliding across it. If, again as was usual, the cold weather lasted for a number of days, then water could be added at some stage and allowed to freeze overnight; the end product was a runway of Olympic skating standard, frequently stretching over a length of many yards.

The excitement came from marking out a designated run-up, sprinting as fast as you could in the conditions and then launching yourself with one foot forward and the other trailing and skidding across the surface, marking the point at which the slide ended with a stone.

It was not unlike competing in the long jump in athletics, yet far more satisfying and much more dangerous, since the potential to fall flat on your face in the run-up or fall heavily on the runway was almost infinite, while walls, doors, kerbstones, people and occasionally vehicles were additional, random hazards.

Of course rules were introduced. Nobody who wore hobnailed boots or shoes, or those studded with segs, was allowed on the runway because that quickly cut up and damaged the meticulously polished track. But this carefully constructed, protected track was a constant source of friction between us and some adults who, if angered, would carry a shovelful of cinders from a recently cleaned fire grate and scatter it on the polished track, destroying in seconds the work of days. Thus were age-old suspicions, enmities and outright hostilities between energetic children and tired adults fostered and encouraged to fester. No wonder the fertile young minds which created such games sought simple, swift revenge.

Two elderly, well-to-do spinster sisters, the Misses Waller, Rhoda and Mary, lived in the large corner house at No. 1 Havelock Street. Rhoda, the elder, had been a Registrar of Births, Marriages and Deaths and was a respected, authoritative presence; her authoritarian, aloof attitude had been inherited from their father, who had been the city coroner. Almost axiomatic of that aloofness to neighbouring adults, she was crotchety with all children, irrespective of their age or behaviour; if you merely stood on her street corner, however innocently or briefly, she would appear waving her arms, shaking a fist or brandishing a sweeping brush. She would scowl and mutter, making her intent clear, and however reluctant and undignified it was, I used to move further away. Throughout this her sister, misleadingly called 'the younger' Miss Waller because her neck was as wrinkled as a tortoise's – I knew because once we had one of those – would stand in the doorway or peer from behind the parlour curtains while 'Waller the elder' did her customary war dance in the process of verbally assaulting us.

One winter's day we had built a high-quality skating run diagonally across Elswick Row, to finish almost outside the Wallers' front gate. It was not only impressively long but it enabled us to get up unusual speed, because it took advantage of the slope of Elswick Row and the camber of Havelock Street. As the quality of the surface improved we found ourselves hurtling off the end of the 'ski-run', over the pavement and crashing into her front gate, which was unlikely to do any damage to the property although putting ourselves at serious risk — which to us was irrelevant. Suddenly there was Miss Waller in all her primitive glory, rather like a well-dressed aboriginal, brandishing the usual broom; but since this time she had what appeared to be seriously belligerent intent, we scattered. To our horror and indignation she produced the well-established means of wrecking the finest track we had ever created, and in a post-race conference we decided, without too much difficulty, that this time there had to be a response.

One of the gang, with greater experience and ingenuity than the rest of us, hit upon the idea — which I later discovered he had plagiarised from *The Beano* — of removing a reel of black cotton thread from his mother's sewing box, attaching the loose end to the handle of the Waller's front-door knocker and retreating to a safe distance. After hiding in the bushes, and by the simple expedient of pulling the thread, the knocker would be activated, bringing one of the Misses Waller to the door to find nobody there. Satisfyingly it worked twice. On the third occasion the curtains parted and two pairs of eyes followed this mysterious process of the door knocker apparently activating itself; but Miss Waller had not been a Registrar of Births, Marriages and Deaths for nothing, and the black thread could just be seen by her eagle-like eyes against the backdrop of snow. She did the unthinkable — collected her broom, left the house by the back door, crossed the road, outflanked us and promptly set about us with the broom. The indignity of that defeat lasted for months until the next Guy Fawkes day when, in a seriously concerted attack, we lit and deposited three 'jumping jacks' through her letterbox. This time there was no outflanking and for a period Miss Waller appeared to accept defeat, gracefully or otherwise.

Entertaining and necessary though these physical diversions were, the fact remained that many more winter evenings were spent indoors, where an ever-expanding range of games and amusements were necessary to keep such a large group occupied. We needed a minimum of formal structure and materials to allow the maximum space for inventiveness, from which we soon deduced that the common denominators were a piece of paper, a pencil and as many players as possible.

The adoption or plagiarising of new games began with 'Battleships', played by two opposing admirals whose fleets were simulated on a chart of ten squares by ten squares, a fleet made up of one battleship (five squares), one cruiser (four squares), one aircraft carrier (three squares but in a triangular shape), two destroyers (two squares), and three submarines (one square). These were plotted at the player's discretion in squares numbered from 1 to 10 horizontally and lettered from A to J vertically. Alternate turns were taken in 'firing' at the enemy by nominating a square and if a hit was scored it had to be declared, following which further turns were allowed until a 'miss' was recorded. A tendency on the part of some to cheat was offset by the early development of parallel charts, one to plot your own fleet and the other of your planned assault on the enemy, with an insistence that these were compared at the end of the game – with extra-careful scrutiny if you were the loser.

A similar game, derived from our passion for reading – which never abated – was a simple form of crossword, utilising a block of five squares by five, with the ability to insert one blank square after each of two players had had twelve alternate turns at choosing a letter, which both players were obliged to use. The winner was of course the person with the most complete words or the greater number of letters used in complete words, counting both vertically and horizontally. If the contest was restricted to two players, as in battleships or crosswords, a series of heats or play-offs was developed and a handicap system introduced. Whatever the game, there had to be an overall winner.

It was a natural progression from this to a more literary style, and so Ma introduced us to the game of 'Consequences'. The difficulty with this was that the outcome was not competitive, in the sense that while the result might give great amusement it was impossible to determine a winner, because everyone contributed to everyone else's verse other than the opening and closing lines. Although 'Consequences' was favoured by my mother, for the valid reason that there were fewer wrangles or heated exchanges over the scoring method or the probity of the players, it initially had a very limited appeal for us. The game was played by taking a strip of paper and with five of us playing to inject six pieces of information – the first was a male name, who met the second, a female name, at the third, which was a venue; the fourth was what he said, the fifth what she said, and the sixth was the consequence. After each stage the pieces of paper were folded to keep the information secret before they were moved round clockwise, each person having committed one piece of information to everyone else's paper with the first name and the consequence being their own. The outcome of the game was a random, frequently amusing tale such as: '(1) The Pope met (2) Auntie Minnie at (3) the "Blue Man". He said (4) "I am playing for Newcastle on Saturday." She said (5) "Do you play the trombone?" and the consequence was (6) they lived happily ever after.' Vincent soon began to inject some slightly more risqué elements into the dialogue which had a greater appeal to Sydney than anyone else; he decided, despite his tender years, that in future he would play only if, as he put it at the time, we played 'Dirty Consequences'. His definition of 'dirty' was to make reference to underwear, usually ladies', and in this he was very much a forerunner of Donald Swann's 'pee, po, belly, bum, drawers' school of smutty humour.

As winter gave way to spring more and more time was spent outdoors, the time indoors was increasingly devoted to homework and the house became a more peaceful environment, although never serene or private.

21

IN SICKNESS AND IN HEALTH

With so many children in the house, a supply of lint, a variety of basic ointments and gauze bandages were regular items on Ma's shopping list. The benefit of bandages of course was that they were reusable and could be washed, ironed, and rerolled ready for further use. It was impossible to play in the back lane, secure though it was, without regularly acquiring cuts and grazes of varying severity requiring home treatment; in most cases that meant bathing the affected part with hot water boiled on the stove, using a pudding basin for the water and a clean, if ragged, old handkerchief to bandage. However, if cuts looked dirty then a quick application of iodine, a painful but effective and cheap staple of everyone's home medicine chest, was needed. Inevitably as I grew up I saw, both at home and in the neighbourhood, an increasing variety of illnesses with varying degrees of seriousness, regularly followed by death.

The first crisis in our household was when Vincent and his long-term friend Frankie Wood, the co-founder of the Green Dagger gang – a name borrowed from a Saturday-afternoon series showing at the local fleapit – were playing in our back yard with an old mangle. The mangle's rollers had lost some of their tightness, the rubber having shrunk to the point where it couldn't extract excess water from wet clothes, yet it was nevertheless – like everything else – believed to have some potential value sometime even if, as it later transpired, it was to be disposed of as scrap. However, Frankie Wood had obviously encouraged Vincent, because of this large gap between the rollers, to try inserting his fingers, whereupon he had turned the handle and severely crushed them. The fingers were split, they were bleeding and the knuckles were badly distorted. My mother's anguish was palpable, but as always was accompanied by a speedy response, a cleansing and wrapping of the fingers, before a visit to the dispensary, as the local free out-patient department was known. For weeks the ultimate fate of Vincent's hand lay in the balance, during which time it seemed eminently possible that he would have to have at least two fingers amputated. But that crisis passed, and apart from acquiring the additional benefit of being able to distort his fingers so he could replicate quite convincingly with his right hand a dinosaur-like shape and movement convincing enough to frighten younger members of the family, he was none the worse. He had, though, suffered great pain and lost fingernails in the healing process, when there was always the possibility – turning my mother white at the prospect – of having them forcibly removed. In the event prayers to his name saint resulted one day in the fingernails being found in the bandages when they were being changed, and thereafter the process of recovery was completed seamlessly.

Not long after that an even more devastating event occurred which was both an emotional and economic crisis. This was because Pop, returning one winter's night from a long day shift and I believe on this occasion – although it would have been extraordinary – without a visit to a local pub, slipped on a particularly icy patch, probably where some of us or others like us had been sliding, fell heavily and broke his leg. He was taken, hobbling with the support of some neighbours, by bus to the local infirmary where the leg was set in plaster. No ambulance, no X-rays: simply a swift response and the leg was encased. However, the economic crisis occurred because no wages were paid by the Corporation Transport for absence, even during certified sickness. The economic crisis was ameliorated by the fact that Pop subscribed regularly both to a Trade Union fund, the Transport and General Workers' Union Benefit Fund, and to a mutual sickness-benefit fund called the Ancient Order of Buffaloes. I well remember my apprehension as strange men appeared in the house, looked at documents, spoke to Pop, nodded, grunted and left some money. I think for a short time the residual loss of earnings, caused by the fact that the sickness benefit in aggregate did not match the whole of his lost earnings, was mitigated by the fact that he was prevented from visiting the local hostelry. However, no doubt by continuing and far-sighted diplomatic negotiations, he managed to reserve some of the sickness benefit money for the occasion when he was released from his temporary imprisonment. In the meantime we had the novel sight of Pop hobbling round the house with a strange, white casing round his leg below the knee, on which visitors signed their names, wrote messages of good luck and tapped healthily with their knuckles. There was then a short period when he hobbled out of the house on crutches, borrowed of course, to and from the pub or the dispensary; but as soon as possible the plaster was removed and without physiotherapy or proper rehabilitation, apart from a short period when he had to be careful about his weight transference, he was back at work and the family economy was back to normal.

We had 'our doctor' in the sense that we were registered as being at least prospective patients of a local doctor; this was known at the time as being 'on his panel'. Not that that was a necessary process in those days; choice was as much by accessibility as availability. We regarded ourselves as patients of a Dr Herman Taylor, whose surgery was on Westgate Road on our route to and from the cathedral on Sundays. But during the first two illnesses I can't remember having seen the doctor visiting us, and most consultations were achieved by patients visiting him. Whatever the illness these usually resulted in a prescription, which was made up at Stewardson's, the local chemist; curiously the prescribed medicine always appeared to be identical, whatever the ailment. It was provided in a tall, clear glass bottle with a cork rammed in to seal it and a large, white label with instructions of how frequently it should be taken glued to one side.

It was made up of three apparent ingredients – some liquid, some dark-brown solids and some pale-coloured solids; when shaken vigorously it assumed a medium chocolate colour and I believed it had the kind of magical properties that were always claimed by one of the proprietary medicines you could buy in the local corner shop – Dr Collis Brown's mixture. If true it was indeed a panacea, capable of alleviating any ailment known to man – as confirmed by the list included in every pack and testified to by the members of a Mount Everest assault team; thus, along with Beecham's powders, Carter's little liver pills, chemical blood, cod liver oil and iodine, it appeared to be a staple of a working-class medicine chest.

As I later learned, consultations with the doctor were expensive and it was no surprise that in descending order of priority, the approaches to seeking cures for ailments were first to supply one's own remedy, second to use one of the patent medicines readily available, third to ask for some advice from the pharmacist, and only fourth, having exhausted all other processes, to consult the doctor at his surgery. By that time whatever was wrong with you had probably taken a firm hold, and may even have rendered the patient incapable of walking to the surgery.

Occasionally there was an attempt by Church or state to exercise preventative medicine and on one of these occasions the Schools Medical Officer, Harry Dixon – the son of Joe Dixon, then Headmaster of St Aloysius – paid a visit to St Mary's. The relationship between the two men suggests that there was an element of nepotism in the appointment, although it could have been a simple coincidence – suspicion always lurked in our minds when people in authority, 'they', were concerned. Harry Dixon didn't appear to have any great authority or reputation and there was a feeling, even by the schoolchildren he attended, that Schools Medical Officer was a role delegated to those with medical aspirations who had failed to progress in other directions. Nothing that ever happened through his many diagnoses and prognoses contradicted that assumption.

It was Dr Dixon who in one of these routine examinations decided that he heard some murmur from Rex's heart and endorsed Rex's record with the words 'VDH', an abbreviation capable of misinterpretation but intended to indicate the presence of a valvular disease of the heart. This was definitely not to be confused with a disease identified by a strikingly similar abbreviation, details of which were carried on a white, metal sign always found in public lavatories.

Whether typical of the times, of Dr Dixon or of our financial inability to pursue this matter, it remained simply a medical record notation until the same Dr Dixon decided that Rex's tonsils were displaying unhealthy symptoms, indicating – to him, at least – that they ought to be removed. Curiously, in a school full of children where tonsillitis was not a recurring problem, there appeared to be an abnormally large number of children selected for this treatment. However, in Rex's case, because the tonsillectomy was to be performed on a child with VDH, concerns were expressed that complications could arise, although these were apparently thought to give insufficient grounds to call for further investigative tests. Nevertheless, in advising Ma and Pop that Rex was now listed for admittance to the Fleming Memorial Hospital for Sick Children, it was stressed that, given his other condition, it would be wise to send him equipped with nightclothes in case an enforced overnight stay was required. This in itself was abnormal, as most of the children were admitted in the morning, had the operation performed and were released later the same day. When Ma took Rex to the hospital for admittance it was emphasised this was purely a precaution and that there was still a distinct possibility he would be released later that day, although it was with more than the usual sense of foreboding that she abandoned him at the hospital with his meagre possessions and returned home.

Early in the evening when Roma had returned from her work, Ma walked the two miles or so across the moor to the hospital, undoubtedly a shorter distance than the two tramcar journeys entailed but certainly a more tiring and time-consuming journey on foot; however, the principal objective was to preserve some money for the return journey home with a sickly child. When she arrived she was told that there had indeed been complications, that Rex was bleeding, he would be kept in overnight and furthermore his condition was sufficiently serious for him not to be allowed any visitors. Ma was advised to return home and to check again the following day – which in effect meant calling at the hospital again, a laborious and time-consuming activity without the compensation of knowing whether or not it would be any more successful. She was again told he was still bleeding, too ill to be allowed visitors and she was advised to go home yet again and await a telegram. She remonstrated, she pleaded to be allowed to see him, she considered camping on the premises: but eventually, disconsolately, she returned home in a state of some distress.

Of course we did not have a telephone in the house, neither did anyone else that we knew, and there were few public telephones in the neighbourhood. It was impossible for Ma, with her workload, to visit as frequently as she would have liked and given the gravity of the illness, visiting times even when allowed would be restrictive. As a last resort the fallback was to check an early edition of the *Evening Chronicle*, looking with great anxiety at the list of patients shown on the back page, sometimes in the late column along with the racing results – because it was a kind of lottery in a way – to check their condition. The patients were listed under 'critical' (usually two or three), 'dangerously ill' (a substantial number), 'seriously ill but improving' (even more), 'improving' (not so many), and 'discharged'. Deaths were not announced, though.

Rex didn't fare much better, as he drifted in and out of consciousness. There was considerable medical concern over his condition and it was only on the third day that he was allowed some food, which was a diet of soft, white bread soaked in warm milk – apparently a fairly standard treatment for patients who had undergone tonsillectomy. Meanwhile, as the complications persisted, prayers were said at my mother's request in school for his restoration to good health, and candles were lit in St Mary's Cathedral.

Ultimately the ordeal was over and Pop went to the hospital to collect him, a sure sign of the gravity of Rex's illness but visibly to my mother's obvious relief. Curiously nothing more was said about his underlying cardiac complication; his VDH remained a Damoclean sword hanging over him until it was removed many years later on his only other known appearance for a thorough physical check-up, his medical prior to National Service. He was declared 'A1' and it was confirmed, correctly this time, that there was no trace of any heart condition, or for that matter any other disease.

Sometime later an even more acute emotional crisis occurred when Sydney, still regarded as the baby, contracted scarlet fever. This was not only a serious illness which required him to be taken to an isolation ward in a special hospital, where we were going to be totally dependent again on the daily newspaper updates for his progress, but also, since this was a 'notifiable disease', we were required to display large, white stickers on the door and the windows of the house with 'ID' in big letters, signalling the presence of an infectious disease.

My mother was distraught. This was not only a serious problem, but made worse because she believed the finger would be pointed at our house as 'unclean'. No amount of comforting or reassurance, that this was an obligation simply to prevent people from unwittingly putting themselves at risk of infection, had any effect; in her eyes we were shamed in front of the whole neighbourhood. For a time she went round the house removing the offending posters, which Roma had to reclaim and replace. In the end the same patience, the same prayers, brought full recovery but not, however, before we had been visited by various relatives nodding gloomily, having cups of tea and discussing similar ailments, and sometimes death, at some length. 'Job's comforters,' Ma usually muttered after they had left.

There was an absence of preventative medical guidance at a time when all remedial medicine or treatment had to be paid for, and it was this potential unaffordable liability that caused the proliferation of proprietary medicinal treatments and promised cures, just as limited finances forced people to adopt their own remedies and treatments, many of which had been handed down by example and word of mouth over generations. In these near-universal circumstances it was strange, almost bizarre, that some consideration should have been given to dental hygiene. Bizarre because none of us possessed a toothbrush; most people shunned the expense of what they regarded as the cosmetic use of toothpaste. For the education authorities to impose a medical examination based on the quality of children's teeth, while ignoring the decaying bodies that housed them, was strangely inconsistent.

Nevertheless, one day a medical team arrived at St Mary's school and examined all the children's teeth, making judgements about the standard of dental hygiene and decay. As a consequence I was instructed to attend a dental surgery to have some teeth removed, not because the teeth were decayed but because they were the original milk teeth and as such were deemed to be inhibiting the growth of my second set which was to last for the rest of my life. What I didn't know, but obviously Ma did, was that this was going to be rather a bloody operation. I was taken by Roma, accompanied by Vincent, to the school clinic for the operation because Ma could never face the sight of her children being hurt even in a good cause, which this clearly wasn't. Roma knew that after the damage that was about to be inflicted on me it would not be possible for her to bring me back unaided.

The dental clinic was in Mill Lane, not far from the Brighton Cinema, about a mile from home; it resembled something that I had read about in newspapers or seen hinted at in films that tried to portray a concentration-camp reception centre. It was cold; most of the walls were tiled and bare; the floors were uncarpeted; and the staff were severe and stony faced. Almost immediately on reception I was removed from my brother and sister, sent to toilets which were none too clean and fiercely cold, before being asked to queue with other children sitting on a long, wooden bench in an unheated, tiled room until the dental team was ready for us. When I was called eventually, on entering the operating theatre I first saw some foot-operated pedal drills – tall, black instruments with what resembled bicycle chains running from the top to the bottom; but I was relieved to see that the chair I was being directed towards was far away from those. I meekly sat in the chair, a brace was inserted between two front teeth, I was given a tube which as I breathed inflated and then deflated a large rubber balloon not unlike the inner case of a football, and slowly I went to sleep under the influence of 'laughing gas'.

When I woke up it was with torn, profusely bleeding gums, having had all my teeth removed except the two which apparently had only been retained to hold the brace. An old white handkerchief was held across my mouth and Vincent carried me home slung like a sack of coal across his shoulders, dribbling bloody saliva down his back. Both my mother and Roma were aghast, but the deed had been done. This operation coincided with a marked increase in the number of German air raids on Newcastle, so that night after night I was woken to be brought downstairs from the bedroom to the notional security of the cupboard under the stairs or on a mattress under the table, leaving behind a blood-soaked pillow case as I began to bleed afresh on others. It was medical care carried out without thought for the individual; it seemed hugely disproportionate to whatever problem it was assumed I was going to have, and left me for a long while permanently scarred and very reluctant to submit myself to dental treatment again.

It was almost with a sense of anticlimax that I found one day, having trodden on a board with a nail protruding which had punctured both my wafer-thin shoe sole and my foot, that what had at first been treated by me as a minor injury had developed into a serious infection. I had developed a large blister on the sole of my foot which was filled with very unpleasant-looking pus, and there were the first signs that the poison was beginning to move along the foot towards the ankle. The pain was severe and any movements seriously impaired. That brought out not the doctor, but one of the age-old home remedies. Some firm, old bread was taken and placed in the bottom of the ever-faithful pudding basin, a kettle was boiled, the boiling water was poured over the crust of bread and the sole of the foot around the blister was anointed with Vaseline with great care to avoid the quick jerking movements I made when anybody went anywhere near the blister, which was unbelievably painful. A piece of lint was measured and cut ready to cover the foot while some bandages were prepared. My mother and Roma supervised the operation and I was asked to lie face down on the settee. Of course I asked if this was going to hurt, in response to which I was told, with Ma's usual calming conviction, 'Don't be silly, it's nothing.' However, when the hot bread poultice was applied to the wound, Roma immediately sat in the small of my back, Vincent held my foot rigid while my mother, having applied the poultice, bandaged it and the yells, screams and tears were met by a soothing 'There there, I know; it's all right, it's all done now.' Indeed, miraculously, it was all right when next morning a rather messy poultice was discarded to reveal a wound that was clean and pink.

Wartime brought a new crop of ailments, partly caused by the conditions in which we all lived and some major deficiencies in our restricted wartime diets. I can seldom remember seeing oranges, certainly never a banana or a pineapple, and fresh fruit was restricted to seasonal, home-grown fruits – principally apples or even blackberries, which we picked every autumn.

The most obnoxious disease was that known as 'scabies', producing large, weeping sores that spread rapidly over various parts of the body; they were no doubt spread by contact, particularly since they were extremely itchy. Once the first sores appeared the scabs would spread rapidly over arms, legs, and body; the treatment was usually the application of either a highly coloured, purple, dye-like substance which was daubed on, or an ointment which consisted of a white cream to which fresh sulphur powder was added. Both treatments were slow and very visible and although the sulphur ointment had the benefits of being more readily available, in some circumstances less obvious and much cheaper, it had a tendency to soil with a bright, green-yellow stain the clothes with which it came into contact. In addition some people, of whom Vincent was one of course, found that their own personal metabolism seemed to encourage the sulphur content to produce a strong smell of hydrogen sulphide, or as we knew it, rotten eggs, the common ingredient of home-made 'stink bombs'; this meant that anyone suffering from scabies was unlikely to be a welcome visitor anywhere.

As with so many of these wartime illnesses and afflictions, hygiene and time were the most important requirements for recovery, in the absence of any highly developed, pharmacological remedy.

While Vincent's stink-bomb-like trail made him a social pariah, Sydney's problems with the same disease were much more painful. Sores invaded his lower body, so he had to have a pair of lint 'underpants' smeared with ointment to try to tackle the infection in the parts affected. The amount of lint used placed a further burden on the inelastic family household budget – one which never stretched to conventional underpants until, paradoxically, children had graduated to long trousers.

These ailments, with the other common scourge of head lice, were a frequent problem during the war and in poor circumstances. However, if the indignity of having large 'ID' posters shown in our bedroom windows and on the front door was wounding, it was much more wounding to be thought of as a household which had 'nits' – although it was impossible, given contact with other children at school, to avoid them. The family had to undergo a very careful inspection, particularly if anyone was ever seen scratching anywhere near their scalp. Then the remedy was clear – to produce a white-enamelled metal plate, a 'fine toothcomb' and a basin of hot water. The victim had to sit with head over the water while the hair was carefully combed with the fine toothcomb to dislodge any nits onto the plate, where they were either immediately despatched with a quick press from the back of the thumb nail, or they fell to a quicker death in the boiling water.

But it wasn't long before I graduated beyond these illnesses to something that seemed at first trivial, but then became serious. It was a dark, winter's night and we were sledging down a section of the unlit road at the top of Campbell Street, which ran parallel to Elswick Row and into Havelock Street. The top of Campbell Street, running steeply down from Westgate Road, was an excellent launch pad for a sledge, so a swift burst of speed running with hands on the sledge to gain momentum, and then a quick dive onto the sledge, could in fact mean that with some luck you could speed the length of the street down to join Havelock Street – 100 yards away.

Unfortunately, on this occasion as I began one of my runs I did not notice that the towing rope was trailing, and so as I made my final, running thrust before diving onto the sledge I trod on the rope. The sledge shot from under me back up Campbell Street, while I carried on forward in an elegant, swallow-like dive, making a perfect, three-point landing on the icy road surface – which promptly split open my chin. I was both dazed and numbed by the fall but got up and although feeling fuzzily dazed, felt fine otherwise and went to retrieve my sledge. It was then that one of the other boys saw me, or rather more importantly saw the blood spilling down my front, after which we had a quick consultation before we went home and knocked on the door, which was closed for warmth rather than security. Roma came to the door, exclaimed 'Oh! My God' when she saw me, said, 'Stay outside; don't let your mother see you', retired inside and reappeared later with some handkerchiefs and a scarf. The handkerchiefs were clapped round my chin, secured with the scarf and off we went to see Dr Taylor.

This was going to be my first visit to Dr Taylor and, although shaken, I was without too much pain and not unduly perturbed by the thought. A few minutes later we arrived at the surgery in Westgate Road, climbed the steps and were directed to the empty waiting room by the receptionist, who told us that Dr Taylor was on his way back from one of his calls. We sat for what seemed an eternity in a cold surgery and gradually, as sensation returned to the chin, so the pain developed. Dr Taylor arrived; there was a quick look at the damage, a wiping away of blood and a further examination, following which he pronounced that the wound would need stitches. Roma, being well trained, enquired 'How much?' – to which he replied that it was 'Two shillings and sixpence for the consultation and the stitching, and a further two shillings and sixpence if you want me to give him an anaesthetic.' This was a classic case of 'Hobson's choice' for both of us, and it became clear that I was to have the 'half-a-crown job' rather than the five-shilling, de luxe treatment.

My immediate response was to pay great interest in Dr Taylor as he opened his bag and looked through the assorted instruments. I was very displeased at what I saw. I am told I went a rather vivid shade of green, which I am sure couldn't have been improved by the stitching operation itself. In addition, although it was effective as it quickly stemmed the flow of blood, it was by no means the most elegant repair job I have ever seen – but it wasn't bad for half a crown.

Yet I was impressed with Dr Taylor. I watched his impassive face as he selected the needle and the gut and set about the repair. I was so shocked by the whole process that I know I neither cried nor winced, but in more ways than one he certainly made a very deep impression on me. Dr Taylor was a man of early middle age who was always beautifully groomed, with immaculate manners to match his grooming, and he had what people regularly referred to as a 'film-star appearance'. Indeed, he looked rather like George Raft, with a small, black moustache and his dark hair very carefully groomed to match his dress standard. He usually wore a dark suit with a white shirt and a plain tie, and outside the surgery he always wore a very heavy, expensive-looking Crombie overcoat and a Homburg hat.

Yet all these everyday mishaps, illnesses and anxieties paled into insignificance when Ma took ill. She was a little dynamo, a source of

endless energy, who neither I nor anyone else had ever known to be ill
before; in truth she probably had never allowed herself to be ill: yet
suddenly she was first consulting a doctor and then being referred to the
Chest Clinic. The reasons for the concern began when she haemorrhaged
and coughed blood, but she made light of it at the time and we younger
members of the family were protected from all knowledge of this.
Vincent, in his final year at the grammar school, was now required – in
the absence of Roma and Alan, the former married, the latter at war – to
pick up the burden, which he did as in so many things without
complaint. To him fell the burden of coming back from school and going
out to get shopping – never easy, but in wartime almost impossible. To
him regularly fell the burden of absenting himself from school on
Mondays to do the family wash, since such heavy work would certainly
have brought on Ma's haemorrhaging even if she had had some
assistance.

But with very little serious medical treatment Ma's condition
gradually worsened, and one day the worst was only too apparent when
she couldn't even get out of bed. Just how bad things were I soon found
out when I was summoned to take a note to the vestry of the cathedral,
to bring whichever priest was available to the house as quickly as
possible. Dr Taylor was now in attendance, an indicator of the
seriousness of Ma's condition; he had decreed that there was a real
possibility of death and although he intended to prescribe a new drug,
he feared 'the worst'. I handed the note in at the vestry, a priest came
quickly and together we walked hand in hand up Westgate Hill to the
house. The crucifix was taken from the wall of the bedroom and placed
on the bed, a candle was lit, the priest opened the black box he had been
carrying, took out some oils in order to administer extreme unction –
the last rites – opened a small bottle of holy water, took out his
vestment, kissed it, placed it round his neck, opened his prayer book:
and I was ushered away from the bedroom door, which was then closed
and the process began.

I now knew how serious it was; I was in absolute panic. The thought of life without Ma was simply inconceivable and I was soon on familiar terms with St Jude, the patron saint of hopeless cases, to whom I prayed incessantly. Everyone else in the household had their own version of prayers and even my father's boisterous good humour (rare) or deep brooding (frequent) gave way to a shell-shocked though strained calm.

But slowly, and over a period of some two to three years, Ma miraculously recovered. The visits by the doctor soon became less regular, the age-old remedy of a heavy poultice around her chest, rather like a bag full of porridge, gave way to a new variation on a theme of patent medicine – alcohol. Ma was short, slightly under 5 feet tall, and weighed about 7½ stone. The conventional wisdom in such circumstances was to encourage the patient to put on weight by eating lots of dairy produce, impossible during the war; but in the absence of that to have Wincarnis wine, 'full of iron and a great restorative', or stout, preferably Guinness: 'Guinness is good for you and it will certainly put some weight on.' Meanwhile, the ever-present household sickness reverted to the usual mixture of cuts, bruises, coughs, poisoned heels, boils and general debility, leavened occasionally by head lice, scabies or some other topical problem.

22

THE OLD SCHOOL BY THE TYNE

A change of school was approaching. Vincent and Rex were already studying at St Cuthbert's Grammar School, having both been awarded scholarships, and I was expected to follow them – which was just as well, as the academic competition at St Mary's was virtually non-existent and only my intensive reading kept me stretched. Even the war had gone quiet, for no longer did we suffer disruptive German bombing raids, and neither did I enjoy the excitement of firewatching with Vincent. The raid that had destroyed Manors Station in September 1942 was now as dim a memory as the blue flames that lit up the night sky, and the caramelised smell which lingered over Newcastle for two weeks after a sugar warehouse had been hit by high-explosive and incendiary bombs. The Allied forces had cleaned up German resistance in North Africa, Stalingrad had been relieved and Italy had been invaded.

In many senses it was as well that I had the added interest of being a newspaper boy because it spawned an incentive, perhaps rather unusually intensively for my age, to keep abreast of current affairs – where 'current affairs' was synonymous with 'the war'. By now I had acquired both an interest in and a knowledge of the First World War from the books I was able to borrow from the Stephenson Public Library. I was encouraged by Ma in my general reading, and by Pop because of his own interest in books about the Great War, some of which he discussed with me. Both of them were pleased at the evidence of my addiction to reading, continuing a habit already acquired by my older siblings and to which they added the encouragement for me to go on pushing at the boundaries of knowledge through my natural curiosity.

However, there was at the same time an ever-present pressure to be outside with other boys, generated by our cramped and well-populated domestic accommodation even after we moved to the more spacious house in Havelock Street. After all, the parlour was out of bounds, being reserved for special occasions which were conspicuous by their infrequency, while the only other room in which we could play or work was the kitchen. Since this was always as active as a marketplace and as heavily trafficked as Crewe Junction, it was seldom a practical proposition; but neither were our bedrooms, which were cold, bare, and not the most appropriate or hospitable fun environment either.

Although school was seldom boring or dull, neither was it particularly exciting. There was a handful of boys, of which I was one, who were 'streets ahead' of the rest and the question that exercised teachers' minds – but never ours – was whether or not we could perform well 'on the day' to obtain a scholarship that would ensure a free place for us at St Cuthbert's Grammar School. They knew that we would have to produce a superior result to obtain one of the few scholarships at the fee-paying grammar school; and they recognised the lifelong penalty for falling at this hurdle. Yet they also knew, although I doubt whether our parents even thought of it, that only four elementary-school pupils in every thousand went on to university at that time. The academic hurdle was at least as high to gain entry to the Royal Grammar School, although a significantly lower mark would have been good enough to obtain a place at Rutherford Grammar School or some others: but they were non-Catholic and for us that was simply out of the question – 'What doth it profit a man if he gained the whole world and suffered' (or at least risked) 'the loss of his own soul?' As Bishop Wilkinson, of Hexham and Newcastle, wrote to his flock in 1890, a Catholic grammar school had been created to meet 'the necessity of a more advanced education . . . if Catholics were to occupy the social position which their numbers would warrant' – but 'without exposing their children to the greatest danger to their faith and morals'.

With long-term planning to reduce the risk of failure uppermost in our teachers' minds, Alan Thornton and I were allowed to sit with the eleven-plus pupils the year before we were due to enter the examination, so as to give us the benefit of a dummy run. We were not official candidates because it was never intended, or so I understood, to submit our papers and its only purpose was to give us a feel for our first important examination. We observed that whole ritual: the instructions not to start until told, not to speak to anyone until the completed papers had been handed in, all eyes watching the clock, and the words, 'Now turn the paper over and print your name at the top, read the questions carefully; if you can't answer a question go on to the next question, and return to all unanswered questions if you have time before the end. You now have one hour fifteen minutes to complete the paper. Start NOW.'

It may not have been obvious to us, but to the teachers principally concerned, Fred Kelly the headmaster and J.J. O'Donnell, its significance to our future was a cause of great concern – so much so that when we sat the examination in June the following year on the usual 'one strike and you are out' basis, I was conscious of their concern by the way they kept standing behind me, and no doubt one or two others, carefully gauging the pace at which I was writing and the responses I was giving to the written questions. As I was completing the short essay question of the 'English' paper I heard Fred Kelly saying, *sotto voce*, 'It will be a great shame if he doesn't get the mark required.' I paused and reread the line I had written, which was a description of people at a railway station 'scurrying like ants', an expression I must have plagiarised because I had never seen ants in my life; yet if I had any doubts they passed immediately and the examination paper was duly completed.

While we were waiting for the results the war became more exciting again, as it entered its final phase. The Allies invaded Normandy in early June, just before we sat the scholarship examination, and subsequently my encyclopaedia of names, people and places began to expand rapidly – Juno, Sword, Gold, Omaha, Utah, St Mère Eglise, Pegasus Bridge, Caen, Falaise and 'the pocket', Montgomery, Patton, Clark and Eisenhower.

Restrictions at the coast had been relaxed in some places, and as the school holidays started I was caught up in a repeating cycle of busy, daily activity delivering newspapers, then back home, out to play games or off to the coast to fish off Cullercoats' pier before returning to complete the evening newspaper round, more games and bed. The news bulletins I heard in the evening were very different now, so confident of ultimate victory, from those which had so dominated the household mood in 1941 and 1942.

Whether it was school week or not the ritual of a weekly bath on a Saturday night in the zinc bath, normally kept on a hook in the kitchen, was often interrupted, as it was on that Saturday night in February 1942 when I heard Winston Churchill at his gloomiest talk to the nation about the fall of Singapore. My mother was about to listen to her favourite 'Saturday Night Theatre' when a brief news bulletin followed by the prime minister's announcement was broadcast, and although those were dark days for adults, seldom did the parental mask slip.

Yet now things were different; our rituals were the same but news bulletins had become increasingly positive and optimistic, with only an occasional setback or threats. As if catching the mood, I heard and was delighted that Alan Thornton had also heard that we had both won scholarships to St Cuthbert's Grammar School. We were the only two in the school to do so, but one other boy was going to join us because his parents could afford to pay the fees. For the third time in six years Ma had to overcome the recurring problem of limited finances by drawing on all her skills to create a 'mix-and-match' school outfit for the grammar school.

She had the same budget limitations, constraining her to purchase from the official outfitters only the school cap complete with badge – a complex working of the school colours of claret, blue and papal gold, with its motto *In Coelo Quies*, an official school tie and a separate blazer badge. These were sold at what Ma, as usual, thought were outrageous prices and I, like Vincent and Rex before me, suffered as the principal in the pantomime of being dragged around those more reasonable if less accessible stores, Todd Brothers on Scotswood Road, Farnon's in Nunn Street, Ward's in Clayton Street and JT Parish in Byker, in her attempt to get an acceptable colour match between the expensive cap and a cheaper blazer at an affordable – in other words rock-bottom – price. Essentially all these shops accepted Provident checks, a form of limited credit that was repaid with interest in weekly instalments collected by the Provy man every Friday night. The shopping process was never going to produce an exact match and some of her colour options left a great deal to be desired, as did the positioning of the badge on the breast pocket. Happily the grey shirt and socks at least presented fewer problems.

While footwear was always a difficulty because of my increasing addiction to football, encouraged by my first visit to St James' Park the previous year which had dramatically shortened the life of our boots, the shopping list was further complicated by the need also to have real football boots. Still, she managed to find a pair in the local shoe shop, Harry Posner's; they had the appearance of having been made from compressed cardboard, but even these boots had *real* studs in the soles. Disappointingly the football strip was not to be black and white stripes but the green of Mann House, while the other houses, requiring red, yellow or blue, had no particular appeal either. The concept of being in a 'house' created some puzzling questions for me. What exactly was it? Vincent and Rex simply said it didn't exist at all. But a house was a house. The *Gem* comic's Greyfriars, a boarding school as St Cuthbert's had been at its founding in 1881, had 'houses'; I had always assumed they were where the 'dorms' – fashionable school slang for dormitories – were located. It was all rather puzzling, but quite exciting and I looked forward to finding out the truth, albeit with some apprehension.

I knew St Cuthbert's Grammar School was going to be different. After all, I had had the benefit of some limited information from both Vincent and Rex, but much of that was about the curriculum and the difficulty of certain subjects such as Latin and French, as well as more mysterious subjects such as trigonometry, algebra and physics. They also told me something of the eccentricities of various teachers, but not much more, and I had no idea of what the school itself looked and felt like.

It was in every sense the antithesis of St Mary's Boys' School in Oystershell Lane; it was set in extensive grounds on the very edge of Newcastle and approached by a long, gated drive leading to the main school buildings and the priests' house. It was sited on the old Roman Road which ran westwards from the school down the extremely steep hill on which it was perched, towards preserved portions of the Roman Wall. The trolleybus on which we travelled to school every day had its terminus at the 'Fox and Hounds' pub, which was the end of the line for public transport from the city and short by 100 yards of the school gates.

Not only did I look out over countryside and far-distant views as I reached the school gates, but entering and walking down the winding, gravelled drive through trees and borders of flowers was a disconcertingly unfamiliar introduction. Had it not been for the jostling crowd of uniformed schoolboys surrounding me I might have looked for an escape, since it felt very like trespassing in some rich man's private garden – which is precisely what it had been until about 1922, when it was acquired and extended by the addition of classrooms. It had been known previously as Benwell Hill House, set in 28 acres of land and the home of the Westmacott family.

The priests' house was the magnificent, large, old stone building which had been the principal house, to which over time had been added a variety of buildings including classrooms and a large assembly hall. There were about 600 boys attending the grammar school, and on that first morning some of the calm of the manicured rural surroundings was disturbed by the seething mass arriving for their first day of a new academic year.

Of course over 100 of the boys like me were strangers and had never been to the school before, while the other 500 were going to move ahead one year to new forms in the unstoppable progression of school life, but with some variation in their location and curriculum. All this change created a scene of barely organised chaos. The new boys were identifiable by their equally new uniforms; some were more readily recognisable than others and I, in a blazer rather more of papal purple than it was of the specified claret, was one. Some wore their school uniform with an air of well-heeled familiarity, some as though straitjacketed for the loony bin, while the remainder just looked uncomfortable and fidgety. That uniforms had to last growing boys for as long as possible, important to all parents given wartime clothes rationing, was evidenced by the sight of blazer sleeves that exceeded by several inches the length of the arm which filled them, or shorts that were closer to the ankle than the knee.

The school was very strange. The intake each year was from the four northern counties, although most of the newcomers came from Northumberland and Durham. We were divided randomly, it seemed, into four classes; but unfortunately I soon found I didn't share a classroom with my closest schoolfriend. I was allocated to 1B and Alan to 1A, a fact learned from searching to find matching name and class number through a number of closely handwritten lists pinned to a green baize noticeboard while jostling for position with 100 other anxious searchers.

Most of the teaching staff were priests and the headmaster was a senior priest, Monsignor Canon J.J. Cunningham. He rejoiced in the nickname of 'Tommy Noddy' – sinful to think, let alone to speak – largely because he had a head that was disproportionately large for his body, neck and shoulders, all of which he visibly had some difficulty in supporting in a normal position. Although he was the only Monsignor I had ever met he had what I regarded as the regulation Monsignor's frown when watching pupils, and he usually wore a long, red-trimmed, black cassock with matching buttons, stretching from his dog collar to his ankles, with his hands most often thrust deep into two side pockets. He was much given to speech making; being headmaster presented him happily with an infinite number of opportunities, and it was soon abundantly clear that his style had been developed from close examination of the phraseology, timbre and pace of Winston Churchill. On appointment as headmaster in 1938 he had introduced a more complex, formal and expensive uniform which stamped his intentions clearly on the school's future direction. If only he had known the anguish he was inflicting on parents such as ours he might well have reconsidered his decision, or even discarded it as not necessarily helping to implement Bishop Wilkinson's aspirations.

Yet some of the other priests were much more intimidating. Father Cassidy, a namesake but happily no relation, had a striking resemblance to Himmler with his bald head and a very dark 'seven o'clock shadow'. He wore gold-framed glasses, as did his German counterpart, or sometimes pince-nez, and he appeared to have some problem with his eyelids, because to change focus he had both to raise his eyes and tilt his head backwards. His black cassock and academic's gown differed only from Himmler's uniform in that Father Cassidy didn't wear any swastika armbands. His reputation was as fearsome as his and Himmler's severe looks implied.

Then there was Father Landreth, who as prefect was the school disciplinarian as well as our French teacher. He was tall, dark and handsome in the rugged way some film stars then were. He always appeared to be wearing a sardonic smile and although he had a reputation for fairness this was difficult to discern from his demeanour or his actions; he looked ever at the ready to wield the cane which he carried and frequently used in the interests of just retribution. He was infamous in our household because of a single incident which had occurred the previous year during a collection he was taking for Lenten alms. He was standing, as was his usual habit on occasions when money was being sought, with a wooden collection box mounted on a flat wooden handle, aggressively shaking it in front of the boys as they went home at the end of the day. Vincent, who left the grammar school at the end of the academic year prior to my starting, had held back on seeing him and assessed his chances of passing through unchallenged or even – although he discarded this thought immediately – of pleading that he had no money other than the halfpenny required to get him home on the bus. Having tried to make himself as inconspicuous as possible he mingled as well as he could in a group of boys going out, but was halted by a sharp prod of the collection box in his chest. He now had no option. It would have to be a long walk home as he took his halfpenny out of his pocket and was about to put it in the box when Father Landreth grasped his hand and said coldly, as he threw the coin to the floor, 'If that's all you are prepared to give, keep it.' Vincent left shamefacedly and Father Landreth's reputation in our household was established. Ma, when told, muttered darkly about the widow's mite and the incident reinforced her well-founded prejudices about the priesthood in general and Father Landreth in particular.

But there were other priests who were much more fun. There was the roly-poly, bespectacled Father Hardy, who played cricket for two quality local teams – Benwell Hill and previously Benwell, the latter sharing a delightful oval cricket ground with the grammar school; and there was Father Crumley, who played soccer with the boys when he took the sports period. His style was to behave rather like an established international playing with lesser professionals, and he was quite prepared to come very close to breaking legs in scything, not always fair, tackles which at least gave some of the bigger boys a chance for revenge through deliberately mistimed challenges.

There was a clutch of lay teachers of whom one, my first form master Jock McGovern, was a barely articulate Scotsman. Others were Tommy Hayes, an ageing Latin teacher with even older teaching methods; Bill Cutter, the overweight physics teacher; Teddy Kelly, a rather civilised,

quiet, engaging man who taught French and music; Gerry Stoddart; and
Bill Spoors, whose occasional descents into bad language suggested he
was a coarsely spoken back-street boy made good and who would have
been allowed to join the academic staff only in wartime. And of course
there was my recently acquired brother-in-law Walter Harnan who was
anxious, from his and my first day at the school, not to be seen speaking
to me, let alone associating with me. I agreed with his approach,
although probably for very different reasons.

Our introduction by Jock McGovern to the syllabus for the year and
our weekly timetables came as a shock. In came most of those subjects
new to me such as trigonometry, geometry, French, chemistry and
physics, as well as a more rigorous teaching of English – now separated
into language and literature – history and geography; but there was to be
no Latin until our second year. There was to be a more structured
approach to religious instruction and my own particular demon, art,
with random spots of music – never taught very seriously – and sport.
Fortunately for us the sport was soccer – what else on Tyneside? – in the
autumn and winter terms, with cricket in the spring/summer.

During that first term, the autumn term of the 1944/5 year, I was
stimulated by the learning opportunity, but preoccupied with the
strangeness of it all. There were so many things that were different about
the grammar school, bearing in mind that my experience of schools and
their teaching methods had been limited to five years or so at St Mary's
and to what I had gleaned from my mother about her school – the Union
British, a 'board school' for the masses, firmly based on teaching by rote
introduced in the 1890s by Act of Parliament – or from the other boys in
the back lane about their own junior schools. Of course the school faculty
and its routines were dominated by priests, unlike St Mary's, and yet
these priests were also very different. They were all extremely serious,
frequently grim, and most of them confirmed my early and entirely
accurate impression of unsmiling authoritarians. They were certainly
totally unlike the young Irish curates who used to visit our house in

Elswick Row or Havelock Street. These priests, with the exception of Fathers Hardy and Crumley, were not the football-playing young men who indulged in a simple 'kick about' in the back lane, still wearing their priest's garb. Yet it wasn't only the presence of priests that brought the school more closely into alignment with the Church than had ever been evident at St Mary's. There were formal prayers at assembly every morning before school commenced, and on Wednesday afternoons the school was assembled for sung benediction. During key months of the Church calendar, such as May or June, the appropriate lengthy 'sacred litanies' were recited every day.

The school's history dated from 1881, since when it had developed its own traditions and had become, as envisaged, an important component in the visible structure of Catholic public life in the four northern counties. Following the restoration of the hierarchy in 1850 and given the swelling numbers of Catholics in the northern industrial cities, mainly attributable to immigrant Irish workers, the need for expansion of secondary education became pressing. Of course, old-established Catholic families had sent their sons to Ampleforth or Stonyhurst, but such schools were accessible only to the very rich. The 'only Catholic grammar school north of Manchester' was to be the answer; by 1881 St Cuthbert's evolved to fill the role, with a mixture of boarders and day pupils. All pupils would be fee-paying and a qualifying entrance examination was imposed for day pupils. Since it was also to be a 'feeder' school for the seminary at Ushaw College, Durham, it was inevitable that a senior priest would be appointed as headmaster. Boarding was abolished in 1937, to be followed in 1938 by the appointment of only its fifth headmaster in fifty-seven years, Canon Cunningham. Shortly afterwards war broke out, the school was evacuated and the buildings were temporarily occupied by the army. By the time Vincent joined St Cuthbert's ranks the school had established a formidable reputation because of its academic standards, from which he, Rex and I who followed all benefited. As with so many institutions, the Cassidys

attending St Cuthbert's was coincidental with a general slackening of
the hold that the 'old English' Catholic families had on education and
privilege, as social structures began to weaken under the pressures
created and fuelled by the war. The obligatory fees were being waived
for high-achieving scholarship candidates, as were mandatory charges
for textbooks.

Yet it was still all too obvious to me, as it was to my brothers, that we
were of a social class that was very much in a minority at the school.
Intellectually and emotionally we were more than adequately equipped
to benefit from its high academic standards, without incentives or
pressure from the school faculty; yet our clothes, lack of social graces and
our speech demonstrated all too visibly that we were from a very
contrasting background from most of the other boys. These distinctions
manifested themselves and were interpreted in a very different way at
home in the back lane.

Our relationships with some of our neighbours underwent a series of
subtle changes in response to our production line of scholarship
successes. In the neighbourhood we were in a minority as Catholics, but
that had seldom created problems; we were different but not uniquely so.
To be Catholics and also clever enough to obtain free scholarship places
at a top grammar school, however, was always more likely to attract some
sneering dislike. In the street we were seen by some as adopting airs and
graces; 'Funny way to do it' was Ma's response, while at school we were
the poor children from lower classes, muscling in and potentially
devaluing standards. Faced with this latent conflict there was a strong
natural motivation to demonstrate by results that we could make a
contribution at school without consciously alienating any of our
neighbours. We were encouraged at home, principally by Ma but also by
Pop, and in my case by the older children too, to be conscious of the
opportunity we had, requiring us to work hard and give of our best: yet
this always stopped short of an expectation or an imposed demand for
specific results. With their backgrounds it is unlikely that Ma or Pop

believed there would be any great change in the pattern of our lives as distinct from theirs, and it was difficult for them to encourage aspirations to entering university or achieving a business or professional role of which they had no experience or knowledge. But the pursuit of learning was, in their eyes, a desirable, worthwhile end in itself and who knew, God willing, what might follow. Ma, particularly, was emphatic and intransigent in ruling out one possible future occupation, for she had seen it all before; bright children from large families and poor backgrounds were ideal material for seminaries and monasteries. Whatever happened we were not going to be priests, thus pre-empting promptings throughout our grammar-school days.

My grammar-school period began with much anticipation, a brand-new uniform, and an opportunity to play cricket and football on real pitches wearing proper kit, at least for football.

At Christmas 1944 as the end of my first term approached I knew that I was doing pretty well, but I also knew I had some serious competition from one or two classmates. In an intensive, two-week period we sat our various examinations, eleven in all, and in the last week of term the form master, Jock McGovern, announced the results of the two subjects he took. He told us that during the week other teachers would similarly announce their results, so that by the time we broke up for the Christmas holiday – preceded by the usual hymn singing and benediction – we would know both how we had fared in individual subjects and what our positions were in the form overall. Finally we were told we would be given a detailed report on our progress, signed by the headmaster, to take home to our parents – something neither Vincent nor Rex had talked about.

While that gave rise to some anxiety in some boys, I was quite relaxed about the prospect. The session taken by Jock McGovern was the last before dinner on Monday and it started unpropitiously for him, as well as for me, because as he came into the class he had another one of his coughing fits. He had served on the Western Front in the First World War and had been severely gassed, resulting in permanently damaged lungs. As he began to read out the results he had a coughing fit and, as was not unusual, it ended with him breathless and with a bloodstained handkerchief clamped to his lips. Eventually, after a short break and a glass of water, he resumed. First the algebra result. True, it was a new subject for me but I knew that I was coping reasonably well. The results were read out as usual in alphabetical order and 'Cassidy' occurs quite early in any listing, but I was totally unprepared when I heard him say 'Cassidy, 37' my mark out of 100. I really heard no more. I couldn't remember what marks my classmates had obtained because I couldn't believe that I had achieved such a shockingly low mark. While I was wrestling with my disbelief and disappointment Jock, who also took us for geography, in the curious way in which unrelated subjects were allocated to the limited staff available in wartime, then announced the geography results. He read these out slowly and I did marginally better, but I was still devastated when I heard my mark was 45.

Having recovered slightly from the shell-shock of the algebra result I listened more carefully to the form master's recitation of geography results and it seemed, because of my position as fifth in the form for that particular subject, that either we were all hopeless or that Jock had marked us in an extremely difficult and highly critical way. Since he was a useless teacher anyway, both were possible.

I was stirred from my introspective gloom by the dinner bell ringing, and while most of the boys either pulled out their packed sandwich lunch or went off to have dinner in the school dining hall, I set off at the double for home before returning for the afternoon session. As I wandered out of the school drive there was no thought of the happiness at the approaching end of term or of the joys of Christmas to come, but only of how could I tell my parents of the results without feeling I had let them down. Still in something resembling an endless nightmare, I started to jog across the main road, looking more to the right where the trolleybus should be waiting at the terminus, some

100 yards away, than over the brow of the hill to my left. When I was halfway across the road a convoy of massive army transporters crested the ridge and was almost upon me. There was a loud blast on the horn, I quickly sprinted to avoid being crushed under the wheels, and as I did so I felt something fall from my pocket and I heard it hit the road. Whatever it was it fell victim, rather better than me being under the wheels I suppose – although that seemed an attractive option at the time – to the progress of the fully laden army truck. When the truck had gone I realised the day was spiralling out of all control, going from bad to worse, because what lay in the road was the remains of Roma's prized Waterman fountain pen: something she treasured which had been given to her by one of her admirers some years before. I had borrowed it, with Ma's permission, only that morning from the sideboard drawer where Roma kept it; I had broken the nib of my pen, and it was Ma's intention that I should replace Roma's pen that evening before its absence was noticed. All that now remained of the prized pen were a few crushed fragments and a stain of Parker Royal Blue ink on the road surface. Not even the gold clip of the pen remained, having no doubt lodged deep in the tread of the monster truck. The fact that the pen was one of the few valuable items in the house and I had been allowed to borrow it only in expectation of some good exam results compounded the enormity of my carelessness.

It was an apprehensive, disconsolate boy who returned home and poured out his tale of misery, and it has to be said that the terminal accident to the fountain pen rather diminished the significance of the ghastly exam results. Ma decided very quickly by applying one of her armoury of maxims, 'What you don't know will never hurt you', not to reveal the fate of the pen, leaving Roma to puzzle for many years as to how and why it had vanished or ultimately how she came to mislay such a prized possession with such a strong sentimental association.

Unswervingly optimistic, I knew things could only get better, while for the Allied forces it seemed to be the reverse. The German armies sliding towards unconditional surrender counterattacked ferociously in the Ardennes and for a few days the nation, and me for different more personal reasons, held its breath; but by Christmas Day all was well.

The rest of the results were extremely good and I finished, in aggregate, first out of a form of thirty-five, with an average for eleven subjects of 80 per cent. I held on to that first place throughout the other two terms of my first year at grammar school.

The Allied forces slowed the German panzer offensive and by Christmas Day it had been halted. By the time we celebrated the Epiphany on 6 January 1945 the British and American forces were moving forward again, I was returning to school for the spring term, and all of us had good reason to remember the near-disasters of late December 1944.

23

THE NAVY FILLS THE GAP

The combined loss of Roma's and Alan's contribution to the household budget was an important factor in Vincent's decision, or his implementation of Ma's decision, to seek paid employment immediately on leaving school. Since he was successful immediately, the pressure to reduce already constrained spending was eased further; but a major improvement in our financial circumstances had already taken place with the billeting with us of three able seamen who were pursuing technical skills courses at Walker Naval Yard.

This unforeseen, unplanned, but largely welcome situation had occurred because Mrs Hetherington's 'fancy man', Petty Officer Jack Harrison, had observed the departures of two grown-up children from the Cassidy household late in 1943, while he was engaged in planning and finding accommodation for the 1944 intake of candidates to attend a new training course in radar and wireless operations. He had the authority to requisition vacant rooms for 'official use', of course, yet he was no stranger to the advantages of voluntary cooperation in the billeting of service personnel. Having made the assumption, incorrectly as it happens, that two rooms and two beds would be available, he called round to finalise matters, hoping it would be to everyone's benefit. Initially the household was divided on the proposal; Pop was 'against', Ma 'for', Vincent indifferent, Rex moodily and marginally against, while Sydney and I were not consulted. The 'against' lobby was based on the disadvantages of having more bodies in already cramped conditions, whereas the 'for' case was built on financial prudence in the knowledge that Vincent would soon be called up even if he did find work quickly. Roma's absence was permanent, as – 'God forbid' – Alan's might become. It was while this evenly balanced position was being debated that someone thought to ask the all-too-obvious question of where the newcomers were going to sleep, and what other space they would require for study. While pursuit of this enquiry revealed that each was required to have an individual bed, access to a non-existent bathroom, ample space for written evening work, and an evening meal provided, Ma's solution that she and Pop should move in to Roma's former smaller room, thus vacating the larger, back bedroom and one double bed for the lodgers, was surprisingly readily approved by the billeting officer. Soon not two but three able seamen, ranging in age from twenty-two to fifty, were living with us.

Ma had had her way as usual and our new additions appeared to love their new abode, deficient though it may have been in space and other creature comforts. In their view this must have been more than adequately compensated for by the family atmosphere, which encouraged their participation in the banter and games of the three younger boys, and by their enjoyment at being chased by Ma out of the kitchen to the parlour, set aside for them to complete their 'homework' while we did ours.

Initially the trio comprised tall, lanky Tom Wilkinson from Accrington, Lancashire; short, wiry-haired Charlie Brindley from Derbyshire; and Reg Broome, the bespectacled, quietly spoken grandfather from 'the south'. Tom and Charlie would turn a blind eye to Syd and I 'stealing' the occasional cigarette from their tins of Players Navy Cut, as Reg pleaded with Roma to let him hold, or better still feed, her new baby and in a very short time the strangers had transformed themselves into fully fledged members of the family. But there were some habits and routines we couldn't share, and while they were with us they began to indulge in the very strange practice of visiting the public baths in Snow Street every week; the absence of a bathroom in Havelock Street, combined with the family's monopoly of the zinc bath and the fireside on Saturday evenings, made some practical alternative vital. It was necessary to preserve our modesty and privacy, yet raised the question in my mind of why this was an option not previously exercised by us — a question emphasised by having heard Pop talk about his 'wonderfully relaxing' visits to a Turkish bath somewhere else in the city. The concept of a Turkish bath seemed to me to be inextricably linked with an opium den, shadowy figures and Sherlock Holmes — none of them compatible with my father's normal activities — from which I deduced he had given up such youthful decadence long ago. There was some tenuous link perhaps with Ma's rejection of any attempt by us to go to Snow Street public swimming baths, part of the same publicly operated complex housing the baths to which the sailors were going.

All our requests to be allowed to go with friends to the swimming baths were met with a rigid, unbending, non-negotiable refusal; the principal reason given was 'The kind of people who use them aren't very clean', or 'You'll catch an ear infection.' Nothing was ever said about our lack of suitable costumes, although there were supplementary murmurings about 'modesty' or the danger from violent conduct. In fairness, Alan had visited a different public swimming baths at Todds Nook when he was at St Aloysius', in a formal attempt to teach all children how to swim; given the ferocity of the nearby North Sea and its freezing temperature even at the height of summer, both the concept and the choice of venue seemed extremely wise. However, this strategy, like so many others, foundered on meeting with reality, when the principal instructor implemented his preferred method of throwing boys bodily into the heavily chlorinated pool — admittedly soon followed by a lifebelt — in the belief that their natural survival instincts would lead swiftly to their acquisition of the basics of swimming adequately, such as an ability to float and dog-paddle. Finally, of course, these public places confirmed Ma's views of the patrons by the presence of the familiar, if mysterious,

white-enamelled, dark-blue-lettered plate warning of the dangers of 'VD'
– whatever that meant.

However interesting our sailor lodgers' visits to the public baths were,
it made no difference to our regime, neither did it lead to any reappraisal
of the desirability of learning how to swim. So we continued to live our
lives unaware of the pleasures of a bath, whether of the domestic, Turkish
or swimming variety.

The third part of the Snow Street complex was the public washhouse
where some housewives did their weekly wash, an activity they embarked
upon early in the morning on the chosen day, which unsurprisingly was
predominantly a Monday. These visits were clearly signalled by the dress
of the women going to the washhouse, and the vehicle they used to take
the dirty clothes to it and from which they returned with the still-wet,
clean clothes. Summer or winter, the adopted dress code was the
regulation, floral-patterned pinny, short wellington boots – de rigueur
given the wet floor of the washhouse – with the whole topped by a scarf,
shawl or improbably a headsquare covering a head littered with curlers,
rollers or paper twists. The vehicle was just as predictably a pram, always
past its prime, which had been handed down within a family and for
which the latest owner hoped to have no further use: something of a
lottery in our neighbourhood, where pregnancy seemed as unpredictable
as the weather. Whenever a pram had deteriorated to the point where it
was going to be used only for 'washing day', the internal bedding and
fittings would be detached and passed on to another mother and infant,
while the vehicle itself continued its decline until it was good only for
sale as scrap or for the wheels and bogey to be dismantled and used for a
home-made go-cart. In the interim the pram had a widely varying
lifespan ahead of it as a useful and convenient laundry vehicle, seldom
used by only one person or even on only one day per week; it was another
manifestation of neighbourly sharing, although those who did this were
most commonly 'those who lived in each other's pockets'. As if to verify
it they would usually push the pram, overflowing with bundles of dirty

clothes and with several enamel bowls perched on top, while talking loudly, and frequently breaking into shrieks of raucous laughter, with a good deal of jabbing, pushing or pointing at each other. Their diminishing cackles would announce their departure as surely as their increasingly loud shrieks would herald their return some hours later. It would have been unnecessary to ask Ma why she shunned the public washhouse in our Elswick Row days, when the weekly washdays were so disruptive domestically; even if she could have tolerated these loud, public displays by those regular users we saw, she didn't dry clothes in public view on a washing line in the back lane – let alone merge her separated 'colours' and 'whites' with someone else's washing or reveal what clothes we wore. Thus did the grand, red-brick, Victorian building, with its red stone fascia reading 'SNOW STREET PUBLIC BATHS AND WASHHOUSE', remain out of bounds for all of us: at the cost of our forgoing the pleasure of soaking in a hot bath or that of swimming on a hot, dusty day – pleasures that would have to wait until some unimaginably distant point in the future.

For the sailors there was genuine regret, in which we all shared, when their course ended. As they sadly prepared to depart to new postings, Reg almost tearfully, they were probably all musing over the highly unorthodox circumstances that had led to three serving sailors sleeping not only in the same room, but also in the same bed; while commonplace for us it perhaps indicated their total integration into our simple family life and its context.

For a brief but financially important period other sailors followed, until the war ended and demobilisation gained momentum; then an even briefer period of civilian student lodgers took over and bridged our financial budget deficit. While we co-existed happily with them, none was as welcome or as easily assimilated as the original three, Tom, Charlie and Reg. I often wonder what happened to them.

24

HOWAY THE LADS

Football, requiring a combination of brute force, endless energy and occasionally delicate skills, is a natural game for boys to play. Since it can be played with a round object of any size, preferably a ball, and both back lanes and parks, though very dissimilar, offer suitable pitches, its universal adoption by working-class children in the nineteenth century was inevitable. In a park a couple of sweaters or coats served as a substitute for goalposts, while chalk marks on a back-lane wall eliminated the frequent, fractious, sometimes violent disputes over whether the ball went over or under the crossbar – since a notional crossbar and goalposts have to exist in the minds of the players when only coats are used as a substitute in a park.

The back lane has many other attractions as a pitch, since the back-yard walls act as the touchlines with the added benefit that the ball is always in play and subtle touches can be achieved by accidental or deliberate rebounds from any back-yard wall. Although the surface of a park is more forgiving when falls occur than is a concreted back lane, inevitably a game played on grass seldom achieves the speed of that played in the back lane, because the ball constantly has to be redeemed from 'touch'. The most common ball used for back-lane football was a tennis ball, partly because it was the most affordable and the most easily obtainable; but it didn't have the same flexibility when used in a park, particularly if the grass is long.

But the back lane encouraged the development of particular skills, of knowing how to run at a defending opponent and by clipping the ball with the outside of the foot, preferably onto a door rather than a wall, achieving a cushioned rebound as you ran round your opponent and on with the ball. I, like virtually every other boy, soon learned the basic rules of back-street football, quickly developing the basic skills of heading and trapping a ball; all this was achieved without having seen a football match any more formal than a school game or, more commonly, scratch sides playing on the Town Moor after nearby pubs had disgorged their customers on a Sunday lunchtime. This was usually an attempt by flabby, middle-aged men to regain lost youth, despite being rendered even more unfit by the consumption of several pints of beer in the two hours or so allowed before the pub closed at 2p.m. In addition to being mildly inebriated they were usually dressed in their 'Sunday best' clothes, complete with collar, tie and well-shined shoes. We were an essential ingredient since we possessed a ball, and with our stamina we would be required to chase and retrieve every ball that went out of play. Sides would be chosen; they would discard coats, tuck trouser bottoms into their socks, and the game would start. Its duration was determined by their ability to stand upright or by the fear of their dinner being thrown on the fire – apparently a common occurrence – if they returned home too late.

It was a strange, tragicomic sight, made funnier by some inept tackles resulting in seriously soiled suits. If the game lasted any length of time the need emerged, which rapidly spread to most players, to relieve themselves. This was a dangerous activity to perform in public, with the attendant risk of a fine for indecent exposure if a policeman chanced to spot the delinquents. It was hardly surprising, then, that a penny or two would be paid for us to act as lookouts. We would walk a few yards away, keeping our eyes on the edges of the moor to the north, south and west for signs of 'coppers' on foot, bike or horseback, while we heard a torrent splashing in the grass accompanied by raucous banter. Eventually the game would be resumed until the players, wearied by the unusually intense activity, would drift away to waiting wives and mothers for their delayed Sunday dinner. We would reclaim our football, collect a coin or two for our pains and before resuming a game of our own watch them disappearing, noisily laughing and jostling.

It was on 9 October 1943 that one of my back-lane pals suggested that we go to a game at St James' Park. Newcastle United, in common with most other league teams from the northern industrial cities, had fielded a strong team during the war because most of their pre-war players worked in reserved occupations – miners, shipyard and munitions workers or the like. Of course some players had been called up, but professional guest players were available from the ranks of servicemen stationed in the area, and unlike many sides in the south this enabled Newcastle to field a very skilful side.

I had been brought up by my father on tales of the great deeds of Newcastle United at the turn of the century and of their Cup wins in 1911, 1924 and 1932. I had heard also from him some of the gossip about the great players of the past who had frequently travelled on his tramcar and to whom he had spoken. St James' Park was only about ten minutes' walk from our house, and we set off on a Saturday afternoon for a 2p.m. kick-off. It was a familiar route since we passed close by St Mary's, Oystershell Lane – soon to be a diminishing memory for me – and past the Dickman's pie factory where we occasionally purchased hot pies with a seriously firm crust, which when finally punctured by teeth shot a stream of hot, molten gravy down the hand and arm holding the pie. But there were no such temptations on this day, not even to buy the broken pies usually on offer at a knock-down price. The money we had was reserved for entrance to the ground: the tuppence required for admittance to the uncovered Leazes Terrace End. It was the eastern boundary of the ground, known then as the 'popular end' because it was the cheapest, yet it rather perversely overlooked and restricted the view from some grand, if decaying, Georgian houses in Leazes Terrace.

We entered through cast-iron turnstiles, a new experience for me, and I had some difficulty in pushing the revolving gate round when the octogenarian gateman pressed a foot pedal to allow it to operate. His face was hidden by a metal grille and I saw only a grubby hand held open, over a shining brass plate with the maker's name engraved on it, to receive my entrance money. Once through that there was still no sign of what was to come: just a grubby, shale, grass and soil bank pitted with weeds into which were set a number of wide, wooden stairways. As we climbed these stairs I saw on the far side of the pitch the emerging outline of the grandstand – not particularly aptly named, since it was a ramshackle, temporary-looking structure of corrugated iron with a convex, curved roof and was anything but 'grand'. It housed the only seats in the ground, those in the directors' box, which were individual seats but surrounded by bench seats with numbered spaces for season-ticket holders; all very puzzling terminology for me. When we reached the top of the steps I saw the terraces sloping down towards the pitch, while to the right and left I could see at both ends of the ground similar terraces studded with anti-crush barriers. A handful of boys watched as the ground staff erected goalposts and nets, but what took my eye was the rectangle of tightly mown, green grass such as I had never seen before. It looked simply magnificent.

Slowly the ground filled up, first with boys then quickly as kick-off time approached with men, as they turned out from the local pubs dressed in suits, some with raincoats and all wearing hats or caps. A local colliery band marched onto the pitch and began to play a series of brisk march tunes, and the atmosphere became noisier and livelier. Then the grandstand seats and the directors' box filled swiftly, with brief greetings exchanged as the privileged few sat down. Standing as we were on the eastern side we could see down the tunnel beneath the grandstand which led to the players' changing rooms, from which the officials, dressed all in black, emerged to be followed by a great roar and a welcome for 'the lads'. I was ecstatic. The players looked magnificent in their black and white shirts, with white squares on the back carrying a red number indicating their position on the field. The black and white shirts, the black shorts, the black stockings with white tops, the brown football boots and the athletic way in which they moved and chipped the ball backwards and forwards were all very unlike either the back lane or the Sunday pub footballers I had seen. And it got better. The ball sped on the manicured turf, the touchline markings were fresh and white, the penalty spot had been repainted just before kick-off, and 'the lads' swept into action. They were fast and the skilful football was thrilling, although I didn't totally understand the meaning of all of the orchestrated shouts of the crowd: 'Shoot, man', 'Wor hoy', 'Get your eyes chalked, ref', 'Tackle him, man', 'Howay, man', 'Get him doon, man.'

While there is no doubt that my memory of that day was enhanced by the raw bleakness of everyday life in wartime on Tyneside, with which it offered such a marked contrast, it was still dazzling beyond my wildest dreams. All the deprivations and disadvantages of Havelock Street and the back lane were banished for the moment. Moreover, there was the thrill of being a fully paid-up member of a new community, a large community of thousands of people, where for the first time in my life everyone identified with the same purpose and passionately, noisily, sought the same outcome. For the men it was escapism from the pressures of wartime life on a grand scale, but for me and all the boys present we were not only watching new heroes but also seeking to learn from them. Meanwhile, the adults were indulging in a further round of bonhomie to follow the beer, cigarettes and raucous humour they had shared indulgently in the pubs around the ground for as long as they could afford before kick-off.

At half-time, with Newcastle leading 4–1, I caught my breath. The band played again and the educational process continued as the cry went up, 'Watch your feet, hinny', or more sympathetically, 'Hey, man, be careful, there's bairns doon there', while the more experienced boys rapidly moved out from the lowest level of the terraces where it joined the boundary wall, to either hop up onto the wall or move along the steps as a flood of foaming, beer-smelling liquid poured down the stepped terraces. It seemed a relatively small price to pay for the joys

I had experienced in the first half, and the primitiveness of the surroundings – bare concrete terracing, no facilities, with the minimal number of almost inaccessible urinals, both creating and exacerbating the problems we were having in keeping our feet dry – was simply part of a way of life 'gannin to the match'.

Since I knew what to expect, the second half passed in a flash. Newcastle had won 5–2 and I had a hero, as I was to have in later years: a player with a large figure '9' on his back. He was Albert Stubbins, a flame-haired, muscular local lad with a kick like a horse, who throughout his mainly wartime career scored 250 goals in 199 games over six seasons. That day illuminated my life, which was permanently enriched by every aspect of the game as I tried to mimic the heroes, see photographs of them or get close to them, watched other games, commiserated with them when they lost, shared the joy when they won. It had become an important part of my life.

From then on it wasn't only football we played any more. It was an attempt to emulate, to get close to, the standards achieved by these black and white-clad heroes. It opened up new topics of conversation with other schoolboys, and even adults, in a way that wasn't as readily available for school subjects like history, chemistry or French. Participation in a 'craze' followed, through collecting action photographs from the newspapers (provided that I grabbed them after they had been read but before they had been converted into lavatory paper – always a delicate timing issue) and ultimately to compiling a card index of favourite players and teams. This was further enhanced through the collection of autographs which, unlike most other collectables I had considered and discounted before on cost grounds, could be obtained only after patient, persistent waiting for the gods to appear after a match or training session.

A small group of boys huddled in limited shelter to avoid the biting cold and the driving rain, leaping to life as the fresh-faced, athletic idol appeared from the players' entrance, carrying his boots in a brown-paper bag under his arm and signing his name, almost embarrassedly, on any scrap of paper before running off to catch his bus or train home.

Home matches at St James' Park were played every other week in a season that opened in mid-August and finished almost coincidentally with the start of the cricket season in the following April; there was the added excitement of an FA Cup Final, usually on the first Saturday in May. Our biggest problem during the season was how to afford to see enough football, and even though I was being allowed to keep some of my hard-earned money from my newspaper delivery rounds rather more readily than previously, I still couldn't afford to go to every home match. There was also a need to be informed fully by the experts as soon as possible after every game, home or away, which meant knowing much more than just the result and the goal scorers. That need led to my initiation into another act in the football ritual, participated in by virtually every male on Tyneside.

On Saturday evening at about 5.30p.m. a group of men and boys would gather outside the newsagent's shop where, given my role as an employee, I was allowed privileged access; most had to wait outside for the big event of the delivery of the *Football Final*, a special Saturday-evening edition of the *Evening Chronicle*. Although it carried the latest news of a variety of sports events, together with all the racing results, its prime purpose – as its title implied – was to carry match reports of the major north-eastern teams, but in particular of course Newcastle United. In the darkest days of winter the match report would be complete when the *Football Final* was delivered, because midwinter days meant early kick-off times, often as early as 12.30p.m. But in the evenings of early autumn, as the season began, or those in spring when it was drawing to a close, with kick-offs at 3p.m., the published match report would be incomplete and there would be an anxious scanning of the late columns for the result. With most of the season played in the winter months, however, the scene was familiar and almost unchanging, following a pattern as well choreographed as going to the match itself.

A crowd would build quickly and people would stand around in the foggy half-light on the pavements, lit only by light from the newsagent's shop and dim street lighting. At best it would be dry and mistily smoky; at worst a dense, icy fog would envelop the crowd. They would be capped and mufflered, with hands thrust deep into their pockets, yet most of them would be smoking cigarettes while stamping their feet agitatedly, which wasn't only to keep them warm. Every vehicle that was heard approaching caused a flutter of excitement until the familiar red van would swerve, brake sharply and pull up at the kerb; the van boy would open the rear doors, pull out a large bundle of newspapers tied with thick twine and throw it from the rear of the van to the street. There the bundle was pounced upon as if it was a gold brick; there was always a scramble to pick up the package and dash with it into the shop, as the reward for being the first to grab it was the opportunity to purchase the first copy. The owner played his part in this quickening drama by hurrying to get his knife to hack through the strong binding, rip off the covering sheets and then with one hand hold out a newspaper while the other was opened for the coins. This was repeated swiftly, over and over again, until the entire crowd had filed quietly to the counter, been served and left. At the end of this routine the newsagent's hands would be black with the still-wet printer's ink from the late edition, and the close of a long day was imminent as the till was emptied and the lights switched off in the eerie silence that followed this short, frenetic burst of activity.

Everyone, as soon as they had their own copy, looked quickly at the headlines – which would be a snappy précis of Newcastle's game: 'Bolton difficult to crack' (bad) or 'Milburn rampant' (good) – and then at the 'Stop Press' column for the other results, the final score of the Newcastle match or further information about scorers. Very occasionally there were noises of pleasure or head shaking, but usually a strict etiquette was observed. For the sake of those queuing in high anticipation for their own copy, it was forbidden, by consensus if not by any rule, to divulge the result in any form. It was as elaborate and as impeccably observed a process as a formal minute's silence on those rare occasions when the passing of a great figure was marked at the ground before a match; it was simply 'not done', even if asked, to quote scorers or scores within earshot of those still queuing. I was now engulfed by the local football culture, which was more than escapism from the drabness of everyday life; it was a way of life for most men, becoming their principal pleasure and motivation.

It was through football that I had discovered a route which led to understanding the adult world by sharing in the camaraderie of the regular football supporter. The concomitant schoolboy activities of autograph hunting, compiling statistics about players and queuing for the *Football Final* simply made football watching a continuous activity. Collectively it meant that anyone who participated in these rituals had to be able to talk knowledgeably about 'the game' with adults and listen appreciatively to their comments; through this I learned to anticipate their joy and predict their despair.

When the war ended servicemen returned home, as everyday life struggled to 'get back to normal' and everyone talked about the time when we could all look forward to a resumption of the kind of serious football which I had never seen: that played within the Football Leagues, with automatic promotion or relegation for some at the end of each season. Happily my involvement and interest in Newcastle United coincided with one of the great periods in the club's successful history as it acquired, through an inspired, early postwar exploitation of the transfer market, key players with whom to mount a serious bid for an early return to the First Division, from which they had been relegated when I was still an unknowing child. Soon great players like Frank Brennan, the Scottish international centre half who cost £7,500; Joe Harvey, who was to become the inspirational club captain for many years for £4,250; Roy Bentley for £8,500; and Len Shackleton, for an astronomical £13,500, joined the club to merge with the plentiful indigenous talent already at the club. That included the two Bobbys –

full backs Cowell and Corbett – and the star of all stars Jackie Milburn, who was to become for me, as for so many others, the greatest player of all time. But there was also the sadness to contend with of losing Albert Stubbins, the heroic, red-headed centre forward of wartime days, who departed to Liverpool for £13,000 – a self-inflicted blow which I couldn't understand at the time. With him Liverpool won the First Division title in the first postwar year. Newcastle finished fifth and failed at their first attempt to gain promotion, in spite of a season of thrilling, attractive football in which one of the highlights had been Len Shackleton's six-goal debut in a 13–0 drubbing of Newport County. In a dismal end to a season that had showed such early promise, United were dumped out of the FA Cup in a 4–0 thrashing by Charlton at the semi-final stage.

The following year, however, provided one of the great climaxes to any season. Newcastle were again well placed for promotion, but after much well-publicised internal discord, resulting in several star forwards such as Shackleton, Wayman, Pearson and Bentley leaving, they still had to win two of their last four games against fellow contenders for promotion. In one crucial week they had to play Cardiff away, and then were due to play Fulham on the following Wednesday night and Sheffield Wednesday on the Saturday, both games at home. On the Wednesday night, with over 54,000 spectators in the ground on a bright, sunny March evening, they almost faltered owing to the referee's human failings; I had already learned that all referees were known to have poor eyesight. Milburn, in one of his frequent, electrifying bursts, collected the ball in the centre circle and instantly unleashed a thunderous left-foot shot that rocketed into the net past the startled Fulham goalkeeper, hitting the metal stanchion holding the net with such force that it rebounded almost to the halfway line. The referee, trailing behind Milburn at the time, reached the erroneous conclusion that the ball had hit the crossbar. As he must have reasoned, poor simple man, no ball could have been hit so hard as to rebound almost to the halfway line if it had gone into the net itself – but 54,000 pairs of lungs roared their disagreement. Then, as the game entered the last minute, the pent-up frustration of the crowd and its unbearable tension were released in a mighty, deafening roar as the linesman flagged furiously and the referee awarded Newcastle a penalty. Amid the tumult and confusion I saw with dismay Jackie Milburn shake his head and walk away with his back to the Fulham goal, while little Geordie Stobbart carefully placed the ball on the spot and walked a long way back before turning quickly and running at full speed towards the stationary ball, watched in absolute silence by 54,000 pairs of anxious eyes as well as those of an immobile Fulham goalkeeper. Many years later Jackie Milburn himself told me that he couldn't even bear to watch; but as Geordie turned at the end of his run in he shouted, 'Jackie, just watch me bleaze this f . . . r in' – and he did. What a night, what joy: but there was still Sheffield Wednesday to come.

On Saturday the excitement had reached fever pitch as I took Sydney along with me to the match, wisely arriving at noon for a three o'clock kick-off to ensure that we got a satisfactory position on the wall bordering the pitch, so that we could see without hindrance. After an eternity of waiting the game kicked off, amid deafeningly encouraging noise from another full house of over 68,000 passionate supporters. Then an early disaster – a foul by Newcastle in the penalty area: a penalty for Sheffield Wednesday that Whitcombe, an English international, coolly scored, causing Sydney to break down in tears. Sad though I was also, I comforted him, promising him better things to come; with Newcastle always struggling to stay on equal terms, it was surprising they got a lucky equaliser in the goal just in front of us, a few minutes before half-time. Immediately after a happier half-time interval Harvey scored with a header from a Walker corner kick and our joy was unconstrained, before once again disaster struck and there were more tears when Sheffield Wednesday equalised, just as the ten-minute flag was being hauled down in the corner between the Gallowgate and Leazes Terrace Ends. It seemed as though promotion had eluded Newcastle United once again almost at the final hurdle, but they were not done; in one of those bouts of frenzied, attacking football for which they became famous in this period, they scored twice in the last few minutes. The heroic goal scorer, Frank Houghton, was seriously injured in the process, contracting TB afterwards, and was never the same player again. But all that was to come; the only thing that mattered at that moment was that Newcastle had won and were going to return to their rightful place in the First Division. What a side it was, and what a hero we all had in Jackie Milburn, who over the next few years was to consolidate his position as probably the greatest, as well as the most popular, player ever to wear a black and white shirt.

Football had become a major part of my life, as it had for Alan, Rex and now Sydney, but strangely Vincent was never drawn to the game and its atmosphere in the way that the rest of us were. However, there were still times when its appeal, perhaps because of the intensity surrounding it, affected him also.

In this period of learning about the passion, the highs and lows of top-quality football, which began while I was still delivering newspapers and reading comics, I noticed a small display advertisement in *The Champion*. It read simply that a game of table football with eleven miniature players per side could be purchased by post from a P.A. Adolph, quoting a post-office box number in Tunbridge Wells, Kent. I was intrigued. Our first experience of 'blow football' had been fun but decidedly unfootball-like, and it had been relegated to the category of games suitable only for young children. This promised to be different, but I wondered whether it was just another over-hyped claim, or was it indeed a game that could be played with skill by eleven players from each side?

The game had a very curious name, Subbuteo; I wrote to P.A. Adolph, sending the required postal order, and before long I had my Subbuteo game. It made the perfect complement to our match-going days, because it did indeed have eleven miniature players on either side. They were small, cardboard cut-out figures to which we glued genuine football-league-club colours before they were mounted in a slot on a semi-spherical base; they were moved by flicking with the fingers to tackle or to kick the miniature football. It certainly did require dexterity and skill, and rather like 'blow football' it enabled skilled merchants in duplicity such as Rex to practise their black arts to heighten the competitive tension. Sunday afternoons were soon devoted exclusively to our own league matches, each of two five-minute halves, in a competitive championship which in true Cassidy fashion quickly led to a redrawing of Mr Adolph's simple rules in favour of a more complex structure. As we grew older the competitive element grew stronger, tensions increased and we were still subject to bursts of outrage at the tactics of opponents; Rex was usually the focal point. He had an unfortunate although premeditated knack, if he was losing, of initially blocking the opponent's goalmouth with a line of his players before crashing the ball with the remaining player and his finger through them into the net. This was one of the many tactics that we outlawed but that was not precluded by the original rules. Even worse, although he elected always to play as Manchester United in the league competitions we held, he added insult to injury by having no compunction, if he lost, about retrospectively renaming his side Lincoln City, thus removing from his opponent as much as possible of the pleasure of victory. This, too, was barred by the Rules Committee. More positively, the committee created an enlarged playing area and surface, discarding the smaller piece of baize sent with the pre-packed kit in favour of a large, old, ex-army blanket covering the kitchen table; using tailor's chalk the pitch markings were redrawn on the blanket to include redefined penalty and shooting areas.

Football, which had insinuated itself into the household by history and birth, was now adopted with passion, becoming a major part of leisure activities for everyone and of conversation for most. Thus it was to remain – for ever. When you choose a football team, you do so for life.

25

PLAY UP AND PLAY THE GAME

The move to St Cuthbert's to join Rex there had a number of unexpected and beneficial results, such as the catalytic effect it had on my interest in cricket, as indeed it had already had on our closest back-lane friends and neighbours Sidney Dansky and Teddy Birkett, now attending Rutherford Grammar School. The reason for this change was fairly obvious, since the width of the back lane imposed limitations on our replicating a cricket pitch there that were much more constraining than they were to a game of football or its junior cousin, 'headers'. Before we had all attended grammar school our cricket resembled the popular girls' games of French cricket – broadly 'tip and run' – or 'rounders'; but we were allowed, indeed obliged, to play our school cricket on a full-sized pitch of the regulation 22 yards in length, with full-sized stumps complete with bails. It was even more exciting as we were provided also with pads, gloves and real cricket balls, even if all this equipment did appear to date from the turn of the century. One size of bats, pads and gloves was less than helpful to someone of my slight build, and try as I might I found it impossible to buckle the batting pads tightly enough to prevent them from sliding round my short-trousered legs when taking a quick single. In addition, neither the sausage-type batting gloves with the wind-on thumb piece, nor the spiky, rubber-backed glove version, encouraged the maintenance of a firm grip on the bat handle. Nevertheless, the thrill of playing a real match of 'eleven a side' over two or three weeks, with deputed umpires and scorers, enormously increased our interest in and love of the game, in itself leading us to more reading about its history, the players, their great feats, statistics, records and the rules of cricket.

At St Cuthbert's we had the additional benefit of being allowed to play inter-house and school matches on the first-class ground that we owned but shared with Benwell Cricket Club, who maintained it. It was on this ground, with a true if lively pitch, that in a house match I saw Rex, bowling at a brisk, medium-fast pace, make a ball lift sharply 'off a length' and hit David Henry, the bespectacled batsman, between the eyes, burying the bridge of the frames deeply into his nose. Few cricket injuries we sustained were as serious as this, although bloody noses were common enough when balls reared spitefully at batsmen and fielders alike from the less-than-true surface of the other pitches, which doubled as football pitches in the winter and on which cattle grazed to limit the care and maintenance the grass would otherwise have required. Those who have played cricket on similar, interestingly rural pitches will know the feeling of alarm felt by a fielder as he runs towards a well-hit cricket ball that seems intent on ploughing through a freshly created, lightly crusted pat, before sending a Catherine wheel of soft, green cow dung flying into his face and body. The temporary blindness caused is followed first by a crushing blow as the ball strikes randomly on his body, and then the stench he wears is unmitigated by the scorn and mirth of his classmates at his misfortune. We rode these minor mishaps secure in the knowledge that we had gained much more than we had suffered, and we became anxious to watch some serious cricket in the summer – hopefully to match the experience of seeing Newcastle United play other quality teams at St James' Park, as we now did in the autumn and winter. We increased our cricket reading and I even bought a cricket coaching manual from a second-hand book stall in the market, with small photographs down the leading edge of each page accompanying a narrative describing the technique for playing a forward defensive shot, a backward defensive push, a cut, an off drive and an on drive. When the pages were splayed and fanned the photographs gave a passable replication of a moving, fluttering image, not unlike a silent film, enabling me to rehearse a repertoire of batting strokes with an old walking stick before the only full-length mirror we had in the house, on the front of a large wardrobe on the landing. From these promising beginnings we graduated, by courtesy of Sidney Dansky's father, to a much improved back-lane game through his producing a new, full-sized bat and stumps, on one of his last home leaves from the Navy in which he was serving. The newness of the bat compensated for its large and unwieldy character, but it was the full-sized stumps, complete with bails, which caused the most concern since they did not lend themselves to being erected on the back lane's concrete surface as readily as they did on the meadow-like Nuns Moor. Unlike Pop, Sidney's father produced the perfect solution in a flash: a solid block of wood in which he burned three large holes with a red-hot poker to match the dimensions of the stumps and bails; this also allowed the base to be removed when we played on the moor.

While the back lane did not permit a wide range of strokes our limited numbers, usually only four or five of us, forced us to use it rather like a practice net, thus avoiding the constant retrieval of the ball which was necessary on the moor but which was a tiring and often frustrating element of cricket played there. To our newly acquired equipment we added a pair of Pop's old tram-driving gauntlets, which were a reasonable imitation of the real thing, for the wicketkeeper and, finally for the back-lane game, a hard, cork-and-rubber composition cricket ball with a mock seam, which we soon found would spit and fly alarmingly from the concrete surface after rain. It wasn't very long before we provided a bucket of water to keep the lane permanently wet, substantially improving our collective abilities to bowl fast and straight, to leap acrobatically to catch head-high flyers when keeping wicket, and to take painful body blows without flinching or withdrawing to leg when batting.

As the first full summer after the war ended we got our first opportunity to see some first-class players, who were to play an invited eleven including some of the best talent from Northumberland and Durham; on a disappointingly damp, grey morning we took the trolleybus directly to the county ground in Jesmond for the match. It wasn't a bit like the pictures we had seen of Lords, Headingley, Trent Bridge or the Oval, and certainly totally unlike Sydney or Melbourne; while more appealing than the grimy Bramall Lane in Sheffield it was given a somewhat macabre appearance by the visible monuments in the cemetery at one end of the ground. It was stranger than St James' Park, where it was obvious from the admission charge at whichever turnstile we used what space was available to us. Here, once we had paid our dues to an old man sitting at a table near the double gates which served as the only entrance for cars and pedestrians, we seemed free to sit where we liked; after much debate we elected to sit on some benches behind a low, white, wooden picket fence, almost directly in line with the stumps which were being set up by the white-coated umpires. We knew this was going to be a very exciting day, but nothing had prepared us for the smiling, welcoming, well-dressed lady who kindly offered each of us a numbered, blue cloakroom ticket with the explanation, 'It's for the raffle of this lovely bat, signed by all the players of both sides.' Our hands already upturned and open towards the 'nice lady' retracted as if we had been bitten by a snake, and the upturned open hand turned rapidly into a clenched fist.

'We haven't any money left, Missus,' we said in a collective shout, with absolute conviction and honesty.

'Don't be silly,' she laughed. 'That's all right; it's free – the bat has been donated by Mr Buist', and with that full, reassuring reply she handed us individually a free blue ticket.

'The raffle will be drawn by the chairman during the luncheon interval, the result announced at tea with a presentation to the winner at close of play. Good luck' – and with that she patted my head and went on her happy way.

'I've got 33; that'll be lucky,' I shouted.

'I've got 99,' said Sidney Dansky, 'which is what Len Hutton scored last week.' That was followed by much musing as to whether winning the bat, which didn't seem in doubt, should lead to a proper game with two sets of stumps and if so, how to procure the extra stumps.

This was all cut short by two simultaneous events as the ground was quietly filling up, so different from the way a noisily laughing crowd used to move seamlessly from the 'Strawberry', the 'Black Bull' and other nearby pubs to the terraces of St James' Park. A bell clanged as a prelude to the appearance of the umpires; and the shadow of a figure of authority fell over us.

'You all junior members?' the blazered, red-faced, clipped-moustachioed man barked.

'No,' we answered as one.

'You the children of members?' he questioned incredulously and aggressively.

We looked at each other more in desperation than hope.

'Don't think so,' Teddy answered with a shake of the head.

While 'the blazer' was questioning us in his voice of authority his eyes were scanning the faces of all nearby adults, to eliminate the forlorn chance that these 'raggy-arsed ruffians', as we heard him call us later, might conceivably be in the care of a senior committee member. In the inevitable absence of any claim he shouted his verdict: 'OUT NOW!' while humbling us further by holding out his hand to reclaim the blue cloakroom tickets, extinguishing our last remaining ray of hope that there might be a silver lining to the cloud now hanging over our first big match. We hurriedly left, almost bringing down the two opening batsmen just about to complete their running descent of the steps from the dressing room.

'Bugger off,' hissed the officious blazer, followed by a shouted 'Not in front of the sightscreen.' With red faces we left in an embarrassed search for seats we could legitimately occupy, with the scornful laughter of members ringing in our ears as the game began. We never did hear the result of the raffle or see the conclusion of the match, because it started to rain increasingly heavily in the lunch interval and we, along with most of the crowd, left with yet another reminder of the Hitler-like tendencies of men in authority – William Brown would have predicted it.

The winter of 1946/7 which followed was even worse than that of 1940/1, partly because the heavy snow and freezing temperatures exacerbated an already serious fuel shortage, with limited coal supplies rationed and almost unobtainable; yet paradoxically it nurtured my emerging love for the game of cricket, such that when the summer of 1947 blossomed I was irretrievably hooked. That same winter the MCC arrived in Fremantle on the SS *Stirling Castle* for the first 'Ashes' series in Australia since 1936/7, with a blend of established Test players like Hammond, Hutton, Compton, Edrich, Yardley and Washbrook and rising stars such as Ikin, Evans and Bedser. In the history of Ashes Test matches the series was destined to enter the record books as one of the most one-sided ever, with one of the greatest all-round Australian sides ever fielded demolishing England by outplaying them in every department of the great game. For me it was an experience of pure magic, in the way that only very young, impressionable children can feel. The context was an important part of the magic: getting up at 4a.m. on dark, freezing, winter mornings in a bare, unheated house where the fire had to be relit to boil the water in the kettle, which had frozen solid overnight. After piling on as many old clothes as possible, tuning in then to a crackling broadcast from famous Australian Test Match grounds like the Gabba, the Sydney Cricket Ground (SCG), Adelaide Oval or the Melbourne Cricket Ground (MCG), hearing Alan McGilvray's soothingly impartial voice and listening to his range of different expressions – sundries, not extras; announcing the wickets before the runs; counting an eight-ball over rather than one of six balls; and his enthusiastic 'That's gone high, wide and handsome' as a batsman went for a big hit. He and Rex Alston, the schoolmasterly BBC commentator, describing strange trees, birds, unbelievably high temperatures, or even the horse wearing boots to pull the heavy roller at the Gabba without damaging a storm-drenched pitch. There were vivid descriptions of the Hill at the SCG, the huge scoreboard at the MCG and the 'Fremantle Doctor', the refreshing breeze that blew over the Swan River every afternoon to cool the cricket ground at Perth. I acknowledged little of defeat or disaster, heard only of gallant rearguard actions and heroic attempts by a new set of idols to stem the march of new opponents in yet another unfair, unequal contest on foreign soil. It was 1939 all over again – war by a different name.

After listening to these faint, ebbing sound waves as long as I dared, I would switch off the wireless and hurry out to the freezing, snowy streets to deliver my newspaper round, uplifted rather than humbled, playing imaginary shots as I went while trying to recapture Alan McGilvray's sunny, drawling commentary.

One Sunday morning in the dead of that dark winter, Ma was returning from her customary 7a.m. Mass with me in tow when, as we trudged slowly through the deep snow, we saw and heard a small boy crying helplessly as he stood near the corner of Havelock Street, dangerously near the Wallers' house. As we drew closer Ma exclaimed loudly and hurried immediately to him, taking him in her arms while murmuring her standard reassurances: 'There, there now. Don't cry; everything will be all right.' He was shivering uncontrollably – not surprising given that he was wearing only a thin vest, shirt, ragged pullover and shorts. He had no hat, coat, socks or shoes. This was not the place to question him further, so Ma picked him up and carried him the short distance to our house while instructing me to bring his empty, home-made barrow, which I handled as if it was filled with snakes or dynamite. Once we were indoors she seated him by the fire, as I watched, giving him a cup of tea to both drink and warm his hands on before resuming her enquiries.

'What are you doing in the snow without your shoes on?'

'Me Da put me out.'

'Why? Have you been a bad boy?'

He shook his head and started to cry again invoking the instantly soothing response of 'There, there now; don't cry, it'll be all right.'

Soon we both knew the truth – he lived not far away, close to Hannah's, the newsagents I worked for, and he had been put out to buy some coal with the few coins he had been given before carting it home in the barrow he had with him. He had lost his way, was petrified with fear at the thought of returning home without the coal, but was too cold to search for the coal merchant's yard and too young to think of an alternative. Over the next hour or so Ma found, God knows where or how, some old socks of ours, a barely serviceable pair of shoes and an old coat which was very crumpled, as it was being used to keep out draughts from under the kitchen door, and much too big for him, but it was warm. She shared out some of our precious Sunday breakfast from the meagre reserves of bacon, sausage, black pudding and fried bread and while I was eating mine with him alongside she quietly went out in search of the coal, returning with some about half an hour later. As the rest of the family gradually appeared and I was preparing to leave belatedly for my paper round, Ma dressed him, gave him a kiss and a hug and walked a little way in the snow with him before sending him on his way.

I delivered my newspapers, worrying about the problems I had because of my late start and thinking with some irritation about the reduced size – more imagined than real – of my breakfast, about Ma's curious behaviour in giving a stranger, however distressed, some of our even more precious clothing, and about the favoured treatment he'd had. Curiously I never heard her mention the incident to anyone subsequently, nor did I ever see the little boy again.

By the time the long, hot summer of 1947 had passed – a wonderful, seemingly endless summer of blue skies and hot sunny days, of countless century innings and nearly 4,000 runs each by the Middlesex twins Compton and Edrich, and when Rex, John Thornton, Alan Thornton, George Allan and me, St Cuthbert's Grammar School boys all, exhausted ourselves day after day emulating their feats – the memory of those memorable midwinter broadcasts from sun-drenched Australian cricket grounds was interlaced with images of that hapless, shoeless, coatless boy shivering and crying. Perhaps it was then that I began to realise that great deeds and real heroes don't always find their way into the record books.

26

LOVE THY NEIGHBOURS

Whether we lived in Elswick Row or in Havelock Street, to which we had moved in May 1940, the majority of the neighbours with whom we were particularly friendly or in regular contact remained much the same, because of the adjacency of the two streets. Following the move our immediate neighbours changed, of course, and our relationships with them unavoidably became just as intense as those with some of our closest friends in the neighbourhood. Similarly the most frequent visitors to the house continued unchanged after our move from Elswick Row, as did the tradesmen from whom we bought.

I never felt that it was in any way curious that we seldom knew the names of tradesmen, who were invariably referred to by a name synonymous with their activity. Even if they were welcome visitors – which wasn't always the case – there was no distinction from those who weren't.

The stick lady, the coalman, the violin man, the ice-cream man, the fish man, the French onion man and many more whose anticipated appearance at a time when their goods or services might be required would result in an instruction from Ma to let her know. 'When you see the fish man in the lane, call me', or 'If you see the stick lady, get two bundles of firewood.' With very few exceptions these tradesmen didn't call at any specific house; they simply appeared in the lane, where their presence was accompanied by a familiar promotional cry such as the fish man's 'Calla herring; fresh Calla herring', delivered in a thick, rich Geordie accent.

There were other purely 'business' callers to the house, who always appeared towards the weekend, usually on a Friday evening; they were better dressed, more discreet and, although always courteous, were less welcome. They called selectively at different houses, unusually at the front door, usually watched by one or more neighbours. Their very presence conveyed to the rest of the neighbourhood significant information about the household being visited.

Similar descriptive names were used for these – the insurance man, the Provident ticket man (known by some as the 'provy' or 'tally' man) and the rent man. They were not unpopular as individuals or less welcome because of their behaviour, but because they exerted financial pressure. Their services were necessary and the scheduled payments had to be made, but if a financial crisis struck – a common occurrence – there was no negotiable delay option as there might be at the corner shop. But there was an option, regularly exercised by some and helped by the timetable-like predictability of the caller, of feigning absence, even if it meant locking the front and back doors, turning off the lights and hiding temporarily in an upstairs room or a cupboard. Because Ma was extremely disciplined with her finances we never had to tell the insurance man, as some children had to, 'There's no one at home', or 'Me Mam's not in.' For some reason that I never understood we didn't have only one insurance man collecting premiums from the house, but several. There was the man from the Royal London, a small, carefully dressed man whose clothes, though neat, were old and who wore an old, country-style trilby which he tipped courteously to whoever answered his call. I always assumed the hat was to give him the appearance of being taller than he was. He was known as 'Snotty' – not because he was aloof, although that was a common term for those people who were acting above their 'station' – but because he unfortunately had an ever-present drip on the end of his nose, winter or summer. To this day I wouldn't know his name, but I can recall him clearly. There were others, from the Prudential, the Royal Liver and the Pearl. Each had a distinguishing characteristic, be it physical, like a moustache, or sartorial, such as bicycle clips on trouser bottoms. The premium books were always kept in the drawer of the 'whatnot' in the hall, from which they would be taken and placed below the mirror with the appropriate insurance premium in anticipation of the call. The front door was always open and the inner glass door was always closed but unlocked, except when gypsies or tinkers were in the neighbourhood, although few visitors would be so presumptuous as to enter or open the glass door to call 'Hello.'

We had a different, more formal approach to neighbours; with them it was normal to address the parents as 'Mr and Mrs', as my mother and father did also. Therefore they always referred in public to 'Mr and Mrs Birkett', for example, even though their son Teddy, who was a talented footballer with a delicate touch, played with us constantly. Teddy was also a natural conspirator, who from the age of five took to smoking and managed to do so without alerting his parents to his habits, something that always remained beyond my powers. He was an only child, something of a rarity in our street, and it was clear that such parents exercised their parental authority much more tentatively and self-indulgently than happened in most other families.

But exceptions were made to the generally observed rule when there was some defining reason for so doing. Winifred Crichton was the music teacher, but as a neighbour she was 'Mrs Crichton' rather than just 'the music teacher'; her husband, however, who was widely recognised as being 'loony', was always known rather elegantly as 'Benbow'. Mrs Hetherington was one of a substantial number of women in the neighbourhood whose husband, for reasons never openly talked about, lived separately in the attic, having been banished from the marital bed and all the living rooms. Since he no longer slept with her in the house she had subsequently taken 'a lodger'. There were at least two categories of lodgers; the first fitted the orthodox definition of someone who stayed with a family as a paying guest because the household had a financial need, satisfied by letting unused accommodation on a board-and-lodging basis. This entailed the housewife providing the lodger with separate accommodation, as well as meals and services such as washing, ironing and pressing clothes. But then there was the second category of 'lodger', who had the benefit of a wider range of more intimate services and as a result was usually referred to in private as 'the fancy man' and was distinguished by more familiarity when discussed publicly. Mrs Hetherington's 'fancy man' was known as Jack Harrison, not Petty Officer Harrison, although he had arrived at the house in the early days of the war to be billeted legitimately while he was serving in the local naval dockyard. He soon expanded his role in the Hetherington household to become a permanent fixture after the war, but he was always referred to as 'Jack Harrison', 'Mrs Hetherington's lodger' or 'the fancy man'.

There were some eccentrics, principally but by no means exclusively in our neighbourhood; ours were the Pearson family – two elderly brothers and two spinster sisters who lived together in a large house in Campbell Street, which backed onto the lane it shared with Elswick Row. The brothers had once run a very successful photographic business from their own shop in Newcastle city centre. The house was known as 'Pussy Pearsons', because they had always kept a large number of cats in the house. Tragically in their later years two of the surviving Pearsons were taken into care, while the two remaining in the house died in unexplained circumstances, their bodies lying undiscovered for days in a house full of cats. Popular rumour was that when the house was forcibly entered by the police to find the bodies there were fifty-seven half-starved cats, some of which had fed from the two Pearson corpses. That gave the house, along with one or two other houses in the neighbourhood, a macabre reputation.

A similar tragedy had occurred in Campbell Street, where a local bookmaker running a patently unsuccessful as well as illegal business had committed suicide by hanging himself from the balustrade. Because of suspicious circumstances the house had also been entered by police, who found the body swinging in the stairwell suspended from an upper floor.

Subsequently we hurried past these houses in daylight and consciously avoided going near them at night. Somehow they, or the deaths of their inhabitants, seemed more threatening, more evil than others where equally gruesome deaths had occurred. At one of these houses, also in Campbell Street, the father had taken his own life by cutting his throat with his own razor while seated at the breakfast table – fortunately, or perhaps deliberately, he was alone at the time. The neighbourhood gossip, out of earshot of the surviving widow and her two daughters, was enriched by Technicolor descriptions of the scene. The family enjoyed the full sympathy and ready support of everyone who knew of the tragedy, to which no stigma or fear was attached, and there was no lack of contact with them.

Two doors away from us in Havelock Street there appeared to be a large family of girls living at No. 9. It was obvious that the girls were extremely popular, because there was a constant stream of male visitors to the house. The woman who owned it was never referred to as Mrs McCoy but always as Rosie McCoy, and that in itself should have communicated to me that there was something scandalous or 'not quite right' about her. However, Ma's patiently disarming explanations of odd happenings were always sufficient to remove or diminish any sense of fear or scandal, and it wasn't until many years later that I became aware that No. 9 was a brothel and Rosie was the controlling 'Madam'.

Every street had its quota of mentally or physically handicapped people. Some were born damaged; others acquired or developed crippling disability. Wilfie Crichton, son of Benbow, was born mentally handicapped and suffered other ailments. Jackie MacHenry was born with one leg much shorter than the other and wore a metal brace on the affected leg, a handicap with which he coped remarkably well even to the extent of playing football, moving with a curious hopping, running and skipping action. Bunter, born John Huntingdon, whose nickname derived from the popularity of Billy Bunter in the *Gem* and *Magnet* comics, fell victim to the rare appearance of a motorcar in the front street by running in front of it and then colliding with it, when the protruding handle of the passenger door slashed his cheek wide open. Sadly for him that wasn't the end of his problems, as he managed to add to the handicap of a disfigured face the loss of an eye, by walking between a darts thrower and the dartboard as some boys were playing in the street. He acquired a glass eye and had a disconcerting tendency, when he was playing football, to remove it, suck it and polish it on his sleeve before replacing it with a flourish, presumably to disconcert the opposition rather than to see better.

There were also those who were different in other ways and whom Ma was less ready to discuss. We had yet another insurance man who succeeded one of our regular callers upon his retirement. We were at first amused but soon scornfully dismissive of this large, foppish, scented man who appeared at our door, extravagantly dressed – a very rare sight in Havelock Street – in a highly coloured, checked sports suit with a large, silk handkerchief billowing from his breast pocket, hair that had been shaped by grip curlers, a moustache which had been carefully trimmed and with a cloud of perfume surrounding him. It was inevitable that we had to add a more descriptive name to the simple title of 'the insurance man' – after all he could have been confused with the other, more normal insurance men – and he became known as George. Thereafter Ma began to issue rather veiled warnings about George, with an instruction not to accompany him if he invited us to do so having met us in the street. The reasons why George might want to do that eluded me, although later many of us were approached occasionally by George who by then was known as 'George the man with a conscience', for reasons which also mystified me.

Very often people were referred to with a subtitle. Where sympathy was felt for them it could be, for example, 'poor old Mrs Dodds'; if they were seen as kind and caring, 'canny woman'; or if they were affected, 'stuck up' or 'snotty'; or if another child was added to the family of an older couple, to avoid the social stigma attached to the real mother, they were called 'poor old souls' and the child 'poor little mite'. Even children had their own slang names for neighbourhood groups, variously referred to as being catty cats (Catholics), proddy dogs (Protestants), Yids (Jews), paddies (Irish), Eyeties (Italian), Chinks (Chinese), or Lascar. Nothing escaped the neighbourhood's attention, and therefore the practice of deciding how you wanted to be known played a conscious part in how discreet or otherwise you were about your private life. But one thing was certain: that the pattern of life in Elswick Row and Havelock Street would have been indistinguishable from that of other neighbourhoods, except only that some neighbourhoods would be poorer and if so almost certainly more violent, while others would be wealthier and then calmer, more influential or powerful. Irrespective of which 'box' you were or were thought to be in, there would be dishonest or disagreeable people whom you would wish to avoid.

This awareness caused Ma and Pop to decide early in their marriage to adopt their very formal approach to neighbours. This formality was established very quickly with any new neighbours, as I witnessed for the first time after our move to Havelock Street. It was defined for and explained to neighbours that unless they had been specifically invited to the house they were required to knock on the outer front door or inner hall glass door and wait for someone to open it. Since front doors were seldom locked and we never had a doorbell, or at least not one which worked, this was an important statement of principle and contrary to the practice of many others who, whether by design or default, allowed many of their neighbours to enter each other's houses at will. Ma's caustic reference to this as 'living in each other's pockets' was an accurate assessment, as well as a denunciation of the practice.

Neighbours frequently borrowed from each other – anything from a cup of sugar or a screwdriver to a gas mantle or dining chairs. As 'borrowing' was a flexible term, indicating more a vague intention rather than a commitment to return or repay, a previously established formal or informal basis was critical to limiting demands. It was as unthinkable to borrow a chair, for example, where formal but cordial relationships had been established as it would have been to refuse almost any request between those 'who lived in each other's pockets'. Ma, employing another of her infrangible maxims in her neighbourly contacts, made her intention of 'beginning as I mean to continue' unmistakable. Of course there was an added benefit to shunning the 'open door' policy; it protected privacy by denying others knowledge of what you didn't possess, as much as how you behaved individually and collectively as a family. If that was misinterpreted, so be it – *Honi soit qui mal y pense*, as Pop would gravely quote.

However carefully structured the approach to neighbours was by parents, there was always the random impact of children's misbehaviour to be considered or repaired. It was inevitable that with so many children of varying age groups playing in the back lane, in limited space hemmed in by the high, brick walls, there would be frictions, occasionally leading to outbreaks of hostility. Most parents understood only too well that there would be incidents and accidents arising from so many children playing so many different games.

Mr Oliver, for instance, showed great forbearance in the matter of the misfortune that occurred the day a young, working Alec Blair, from the other side of Elswick Row and probably then in his late teens, collected a tennis ball which had been smashed past the bowler by a batsman playing in front of stumps chalked on the wall at the bottom of the lane. Alec responded by picking up the ball and with an intentionally hard kick made perfect connection to send the ball sailing high in the air, clearing the back-yard walls at the bottom of the lane, probably a distance of some 50 yards. It went through a ground-floor window of the Olivers' house, and unfortunately they had their wireless set adjacent to it; the ball explosively smashed the valves in the back of the wireless set, rendering it useless. Mr Oliver rushed out and protested vehemently, but his gaze was directed by us towards the swiftly retreating back of a by then unrecognisable young man. He did no more than shake his head sorrowfully before retiring indoors muttering, while we continued with the cricket match. Other people were less tolerant.

One of our neighbours was a Mrs Johnson, a slatternly, unkempt woman whose personality matched her appearance; she had two daughters who lived further up the lane, near Wilson's Lamp. One day she determined to exact a penalty for some grievance, real or imagined, against the Cassidy family – or rather against Vincent in particular, who apparently was believed to be guilty of some transgression. Even for Elswick Row the resulting behaviour of Mrs Johnson, who was always referred to by my mother as 'Dirty Johnson', was unusually extreme. She appeared, as unkempt as ever, in the back lane and in a loud voice addressed Ma from the centre of the lane, so that she could see from her chosen position the scullery window at which Ma eventually appeared. I could hear a torrent of angry, abusive language being directed upwards, and although I couldn't see the person hurling the insults there was no doubt whose voice it was. Eventually the recapitulation of the alleged errors, omissions and offences concluded with the demand that Vincent should surrender himself for retribution. Ma, however angry she was, maintained an icy dignity and simply said, 'Go away.' That seemed to enrage 'Dirty Johnson' considerably; her response was, 'Don't you talk to me like that, you and your fat bloody Irish husband.' Ma's response was an even more icy 'Go away.'

'Come down here and I'll murder you.'

'Go away and stop behaving in such a common way.'

This was tantamount to lighting the blue touch paper.

'Come down here and I'll show you who's common. You are not the size of three pennyworth of copper.'

Ma rose to the challenge with an unusual, if temporary, descent into the language which 'Dirty Johnson' would certainly understand.

'If they cut off your belly and stitched up your mouth you wouldn't be half my size. Now go away.'

With that the scullery window was slammed shut and Ma returned, apparently calmly, to her culinary activities.

From time to time there were also incursions into our territory, or onto the boundary of it, by less desirable people who were not neighbours but were related to, or in some relationship with, some of our immediate neighbours. There were two families, both of whom lived in the Scotswood Road area, that were seriously 'bad news'. One comprised well-known lawbreakers who often found themselves in trouble with the police, in court, and not infrequently in gaol. The other family was not quite in the same class, but as their natural heirs they indulged in petty crime and were given to unprovoked outbursts of violence. This seemed to occur with both junior and senior family members, irrespective of their age. In the early years of the war I was walking along Elswick Road carrying a toy farmyard, owned by Brian Rose ('Rosie' to all his friends), from his house in Summerhill Terrace to Elswick Row. I felt particularly pleased since I had been given the privileged role of carrying the farmyard, a large wooden, green-painted board. As Rosie and I were excitedly talking and walking side by side, the youngest of the troublesome clan, Dougie, who would have been about my own age but who was certainly of much heavier build, apparently took a dislike to me – probably because I appeared to be the owner of a desirable object. Without breaking stride or exchanging a word as we passed each other, he simply lashed out with his fist, hitting me squarely on the nose and causing a torrent of blood to disfigure the farmyard. When Vincent saw what had happened to me he set off in search of the offender, found him and threatened, in a reversal of roles from his relationship with 'Dirty Johnson' and family, to wreak vengeance if that ever happened again. However, he was told, not very politely, that if he did an older member of the clan would 'do him', so Vincent, in true Falstaffian style, decided that the better part of valour was discretion and retreated.

Happily flashpoints like this were infrequent, but I learned from them that it made good sense to play to your strengths, whatever those might be. Ma's mental and verbal agility had demolished a superior physical force by commanding the high ground, both literally and metaphorically, whereas Vincent's attempt to threaten superior physical strength was rendered impotent by the threat of other superior reinforcements being drafted in.

In contrast there were occasional glimpses of a better, more attractive or at least more affluent way of life. In Roma's early days at work one of her young colleagues invited her to Sunday tea with her family, and amid great excitement Kitty McDonald called for her in a car driven by her father. Since no one in the neighbourhood owned a car and very few were even seen in our street this caused great excitement, evidenced by the gathering of small boys around the car and much twitching of lace curtains in neighbouring houses. Roma's breathlessly admiring description on her return of the house, the table settings, the carpets, the curtains and the ornaments, omitted any reference to the meal, enabling Ma to inject some balance with a gently reproving rejoinder about the dangers of placing personal and domestic adornment above the feeding of body and soul.

Some years later Vincent found himself much admired by a young woman who demonstrated her intent by inviting him home to meet her parents. Jacqueline lived a few streets away in a much superior neighbourhood, with a bank manager for a father, and her family displayed some obvious trappings of wealth. Ma's ever-present concern about her favourite son falling victim so easily to female charms was at least partially mitigated by this knowledge. On the appointed day Jacqueline called for Vincent, who met her at our front door and they set off for Clifton Avenue, off Grainger Park Road. It was a normal part of our privacy protection even in these circumstances to make sure that our threshold was not crossed at random, and therefore none of us would have seen anything strange in Jacqueline calling for Vincent, or of her being kept waiting on the doorstep until he left the house with her.

As they arrived at her parents' home Vincent was aware of the father's presence at the downstairs front window, while in the garden, a neat and well-kept patch of lawn and flowers, a gardener was busy attending to his duties. It was clear that Vincent was under observation as they entered and closed the creaking iron gate behind them. As they walked up the short front path to the front door the gardener straightened, turned round and greeted Vincent with 'Hello, Vince – how are you?' 'I'm fine,' said Vincent, a harmless enough exchange in itself since Mr Goundrey, a neighbour of ours in Elswick Row and well known to us, lived in a house virtually opposite ours backing onto the common lane that we shared. It was true that the Goundreys had even fewer possessions than we did. They had even less living space too, occupying only one upper floor on which the parents and all four children lived. They shared a kitchen, as well as limited toilet facilities, with all the other tenants of the house. Their youngest child had been born seriously mentally handicapped and was often seen, dressed in nothing other than a short vest or blouse, shuffling about on his bare bottom in the concrete backyard. Poorer the Goundrey family may have been, but their circumstances were within the normal range of the neighbourhood. Yet these thoughts occurred to Vincent only retrospectively, since he was greeted by Mr Langley, the father, with a rather chilly enquiry as to whether, and if so how, Vincent knew the gardener, Mr Goundrey. This was presumed to be the case because it would have been unlikely for the gardener to have spoken to Vincent without being invited to speak, or without any knowledge of him. Vincent, of course, readily acknowledged that they were neighbours and indeed that he knew the whole family. After all Frances, who was Alan's age, had married a McGuinness; they were related to the Tamms, and Edith, who was slightly younger than Vincent and was developing into an attractive young woman, appeared to harbour romantic notions about him – or so he thought. Perhaps it was only the male line that was physically deficient, since the father bore a striking resemblance to Quasimodo and the eldest son, Billy, was partially blind and given to bouts of eccentric behaviour such as singing loudly, with bulging veins and trembling epiglottis, on the upper deck of trolleybuses as if it was the stage of the Theatre Royal – admittedly to the amusement rather than irritation of his fellow passengers. It must be assumed that Mr Langley had some of this wider knowledge of the Goundrey family and its circumstances, because his cool reception continued through an increasingly frigid meeting. Vincent certainly didn't offend anybody during the visit; he didn't manage to spill anything on the damask tablecloth, neither did he cool hot tea by blowing on it or waving at it with a cap, probably only because he didn't carry one with him at the time; yet that visit signalled the end of his promising affair with Jacqueline.

The bonds of our community certainly supported most of those within it, and every neighbourhood had high, if invisible, barriers to entry, particularly to those of a lower social order. The exception to this unwavering rule was usually provided by immigrants, of whom there were an increasing number, in the main those fleeing from persecution elsewhere. Jews from Central Europe were the most obvious, but they were by no means the only ones, and of these Maurice Lichtenstein, always known as 'Maurice Light', was typical. He had some money, great talent as a tailor and an insatiable appetite for work. He ran a shop on Elswick Road where he patched, repaired, enlarged or reduced clothes on demand. Of course, he also made suits to measure, but in our particular neighbourhood this was highly unusual and he seldom had the opportunity to exercise his skills in that direction. More frequently the need was to 'take in' or 'let out' clothes that had been either handed down or acquired from second-hand shops – or, even more frequently, passed down from the recently dead to the living. Apart from his name above the door, his shop window advertised his trade by means of a man's formal suit jacket apparently ripped open, displaying bold stitching to show how garments could be made up, altered or repaired. His short walk from his shop to his home took him via Elswick Row, along

Havelock Street and up Campbell Street. His dress, summer or winter, was always the same – a brown hat, a large overcoat worn over a double-breasted suit, with the overcoat hem almost touching the uppers of his large, cracked, brown shoes. He was short and stout, with feet which seemed more proportionate to his waist measurement than to his height. He walked dragging his feet sideways, as though consciously trying to keep them in a position resembling the hands of a clock showing ten minutes to two. Consequently the brown shoes were badly down at heel and sole on the inside, yet virtually untouched on the outer. His shoes looked, as we boys often remarked, as if these were the same shoes in which he had undertaken, with the Israelites, their long march in search of the Promised Land. As he embarked on his short, familiar, daily journey he very seldom acknowledged anyone he passed, but he sang or hummed gently – presumably to amuse himself, although clearly audible to those, like us, around him – while wearing a tortured smile on his shiny, sweaty face. He was as inoffensive and self-contained as anybody could be, neither influencing nor being influenced by the intensity of the activity around him.

And like so many others in the neighbourhood he had arrived and stayed, rather as a piece of driftwood did on Cullercoats beach, neither completely strange to, nor permanently a part of, his new surroundings.

27

AL JOLSON AT THE PICTURES

The king may have seen his first 'talkie' in 1933, a few days before I was born, but so far as my father was concerned – and it was a story he recounted often – he would remember vividly the day in 1929 when the tram on which he was conducting – 'Fares, please' – passed the Stoll Theatre on Westgate Road as people were 'coming out of the pictures' at the end of the performance. He was astounded to see that the vast majority were in tears and many men were comforting their apparently inconsolable wives, a strange enough sight in Newcastle. The film was *The Singing Fool*, a sequel to *The Jazz Singer*, which became famous as the first talking movie because Al Jolson spoke a few words and sang in it. What he sang in *The Singing Fool* was the tear-jerking 'Sonny Boy', which was much more a story of everyday life than most people perhaps liked to admit; but it was certainly that song which had touched the hearts and minds of the people leaving the cinema.

However, I hadn't heard this at the time I was taken to see my first film. The memories of that are extremely vague and I am reliant totally on what my father, not always the most reliable of historical sources, told me about it afterwards. That it was my father who took me, unaccompanied by any other member of the family, was in itself a minor miracle. The film was *The Mutiny on the Bounty*, with Charles Laughton playing Captain Bligh. My first appearance at the 'pictures' was marked by my becoming extremely upset with Captain Bligh's behaviour towards Fletcher Christian; I began shouting at him and couldn't be silenced, to such an extent, my father tells me, that he had to remove me from the cinema. Whether or not he then went to an adjoining public house and stood me in the doorway while he recovered his dignity, I am not quite certain. He would deny it, I'm sure; but that event became much talked about at home, particularly since we had been in expensive seats at the newly opened and upmarket Queen's Theatre, just off Northumberland Street. It was many years before I was taken to the pictures again, and never again in the rest of my life by Pop.

The growth in popularity of the cinema led to the creation of low-priced, Saturday morning or Saturday afternoon shows for children. Not far from us, near the Big Lamp at the junction of Elswick Road and Westgate Road, was the site of an old cemetery created for plague victims in the nineteenth century; the now-deconsecrated graveyard included an old church which had been crudely converted into a picture house. It faced another graveyard and sat in the middle of a warren of decaying, old, terraced houses, many of which were flats in what was an extremely poor and unattractive district. This picture theatre was, with unselfconscious wit, called The Gem, and since it ran a programme of different films most nights during wartime many people went more than once a week, while it also developed the Saturday afternoon matinée for kids. It had the unassailable attraction of being very cheap! The films were old, usually short films by Laurel and Hardy, Charlie Chaplin, the Keystone Cops, and the Three Stooges. These were, of course, laced with more gripping serials like *Flash Gordon* or *The Green Hand*, and Westerns like *Riders of the Purple Sage*, *Hopalong Cassidy*, and *Johnny Mack Brown*, accompanied by a multitude of early horror films frequently starring Boris Karloff. Yet it was the Three Stooges who really grabbed our childish imagination – Curly, Mo and Larry. Clumsiness or questioning by Curly or Mo always brought a violent physical response from Larry, usually a flurry of punches, a poke in the eye, kicks or a blow with a mallet to the head, at which we all laughed heartily.

The Gem cinema was a unique institution, which because it was cheap and in a poor district was run like an institution in a police state.

Children queued up with their ticket money for some time before the doors opened – a random timing no doubt calculated to cause maximum inconvenience to balance the low cost – after which the patiently queuing customers were directed by an officious petty bureaucrat to the first empty seat, starting with the extreme left-hand side of the front row. The seats were filled in strict sequence left to right, front row backwards to the entrance. No choice was allowed and there was no concession to customer service. The seats were old, mostly torn and sagging, and the air stank. The man who supervised all this was a thin, old, bedraggled, moustachioed, mean-looking veteran of the First World War who was dubbed very quickly by Vincent the 'Confiscator', because if you carried any article to which he took offence it would be confiscated. If you yourself fell foul of his strict rules, you were 'confiscated', which meant being ejected without recourse. Children were packed in and when, as was the norm, I was taken along by Vincent and Rex, sometimes with Sydney also, they would be expected or instructed by the 'Confiscator' to seat us on their knees. Everybody wanted to avoid the front row, where the viewing angle required you to crane your neck backwards at an unseemly angle in order to see the screen. A double-jointed neck would have helped but none of us possessed one, so we always saw grotesquely distorted images whenever we were unlucky or unwise enough to be near the front of the queue for admission. But avoiding the front row did not avoid all potential risks.

Some delinquent children would regularly gain unpaid entry via the toilets, sited in a corner between the front row and the screen. One of the delinquents would pay to enter early and would go to the lavatory, open the emergency fire doors to allow in the others, usually two, and then swiftly, in order to avoid instant ejection by the 'Confiscator', they would forcibly eject someone randomly from an occupied seat and sit with an innocent expression, while the displaced victim was thrown out for being without a seat. Everyone knew this happened. No doubt the 'Confiscator' did too, but we happily survived for a long time without falling prey to the seat-grabbing louts until on one Saturday afternoon, when we were early because we were extremely anxious not to be locked out, we became unwilling victims. We were bundled unceremoniously onto the floor in the aisle by the lavatory invaders, to be evicted instantly by the 'Confiscator' despite Vincent's protests of innocence; left with no other option, we trailed home. When Ma saw us a few minutes later and found out what had happened, she immediately donned her coat and hat, picked up her bag and marched us back to The Gem. There was a very swift showdown. Powerful though the 'Confiscator' was he was no match for the formidable Ma, who dismissed him with a volley of perfectly proper but scathing language and insisted, particularly since Vincent was still holding our tickets, that we should be readmitted. There was no further delay, and so confident was she of victory that she didn't even wait to see us safely in our seats but marched off. Unfortunately, since the cinema was packed, the 'Confiscator' meted out rough justice: two small children were unceremoniously evicted, equally unfairly, and we were in.

We graduated from the 'fleapit', as we referred accurately if unflatteringly to The Gem, to other local cinemas offering the same types of film, always in black and white and mostly talkies; many of the local cinemas developed the concept of 'Saturday Children's Matinées'. Some were held on a Saturday morning, but most were on Saturday afternoon. They were cheap, although not as cheap as the 'fleapit'; but gradually, towed along by Roma who was the most avid cinemagoer in the family, and later by Vincent, we graduated to the higher-priced, city-centre cinemas. We didn't have any fixed amount of pocket money and therefore money obtained for a visit was gifted by Roma, Alan or visiting relatives – although particularly in the summer we had the benefit of income from 'hoy oots' at weddings. Occasionally, for a special treat, Ma would gather us altogether and take us en masse, with the benefit that when accompanied by a parent children under sixteen would go in for half price, and those under six or thereabouts would go in free. Even when I was eight I could be passed off as being younger than six.

Although microscopic scrutiny might suggest we were all related, Sydney's sturdy body, round face and jet-black hair indicated he was from quite different stock from my thin, weedy build and brown hair. Rex's dimpled cheeks and kneecaps and mass of blond, curly hair gave him a likeness more to Shirley Temple than to Sydney or me, while Vincent looked rather like a garden plant that had been overwatered and left in the sun, achieving straggly height without the comfort of apparent means of sustainability. Ma, being small and slight and often wearing an oversized coat just in case she grew more, with an inappropriate hat rammed on her head, looked as if she might have rounded up these street urchins and was passing them off as her own in order to gain unjustified benefits. Indeed, having purchased tickets at the box office of the Olympia in Northumberland Road she was challenged once by the doorman to whom she presented two tickets, one full-price for her and one half-price for Vincent, not only with a question but an accompanying statement. 'Are these all yours? You know you can get into trouble for taking in other people's children under false pretences.'

Ma, never one to duck a challenge, bridled and said cuttingly, 'Don't be impertinent. These are only some of my children, and I am not in the habit of carrying birth certificates with me when I go to the pictures' – and with that she retrieved her two tickets, brushed him aside and went to find seats for us. Coming as it did soon after our experiences with the 'Confiscator', it reinforced our view that old men in uniforms were a serious threat to cinematic enjoyment.

There were basically two kinds of cinema in Newcastle: the rare, new, purpose-built building like the Odeon and the Essoldo, both of which opened in the late 1930s shortly before the war; and the others, consisting of those that had been used for other purposes – principally but not exclusively entertainment, and including two former music halls, the Stoll and the Gaiety. They were instantly recognisable as old music halls, not only from the style of the exterior of the building but also from their large, bare balconies with seating no more comfortable than a Roman amphitheatre. There were others that had been dance halls, and the odd church conversion, as was the case with The Gem; predictably, since it had been a church in a graveyard for plague victims, we often discussed the possibility that 'the Confiscator' might, Dracula-like, return to his coffin in the graveyard after every performance. The Gaiety's attractions were that it was low priced in the balcony, and also it showed more recent films than The Gem. Once you were in you could almost smell the greasepaint atmosphere of an old music hall, but it was without the trappings that made watching a film in the small, plush Grainger theatre so luxurious. There was no concession in the Gaiety to the developing trend towards a high-quality, properly installed screen, or to modern seating, carpeting or sound effects. Although you didn't get the electric organ coming up from beneath and in front of the screen to welcome 'patrons', as they were called at the Odeon, you did often get a pianist on the stage, sometimes accompanied by a violinist. But the atmosphere was perhaps more realistically set by the dank bareness of the concrete staircase that led from the box office at the side door to the balcony, and its associated smell of urine.

Since the first talkie was released only in 1927, as Vincent was being born, most of the films we saw at the lower-priced cinemas were in black and white; but just before war broke out two new cinemas were opened almost coincidentally with the release of two of the first major Technicolor films, *The Adventures of Robin Hood* followed by *Gone with the Wind*. Both were beautifully made and both had a wide appeal; I didn't see *Robin Hood* until the early 1940s, but it remained my favourite film for many years. The appeal of both films was that they had big Hollywood stars, and there had been nothing remotely like their scale, grandeur, complexity and quality before they were screened.

For the Roman Catholic Church *Gone with the Wind* presented a new problem, that of glamorising immoral behaviour; the Church felt obliged to speak out, publicly forbidding Catholics to see the film. Canon Wilkinson read out a pastoral letter from the bishop on this theme, and devout and dutiful as she was, Roma still succumbed to her growing obsession with the cinema by ignoring this edict. She returned enraptured by *Gone with the Wind*, as far as I could tell with her morals intact, as ecstatic about Clark Gable's performance as she had been over that of Errol Flynn in *Robin Hood*. It was her desire to see these films again and again which granted me an early complimentary visit, although as a consequence I almost lost my left eye.

Impressionable boys don't simply watch that scale of adventure, for never before had it been possible to see such realistic sword fighting as took place between Robin Hood and Guy de Gisbourne. Of course I had read about it in books, but in the cinema it wasn't left to the imagination: it was there, real, moving on screen, with Robin as the hero holding off and overcoming not only the villainous Guy de Gisbourne but whole armies of Norman foot soldiers. Not long afterwards a group of us visited St Paul's churchyard with sharpened penknives, cut off some stout branches, trimmed and shaped them, rapier-like, found pieces of cardboard with which to create sword handles and then indulged in very realistic sword fights. With the railings having been removed from around the churchyard, as they had from the fronts of all our houses, we were able to re-enact some of Robin's leaps from battlements to ground while continuing the sword fight, and by throwing open the iron outer gates to the churchyard we would carry on our sword fight up and down steps and around the church. It was a very realistic setting – perhaps too realistic, for in parrying one lunge at me I deflected Sidney Dansky's 'sword' which entered my left eye socket deeply, pushing the eyeball back in the process. It was very painful, the eye was red and my vision blurred, but I thought it unwise to reveal what had happened. In reality I had been extremely lucky. I could so easily have lost that eye, whereas even though my sight gradually deteriorated, no one discovered for at least ten years afterwards that I had a very badly damaged eye which required me to wear glasses. Perhaps at the time it happened I didn't want to risk the Ronald Reagan/Robert Cummings incident in *Kings Row* and have my eye, Bunter-like, removed by a sadistic, psychopathic surgeon.

This was the 'golden age' of the cinema – in some ways inhibited by the Second World War, but in other respects providing an almost perfect programme for boys, a rich diet of war and patriotic historical films.

Happily, despite the war, there was still a regular flow of major new releases from the United States. There were the fairytales and fantasies: Disney's *Snow White and the Seven Dwarfs* and my own favourite, *Pinocchio* – which reduced me to tears when I thought Gepetto had retrieved a dead Pinocchio from the sea – *The Thief of Baghdad* and *The Wizard of Oz*. Vincent preferred the high drama of *The Maltese Falcon, High Sierra* and *Casablanca*, all with a new hero, Humphrey Bogart, as well as *This Gun for Hire* and *Gaslight*. Rex preferred *Kings Row, Five Graves to Cairo, Double Indemnity* and *Ministry of Fear*. Ma preferred Bob Hope and Bing Crosby in *The Road to Zanzibar, The Road to Morocco, Going My Way* and *The Bells of St Mary's*. Sydney loved *The Black Swan* and *The Sea Hawk*, and precociously *The Wicked Lady*, whereas Roma had a truly catholic taste and at least until 1944 fed this obsessive interest with her regular diet of news from *Picture Goer* and *Picture Show*, the two weekly filmgoers' magazines of the period.

As a family we shared our views of the pictures we saw, as we did of the books we read. For the younger members of the family the cinema was more accessible, if more financially constrained, but we developed our own list of favourites and classics which would often be the subject of heated debate. As the tide of war changed, so too did the content of films. Gradually the focus on war films declined to be replaced by more dramas, often articulating major social themes: *The Lost Weekend*, about the problems of alcoholism; *The Odd Man Out*, about the IRA; *The Snake Pit*, about the plight of patients in mental institutions; and as I was leaving school *The Third Man*, set in Allied-occupied Vienna and coinciding with a sequence of enduringly popular British comedies from the Ealing Studios – a welcome relief from the enforced patriotism or the gloom and madness of war.

The propagandist, adventure-laden, heroic films produced between 1939 and 1945 had been perfect for me and my age group growing up in wartime, whereas the immediate postwar period brought the cinema much closer to convergence with my own rapidly accelerating explorations of literature and music. I could now see in retrospect that *Robin Hood* had appealed to me in two very different ways: through its realistic 'blood and guts' fighting scenes, and because of the quality of the music score by Erich Korngold. Similarly Richard Addinsell's 'Warsaw Concerto' in *Dangerous Moonlight*, and Tchaikovsky's first piano concerto in *Song of Russia* – first heard merely as background music to war films about Germany's onslaught on Eastern Europe – were added to the other family favourites such as the Manchester Children's Choir singing 'Nymphs and Shepherds', Ernest Lough's 'O for the wings of a dove', Marian Anderson's 'Softly awakes my heart', as well as songs and operatic arias by Caruso, Gigli, Tauber and Dawson.

Bogart and Peter Lorre became archetypal characters for us, and through these Vincent led us into Raymond Chandler with Philip Marlowe. Laurence Oliver's *Henry V*, and later *Hamlet*, reinforced my burgeoning interest in Shakespeare, which converged with my study of *Henry IV Part 1* for school certificate. *Brief Encounter*, *The Third Man* and *Brighton Rock* made us all fans of Graham Greene, as well as strengthening our musical interest. While James Mason's seedy, desperate gunman in *Odd Man Out* led us to the conclusion that R.C. Sherriff was much underrated for this screenplay, he was already well known to us for the First World War drama *Journey's End*; we had acted in it at school, as it appeared most other schoolchildren of the same age had done also.

Many of these films were to become 'all-time greats' and as such were universally enjoyed; but we compiled, typically, another list of quirky films, seen by us as memorable classics either because of their quality, even if it was not generally recognised, or because they were unbelievably awful. Included among these were *The Foreman went to France*, *The Next of Kin*, *The Deer Slayer*, *Waterloo Road* and Hemingway's *The Killers*.

For sheer excitement and escapism – desirable if rare achievements in wartime and its immediate aftermath – going to the pictures was second only to going to the match, but it had a wider appeal to the non-football-playing population. However, it was about to be dealt an almost terminal blow, as I matriculated from grammar school, by the government's life-changing decision to push ahead with the 1935 commitment to provide a public television service as soon as possible.

Shortly after I started work in August 1949 I saw for the first time the biographical musical *The Jolson Story*, first released in October 1946 and already a box-office hit. Jolson had re-emerged from the shadows by entertaining American troops in the Pacific during the closing stages of the war and had effectively relaunched his recording career, which had been all but dead and buried before the war. Yet the film's lively, nostalgic tunes and simple lyrics were a breath of fresh air in the late 1940s, just as they had been for the American GIs in the Pacific; the songs had the same enthralling effect on them as they had had on their parents in the 1920s and 1930s audiences. It was Jolson who had personally ushered in talking pictures twenty years earlier with *The Jazz Singer*, a far-distant cry from going to the old silent pictures, when he seemed to be saying once again his famous phrase, 'You ain't heard nothing yet.'

The advances in technology brought colour, sound, serious acting, realistic scenery, outdoor locations and animation, and over the next two decades these propelled cinema-going into the top place as an adult entertainment activity – but not without cost to the music halls and variety theatres which had provided the stage for Al Jolson's first career.

In this final flowering of his career he would soon be seen as being among those bringing the curtain down on the big screen's 'golden age'. The ending of the cinema's dominance was being publicly and increasingly signalled by a series of small steps, such as the announcement by the BBC in November 1949 that it was buying Lime Grove Studios from Rank Films.

Nothing is for ever, is it?

28

MICKY THE MONKEY AND OTHER TALES

*M*icky the Monkey may not have endured as my favourite story, poetic though I found it in my earliest days, although it was almost certainly one of Ma's childhood favourites and, through her, our common introduction over a twenty-year period to the charms of bedtime stories. Micky, who 'went out one day' was followed by a familiar series of better known fairytales of which *The Three Little Pigs* offered Ma her best opportunity to display a range of actions and voices as the big, bad wolf tried to blow the house down. *Aesop's Fables* was the next compendium of moralising and instructive tales, all of which encouraged me when next in line for tuition to start reading for myself, and so avoid the pleading necessary to have my own favourite tale repeated. Since most of the books we owned were from my father's limited but highly prized collection, they were inevitably out of reach initially, both intellectually and physically, so that I remained dependent on other people to provide suitable reading material. We had all learned the alphabet and our initial vocabulary of words from Ma's own handwritten examples; this was partly to blame for my initial disappointment with junior school, where the only difference from home was that we were given dog-eared primers to teach us what I had learned more than a year earlier.

In the interim I enjoyed the new comics *Dandy* and *Beano*, which had the good sense to start publication as my reading needs increased; to them I added *Film Fun*, with its reliance on popular characters well known to us, like Laurel and Hardy. While the picture comics helped me to improve my reading skills, they were only a short-term bridge to the longer, more satisfying tales in the *Adventure, Rover, Wizard* or *Champion*, although all included memorable characters such as Desperate Dan, Lord Snooty, Pansy Potter, Keyhole Kate, Wilson, Alf Tupper, Clickyba and many others who survived long after my regular comic-reading days gave way to 'real books'.

By the time the class reading at school had progressed to more imagination-stretching literature, I had been enrolled as a member of the public library and had begun to deliver newspapers, both events that provided an enlarged and interesting range of free, readily accessible reading material.

The local public library, the Stephenson – named after one of the great local heroes, the engineer best known for his pioneering creation of 'people moving' locomotives – was near Elswick Park, which we frequented and which was within easy walking distance of our house. As with so many of my activities my first experience of the library was being taken along by Vincent and Rex while they went through an exciting ritual of returning books, having their record card marked, and their ticket returned to them before the books were prepared for return to their allotted place on the awaiting shelves prior to reissue. Subsequently, when they had made their new selection, a slip was removed from a holder inside the book's cover, the book would be stamped with a 'return by' date and the slips would be held with their record card until they were returned by the due date, in default of which an unaffordable and progressive fine would be levied. Best of all, I could pretend to be considering the relative merits of different books, and occasionally would remove one from those shelves I could reach to examine it intently on the nearest vacant reading table. The library housed an unbelievably large collection of books, and although most were beyond my understanding there were some more accessible than others, usually with large print, coloured drawings or photographic illustrations. It was through the latter that I became precociously interested in, and subsequently knowledgeable about, the conduct of the Great War.

Going to 'the Stephenson', as we referred to it, gave me an insight into how perceptive the Victorian benefactors had been in creating the concept and then opening a nationwide network of public lending libraries – extended later through the addition of reading rooms which the general public, library members or not, could visit at will during the long opening hours to read any of the daily newspapers, as well as a selection of current magazines. It was a haven for more than the unemployed during the darkest days of the depression and helped to sustain a working population who were hungry for knowledge and self-education, but who did not have the financial means to achieve it otherwise. It was the same adult population that we had as neighbours, as fellow members of the congregation at St Mary's for Mass on Sundays, and with which I began to mix as later I visited St James' Park for football matches.

Before long I, too, was enrolled as an individual member of the public library and had my own membership number, ticket and record card – only to find that first Vincent and then Rex gravitated to the much larger, better-stocked Central Library on Oxford Street. I was mortified and envious, feeling snubbed; once more I had thought I had reached their level, only for them to move tantalisingly ahead of me again. Yet consolation was soon provided by the fact that at the Central Library most books were chosen from a card index and brought to you by the librarian, which wasn't remotely as interesting as choosing your own books at will from shelves packed with as many different shapes and sizes of book as there were potential book borrowers. You may indeed not be able to 'tell a book by its cover', but I found it a very good guide – with the added benefit of gauging its weight, feel, print, smell, paper quality and binding, through which books also appealed to me.

The factor which swung the balance decisively in favour of the local Stephenson library for me was that it stored all the books on offer in one large room. There was a children's section, but that was only to aid selection; it did not prevent anyone entitled to use the library from browsing at will, a facility that I exploited to the full initially in my wartime search for books on the Great War, particularly those by Captain Liddell Hart. In contrast, at the Central Library children, defined as those under fourteen, were not allowed even to visit the adult library which was housed in a separate wing.

We borrowed books from the library on a weekly basis by choice, because as a rule two weeks were allowed for books to be read and we were all constantly reminded of the need to avoid paying fines for the late return of overdue books. There was no chance of such lax ways remaining confidential because reminders were issued by the library with details of the accumulated fine 'to date', which would bring a sharp rebuke from Ma about wasting money – a very serious crime in her eyes. Such lapses were few and far between as my love of books developed, a passion increased by the enjoyment I got from the contents as well as from the currency they gave me to exchange this knowledge with others. I simply could not devote enough time to this most satisfying hobby and soon began to read in bed at night before going to sleep, which in 5 Havelock Street in wartime meant by torch under the bedclothes, because we couldn't afford removable blackout screens. Once the benefits of reading had been tapped and the love of books created, a series of opportunities followed and new pleasures emerged as I explored second-hand bookshops and stalls in the Grainger Market. I began regularly to spend hours, normally every Saturday, at the Book Room in Brunswick Place, where browsing through the newly published books and enjoying the smell, feel and colour of them gave pleasure as intense as an exciting match at St James' Park. One Christmas I bought my first brand-new book, *Congo Chains* by Major Charles Gilson, an adventure story set in Africa, and through this extravagant splurge of the Christmas-box money I had been allowed to keep I discovered not only the joy of ownership, but also of handling a book which no other person had touched or read before me. Such episodes were going to be rare but collecting books was not, since I had now discovered William Brown and his family – father, mother, Robert and Ethel – his gang of friends Ginger, Henry and Douglas and the insufferable Violet Elizabeth Bott, as well as dozens of eccentric vicars, visitors, villains and village fetes.

It was through William, an outrageously unkempt, daredevil schoolboy, that I learned about middle-class life – of tennis clubs, of people who owned motorcars, employed cooks, cleaners and other servants and of all manner of strange habits; and while Richmal Crompton knew how to appeal to any boy's emotions, I doubt whether she realised fully the social educational value of the stories from which we all derived such intense enjoyment. The exploits of her famous schoolboy in *Just William, William Again, William the Outlaw, William the Conqueror, William the Pirate* and many more that followed created an irresistible urge to collect 'the full set', which was available in the Book Room yet unachievable on cost grounds, except by reverting to recognised second-hand bookshops like Robinson's in the Grainger Market; other market stalls, jumble sales and a variety of other sources also enabled my motley, often dog-eared and battered collection to grow at a reasonable cost, if sometimes agonisingly slowly. Pop had offered the first evidence of the pleasure to be derived from a collection, even if it was an extremely limited one; Roma had followed with an extensive, if conservative, taste in classic authors such as Jane Austen, accompanied by more modern humorists like P.G. Wodehouse, Jerome K. Jerome, Damon Runyon and Stella Gibbons – editions which she bought regularly in the new Penguin paperback series. Vincent invested more in a wider range of contemporary novelists, while maintaining his classics reading by borrowing from the library. The house rules dictated that you could borrow someone else's property only with their permission, which was usually forthcoming but could not be taken for granted, although we all now had free access to Pop's books. Encouraged by Vincent's melodramatic recapitulation of Jack the Ripper's deeds, Dr Harvey

Crippen's murder of his wife Belle Elmore and of his bricking her body up in the walls of their respectable North London house, and of the even more gruesome tale of Fritz Harman – styled 'the Butcher of Hanover' after he had murdered more than a hundred post-Great War refugee children and sold their dismembered bodies as 'pork' – we all fought to read *The 50 Most Amazing Crimes of the Last 100 Years*. It was one of Pop's favourite books and through it we became familiar with lurid murders, evil monsters and the towering skills of the great barristers – Marshall Hall, F.E. Smith and many others. *The Body in the Trunk, The Brides in the Bath, Landru the French Bluebeard, Adelaide Bartlett, Madeleine Smith the Poisoner, Thompson and Bywaters* and the rest were the ideal sequel to *Little Red Riding Hood* or *Ali Baba and the Forty Thieves*, offering hair-raising, bloodcurdling tales to make you race through the shadows on the dimly lit stairs to a cold, dark bedroom and leap into bed before a hand – usually Vincent's – could grab your ankle through the banisters and you succumbed to a restless night of haunted images. It all made us even more anxious to read, hear or discuss the macabre details or revel in the skill of the prosecuting counsel in bringing such evil-doers to justice, with the judge finally donning his black cap to utter the fearful words, '. . . to be taken to a lawful place of execution, there to be hanged by the neck until you are dead'.

As the war ended and the BBC began to develop new, peacetime programmes to replace the frequent wartime news bulletins by Bruce Belfrage, Frank Phillips and Alvar Liddell, the political broadcasts of doom, gloom and disaster, or the patriotically inspired music programmes to encourage increased factory productivity, such as *Workers' Playtime*, a convergence began among our widening literary tastes, my own school English literature syllabus and some of the new Light Programme's output. Soon we as a family were committed listeners to the weekly episodes of Francis Durbridge's *Paul Temple*, with its familiar signature tune of 'Coronation Scot', to Conan Doyle's *The Lost World* and the blustering Professor Challenger, or to more intellectually stretching excursions such as Dylan Thomas's *Under Milk Wood*. These were leavened by the equally enjoyable weekly episodes of *Take it from here* with Jimmy Edwards, Dick Bentley and June Whitfield, a natural successor in appeal if not in style to Tommy Handley's 'I.T.M.A.' Theoretically homework had to be finished before we were allowed to put aside pen and paper to listen to these broadcasts, usually between 8 and 9p.m., but since Ma was a committed listener supervisory rigour often lapsed temporarily.

There were increasing links between the cinema and literature, which accelerated the extension of my reading to more grown-up themes. At home we had all enjoyed Robert Donat's performance as Richard Hannay in *The Thirty-nine Steps* and since we had read, even in our last year at junior school, some of John Buchan's other novels such as *Greenmantle* and *Prester John*, none of these stories presented insurmountable intellectual problems. However, having been gripped by Walter Pidgeon's performance in the film *Manhunt*, I required a lot of help to fully appreciate Geoffrey Household's original book *Rogue Male* on which that film was based.

It was a combination of cinemagoing and Vincent's pioneering reading that led us all to become Graham Greene fans; but it was Ma's desire to merge the spoken word of the wireless with our rapidly increasing vocabularies that motivated her to create a new, more appropriately advanced game for all of us, and her in particular, to enjoy. It was perfect for us, requiring nothing more than that which we already possessed – a plain, green-painted wooden bench seat, always referred to as 'the form', with the only other essential ingredients being our own imaginations and developing verbal fluency. The rules were simple and seemingly incontestable. Each one of us was obliged to stand on the form and speak for two minutes on a subject given by one of the others. Heckling was allowed, particularly if the speaker hesitated unduly, a tactic quickly and unsurprisingly adopted by Rex, and we were allowed to shout corrections of fact at the speaker also. Ma used to keep time as well as adjudicate and generally maintain a semblance of order, while listening in rapt, smiling admiration at the verbal and mental skills exhibited by her brood. Her own simple literary tastes, to which we had been introduced through *Micky the Monkey*, also accommodated the mandatory weekly edition of the *News of the World*, but 'only for the fashion and spot-the-ball competitions' – or the romantic stories of Ethel M. Dell or Ruby M. Ayres, for both of which I was regularly sent to Boots the Chemists' Lending Library in spite of the fact that this was a fee-paying service. The reality that our knowledge and tastes had outstripped hers was a source of pride for her, as testified by her evident joy at the fierce way we competed in the last game she ever created for us.

29

BIRTH OF THE ANTI-HERO

Statistically Vincent, born in 1927, was in the middle of the surviving family, Roma the eldest having been born in 1919 and Sydney the youngest in 1935. He also charted the rise and fall of the height of the family, since he was the tallest. As a child he had some very different mannerisms and was the only one of us to have a stammer, very pronounced in his early childhood but which declined and eventually disappeared in later years, mirroring King George VI's progress. He was the first to have a serious accident: the incident with the mangle that nearly cost him the fingers of one hand. And this set a pattern for accident proneness, which he did his best to live up to for the rest of his childhood and adolescence.

My earliest recollections were that Vincent was more accessible than Roma or Alan, who were too old to be involved in many of our activities, except occasionally when playing collective parlour games at home. Vincent was always on the fringe of my activities initially, yet always seemed within reach whether he was reading, going to the pictures, creating or playing games. Sometimes the younger children were included, but if they weren't I often heard about, or saw, what he was doing. Unconsciously but inexorably he became a family trendsetter. If he talked about a book, from the age of seven I subsequently tried to read it, not always with success. If he went to the pictures without me, most often accompanied by Rex, and they talked about a film enthusiastically afterwards then I would try to go to see the same picture. If they played a game I wanted to understand it, even if I wasn't allowed to be part of it.

Since Alan had failed his scholarship examination, Vincent became the first of the boys to win a scholarship to the grammar school; with a combination of his two natural gifts, accident proneness and comic timing, his intended first day there coincided with the outbreak of the Second World War. Not only did war postpone his joining the grammar school until our return from Aspatria but also, since St Cuthbert's continued its evacuation for a short while longer than us, he was obliged as an interim measure to attend a girls' grammar school in a nunnery – Fenham Convent, which Roma had attended until 1935. Eccentric or at least unorthodox for some, it all seemed pretty normal for Vincent. In retrospect I believe his time in the convent was responsible for a latent urge to take a premature interest in girls. This was yet another first since Alan, who was three years older, had indicated no such tendency – at least not to Ma's knowledge; she would have policed it carefully but would never have encouraged such an interest. Curiously, Pop had openly assumed the role of guardian of Roma's morals and future, while it was Ma who zealously oversaw all the boys' developing relationships with the opposite sex.

However, after Easter 1941 St Cuthbert's eventually returned from its self-imposed exile in Cockermouth, Cumberland – not far from Aspatria where we had been sent as primary-school children – thus enabling Vincent to join them after his short and undoubtedly pleasant interlude at Fenham Convent. He progressed well and his interest in and knowledge of literature expanded enormously. His mathematics probably held him back but not seriously, although he was now studying at a level where no one in the family could help him.

It was in the academically crucial years when he was in Forms IV and V that Ma became seriously ill and Vincent, with his self-sacrificing readiness to take on burdens, responded to the need by absenting himself from the grammar school on Mondays, to do the physically demanding weekly washing which Ma would have been incapable of doing. This involved using the Pattinson's washhouse, which in turn meant carrying paper, sticks and coal to provide a fire, clearing out the ashes from the fire's last use, carrying buckets of water from our scullery to next door via both backyards and the lane, before the principal activity of washing could begin. There would be several loads to be subjected to differing degrees of 'steeping' in cold water, boiling in the copper over the by-now-raging fire, soaking in 'dolly blue', rinsing, wringing and finally 'pegging out' if the weather permitted, or folding the wet clothes in a basket for drying indoors around the kitchen fire if it didn't. Vincent would then have to clear everything away, supervised by Ma when she was well enough, and frequently interrupted by the large, perspiring presence of the bare-armed Mrs Pattinson with her loud, cackling jokes and hefty blows to his arms to ensure he was taking a proper interest.

But there were other tasks most days, done in his school lunch hour: particularly the heavy shopping, often where long queuing was required.

None of this made him very popular within the class. It didn't contribute much to his examination results either, which were affected to a degree, but it did ensure Ma's survival. His declining results were noticed, of course, since in one term he finished thirtieth out of a class of thirty-one, whereas he had normally achieved a position in the top ten, with a high of fifth. His form master at the time, Mark Mulcahy, in discussing Vincent's regular absence with him – presumably to stifle any tendency to truancy – simply said 'If you have to do it, you have to do it.' While that wasn't the most sympathetic response possible, it probably would have been extremely difficult for the school in wartime to have offered an alternative to replace the lost teaching input and also it would have been virtually impossible for Vincent to have accepted it, given the time he needed to devote to his domestic chores. Because of the critical nature of their earnings to the household budget none of Pop, Roma or Alan could be called upon to deputise for Vincent; it was during this period that Roma was married, not without tears and misgivings on her part, and Alan joined the RAF.

Subsequently Vincent left St Cuthbert's at the end of the summer of 1944, having underperformed according to his potential but nevertheless achieving matriculation standard in the school-leaving certificate, while Rex was completing his second year there and I was about to start my first autumn term in September.

Perhaps Vincent's declining attendances were wrongly construed as a lack of interest in school, or perhaps it was the fact that we were still a nation very much at war; but more probably it was because of the lack of both earnings and expectation within the household that there was no suggestion of his staying on at St Cuthbert's as a sixth former to prepare for university. In any case Vincent knew, as did Ma and Pop, that when he left school in July 1944 he would be required to 'join up' as a conscript in November the following year, when he turned eighteen.

He left school on a Friday afternoon in July, and early on the following Monday morning presented himself at the Labour Exchange to seek work. There was, after all, no alternative. He had no income. The household could not support him in any activities, and he could no longer look upon the remainder of July and August as the school holidays.

While his principal interest had long lain in literature, as with most of the family, he had also demonstrated a keen interest in chemistry, probably as a by-product of his addiction to novels based on strange results from scientific experiments which went wrong or involved strange scientific methods to execute or to solve crimes. This interest was well known in the neighbourhood and as a result Vincent was given a mysterious Swedish gadget by Mr Saville, who lived near the corner shop. It was a large, polished, wooden box with electromagnets attached by wires to two brass tubes, designed to give a therapeutic electric shock to the person holding them when a handle which caused the electromagnets to revolve was turned vigorously. Vincent, quoting from H.G. Wells, Mary Shelley or Bram Stoker, would mutter some mumbo-jumbo and ask us to hold the handles, while another was asked to pray with a crucifix in hand ready to ward off any danger of a metamorphosis to a Frankenstein, Dracula or Mr Hyde. Less dramatically, but intriguingly, he created invisible ink by dissolving copper sulphate crystals in water; having written a cryptically sinister message invisibly, he would then assume the role of Sherlock Holmes to make a sepia-toned, handwritten message appear by passing the paper over a lighted candle or in front of the fire.

His early attempts at experimentation had been frequently frustrated by a lack of raw materials. In response he had borrowed from the Public Lending Library a large volume entitled *One Hundred Things a Boy Can Do*, which described a number of simple experiments aimed at stimulating boys' interests by using materials available in every household to achieve some exciting trials and results. Laudable though this was in attempting to provide the basic ingredients from household waste, without the need for pocket money, the book was not written in full knowledge of the consumption pattern or circumstances of the Cassidy household. Vincent, confronted with a number of extremely interesting experiments which he would have liked dearly to undertake, read with sinking heart of their various requirements: 'Take one of your father's empty cognac bottles' or his 'empty cigar box' – preferably the size that had originally held '50 Havana cigars' – to the final *coup de grâce*, 'Take a discarded champagne cork'. The pursuit of wider experimentation on a zero financial budget was abandoned, and it was back to the sixpenny chemistry set at Christmas with its precious test tubes, litmus papers and copper sulphate, leaving a suppressed longing – never fulfilled as a non-earning child – for the five-shilling chemistry set with a Bunsen burner, tripod stand and distillation flasks; or of course the ever-present hope that some gem would appear as a gift from someone, or affordably in some second-hand shop.

His interest in matters scientific must have had some effect on the Labour Exchange official who sent him to Richardson's Leather Works on

Scotswood Road. It was at the junction of Dunn Street and Crucible
Lane, the latter's name confirming that it was in the heavily
industrialised part of Newcastle: very unhygienic, very dangerous, very
run down and very close to the River Tyne. The leather works had been
founded by the eponymous Mr Richardson in 1780 and had been
pouring its pollutants in to the 'coaly' Tyne unceasingly ever since.

There was a vacancy created by the departure for National Service of
one of the scions of the family who had been styled Assistant Works
Chemist – no doubt a title assigned to him simply because he was a
member of the family rather than because of his duties, since the
organisation did not need an Assistant Works Chemist. The Works
Chemist, a late-middle-aged Jewish scientist, interviewed Vincent. There
was no discussion about pay and conditions, but neither was any
alternative offered by the Labour Exchange – or sought. Dr Goldman
offered Vincent the job; he accepted and started as required the following
morning at 8.30a.m. Dr Lionel Goldman had, like so many others,
escaped from persecution in Central Europe and even in 1944, when the
danger of a Nazi invasion had passed, was frequently given to displays of
extreme agitation if there was the slightest temporary setback in the
Allies' successful pursuit of the war. He took readily to Vincent, who was
a diligent, knowledgeable and extremely willing pupil and very happy in
his work. His title was Laboratory Assistant, however, rather than
Assistant Works Chemist: *Plus ça change . . .* , Vincent might have mused,
fresh from his French oral examination for his school certificate, as in his
lunch hour he trekked home up near-vertical streets to have some dinner
– or more often to ensure that if any shopping was required he would do
what could be done.

Perhaps it was because Vincent was unusually yet instinctively
decisive in this case, having taken the job even if it was the only one on
offer, that he was encouraged by Dr Goldman to continue his studies for
an intermediate B.Sc. It was consistent with his schoolboy experiments
and now his work, but at odds with his natural affinity for language and

literature. Yet he readily agreed to do a 'night school' course requiring four nights' attendance, Monday to Thursday each week, to study chemistry, physics, pure maths and applied maths, one subject per night, in the old Rutherford College. I found out some five years later that this was an old, decaying, Victorian building with stone floors, classrooms lit by gas lamps, old, battered, discarded school desks and no central heating. It didn't have Thomas Gradgrind as Principal, but in other respects it was pure Dickens.

Vincent's workload consisted of walking to work, working in the morning, walking back home and doing chores at lunchtime, walking back to work, working in the afternoon, walking home for tea, before walking to Rutherford College to study and then walking back home again. It was borne with the quiet, uncomplaining cheerfulness and self-deprecation that had now become Vincent's dominant characteristic as he made some important contributions to family life. First there was a fund of stories provided by his new colleagues and surroundings, in which Dr Goldman figured prominently. While we all enjoyed hearing his stories of mishaps, misdemeanours, miscreants and madness, no one enjoyed them more or laughed as much as Ma. She laughed until she cried and Vincent, with his new-found confidence, would tease her with increasingly risqué 'shop floor' language, previously forbidden at home. Second, he made a welcome financial contribution to the household, to everybody's immediate benefit; and third, he was allowed by Dr Goldman to bring home some chemicals to improve his home laboratory in the attic. This had a catalytic effect on the attic, which now began to be a centre of family interest, although not without its dangers from time to time. Our long-established habit of having a variety of pets at home led seamlessly to the notion of breeding mice in the laboratory as subjects for scientific experiments. However, Vincent, as any one of us could have predicted, was much too squeamish to subject them to dissection; the worst fate to befall them was being propelled out of the attic window attached to a home-made parachute, enabling them theoretically to float down from the rooftop to the backyard or lane, thereby testing the adequacy for the purpose of an old handkerchief tied with thread to a cardboard harness holding the mouse.

Happily that worked sometimes but not altogether to the mice's benefit, because not long after this particular experiment the key to the attic – which by then was locked to keep out unwanted people while experiments were in progress, or the ever-present cats at any time – was temporarily lost. It was two weeks before it was found, by which time the mice – or rather the sole surviving mouse – had resorted to cannibalism to survive. Without vivisection Vincent had his torn bodies, or what was left of them, for scientific research; they were promptly preserved in formaldehyde and bottled in glass jars to demonstrate the seriousness of his attic laboratory. He had unintentionally reared a suspiciously large, black mouse with a very long tail by his experiments, as he rationalised – an outcome that delighted him. Unfortunately 'Black Joe', as he was renamed, later 'did a Colditz' and having gnawed through cage and skirting boards escaped, never to be seen again.

More alarmingly, however, one day another experiment went wrong and the house had to be evacuated as a large, rolling cloud of green chlorine gas descended the stairs from the attic and, like some malevolent spirit, flowed more or less past the bedrooms and down further flights of stairs to the hallway. Vincent, having donned his gas mask, told us with great clarity of thought – if in muffled tones from behind his steamed-up, protective, government-issue gas mask – that its descent was due to the fact it was heavier than air. This incident did nothing to encourage us about the safety of his work or the wisdom of receiving a wider range of chemicals from the good Dr Goldman: but Ma only laughed till she cried and that was that.

In the late autumn of 1945, when I was approaching the end-of-term exams at St Cuthbert's with much greater confidence than I had the year before, Vincent departed for his National Service. He had been served with his call-up papers earlier in the year, had undergone an initial medical examination in Newcastle and was required to travel to Richmond Barracks in Richmond, Yorkshire to undergo his initial training – twelve weeks of 'square bashing'. It was an awful morning. Vincent appeared extremely nervous, although he claimed he wasn't, and Ma was distraught, as well she might have been. Vincent was not only a source of major support in his selfless, uncomplaining way but he had also blossomed into a natural raconteur, fed with endless new raw material from his unsuspecting colleagues, while the eccentric Dr Goldman provided a useful opportunity for lampooning – all of which had the effect of keeping the younger children in good humour and my mother in semi-permanent paroxysms of laughter. This had stimulated and been a major factor, along with the mysterious 'M & B' tablets she had been prescribed, in Ma's miraculous recovery to reasonably stable good health.

Since the war was now over the dangers of active service were clearly much reduced, although there were still highly dangerous areas of the globe to which he might be sent. Yet in these circumstances the gloom that accompanied his departure was in marked contrast to the heroic way in which Alan had marched off to face real danger almost three years earlier.

Vincent's brief home leave at the end of the 'square bashing' and before his next posting was due to a combination of the obvious and the ridiculous. The obvious was that he had been identified from the intake as someone of 'above-average intelligence' and the ridiculous was that he was classed as a 'young man of good physique' – which meant he was earmarked for officer training and was to report to an OCTU (Officer Cadet Training Unit) at Buller Barracks in Aldershot. The second parting was again difficult, but with at least a hint of optimism due to the fact that he had survived his first twelve weeks without any catastrophic mishap. It was with a mixture of mild disappointment, overtaken by relief, that Ma and Pop found out a few weeks later that Vincent had failed his WOSB (War Office Selection Board). Once again had we, the younger children, known what was involved in the selection process we could have predicted the outcome with some certainty, after our experiences with Vincent in Aspatria.

In brief it was the cumulative evidence of three incidents which had rendered his promotion to commissioned officer improbable, to say the least. Early doubts must have registered on the first leg of the assault course, where budding officers were required to undertake a series of strenuous physical tests and to demonstrate their ability to lead a subordinate group over the most hazardous parts of the course. An early hazard entailed scaling a 15-foot-high wall and required the leader to create a pyramid of subordinates over which he could climb to the top of the wall; given his familiarity with hazardous, high, broken-glass-topped walls in the back lane, this should have been easy. Having reached the top, his task was to lean down, locking his body around the top of the wall, and help to haul up the others. Vincent successfully reached the top of the wall but was immediately assailed by an attack of vertigo, which could only be relieved by his lying flat on the wall and asking the others to make their own way, unaided by him, to the top before building a pyramid on the other side to help him down to the ground – precisely what he would have done had he been faced with a similar situation in the back lane. The final result, while satisfactory, was not thought consistent with inspirational leadership. However, that in itself was not a terminal blow, as the War Office Selection Board believed that he could acquire, by coaching, some elements of physical bravery.

The second test of significance was an orienteering exercise in which the aspirants were initially blindfolded before being individually dumped in the countryside at night, armed only with a map and a compass, to find their way back to the camp several miles away as quickly as possible. Their chosen route, the means that they used to complete it and the time they took were all important elements in the assessment. In the early hours of the following morning when Vincent was well on his way back to camp, having successfully overcome some

difficult hazards for an urban dweller, he was spotted by an elderly lady
in a nearby village who, observing him trudging rather disconsolately
back to camp, felt very sorry for the lonely, tired and hungry young
soldier. All were true, of course, but she probably hadn't gathered that he
was also on an important, promotion-determining exercise, and he didn't
tell her. She approached Vincent, who in his usual polite way listened
while she asked him whether he was tired – to which he truthfully
answered 'Yes.' She then told him that he looked very much like her
'own dear son', who currently was also serving 'in the army somewhere
overseas', and she wondered whether he would like to come back home
with her to have a cup of tea to refresh himself. No doubt he felt to do
anything other than accept would be uncharitable and ungrateful, and so
he accompanied her. He soon realised that, in addition to the attractive
and comfortable interior of the cottage, it had a substantial library with
piles of books lying about which gave him an hour of rare pleasure. Even
better, he came away some time later with a pile of *Lilliput* magazines.
Lilliput was very popular, not only because it had a wealth of well-
written articles, but as I discovered much later it also included in every
weekly edition a tasteful, black-and-white photograph of a nude female.
Buoyed by this physical refreshment, and with the prospect of
intellectual stimulation from the pile of *Lilliput* magazines, Vincent was
in a reasonably chipper state as he walked briskly through the camp
gates. He was immediately set upon by the sergeant major in charge of
the exercise, who with a carefully chosen selection of expletives from his
extensive vocabulary of obscene language, wanted to know where
Vincent had been. It seems reasonable to assume that he was less than
amused at the tale that Vincent poured out, but it was probably so
outrageously unmilitary that he may well have thought it wasn't entirely
true either.

Regrettably the third incident sealed Vincent's fate, since it involved
the same sergeant major. Ma, ever conscious of her absent serving son,
had decided to make some home-made toffee which she believed

Vincent would love, particularly since it was prepared with the then rarity of desiccated coconut sprinkled liberally on top. It was firmly wrapped in reused brown paper, with a brief, handwritten letter enclosed, and the small package was posted to Vincent at Buller Barracks. During the day Vincent was told there was a parcel for him, which he had to collect at the barracks post office. Pleased and intrigued about the possible contents, as he entered the regimental post office he saw a parcel on the counter which, without any further thought, he assumed was his. The fact that it was an extremely large parcel might have given him a clue, but it didn't. He quickly became deeply engrossed in the unwrapping process, tearing at the paper with a rare ferocity, to reveal a massive Harrods hamper. He could hardly believe his eyes. Had Ma won the *News of the World* fashion competition at last? While the lance-corporal on duty was sorting other packages for collection, the sergeant major who had interviewed Vincent on his return from the failed orienteering exercise came in. He immediately barked, 'What the bloody hell do you think you're doing, lad?' and prodded Vincent very sharply in the chest with his parade-ground stick. Meanwhile, the lance-corporal returned with a number of parcels, including the miniscule packet for Vincent. This was followed by a bizarre, heated conversation among the three parties in which the sergeant major initially accused Vincent of trying to pilfer from the major's parcel, and then attacked the lance-corporal for giving Vincent the wrong package. Vincent, rediscovering his stammer, waited for the storm to subside. He made some extremely unhelpful interjections in an attempt to explain that having been told there was a parcel he had assumed, since the major's Harrods hamper was the only package on view, that it must be his. It was all too much for the sergeant major.

Not long afterwards Vincent was interviewed by the Board and told that he had failed the course and that he would now be sent to a technical unit to learn touch typing, since his intellectual standards suggested that with this additional skill he would make a suitable administrative officer somewhere. However, his attendance at the OCTU meant that as compensation he was awarded two stripes to become a full corporal, which seemed to be appropriate in more ways than one. After all, it left the real warrior and elder brother with an active war record – Alan – as a flight sergeant, and Vincent with the junior rank of corporal.

Their two paths were to cross shortly, however, in a most unexpected way, but not before they had each had a leave at home in preparation for a move overseas. To where they were being sent was never made clear. They didn't know themselves, since all they were told was that they were being posted overseas to a warmer climate and more appropriate kit had been issued. As the war was over, Ma was confident that Alan was now out of immediate danger and reassured by the fact that Vincent, having failed his leadership test, was going to be in a less exposed position than if he had been promoted. Pop, who took male parental pride in being seen in public with his uniformed eldest son and his Australian aircrew, was no doubt disappointed that in Vincent he wouldn't now have a son with an officer's uniform, complete with Sam Browne belt, swagger stick and holster. Reflecting their different personalities, Alan's tales at home were of danger and heroics, while Vincent's were in the usual self-deprecatory tone emphasising human frailties, not least of which were his own. What neither we nor they knew at the time was that Alan was headed for Khartoum via Cairo, and Vincent for Tel El Kebir. After separate, happy homecomings, brief festivities and quietly sad departures, they were both gone again.

Alan was shipped by sea with some other crew members and support staff complete with Lancaster bomber spare parts, and Vincent set off through France by train. Some days later, having disembarked temporarily in Toulon, Vincent was walking along a street in the small town of Hyère when he saw a young man in Royal Air Force uniform with an unmistakable figure coming towards him. It was Alan. The two had not met for over a year and neither had the slightest indication that the other was abroad, let alone in the same small, provincial French town. Typically both were making for a public toilet and even more typically Alan's first enquiry was to see whether Vincent could either accompany him to a café for a drink, or if not lend him some money so he could have a beer. As Vincent had thought when he went to Richardson's for a job, *Plus ça change. . . .*

But this happy coincidence was the harbinger of better things to come, from which Vincent was to develop many of his emerging eccentricities.

30

AN UNPROMISING PEACE

Although the end of the war came suddenly it did not happen unexpectedly: indeed, in many respects it was something of an anticlimax. After all, the Allied forces had made continuous progress on all fronts since winning the pivotal battles of El Alamein in the Western Desert and Stalingrad in the East, and retaking the Philippines in the Pacific. The D-Day breach of Germany's Atlantic Wall had been followed by steady, sometimes excitingly rapid advances that mirrored the Eastern Front in only rarely encountering sustained German counterattacks to recover lost ground. Russian dominance in the East, America's in the Pacific and that of the Allies in Western Europe simply confirmed that ultimate victory was inevitable; it was a matter of when, not if, although Germany's last throw of the dice in Europe was to launch the V1 and V2 doodlebugs and rockets – an unpleasant, and for many deadly, reminder that 'It wasn't all over yet.'

On Tyneside air raids were now sporadic, although one of the more bizarre attacks was by a lone German bomber that had somehow penetrated home defences by flying at very low altitude in an attempt to attack warships on the Tyne. I and three or four other boys were playing 'guessy in the window' outside the corner shop when we heard and saw an aeroplane with Luftwaffe markings climb near vertically before rolling and dive-bombing some target out of our sight on the Tyne. The unmistakable reverberating 'CRUMP' of the bomb exploding made us stop and stare again at the sky where we had last seen the aircraft. There was now only a cloud of dark smoke slowly rising until suddenly the same aeroplane, now head-on to us and flying just above or between the houses, breasted the bank of the Tyne with machine guns blazing. We scattered and stupidly ran up Elswick Row, remaining in the line of fire, which spat noisily as it kicked up the tarmac road surface; and then suddenly the plane had gone, roaring just above rooftop level as it made for the coast and safety. Its mission had been a failure because it missed its naval target and managed only to interrupt our bread supplies; the bombs had hit Spillers flour mill on the south bank of the Tyne. Tempting though it was to think that the Luftwaffe had focused on us as their secondary target, we realised that they were probably only lightening their load as quickly as possible to achieve a swift, safe return to base. Dramatic as it was, it was made more so by its rarity late in the war, whereas in 1941 and 1942 serious air raids had been a regular occurrence – as had been our collections of jagged lumps of shrapnel, some still too hot to handle, shellcases or incendiary bomb fins after such raids.

There was, of course, widespread relief and joy when 'Victory in Europe' was confirmed; it was followed by a brief period of intense, reckless partying by adults in which we joined by creating and lighting bonfires.

But the voice of reason – or was it Mr Churchill? – brought everyone down to earth on 8 May by reminding us that the war wouldn't be over until Japan had also been forced to accept 'unconditional surrender'. 'We may allow ourselves a brief period of rejoicing, but let us not forget for a moment the toils and efforts which lie ahead.'

'Japan with all her treachery and greed remains unsubdued.'

'We must now devote all our strength, our resources to the completion of our task.'

To my consternation, sorrow and confusion we became aware that even before that was achieved there would be a General Election, because in these joyous moments of victory we had to prepare for peace, which meant the Great Man submitting himself to the will of the electorate. What a scandal, I thought: what ingratitude. I was reasonably well informed about current events because of my newspaper delivery round, my general reading and by my increasingly serious study of modern history at the grammar school: so that when I read on a poster outside St James' Hall, the boxing and wrestling arena opposite the Gallowgate end of St James' Park football ground, that the prime minister would be holding an election meeting, I determined to attend. The hall was filled with workers who outnumbered the 'toffs' present by at least ten to one, with the former easily identified by their cloth caps and silk mufflers. The Great Man looked magnificent in his pinstripe suit, trademark polka-dot bow tie and gold-watch-chain-bedecked waistcoat, his thumbs constantly finding rest in his waistcoat pockets between his bouts of debate with a hostile, though respectful, heckling audience.

'Why', I asked Pop afterwards, 'why do they dislike him so much? He's brave and tough and he's our prime minister. He has beaten Hitler, as he said he would. Is he going to lose his job?'

Pop smiled indulgently. 'Well, he doesn't get everything right, you know. There was the Dardanelles, the Sydney Street siege – fancy using machine guns here in London – and the way he behaved during the General Strike.'

'But that's not a good enough reason,' I protested.

'Perhaps they know he's a good war leader but shouldn't be trusted in peacetime.'

'Do you think that?' I demanded.

Pop looked at me gravely and said slowly, 'Yes son, I'm afraid I do.'

And in a landslide vote on polling day, 5 July, the Labour Party came to power and Mr Atlee, the cartoonists' 'Uncle Clem', became prime minister on 26 July. He, not Mr Churchill, would prosecute the rest of the war. Within weeks the first atom bombs were dropped on Hiroshima and Nagasaki, Japan surrendered and at least nominally the world was at peace again, just as it had been when we were at Cullercoats 'before the war'.

As the end of that year approached everyone talked about the men away at war being demobbed and returning home; of the end of food and clothes rationing; of the rebuilding of bomb-damaged and old houses; of the end of air raids, the blackout and queues; of seaside holidays to come; of plentiful beer and cigarettes; and of the prospects for promotion to the First Division for Newcastle United. Many who read more widely, like Pop, also talked incessantly about the Beveridge report, pensions for all, the prospects for free health care, free education for all, decent housing and the other changes that had been promised 'after the war'.

But for me there was more sadness than joy, and it increased over the next year. The newspapers I delivered weren't as compelling, heroics were no longer splashed across front pages, and there wasn't the excitement of bombing raids, of crashing anti-aircraft guns and smoking shrapnel showering the street.

What was going to replace thrills such as the night Vincent, who was a firewatcher on a school roof, urged me to help him pour sand on a spluttering incendiary bomb to extinguish it, or Pop's allowing – even encouraging – us to watch an aerial dogfight in the night sky over the Tyne? Now the sightings of camouflaged tanks rumbling down the West Road were few and far between, and even the distinctive, throaty engine noise of Spitfires and Hurricanes from RAF bases at Ouston and Bulmer had almost ceased. Uniformed servicemen were being replaced gradually by neighbours returning in ill-fitting 'demob' suits and, contrary to expectations, rationing continued, shortages got worse and queues much longer.

Still 1945 had its moments. In April Alan had married May, a tiny, pretty, doll-like girl with a soft smile and gentle nature who finally completed Alan's transformation from problem child to paragon of virtue. They married quietly at St Mary's while Alan was on a brief leave and May, who was an orphan from a similarly poor background, moved in with us.

Ma, who was extremely wary both about visitors and predatory females near her sons, also fell under May's spell, like everyone else.

The football leagues and the FA Cup restarted in the late summer, after the Victory Tests between England and the Dominions, and at least this offered some promise of compensation in 1946.

School was going well; I was becoming used to being top of the form and I enjoyed the new Latin studies in Year 2 as well as being a member of the school choir, newly re-formed now that we had a relatively young choirmaster, Teddy Kelly, back from war service.

Ma was naturally distressed that Vincent was needed for army service, because our needs were greater than His Majesty's now that Hitler was dead and the war over; but I harboured just a glimmer of hope that Vincent would turn out to be yet another family hero.

Christmas 1945 was happy, although a shadow overhung it not only because of the by-now-familiar shortages of everything that you wanted but because these were made more acute by the absence of the three eldest children, all of whom had until recently, over varying periods, contributed to the household income. Yet it was their absence rather than the loss of their income that weighed so heavily. Roma was married, with a baby girl and another baby expected; Alan was preparing to transfer with his re-formed bomber squadron but without his Australian mates to the Far East; and Vincent was completing his initial training at Richmond. Of those still at home Rex was preparing for his school-certificate examinations in the summer, Sydney was about to sit his scholarship and, although we younger children didn't know it, May was pregnant.

I looked forward to my first live FA Cup competition, about which I'd only read, and to my first real Test Match series, England v. India (before Partition); together these events might just compensate for the loss of the war and its daily roller-coaster of victory and defeat. During the war everybody thought and talked in terms of three time periods, which infected every conversation: 'before the war', 'during the war' and 'after the war'. Nobody seemed to think of intermediate points in time and of course nobody questioned 'Which war?' Through war I had become familiar with the concepts of death and of temporary absence suddenly becoming permanent. I had seen the grief-stricken and been discomfited by the intensity of their pain and sense of loss. Since we had kept animals throughout my childhood I had been exposed gradually to the inevitability of death, with its pain and sense of helplessness after the loss of much-loved friends. We were also encouraged to grieve through the burial ceremony, even when this was as trivial as the chewed remains of a mouse buried in an old matchbox. There had of course been neighbourhood deaths, some in tragic circumstances, as well as those of relatives when Ma and Pop were visibly upset, although emotionally we children were hardly touched.

Nothing had, nothing probably could have, prepared me for the anguish which wrapped the house like a mourning shroud on 1 March 1946. May had not been very well for some time, although it was of course winter, the house was as usual cold and damp, the air outside was foggy and since we had to nurse our restricted supply of coal very carefully, the house never became really warm. She was still working and her pregnancy was straining her limited physical reserves. None of the concern that Ma and Pop felt was articulated, so I was surprised when Alan suddenly arrived home on 'compassionate leave' and the atmosphere became much more subdued than I had experienced when he was on leave before. Nevertheless I went to bed, after having completed my homework, to a very cold bed in a palpably sad household. When I was woken by Ma at six the following morning, 1 March, for my early-morning paper round I was very surprised to hear raised voices at that time of the day, and my pleasant surprise at finding the kitchen lights on and a warm room with the fire burning brightly was removed by the sight of Alan, still in his uniform, sitting close to the grate and sobbing relentlessly, with tears streaming down his cheeks and dripping from the fingers in which he held his head. Ma had a comforting arm round his shoulders, patting gently and saying repeatedly 'There, there', while he sobbed, '. . . she said I can't see you, but I know you're there; look after Ma . . .'; and then the voice choked and after a pause it was all repeated.

Without moving, Ma told me quietly to have some tea and bread and to hurry home after the newspaper delivery round was finished, because I would have to take a message to Roma before I went to school.

Hardly pausing, I was back in less than an hour to find Alan and Ma in the same positions. Her eyes were tired and tear-filled but her grip didn't falter and I was despatched, without a word, on my bike to Roma's house. When she opened the door to my knock she was visibly alarmed saying sharply, 'What are you doing here? What's wrong?' but I couldn't speak. I simply thrust into her hand the still-sealed tin of cigarettes that Alan had brought for Walter, together with Ma's note. She read it and immediately burst into tears. I still didn't know anything, but the accumulated suffering I had been surrounded by for the last twenty-four hours gathered me up and I too wept uncontrollably. I heard Roma explain through her own mist of tears to Walter that May had died during the night because latent TB had been unleashed through the stress of pregnancy, and the baby had been stillborn.

I was sent on my way, my misery matching the cold, damp day, my eyes still red and smarting; cycling at speed down Arthur's Hill towards home I positioned myself to turn right as I approached Campbell Street. I saw a bus approaching but I had a lorry not far behind me so I turned swiftly, overlooking the fact that the front wheel was in the now-unused tramlines. I was thrown violently off in front of the bus, which mercifully stopped within feet of me while the bike crashed, and the lorry careered past. Shaken, bruised and with my tears flowing again I retrieved my bike and escaped the wrath of the bus crew as fast as my legs could carry me and the damaged bicycle.

Alan was still sitting, a dejected, crumpled, lost soul. His heroic stature was gone, his beloved May was dead, his baby would never see the light of day; his war was over, his Australian colleagues had gone home and he was not yet twenty-two.

If this was the joy of peace, bring back the war.

31

SEX AND THE SCHOOLBOY

It was September 1946 and I was still thrilled by England's performance against India in my first summer of Test matches, during which a new hero, Alec Bedser, had emerged as a Test match star of the future with his 7 wickets for 49 in the first Test match at Lord's in June, followed by 7 for 52 in the second at Old Trafford in July. After the barren years of the war, and with my increasing love for cricket fuelled by the reading I had done about pre-war players and Test matches, I was obviously looking forward, almost obsessively, to the first postwar Ashes Test series in Australia in the winter. There had of course been a drawn Victory Test series against the Dominions in 1945, with three of the matches played at Lord's; each side had won two matches, with one match drawn. The series was more symbolic of victory in the war than it was indicative of a readiness to play Test cricket and the scorecards showed that most of the players on both sides were still active members of the armed services. Better still, I claimed a personal interest since many of the Australian players were serving as operational aircrew in Alan's bomber group. But the return to apparent normality led to my thinking about the great adventure that the lucky cricketers who had been chosen to tour Australia would enjoy when they landed in Fremantle later in September, after a month-long cruise. That, at least, for the first time since 1938 when the last Ashes Test series had been played in England, would be over high seas freed from the threat of U-boats. But with the drawn series in 1945, the crushing of India in 1946 and the fact that Hutton was set to continue where he had left off after his world record innings of 364 in 1938, there seemed to be grounds not only for optimism but for endless schoolboy dreaming of great sporting victories to come.

For my part, therefore, it was entirely innocently that I read out loud, as I had been instructed to do by Father Cassidy, a chapter in the book of essays which was part of our required reading during my third year at St Cuthbert's. From the beginning of that academic year through to my leaving St Cuthbert's in the summer of 1949 I knew every piece of required reading in the English literature syllabus almost by heart because, for whatever reason, Father Cassidy determined that these lessons should consist of me reading in preparation for the analysis and discussion in which the whole class participated later. Pride insists that he did so because I was unquestionably the best reader in the class, with an ability to phrase the spoken word better than the others, but reality suggests there was some other reason – perhaps, unworthy though it seems, that he believed that if I wasn't reading I would be paying less attention, to the disadvantage of the class as a whole. Whatever the truth, on this particular day I read very carefully a line which read, 'a woman whose breast no hand had touched except the hand of time'. Immediately those nearest to me, and some others, began to snigger; I had no idea why they were sniggering, but hearing suppressed schoolboy giggles is rather infectious and creates a difficult atmosphere to continue with serious reading.

Father Cassidy, who was not given to a lightness of touch anyway and whose closely shaven dark jowls, bald head, black academic gown and pince-nez lent him a particularly sinister appearance, said quietly yet threateningly – he never shouted – 'Silence.' But schoolboys, even in the presence of such a malevolent figure as Father Cassidy, are seldom quietened quite so easily. He marched up the aisle towards me, banged a cane upon my desk and hissed at me, 'What are you sniggering at, Cassidy?' I told him I wasn't, which of course wasn't true because I was, but then in truth I really didn't know why I was sniggering other than because everyone else in the class was suppressing giggles. He moved me then, from my preferred position towards the back of the class nearest to the window, to a seat in the front of the class immediately adjacent to the door and ordered me to continue.

Subsequently I could not rid myself of the puzzle as to why my schoolmates had laughed. Of course I asked them, which only made them laugh more. I then began painstakingly, over a period of some weeks, to wrestle with this issue and to try to form a pattern from previous events which had caused me to puzzle and which might provide me with clues. Yet however much I struggled, the words 'a woman whose breast no hand had touched except the hand of time' still made no sense.

From my infancy I had known that there was a difference between boys and girls, although I really found it difficult to understand what the difference was. The closest I ever got to understanding was through Roma's skill in determining the sex – not a word we used – of the regular output of kittens that our cats produced. She had a habit of holding the kitten by the fur at the base of the neck, quickly inverting the animal in one hand, parting its rear legs and peering, after which she would pronounce authoritatively 'That's a boy' or 'That's a girl.' Occasionally I was curious enough to follow this process closely, but could see absolutely no difference whatsoever. It was just another one of the skills that older people possessed, as Ma demonstrated frequently when she knew, as if by magic, when I had been lighting fires or smoking in the air-raid shelters. Roma had her own bedroom until she was married in 1943 and in spite of the lack of privacy on our bath nights, it was always arranged – although I never thought deeply about it – that she, and presumably Ma, bathed at a time when everyone else was excluded, meaning that there were no accidental revelations.

My new retrospection also reminded me of my puzzlement at terms used in preparing for our first confession, which had to precede the first Holy Communion. In this, following the by-now-familiar teachings of the catechism, I could recite most responses to the questions posed on

Christian doctrine, although I struggled with the meaning of some of the Ten Commandments or the Seven Capital Sins. With the retentive memory I had already developed I could recite these without difficulty, and that often gave adults the impression that I understood them equally as well. The sixth commandment, for example: 'Thou shalt not commit adultery', didn't seem to apply to me, since it went on to explain that it forbade 'all sins of impurity with another's wife or husband' – which superficially meant I really didn't have to worry about it. However, in the expansion of this I also learned that the sixth commandment 'forbids immodest songs, books or pictures because they are most dangerous to the soul and lead to mortal sin'. The Seven Capital Sins gave me a problem in that the third, lust, I found barely distinguishable from gluttony or covetousness, yet the factor in common with adultery seemed to be the sin of 'impure thoughts, words or deeds'. Despite this lack of real understanding I felt it was not unreasonable to include this in my catalogue of sins when I made my first confession and I therefore included the desire to be forgiven for impure thoughts, which I felt was a fair reflection of my desire on occasions to strangle Sydney when he disrupted a game we were playing.

Some years later, but long before the defining words of 'a woman whose breast no hand had touched . . .', I had the misfortune to go to confession in the cathedral when we had a visiting missionary. I disliked these missionary visits because they tended to preach fire and brimstone at great length, ensuring that Mass took longer than it would have done normally. But this was the first occasion when the avuncular Canon Wilkinson had given up his confessional to the visiting priest. As I trotted out my now-familiar catalogue he seized upon the impure thoughts and asked me whether I meant by that 'girls'. I didn't, and said so. He then asked 'Was it with others?', to which I again said 'No.' That enabled him to leap erroneously to an alternative conclusion, causing him to enquire 'Did you bring forth the seed?' This posed a serious puzzle. I had no idea whatsoever what he meant, and rack my memory as

I could I found no trace of gardening in the associated sins or sinful circumstances. He repeated the question again, more sharply, and both because I still had absolutely no idea what he was talking about and for the sake of good order, I said 'Yes.' Apart from a heavier penance than normal, that seemed to be that. I left with another minor puzzle, soon relegated and buried deep in my memory bank.

In my first term at St Cuthbert's I was leaving for home after morning lessons when a group of boys who sat near me and who took sandwiches to school for their dinner got out a copy of the *News of the World*, looked carefully around to ensure no one in authority was present, and proceeded to discuss some of the contents. The subject matter eluded me. I knew, however, that they were not studying the fashion competition, which Ma always insisted was the reason she took the newspaper, neither was it the 'Spot the Ball' competition. They had gone immediately to inside pages, whereas I knew from my delivery rounds that all sports reports were normally on the back page and if Harry Atwool, who was a talented footballer and captain of the school juniors, was going to look anywhere surely it would have been first at the back page. As I disappeared from the class I overheard terms such as 'a GI in a serious assault case accused of . . .', 'uncontrollable flesh . . .'.

And then there was the case of Marion Fitzgerald. Marion, the elder of two daughters, was probably somewhere between Rex and Vincent in age, and the Fitzgeralds' back door in Elswick Row had been directly opposite ours when we lived there. One Sunday we were playing 'double headers', requiring two teams of two to compete against each other. One partner headed the ball towards the other, who then had to either nod the ball back to the other partner, or attempt to score a goal by heading it into the chalk-marked goal, past the competing pair across the lane. They, as defenders, were allowed only to control the ball with head or body but not with the hand. It was played with a tennis ball and quickly made us extremely accurate and powerful headers of a ball – if at the cost of recurring headaches. During one of our exchanges in this post-Mass, pre-dinner session, the ball went off my head and over the Fitzgeralds' wall. The rules were clear: if the ball was 'lost' off your head, you had to retrieve the ball. Fitzgeralds' was known as a house where you could knock on the door and the ball would be handed back, whereas the Clarksons who lived next door would deliberately allow their small, bad-tempered dog out of the house to savage the ball and would ignore any request for it to be returned. It seemed clear, after an appropriate time spent banging on the Fitzgeralds' back door, that there was no one at home, and so with a little assistance I climbed to the top of the wall and was about to crawl along the top to drop into their yard when the door to the rear of the house opened and Marion ran out, completely naked, with a stream of long, ginger hair flowing behind her. She picked up the ball, threw it quickly over the wall and in turning to run back spotted me on top of the wall, smiled demurely, swiftly re-entered the house and closed the door. It was all somewhat unreal – rather like a more revealing version of one of Arthur Rackham's fairy paintings, with which I was quite familiar from books we had borrowed from the public library. Marion was different, but no more than that, and as I dropped back to the lane I didn't mention the matter to the other three – who in any case were disinterestedly chatting about football – and the game continued.

As I mulled over these previously unconnected incidents, which I knew intuitively had some connection with the now haunting words 'a woman whose breast no hand had touched except the hand of time', my confusion increased – as did my determination to solve the riddle. But how?

Several weeks later, on an impulse, I decided to share my problem with Bunter. He was slightly younger than me and he looked at me incredulously. He didn't laugh; he simply looked grave and said, 'A breast is the same as a tit. Have you never seen a tit?' Now to the best of my knowledge at that stage a tit was a bird – information I had only recently gleaned from John Peace, a talented artist although seriously dull in every other respect, who was in my form at the grammar school. In showing me some of his beautifully drawn wildlife studies he had shown me, inter alia, various tits. His watercolours and pen-and-ink sketches had been good enough to be displayed in a major London public gallery as a finalist in a national competition. This didn't prevent his father from threatening that if his exam results didn't improve, he would be withdrawn from the grammar school and 'be sent down the mines'.

At this explanation Bunter looked even more incredulous and I began to regret my pursuit of the elusive answer to my torment.

'Come with me,' he said and we walked down Elswick Row, along Elswick Road and up towards the back of one of the surviving houses in the decaying remnants of Elswick Street. He knocked on a back door, a woman wiping her hands on the customary crumpled pinny came to the door, and he asked her if Mary was at home. He was told 'Yes', to which he then asked 'Can I see her?' Mary, whom I hadn't met before, was tall and gawky with lank, dark hair over a long, pale, sad face; she came out into the cold, gloomy lane and closed the door. Bunter looked into her face and said, 'Denis has never seen a tit; would you show him?' She looked me up and down but didn't answer. She simply pulled up her sweater, rolled up her blouse underneath, cupped her breast in one hand and held it out for inspection.

Bunter said 'That's what they were talking about.'

I said 'Oh.'

Mary said 'Is that all?'

Bunter said 'Yes.'

Mary replaced her breast, adjusted her clothing, went back indoors and that explained that. But it didn't. I now knew the words, but I still could not understand why the other boys had laughed – yet it was quite clear from Bunter's dismissive incredulity that this was not an issue to be pursued any more at this stage.

And for a time I stopped puzzling about girls and related matters. I stopped questioning how one would know when one was 'offending holy purity by looks, words or actions' and I was seldom in danger of contravention by 'immodest songs, books and pictures'. I clearly understood the spiritual health warning the catechism gave that if you did indulge in such things 'they are most dangerous to the soul and lead to mortal sin', and I made a firm purpose of amendment to drop impure thoughts from my catalogue of sins. That is, until Jane Russell and *The Outlaw* began to hit the headlines.

I was a cinema addict, as I had been since the early war years and as most other people in wartime Britain were. The brake on my addiction was the cost, which even in the low-value, low-cost 'fleapits' we frequented still constrained indulgence of my passion. Occasionally major new movies appeared which for one reason or another you simply had to see, and it was useless waiting for these to appear at The Gem or the Gaiety; too long even to wait for them to find their way to the middle-order picture houses such as the Brighton or the Plaza. There was nothing for it but to beg or borrow money to go and see them. Vincent's pioneering in this field, as well as in books, had led us to adopting *Odd Man Out*, with James Mason, as one of our cult films, following earlier wartime favourites such as *Nine Men*. But this time the impetus to see it came from my friend Alan Thornton, not from the family.

There were two substantial barriers in the way of my going to see *The Outlaw*. The first was that I couldn't be admitted under the age of sixteen unless accompanied by an adult, and there was no chance of Ma or anyone else in the family taking me to see this film. The second was that while Alan Thornton could dress older than his years and, given his stature, pass as a sixteen-year-old, I had no such hopes. Nevertheless we decided to try, having worked out an elaborate ruse whereby Alan would get to the box office and with his bulky figure block the ticket window, so I could be seen only vaguely in the background, and he would buy the two tickets. It worked and in we went. It certainly wasn't the best cowboy film I had ever seen, and although I now knew what to call the heaving flesh that threatened constantly to escape from Jane Russell's low-cut blouse, I wasn't moved particularly by it. Neither was I excited, as appeared to be the case with certain people at the back of the cinema, by the sight of the heroine slipping naked into bed beside Billy the Kid, who had been seriously wounded, in an attempt to rid him of his fever. Yet nevertheless *The Outlaw* had a most profound impact on my sexual learning curve.

The film had caused such a sensation that the Vatican had been obliged to warn Catholics not to see it, because of the danger of spiritual corruption; but inevitably that simply made more people – not excluding Catholics – even more anxious to see it. *The Outlaw* was promoted by a racy poster campaign in which Jane Russell proudly displayed her principal assets, and the words that accompanied the pictures on the poster passed into everyday usage. 'Mean, moody, magnificent' was the description of Jane Russell and the story was about love and adventure. It was widely talked about by the boys in the class, most of whom had seen it and most of whom had derived rather greater pleasure from it than I did, but at least I didn't feel excluded, because I too could say I had seen it.

At this time we had a history master, Father Vincent MacLean, who looked the human embodiment of a caricature. He was a tall, shuffling, stooping and gentle man with a very warm smile but, oddly for a priest, he had a crewcut, GI-lookalike hairstyle which gave a strong impression that he had been frightened by a ghost, since the hair grew vertically from his head rather like the pile on coconut matting, or the grass on St James' Park football pitch before it was cut. This rather odd appearance was certainly not improved by his wearing of rather large, wire-rimmed glasses which gave him a vaguely owlish appearance. He was exceedingly bright, had clearly been a very successful history student; not only did he teach us European history but he produced his own history books which he duplicated on an old Gestetner machine. The covers were sheets of plain, coloured paper and these small books were stapled on the left side. I had never seen home-made books before.

No doubt in an attempt to show off my new-found knowledge to my classmates – certainly it was driven by exhibitionism, since the knowledge I possessed was less than I implied – I decorated the cover of my book with the words 'Father MacLean's History of England'. Inspired by John Peace's work I drew in the centre quite a good caricature of Father MacLean's outstanding features of owlish glasses, dog-collar and vertical hairstyle, surrounded by the words: 'mean, moody, magnificent, thrills, spills, love, adventure, Vincent MacLean's History of Europe, 1841 onwards'. I proudly but foolishly showed it to one or two members of the class who enjoyed the joke as did I until . . .

As Father MacLean entered the class a cry of 'Use Cassidy's copy' went up, in response to his request for a copy marked at the page we were currently up to in our studies. At the speed of light I removed the book and buried it in my desk. The gentle, smiling Father MacLean towered over me and asked politely for the book. 'I haven't got it.' 'He has,' the cry went up. The tussle went on for some time until I realised all was lost and I handed over the book. He looked at it, a great cloud came over his gentle face and he walked out of the classroom. A few minutes later he returned, asked for another copy and the lesson started. I breathed a sigh of relief, sadly prematurely. A few minutes later the headmaster, Monsignor Cunningham, opened the classroom door, beckoned me from my position immediately next to the door to come out and when I joined him said severely, 'Come with me.' This was a succession of events I had never even contemplated and after climbing the deeply carpeted stairs to a part of the priest's house I had never been in before, I entered his study – huge, warm, expensively decorated with oak panelling, a massive leather-topped desk, a library of books, some burgundy leather armchairs and a coal fire burning brightly in the hearth. He told me to stand in front of his desk. There, lying in front of me on top of the desk between us, was my customised history book, bearing the words and the caricature. He picked it up by one corner as if it was a disease-ridden corpse.

'Is this yours?' he asked.

'Yes, headmaster,' I almost whispered.

'Did you do this yourself?'

'Yes, headmaster.'

'Did you do this here in the school?'

'No, headmaster.'

'Then where did you do it?'

'I did it at home.'

'At home?' he thundered. 'Where were your parents?'

I thought quickly. 'They were out at the time.'

'Both of them?' he asked.

'Yes, headmaster.'

'Where were they?'

By now I was trapped in my own web. Ma hadn't been out; it seemed reasonable to offer that as protection for them, if not for me, but now I was lost, so I stumbled on.

'In the "Blue Man".'

'The "Blue Man"?' he almost shrieked. 'What is the "Blue Man"?'

'It's a pub, headmaster.'

It was an unwitting masterstroke on my part because the original subject of his anger – me – was now revealed to be only a poor, defenceless child whose uncaring parents had left him at home on his own while they disported themselves in unseemly enjoyment in a public house.

'You know you deserve a thrashing for this?' he said, picking up a cane and banging it on the desk too convincingly for comfort.

My heart sank, but stoically I replied, 'Yes, I do.' I had already discovered that when the game was lost it was far better to agree with the holder of power than to disagree.

'Before I burn this filth, tell me – do you associate with girls?'

'No, headmaster.'

'Do you have impure thoughts about girls?'

'No, headmaster,' I replied, absolutely truthfully, while withholding my recently acquired knowledge that girls had breasts and that tits were the same things.

'Then why do you use language of the gutter like this?'

Now I could see the connection. Now my mind went back to 'whose breast no hand had touched'. Now, at last, I saw the connections among all those previous events – Vincent's *Lilliput* pictures and *The Outlaw*.

'I just saw them on a cinema poster,' I said, more or less truthfully.

'I want no more of this,' he said, casting Father MacLean's *History of Europe* into everlasting fire, 'and I shall write to your parents about it.'

To the best of my knowledge he never did write to my parents, although I suspect he had a long talk with my unfortunate brother-in-law in the staff common room, and I have little doubt that Walter would have been discomfited. I did, however, feel obliged to pass on some of the story – leaving out any reference to my newly found knowledge of impure thoughts – to my parents, who somehow managed to contain their mirth. I was ultimately let off with a caution never to do anything as silly again, but in addition to remember Monsignor Cunningham's words and to have nothing to do with girls.

By then the England team was preparing for a visit from the Australians after the glorious summer of 1947, in which the record-breaking feats of Denis Compton and Bill Edrich had contributed to a resurgence of optimism. In more than a cricketing sense that summer compensated for the awful fuel and food shortages in one of the coldest-ever winters. Hopes were high and for the moment, girls and sins of the flesh were forgotten.

32

HAVELOCK RANGERS

Gradually but inexorably the pull towards devoting all of our free time to just two games, football and cricket, continued: a process encouraged at school, in the back lane and indoors at home, as well as shared by our school friends, back-lane pals and brothers; only Roma, who didn't live with us any more anyway, was untouched by this shift.

The passion and excitement of watching Newcastle United had been stimulated by the resurgent team's postwar reputation for fast, skilful, attacking football spearheaded by 'Wor Jackie', as Milburn was affectionately known. Although a major trophy continued to prove elusive, it was the thrilling quality of their play which had us all packing the old St James' Park stadium irrespective of opposition or weather.

Since our earliest days we had played our own committed brand of football in the back lane, before graduating to games on the moor and then to more formal and competitive matches at school. Indoors we had progressed through the soggy papier-mâché pipes of blow football to a seriously competitive 'league' of Subbuteo games, after a predictable redrawing of the rules to suit our collective mental agility and Rex's ability to exploit ingeniously any loophole in them. Inevitably the principal casualties in all of this were the other childhood games we now abandoned almost without trace, and since Ma had always been a player in these, she too was in danger of being made redundant as a competitor – although still in regular, if less frequent, demand as the supreme authority to whom irreconcilable differences could be referred.

That also explained how she came to develop, at about the same time, the public debating game she had created and managed with such enthusiasm.

Yet there was still a major gap in our gamut of football activities that was glaringly obvious at weekends, particularly on the ones when we didn't, or couldn't afford to, watch a game at either St James' or Redheugh Park; the latter was where Gateshead played their own brand of violently robust football, usually on a muddy pitch on murky winter afternoons. We were too young to be Sunday pub players except on an impromptu basis, and then it was our ball rather than us that was required, while school matches or youth-club games – we weren't club members anyway – were played only on Saturday mornings or afternoons, That left Saturday evenings in autumn and spring, together with Sundays throughout the year, determinedly without any formal, competitive games.

The imperative to correct this came from Rex who, having left the grammar school and taken paid employment, invested his accumulated cash reserves in the acquisition of a new, size 5, brown-leather Webber football, 'as used in FA Cup Finals and International matches'; this he displayed proudly once he had inflated the inner case and carefully inserted and tightened the thick leather lace. It had cost him 'a small fortune', amply repaid by the admiring, occasionally envious examinations he allowed others to indulge in. They would squeeze the ball to ensure it was inflated to regulation pressure, hold it as if to 'throw in', or hug it goalkeeper-like to their chest, but no one was allowed to bounce the precious ball on the pavement, even though we had no grass available for the purpose. 'This ball,' declared Rex with great solemnity, 'marks a new beginning; we shall have our own football team' – a vision enthusiastically adopted by all of us, except Vincent, of course, who although a devotee of the indoor, table-top variety studiously avoided watching or playing the game while in pursuit of his principal outdoor leisure target – girls.

We had soon enlisted all our regular neighbourhood companions, although that created a need to invite some other, more peripheral acquaintances to join in. We were obliged to relax our selection criteria to take much more account of 'availability' than we did of 'skill' or 'positional balance', and while we were doing that there were other tricky decisions to take: what to call this thrustingly ambitious team, who would manage and captain it, what would its colours be and where would we play our home games?

Since it was Rex's ball there was no serious objection to his being a goalkeeping captain, as he had already followed Alan in demonstrating skill, agility and fearless courage in this position. Both had been encouraged by the example of Tommy Dawson, the Gateshead FC goalkeeper who had on more than one occasion lost his cap to the flailing boot of an opposing centre forward as he dived at onrushing feet. Neither was there any question over the automatic inclusion of Teddy Birkett as left winger, nor of Sidney Dansky, a rampaging left half with a kick like a mule in either foot. Bunter's one good eye and Jackie McHenry's one good leg were deemed more than adequately compensated for by their enthusiasm and energy; Sydney's and Josie Leahy's lack of inches and years made selection of both marginal; I, as the newly appointed match reporter, was another automatic selection. Rosie was yet another talented certainty, while Jamie Langley would have been had he been a friend as distinct from just a neighbour, his relegation being due to an unreliable temperament. But 'Beggars can't be choosers', as Ma would regularly remind us, and with the addition of Reggie Wood, who possessed great speed and strength with his ability to get to the byeline before pulling back fast, head-high crosses, we took to the field as 'Havelock Rangers', in a harlequinade of coloured strips, against a more regularly playing neighbouring street side.

It was neither the most successful nor encouraging effort, in spite of some top-flight performances. Rex made a string of good saves, as well as keeping out two penalties; Sidney Dansky kept a powerful grip on the opposition forwards, although inevitably at the expense of not supporting his own; while Reggie Wood scored a brilliant goal and made one for me with a fast cross, which I converted with a flying header at the cost of a severely grazed forehead. Surprisingly Teddy Birkett had a poor game, if only because his stamina didn't match his ball skills; the opposition scored two of their four goals while he was off the field, squatting near the touchline smoking a cigarette to recover his wind. Both Sydney and Josie were overwhelmed by the physical strength of the much older opponents, while Jackie McHenry's hop-skipping action had bogged him down on a muddy pitch and Jamie Langley's suspect temperament had resulted in a disinterestedly lightweight contribution. We needed to recruit more players with greater weight, skill and guts, as well as to remedy our inability to recognise our own side, preferably by reducing our rainbow-like collection of different coloured strips. In the meantime I knuckled down to the improbable task of writing, and typesetting on my John Bull Printing outfit, a match report honest enough to be recognisable, stimulating enough to motivate those available for selection, yet short enough to enable it to be produced at all, given the limitations of the three-and-sixpenny printing set.

Our next-door neighbour produced a partial solution to both problems. Raymond was in our target age range, being between Rex and me, but was not one of our friends – partly because he had fallen short of Ma's strictly applied code of honesty. After legitimately selling us a bottle of his unused, free school milk at a heavily discounted price, he adopted the practice of watering it down before decanting it into a number of used bottles, thereby increasing his income. The scam was not difficult to detect and these transactions were immediately terminated diplomatically, without any anger or rancour, so as to retain our much-valued privilege of using the Pattinson's washhouse facilities for the weekly task without recourse to the public facilities in Snow Street. But since desperate need requires an extreme solution Raymond, having become aware of our recruitment programme, offered not only his own services – not so highly prized as to override our reservations – but also those of a nearby cousin, Billy Bennet, who was an accomplished and robust footballer. He was also aware that we had decided to appear in shirts of a common colour, even if we couldn't afford proper football shirts, and in a hasty moment had announced that colour would be white, for which we would prepare hand-painted, black team numbers on sheets of white parchment to be stitched onto the shirts. Since Billy Bennet worked in a small textile factory and immediately offered to sew each number onto the appropriate shirt, the deal was clinched, and with that renewed optimism endemic in watching or playing football, we began to make preparations for our next match, which was soon arranged. In spite of our careful planning half the team, of which I was one, turned up for the match without a numbered shirt because the shirt was also needed for school and was unavailable for pre-numbering. Our new recruit shamed us all by appearing in an old, worn, off-white vest which had both seen better days and been cleaner, if not whiter, in those days; while those team members who appeared properly dressed were soon sorry they had done so since it began to rain steadily soon after kick-off, causing the black numbers to 'run' and inflict permanent ink stains on good white shirts. That the numbers soon became sodden with rain, which with the added assistance of rugged, clutching tackles and a number of falls made us all numberless by the end of a bruising game – which we again lost – seemed irrelevant as the final whistle blew. We knew we had yet more problems to solve: how to 'level the playing field' by recruiting our own referee to officiate in these games, as well as how to explain to exasperated mothers how a stitched strip of parchment appeared suddenly on an ink-stained white shirt.

More hard work, more thinking, some tough decisions – including sacking Billy for appearing in such a dirty, inappropriate garment – all followed. Eventually the hard work succeeded, with powerful assistance from our own referee, and we won our next match 4–2 in another hard-fought game on an undulating pitch at Blakelaw, on a gusty, sunny evening and in front of a sizeable partisan crowd. We were on our way, thanks to Rex's Webber football, and my match report was fulsome in praise of our stars Birkett, Wood, Dansky and 'our brave custodian' Rex; that popular phrase was borrowed from the *Football Final*, as the John Bull Printing Outfit worked overtime.

By now cricket also was firmly established in our sporting calendar; we lacked a Subbuteo equivalent, although we had regularly played a pocket version known as 'Howzat' which comprised two metal dice. One of them gave a value to runs scored, while the other determined the outcome of a 'Howzat' appeal, and both were contained in a small, tin box exactly the size of the old pre-war gramophone needle box. While this satisfied the statistical element in the fanatical cricket-watcher's make-up, it lacked realism, more particularly any element of skill, and so 'Howzat' was doomed to remain an occasional distraction for those rainy days in the cricket season when the scheduled wireless broadcast was substituted by Elton Hayes strumming his guitar while singing 'The owl and the pussycat went to sea in a beautiful pea-green boat . . .'

That was the situation until one Christmas Day when, in an inspirational, Archimedes-like moment, we created the game we had been seeking as a heated discussion was taking place about the relative merits of a number of leading Test cricketers. In pursuit of the argument an old table-tennis ball was produced to illustrate spin, Pop's much-admired, tortoiseshell–backed, long-handled clothes brush was similarly used to demonstrate scoring shots; and before long the thoughtful, if partisan, debate had been succeeded by a seriously competitive, miniature game of cricket, with our draughts board propped against the sideboard as the wicket. The active players – batsman and bowler – were required to kneel, an activity which itself demanded trousers be rolled to the knee to avoid damage, and although the lack of space in the parlour ruled out catching fieldsmen, we soon ordained that armchairs and table tops could be designated as fielders. Bowling which began as a gentle spin generated by rotating the ball swiftly between the bowler's palms soon progressed to a powerful, underarm delivery with a ping-pong ball seamed with Elastoplast, leaving the prostrate bowler flat on his face from his 'run up' and the batsman ducking out of the way of a head-high bouncer. There were two inevitable consequences. The first was that a hook by a ducking batsman smashed the reinforced ball into Ma's only precious ornament, a statue of a pink-gowned Victorian lady covering a ceramic base full of scented potpourri, shattering it to provoke Ma's only really serious display of anger and distress I ever saw. The second swiftly followed: banishment to the attic.

The second mishap turned out to be a happier occurrence than its cause, since it led to the rapid development of the newest, most physical and exciting game we had ever created, with the semi-plagiarised title of 'Atticeo'. The attic had previously been monopolised by Vincent and Rex, first for quasi-scientific purposes, and then for a complicated, chess-like war game played out in re-created theatres of war such as the Western Desert or the Russian Steppes. As always the rules were extremely complicated, mainly governing logistical issues while controlling the complement of arms, tanks and guns each side was allowed to have, which were then represented by cut-out paper shapes. Reality was represented by a dart which was 'fired' at opposing forces, deemed as killed or destroyed if punctured by the dart; I was endlessly frustrated at being banned from these arcane games because I 'didn't understand how to play'. With the combination of our discovery of a satisfyingly realistic game of indoor cricket and the slow return to peacetime activities, Sydney and I could participate on broadly equal terms, while Vincent's lack of cricket-playing knowledge was compensated for by his unusual ability to make a ping-pong ball spin: a direct consequence of his mangled fingers from which he now derived some benefit – at last. The hard surface of bare floorboards helped spin and pace equally, while the larger free floor area gave scope for more complexity in field placings – with open-topped boxes doubling as fieldsmen – scoring and the length of the pitch. We were soon playing two-man teams, employing an umpire and scorer from the two inactive players at any time – a particular necessity now that higher-order batsmen were given an extra life to reflect their demonstrated skills in real life. It was heady, active, ultra-competitive stuff which as the games assumed more importance became even more tense, and the accruing raw statistical data was a source of either pride or irritation.

At the height of Atticeo's appeal I suffered the first of many subsequent bronchial asthma attacks – Dr Taylor's description rather than mine; and in the period of enforced idleness at home I carefully, diligently and accurately generated a Wisden-like compendium of records, omitting no important fact, whether of batting or bowling. Most were subsequently quoted with the same love or conviction as the real thing, until another crisis occurred over another Christmas period.

In a particularly tense Test match I – or rather Len Hutton – was given out, a decision which I believed was incorrect, unfair and deliberately biased. I repeated my opinions endlessly until I was forcibly evicted; the game, to my annoyance, continued. Disconsolately I went down to the kitchen where Ma was busy preparing dinner and, although surprised to see me, she read the signs of a serious 'fall out' accurately as I looked at my carefully catalogued statistics, mentally incorporating the effect Len Hutton's unfair dismissal would have on his batting average and ranking. As red mists of hurt and anger descended I walked over to the fireplace and burned all the records I had compiled so painstakingly, with feelings not of loss but of revenge; but it left me even more dissatisfied. Not long afterwards the three remaining players returned, ignoring me in their search for my ultimate reference book; when I told them calmly what I had done, they seemed for a brief moment frozen in disbelief before they fell upon me with a barrage of punches, pushes and abuse. Ma, who tactfully had remained absent at first, returned to remonstrate with them; then to tell me quietly when they had gone that I had 'behaved very badly', and that 'such dog-in-the-manger responses' were always contemptible.

Ultimately the rift healed, yet because the records were never re-created we all lost something from our potential future enjoyment; while I continued to feel that my contribution in compiling the records voluntarily had not been fairly valued in the first place, others suffered too. Vincent developed a serious case of 'housemaid's knee' from hours of batting and bowling with bared knees on bare floorboards; Rex's pursuit of a suspect, loose-limbed, fast-bowling action threatened his right shoulder joint; while Sydney continued to be frustrated by his inability to top either batting or bowling averages.

At the time it had all seemed a matter of life and death . . . only more important.

33

ALL CREATURES GREAT AND SMALL

Everyone in the neighbourhood appeared to keep pets, the vast majority being cats and dogs, although a variety of other animals such as rabbits, mice, tortoises, goldfish, small songbirds and pigeons were also common. Cats and dogs usually served the dual purpose of providing a domestic pet while protecting the household, the former from the ever-present problem of mice and the latter to deter potential intruders.

Tortoises and goldfish usually appeared after the Race Week Fair, the Hoppins, in late June, where they were a popular prize from one of the many stalls for 'hoopla', 'roll your penny', clay-pipe shooting range or similar activities. Both of them had brief periods of residence in our house, but we soon became bored with a tortoise which hardly moved, while the goldfish – a mistake never repeated – lasted about a week before being shovelled out of its shallow pool to provide Topsy with a tasty fish supper. Canaries or other songbirds were never kept by us, reflecting not only Ma's dislike of caged birds and our inability to afford one but also her pragmatic decision, based on the goldfish experience, that with our highly successful mouse-catching team of cats no bird would have survived Topsy's or her successors' attention for very long. For much the same reason mice and their relatives in the animal kingdom, such as guinea pigs and hamsters, could have been useful only to provide training material for our large cat family in the often silent art of killing – in which they needed neither training nor encouragement.

So they, too, were shunned until our move to Havelock Street, when Vincent began his creation of a serious laboratory, where the attic provided space previously unavailable for his new activity of breeding mice 'for experimental purposes' – although no one but Vincent would have so readily obtained Ma's permission to do so. But after a few months of frustrated, prowling cats trying to get at their prey, the mice resolved the cats' and Ma's latent dissatisfaction with this pointless programme by 'going cannibal' and eating each other.

Pigeons were kept usually by those men who had an allotment on which they could build a 'cree', but occasionally a cree or loft of less dramatic proportions was erected in a neighbour's backyard. Regrettably this frequently created neighbourhood tensions because of the inevitable interest of the extensive cat population; the wanton killing of an expensive or much-loved racing pigeon – for that was the raison d'etre of these birds – was usually followed by the mysterious death by poisoning of a cat in an act of random retribution. The time spent by 'pigeon fanciers' with their birds, their despatch to distant race start points, the anxious watch from the cree for the returning, seldom victorious bird, together with the cash and care which accompanied the hobby, caused Ma to collectively dismiss fanciers and their activity as 'common'.

We never kept more than one dog at any one time, but our cats were even more fecund than the Cassidy family and we had a succession of litters over many years, temporarily swelling the numbers in residence until the newcomers 'could be found good homes'. At the time I was sad as a batch of new, playful kittens were farmed out, but surprised that most had been sexed by Roma's simple technique as 'toms'. It was many years before I discovered that most females were swiftly put to death by drowning – tied in a sack and deposited, mafia-like, with a brick counterweight in a bucket of water. It was a common, necessary method to control a population growth that always threatened to get out of hand, although it had been known for one of our cats to kill off its own offspring. Some of these cats became obsessively possessive with newborn kittens as though, with a highly developed, feline sixth sense, anticipating their likely fate. They would attempt to move their offspring, however numerous, to a safe hiding place under cover of darkness, even though this meant forgoing the warmth, comfort and apparent security of the traditional cat maternity ward in the defunct hot-water chamber of the kitchen range. When one of these 'moonlight flits' was frustrated and the day-old kittens were retrieved by us from the bottom of a cupboard and returned to their original spot, the mother killed two of those returned in an extreme show of displeasure. On another occasion the mother, having successfully moved six of her seven-strong litter up four flights of stairs to a secure spot near the attic, accidentally dropped one she was carrying by the nape of the neck down the stairwell, where it unluckily fell on a protruding nail from which it hung bleeding before dying untidily. Nevertheless it was a death no more grotesque than some of the human suicides which occurred in the neighbourhood.

Our cats were always well cared for and much loved, but they, like every other resident, were required to contribute to their upkeep one way or another. Some became legends in the family's history; of these Topsy, a large tortoiseshell cat that lived for well over twenty years, was the undisputed queen of her time. She defended her and our territory in Elswick Row, particularly the back yard, and neither intruding people nor other animals were safe if she decided they had no right to be there. On one famous occasion she watched malevolently as a large, black dog strayed into our yard; as soon as Ma opened the scullery window to 'shoo' it away Topsy, old and poor-sighted as she was, leaped onto the dog's back, riding it rodeo-like as it fled yelping under the sustained attack of her claws. Yet our cats were consistently at their best catching mice within the house, often shepherding them into our view to demonstrate their virtuosity, teasing a hapless mouse by allowing it to escape temporarily before springing into action and playing a deadly game of football with it between their front paws.

Our dogs played a very different role, nominally that of guarding the house; most developed a ferocious-sounding bark which was at odds with their common trait of gentleness. The death of a dog was followed by an interval for reflection before a replacement was adopted, literally. I knew only three of our dogs, and two of these were long-lived animals that just happened to follow Pop home and decided to become permanent residents. Pop loved his dogs and would look forward as much as they did to their late-night walk after his customary pub visit; he did seem to have a Pied Piper-like attraction for all of them. It was how we acquired them in the first place, how he walked them at night, and it was the cause of the death of the third dog, which was accidentally killed as a puppy. Loch, as it was named after its long-lived predecessor, followed him on his way to work one morning, unbeknown to him, and when Pop boarded a trolleybus to get to his duty start point, it tried to follow but slipped and fell to its death under the bus wheels. We were all distraught at its death and the tragic circumstances, which affected Pop most of all. There was a longer interregnum than usual before Roger, as he was named by us to rhyme with lodger, trotted aimlessly into our lives by following Pop home to Havelock Street from the 'Blue Man'. To the untutored eye he was a nice-looking, black and white collie, almost the archetypal sheepdog. He was quick-witted, obedient and happy to share his lodgings with the already resident cats, rabbits, hens and ducks. He was gentle with children and quietly watchful over babies. Like his new owners he bore his mongrel breeding and poor status with dignity, and established himself quickly as a family favourite. He loved joining in our ball games and was an excellent additional fielder in our cricket matches, risking his teeth more than once to catch a hard cricket ball; the only drawback was the slimy saliva coating he added when coaxed to return it. However, he was banned from any game of football, because his speed and impetuosity often upended someone, with potentially near-fatal consequences. When scolded for such foul play he would retreat, head bowed, a limp tail between his legs and lie with sad, pleading eyes with his head resting on his front paws.

In a cramped, overpopulated house the dog's ever-mobile presence would occasionally cause Ma to chastise him with a cross 'Roger, get out from under my feet', a near-impossible task anyway; while Pop, in his more liverish moments, would simply but sharply say 'ROGER!' and immediately the obedient dog would collapse in a heap of contrition, lowering his eyes and apparently begging forgiveness. We all swore that he had an inbuilt alarm clock enabling him to appear at our front door just before 10p.m. every night, when he would sit upright and very still, with his head inclined towards the 'Blue Man' in the direction from which he knew Pop would be returning. Long before Pop was in sight his tail would start up, beating slowly and rhythmically at first but quickening as Pop, still inaudible to us, approached, until he could sit no longer. He rose on all fours, whimpered, bashed his tail on anything within reach and his eyes would implore the watcher to open the door and release him to greet his returning friend. If we succumbed, it was frequently dangerous for Pop, who walking slowly while musing over his last domino hand, might be hit in the chest by Roger's flying paws in an unwanted display of affection.

Yet one night Roger didn't return home – a cause for only mild concern because, though rare, it had happened before; but when he didn't appear the following night a full-scale search-and-rescue plan swung into action. Streets were walked, people were questioned, police stations were visited, notices were erected and finally a notice was inserted in the *Evening Chronicle*'s 'Lost & Found' column:

Lost – Black & white collie type dog, answers to name of Roger. Reward. Cassidy, 5 Havelock Street.

It was expensive but fruitless. Days turned into weeks and there was no sign of Roger, noticed by all of us in his absence more than in his presence. Grieving is impossible without a body and encourages a false optimism, which as weeks passed simply extended our collective sense of loss; reason suggested he had been run over by a heavy vehicle while mooching around the abattoir on Scotswood Road for juicy bones.

On one of the many Sundays after Roger was last seen Ma rose early as usual to prepare for 7a.m. Mass and, having made some tea, was about to go upstairs to wake me to join her when she heard a familiar whimpering sound outside and a frantic if feeble scratching at the front door. She opened it to be almost overpowered by Roger hurling himself at her, tail wagging, yapping and licking every visible area of skin, which seldom was more than hands and face. Before she could remonstrate with him for his overexuberance he had left her, scampered round the kitchen which he left on finding it uninhabited, turned, skidded on the passage floor and tore upstairs through the open door of the large bedroom where four of us were fast asleep, Vincent and me in the bed nearest the door with Sydney and Rex in that under the window. I never want to repeat the sensation of being trampled on by a large, demented dog, even if it was greeting rather than attacking us. The pounding, slipping and scratching of those paws through the blankets, the loud whimpering and frantic licking were less than the ideal way to wake up from a deep sleep. As we woke we all instinctively shouted, 'Oh, stop it Roger', paused, then looked with amazement at this deliriously happy creature and beyond that to the grimy and emaciated, red-eyed shadow of his former self. As incredulous joy at the reunion subsided the dog collapsed, footsore and feverish; it required two weeks of devoted nursing, accompanied by two visits from the vet, before Roger began to recover. The vet's diagnosis was that he had probably been 'taken by gypsies' and had been badly treated, until he had escaped and walked 'many, many miles' back home to Havelock Street. This had exhausted him, he had contracted 'hard pad' and nearly died. It also caused a major change in his behaviour; he ceased his nightly wanderings, prepared now to wait more patiently for his nightly walk with Pop after his habitual visit to the 'Blue Man', and his internal alarm clock kept better time than ever before.

Roger was different from all our other domestic pets. He was more a member of the family, while all the others belonged to one of us – except of course the cats, because we all belonged to them. Bright and companionable though Roger was, he needed us; he was dependent on Pop for his nightly walks and, like the rest of us, on Ma for his meals. Our cats knew we depended on them to keep the house free of mice, probably sensing that Pop could not have set the simplest of traps without the risk of serious injury, which neither he nor the household budget could afford. They simply used us and happily, because they appeared to like us as well, we co-existed.

The first pet I had that I picked and paid for myself at the pet shop in Nun Street was a jet-black rabbit, which I promptly named Jasper. I fed, cleaned, nursed, played with him and even bought his oats and carefully mixed them with tealeaves for his favourite meal. He rewarded me by being a close companion in a way which no one else and their rabbits could replicate: not 'Mr Patch', Sydney's giant rabbit which he had won in a school raffle, not 'Chocolate Drop', Rex's rabbit which vanished under a coal delivery, and not Vincent's 'Whitney' or 'Einstein', neither of which was as bright as their names implied.

Jasper was a talented, instinctive performer who would lie on my knees on his back, all four paws in the air, to be stroked, his head hanging limp, perfectly still except for his twitching nose and whiskers. When I was doing homework he would hop into the kitchen from the back yard and snuggle beside me while I worked, happy just to be there.

It's true that most of our pets had eccentric habits, for Jenny, one of our more productive hens, would sometimes try to emulate this by sitting on my head if I was lying on the floor working. Donald the duck would start quacking noisily as soon as my mother made her appearance in the kitchen every morning, and would not stop until she had opened the back door to allow Donald to nestle her neck, head and beak on the fur trim of Ma's slippers. Usually Ma walked down the stone steps to allow Donald to do this, but if it was raining she would explain this patiently to the duck while beckoning to it, whereupon it would laboriously quack and struggle up the steps to the doorway to get its obviously necessary daily quota of attention. She was undoubtedly Ma's duck.

Unlike the other inhabitants we rarely had internal disharmony among our menagerie of pets, although there was one notable exception. It was a cockerel bought as a day-old chick and reared initially, like all the others, in the warmth of the kitchen range. Despite the care it received it almost died in its first week but was resuscitated, fed with a fountain-pen reservoir and ultimately it survived, though severely handicapped. It bore a striking resemblance to Quasimodo, with a hunched back, deformed neck and limp coxcomb that permanently hung low over one eye. Perhaps unsurprisingly in these circumstances it was very bad tempered, with an unpredictable tendency to attack the ankles or legs of people crossing the yard to use the outside lavatory; since this was the only lavatory we had, no one could be sure that they would make their ground safely. While sometimes it would crow, strut and peck the ground, ignoring any human presence, that could not be taken for granted. Therefore we frequently carried a walking stick to ward off this mad creature if it decided to be unfriendly, particularly on dark nights which provided the biggest threat of its ambushing any toilet-bound prey with a noisily frightening, wing-flapping, screeching attack on the ankles. For some reason Roma's husband Walter seemed very prone to attacks from this evil-tempered misfit, yet it lived longer than intended simply because the chosen executioner, our neighbour Mr Pattinson, was repulsed by the aggressive bird several times before justice was finally done. Even though toilet visits returned to normal, with an eye on the weather rather than the chicken run, this most difficult of our animals had the last laugh, being as tough in the pot as it had been on our ankles.

There was one other form of life, which gave us as many problems in their death as they did when they were alive: flies. The common housefly was a pest and the only methods of control available were a fly swat or flypaper. The former was impractical except for occasional flies in late spring or early autumn, and required too much energy and space to employ effectively. The latter worked, but the poisonous, sticky paper was always hung from a light fitting, like an unrolled 'Box Brownie' film. Naturally that meant it was more or less central to the kitchen table, where after a few days it would be well studded with dead flies of a variety of sizes and colours together with a number of recent victims, stuck by a leg or a wing, buzzing violently. Occasionally one of these managed to free itself and fall, still buzzing – we hoped onto the table rather than the food. The sight of this sticky fly graveyard dangling over the food did little for my appetite in general, or for the attraction of steamed sultana sponge in particular.

Throughout our childhood years both in Elswick Row and Havelock Street, in sickness and in health and irrespective of their own heavy workloads, both Ma and Pop cared for the household pets and were gentle, though firm, with any they met outside. They hated to see ill treatment of any animal almost as much as they did of children, and always impressed on us how important it was to care for those who were dependent upon us individually or collectively. Pop's attraction to, and desire to keep, stray dogs which chose to live with us were mirrored by Ma's 'championing' of the cause of ill-treated animals whenever she chanced upon them, although not always with the intended consequences.

On returning with her one day from a local shopping trip with a heavy load of vegetables we came across a scruffy rag-and-bone merchant savagely beating his mangy, sad-looking horse, which seemed too tired to continue. Ma promptly remonstrated with him, shouting 'Stop that! Stop that at once, do you hear?' He had heard, because he turned his head, looked witheringly at her and continued whipping his long-suffering, helpless horse, which stood stock still with lowered head. 'Stop it, I said. You big bully, stop it,' she shouted as she closed on him, but since he gave no more indication of stopping than the horse did of starting, she decided on direct action. Putting down her shopping bag beside me, she threw seven pounds of large, soil-covered potatoes at the cruel owner. Every single missile missed its intended target but hit the poor horse, which several times raised its eyes with a look of pity, as if imploring her to find other, better-deserving objects for her 'do-gooding'. Probably with this in mind it shuffled slowly forward, the rag-and-bone merchant stopped beating it and jumped up onto the heavily laden cart, as Ma shouted after him, 'If I see you doing that again I shall call the police' – and we began slowly to reclaim our potatoes from the gutter where they had rolled.

All of this helped me to understand life and death, why relatives, neighbours or friends differed as much as they did, and how some people were so attractive while others were so repulsive.

Poor Roger!! Poor Jasper!!

34

STAYING ON?

I began my last year at St Cuthbert's concerned about how England were going to recover from another lost series against the most complete Australian cricket XI that most shrewd commentators had ever seen, although buoyed by the knowledge that Don Bradman would never again put them to the sword after his 'duck' in an emotional farewell appearance at the Oval. Another concern was how Newcastle United were going to succeed in their quest for the First Division championship, for which they had made a promising start. Both these matters outweighed any worries I might have had about how I was going to perform in my matriculation examination in the early summer of the following year; probably just as well, since the academic year began with a few minor trials and rapidly got worse as the year staggered on.

On a promisingly sunny, bright, early October Monday morning, having by then given up my paper delivery round, I discovered that my school shirt had not been washed. My suggestion that I should wear it for one more day was flatly rejected by Ma, on the practical grounds that this would only defer rather than solve the problem. Her solution, which to me sounded no more practical and even less desirable, was to wear one of Pop's two soft-collar-attached shirts. The rest of his wardrobe consisted of round-necked shirts worn with a separate, highly starched collar, attached by two collar studs in a process I had watched many times and which seemed synonymous with bad temper, rising blood pressure and muttered blasphemies. My major reservation, however, concerned our disparity in size; Pop had an egalitarian 46-inch measurement for both chest and waist, while I didn't know my equivalent statistics, although I had heard others observe of me that they 'had seen more fat on a greasy chip'.

Ma was at her most persuasive and having cunningly said if it was such a bad idea perhaps I should absent myself from school that day, she produced and put on me, swiftly buttoning the front, a cream Van Heusen shirt that felt and looked as if it was an ultra-large, mothball-scented sack. As I opened my mouth to protest, Ma smiled warmly and said, 'Oh, you look very smart, so grown up; oh, it suits you down to the ground' – a pretty accurate description, since the front and tail of the shirt reached my ankles. As she saw my dismay returning after the emollient words, she added, 'Just hitch it up and pouch it slightly over your trouser belt. Look! Just like this. There now, that's fine, isn't it?' Well, no, it wasn't; but since the cuffs on the sleeves of the shirt bypassed my hands by at least a foot – 12 inches, that is – I was in no position to interfere, but I did miserably point out this further problem. 'Don't be silly, that's nothing. Just roll the sleeves up.' By the time she had finished this gave my forearms an appearance rather like Popeye after he had eaten a tin of spinach, but I was still not completely satisfied, particularly as my downward survey revealed that the buttoned neck of the shirt hung somewhere between my throat and my navel, although much nearer the latter. Ma was now at her most incisive and persuasive, to the point where she headed off any imminent further question before I had time to form the words by her next imperative: 'Now fasten your tie tightly and the collar . . .' – an improbable 17 inches in circumference, much nearer my chest or waist size than my collar size – '. . . will look as if it was made to measure.' It wasn't quite as she had predicted, but it did fit tightly around my throat; in the process, though, the collar points crossed over each other – something not many people have achieved before – and the knot, together with most of the school tie, disappeared under this profusion of cream cotton. On went my school blazer, admittedly covering most of the bulging shirt overhanging my trouser belt, but constant adjustments were required to prevent intermittent appearances of shirt tails down my trouser legs, as well as to disguise the cause of my bulging forearms and the extraordinary collar I was wearing.

Ma sent me off cheerily with a few more complimentary remarks about my smart appearance as I made my way to Gloucester Road, only a few streets away, to collect my long-standing friend Alan Thornton, before we went off to school by bus together in the regular, daily routine. By the time I arrived at his door, No. 121, I had swallowed Ma's propaganda 'hook, line and sinker'. I knocked, the door opened, Alan appeared and his whole face changed, as though a strong, unpleasant smell had affected him. 'What the . . . what are you wearing?'

'Oh,' I said, as nonchalantly as I could muster, 'Ma bought me a new shirt on Saturday, but it's too big; she'll take it back, though.' I thought as I said this both 'He'll know it's a lie' and 'Why didn't I tell the truth?' – but Alan, good friend that he was, just grunted, snuffled, put his satchel on his shoulder and said 'Come on then, or we'll be late.' And that, I thought, was that: but it wasn't. Later that morning, after a number of disbelieving stares at my front, I was confronted by one of the school bullies as we were queuing to return to classrooms after the morning break. Dougie O'Brien, who paradoxically was a friend of Alan Thornton's, sneered at me: 'Big Nose' – he was always full of compliments – 'what's that you're wearing, your granddad's shirt?' at which the many boys who heard his remarks chortled, relieved not to be the butt of his comments themselves. 'Better to have a big nose than a bird brain,' I retorted, which had the less desirable effect of infuriating Dougie to the point where he was about to leap at me, in spite of the protective presence of the nearby Father Hardy who was supervising the mass return to the classrooms; but Alan, who was in the same class, put a firm restraining hand on Dougie's arm and said loudly, 'Leave him alone!' – which he did.

By the end of the day I was familiar with this strange garment that frequently escaped down my trouser legs, spilled out from the front of my blazer or shot down my arms covering my hand entirely to flap wildly, as if I had an empty shirt sleeve – not unlike a boy at St Mary's who had been born without a left arm but with a perfectly formed hand under his armpit. However, Ma must have been concerned about how I had fared, in spite of the encouragement she had given me earlier in the day; I responded with a reasonably accurate report on how my dress was received, but omitting any reference to Dougie O'Brien's taunts.

In truth I felt quite lucky to have escaped the ridicule with which Vincent had been greeted regularly when he appeared wearing daily as an overcoat a nip-waisted, frocked evening coat, complete with flared, pleated tails, satin-faced lapels, top pocket and buttonhole. As might be expected this expensive and unusual coat was a free hand-me-down from a diminutive, recently deceased friend of a relative; when it was offered Ma accepted it without hesitation and Vincent wore it, though not by choice, throughout the winter of 1942.

My eccentric choice in school clothes was quickly followed by a more serious problem which caused me to miss some of the autumn term and most of the Easter term: the first of many attacks of bronchial asthma, caused no doubt by the perennial cold and dampness in a decaying Victorian house where the air was full of coal dust and fine particles of ash, together with animal hairs of many varieties. If it was predictable and unavoidable, it was random in its choice of victims; only Ma and I succumbed to its grip, which by Easter had me for the first time dropping out of the top three in the class to sixth. This result was so bad, apparently, that it warranted my being summoned by the headmaster for the second time in my career at the grammar school; he again questioned whether or not the problem underlying my poor performance was girls, although happily on this occasion he did not imply any contributory negligence on the part of my parents because of their visits to the 'Blue Man'. I took the opportunity to tell him that my 'chesty' condition had been deemed serious enough to warrant a house call by Dr Taylor, although his impassive expression indicated he had not grasped fully the significance of this investment; as a result I omitted any reference to the fact that I had attempted a game of chess with Dr Taylor on one of these visits, if only to seek full value for money.

With only intermittent attacks and an average attendance record in my final term, I sat the University Matriculation examination during two very hot weeks in June. In pursuit of the security thought necessary on these important occasions all the windows were closed, causing the classroom to overheat so badly that I fainted, as did several other boys on different occasions, following which I was allowed out, but could return to complete the examination paper only if I remained under surveillance during the entire period away from the room. Luckily it was only a 'fainting fit', not dysentery or anything else requiring visits to the school lavatories, and I resumed, completing the examination paper after a restorative glass of water in the more normal temperature of the school assembly hall.

Monsignor Canon Cunningham, Vicar-General of the Diocese and Headmaster of St Cuthbert's, was not finished with me yet, however. In a process which began with a general talk to everyone in the fifth form sitting their matriculation examination in 1949, he reminded us 'of the need to build on and make full use of the education' we had received so far, although warning gravely that 'it would not be appropriate for everyone to undertake further formal education'. He ended by telling us that it was within his remit, and his alone, to invite the most gifted students to return and join the sixth form to study for an intermediate degree before going on to university, or to undertake further study for the priesthood. We were all to discuss this with our respective parents before his next meeting with us the following week, prior to the school concert and speech day to mark the end of the academic year, and for most of the fifth-form pupils the end of their formal education also.

I duly passed on his broad message but was involved only in passing in the weighing of factors before Ma's decision was reached swiftly, following which her summing up was a model of clarity and brevity. Finances were central, of course; Roma was not mentioned because by then she had been happily married for six years and already had three children. Alan was going to remarry shortly; Vincent was studying at King's College, Newcastle on a National Service Grant which was barely able to support him; Rex, after a brief period working at the Public Assistance Bureau, had embarked on the long road to membership of the Pharmaceutical Society of Great Britain by means of a formal apprenticeship with Timothy Whites & Taylors, which included his paid study at Sunderland Technical College between practical learning behind the counter at various branches. Ma's conclusion had an Euclidean simplicity – at best I could pursue some similar, non-contributory but self-supporting role; at worst I could take up paid employment until one of them was making a contribution; or I too could follow Vincent, after the end of my expected National Service in four years or so, and in the meantime I could pursue an intermediate degree at night school, something Vincent had attempted with a singular lack of success. Ma made it clear that staying on at St Cuthbert's was not an option, although both she and Pop encouraged me to keep further study in mind when 'things' – a euphemism for domestic finances – improved; yet another 'big ship' required 'to sail up Dean Street'.

The events which followed seemed to indicate that somehow news of this decision-making process had been leaked to a higher authority, as I was first nobbled by a sympathetic Father Hardy, expressing the hope that I would stay on to pursue 'an outstanding teaching career', which he believed would lead to a 'headmastership before you are thirty-five'. That was a reference point so far distant as to be unimaginable to a sixteen-year-old who genuinely felt he would be lucky to reach thirty after his recent bouts of 'chest problems'.

The second review of my prospects and intentions was conducted more publicly and less sympathetically by the headmaster, in his promised collective final discussion of the likely candidates for further study, some of which were going to be conditional invitations to be confirmed when the matriculation results were known sometime in August. He had clearly decided upon a full frontal assault on me, which opened well enough as he explained that in announcing the names of those he wished to invite to become sixth-formers in September he would explain the grounds on which he had decided they should pursue the arts or sciences curriculum; however, before so doing he was 'inviting Cassidy, the only boy in the fifth this year whose work and potential merit inclusion in either, to make his own choice'. It was a generous public assessment, yet its manner suggested he had decided what I should do and he was not in a mood to be trifled with, which in any case was not my style with senior priests.

'I don't know, Headmaster, whether I can stay on,' I stammered, hoping he would leave it at that – but I couldn't have been more wrong.

'Have you discussed it with your parents?' he pressed, perhaps thinking 'or have they been at the "Blue Man" every night?'

'Yes, I have,' I replied, conscious that all the ears and most of the eyes of the class were focused on us, he standing rocking gently near the door, hands thrust as usual deep into the side pockets of his cassock, towering over me as I sat at my regular desk nearest the door.

'And?' he questioned.

'They don't know if I can stay on.'

'What on earth can prevent you from staying on?' – his voice level rising as he addressed the rest of the class over my head, forcing me to utter the words I was trying to avoid.

'They' [it's always 'they' and 'them' in this world] 'don't think we can afford it,' I said embarrassedly, feeling the colour rise in my cheeks and hoping that at last he would be satisfied.

'How can they not afford it? They're not losing anything; they have never had any earnings from you; they won't incur any extra costs, will they?' There was nothing further I could add. I just sat and stared, waiting, praying for the storm to pass, which it did as the Very Reverend Monsignor Canon Cunningham, Vicar-General of the Diocese, his face thundery and reflecting his frustration, ultimately turned both his gaze and attention to the rest of the class. I longed to protect my parents by saying 'I am not staying on because I don't want to', but it would have been a blatant lie and the words wouldn't form in my confused, humbled brain.

When the inevitable review took place at home later, Ma muttered darkly about the 'stupidity of priests' and the more obvious, 'They couldn't understand, could they, living as they do?' There were some indirect attempts made for the decision to be altered through my brother-in-law, now an established member of staff, but whatever they were or from whom they came the die was cast.

School broke up on a sunny, late July day; farewells were said after the school concert in which I continued to play a part as a member of the choir, knowing that I would be paying an early visit to the Youth Employment Bureau the following week to find temporary employment until I could resume my studies somewhere, somehow, sometime in the future, for which the Matriculation results due in mid-August would give some guidance.

It was a sad, humbling end to five wonderful years during which I had been so happy and had learned so much; yet I felt that even in the process of leaving I had neither done myself justice nor managed to bridge some mysterious social gap which seemed to separate me from many of the other pupils and most of the faculty. I hoped the examination results in August would be good enough to minimise it.

Early reflection confirmed my intention to follow Vincent in a night-school course, although I decided to defer further choice until I had more details to match against my own imminent Matriculation results and my forthcoming job search. I also hoped that whatever I did it would prove more financially rewarding than appeared to be the case with Vincent or Rex, neither of whom seemed to have 'two pennies to rub together'. Of course Rex was in a long apprenticeship and could expect little pay after his tuition fees had been paid for by his employer, and given that the time he spent in various Timothy White's shops was undertaking supervised dispensing of prescriptions. His standards of dress improved visibly, though, suggesting how any surplus funds were being deployed.

Vincent had found his night-school studies difficult, particularly in pure mathematics, which was probably due to his own enforced absences from St Cuthbert's at a crucial time academically because of his role as 'carer in chief' to Ma. His choice of an intermediate B.Sc. course had been more a function of his work as a laboratory assistant at Richardson's Leather Works than a desire to choose science over arts, while the university science degree course he was now going to pursue was itself required to be a continuation of the previous night-school studies to qualify for the National Service Grant, without which he could not have attended university. His determined efforts to conquer his weakness in mathematics caused one of his tutors to plead with him to move his position from the front of the lecture theatre to the rear, because his intense yet deeply uncomprehending stares were disturbing her concentration. It was both a prophetic and pathetic appeal – it was not going to work because it was the wrong syllabus, chosen for the wrong reasons and ultimately made obligatory by financial necessity.

Soon, even with this funding, the lack of residual financial headroom was to be underscored for Vincent as he was planning his entertainment options for the Christmas festivities later that year. By then he had the benefit of a bank account, periodic bank statements and a chequebook – the first person in the family to achieve this status – with which to control and chart his income-and-expenditure pattern. But even elementary mathematics was not his strong point, and he felt the best course was to go armed with chequebook and pen to the Lloyds Bank branch he used normally for his transactions, near the Big Lamp. It was the Friday preceding Christmas and it was packed with people similarly anxious to withdraw a substantial amount of cash necessary to see them through the expensive process of 'eating, drinking and being merry'. When Vincent reached the counter the usual impeccably groomed, middle-aged, moustachioed and beautifully spoken man enquired what service Vincent required.

'I would like to make a withdrawal, please,' was his answer.

'How much would you like, sir?' was the irrelevant yet understandable response.

'I would *like* £50,' Vincent thought sarcastically, but replied 'I'm not sure,' and as he saw the teller's eyebrows arch and then pucker, added 'I mean, I don't know how much I have left.' There were irritated murmurings from behind of 'Hurry up', 'I've got better things to do than stand here while he makes up his bloody mind', 'What's going on?', 'Who's he think he is, Carnegie?' as the teller said patiently and politely, 'I'll check your account balance, sir; just a moment' — and with that he left, to increased rebellious mutterings. Vincent kept his eyes fixed on his open chequebook, pen poised ready for action as if signalling his understanding of the mob's concern and his own readiness to hurry up once the bureaucratic necessities had been dealt with by the guardians of his personal wealth. The man returned, took a piece of paper on which he wrote deliberately as he said, 'Your current balance, I believe, sir', folded the paper and passed it confidentially to Vincent to avoid revealing it to the eyes of the craned heads behind the customer as he waited. Vincent unfolded the paper and saw the written '1s 6d', replying as steadily as he could, 'All of it, please', before writing the cheque while the impassive teller questioned, with another quizzical arch of the eyebrows, 'How would you like it, sir?' Vincent finalised matters with a sad 'Silver, please', as he held out his hand to receive three small, silver coins.

These experiences only confirmed what I knew already: that guidance on further education, career planning or financial management was unlikely to be forthcoming from within the family which had provided my only, yet hitherto infallible source of advice. As I went off to the Youth Employment Bureau it was Friday 4 August, the Queen's birthday, the thirty-fifth anniversary of the outbreak of the Great War and the day before the August Bank Holiday weekend.

I set off, carefully dressed in my school uniform because I had nothing more impressive to wear, but with the benefit of a clean shirt and a carefully knotted school tie. Ma said I 'looked the part', but whether that meant as an aspiring boss or the village idiot wasn't clear. It was only a short journey to the Youth Employment Bureau in the city centre and there were, surprisingly I thought, few people around as I made enquiries about whom I should see to find out what jobs might be available for a recent school leaver, who expected shortly to be notified of a very satisfactory Matriculation examination result.

I was soon directed to a middle-aged, cigarette-smoking man whose fingers were stained a deep yellow by years of tobacco smoke, as were his left nostril and the eyebrows above it. He unsmilingly nodded for me to take a seat as he asked me what I wanted to do, to which my only answer was 'Work', which made him ask rather curtly 'What kind of work?' I answered in a circular conversation with a further question, 'What work is available?' He then persuaded me to tell him what my strongest and weakest subjects were and it must have sounded rather immodest as I told him I didn't really have any weaknesses except art and I was not looking for work as a painter. He clearly inferred from this exchange a superior air on my part, whereas it was simply schoolboy frankness. He looked at a card index, checked it with a sheaf of papers, took a small piece of brown card from his desk, scribbled a name on it and handed it to me. 'I think this will suit you well,' he said. 'It's a job for an office boy, with promotion prospects to Junior Clerk, and with possibilities for further advancement dependent on your capacity for hard work.' I began to tell him about my experience as a paperboy and the unsolicited recommendation from Mr Hannah, but he cut me short by saying I should present myself that afternoon to the Chief Clerk, a Mr Lindsey, whom he would be ringing shortly to tell him that I was on my way. He gave me the brown card, which gave the address as College Avenue, Haymarket, gave me instructions as to how to get there and said 'That will be all.' The whole process of career guidance and the range of prospects open to me had taken approximately ten minutes, and I was invited to leave with several hours to fill in before I could see Mr Lindsey.

As I left the building it occurred to me that I didn't know the name of the company, unless that too was Lindsey; therefore I had no idea whether it was Lindsey's or some other name, or more importantly what kind of business this company conducted. I looked more carefully at the card and saw the name 'Dunlop' written in capital letters, with the address repeated. The matter exercising me most now was how to keep myself in as pristine a condition as possible until 2p.m. when I was due to meet this Mr Lindsey, so taking great care I retraced my steps home, praying that no accidents would befall me to mar my presentable appearance. When I arrived home Pop was still in the kitchen as he had a late shift that day in his more recent capacity as a route planner at the Wingrove bus depot, where he worked in a three-man team allocating buses and crews to the various routes operated.

I gave him a word-by-word recapitulation of the conversation, after which he said thoughtfully and apparently knowledgeably, 'Dunlop; oh, that's a very good company. We have Dunlop tyres on all the buses and they are very reliable – but I am not sure about the people who run it.' That puzzled me and I asked whether he had ever worked for Dunlop. 'Oh, no,' he said 'it's the man who is or certainly was chairman, Sir Eric Geddes; he's the villain who was responsible for crushing the 1926 strike and for reducing unemployment benefits, known as the "Geddes Axe". Anyone who would do that will have to be watched.'

Armed with this useful bank of knowledge on Dunlop I presented myself at the reception desk in College Avenue, behind which stood a very small, youngish man whose head cleared the counter by no more than a foot; he looked rather like a plaster bust that had been dropped onto a very hard surface. He phoned to announce my arrival, was asked to send me up, and I made my way up a winding staircase to the first floor of a simple building where the smell of rubber was powerful and if unsurprising – it was the Dunlop Rubber Co. Ltd, after all – was not unpleasant. There was a thick, dark-brown lino covering the wooden staircase and upper floor; what exterior brickwork was visible had not been plastered but was painted brown to waist height and cream above that; and the majority of the internal office walls were wooden partitions, mostly with clear glass above waist height but one, uniquely, had frosted glass.

It was in the last of these small offices before the corridor ended and opened out into a large, open, desk-filled office – one of only two with a small piece of coconut matting outside the door to signify status – that Mr Lindsey was sitting at a roll-top desk, writing carefully. He asked me to sit so that I was facing him, with my back to what he told me was the general office in which most of the office staff worked. He was patient in describing the functions which were carried out there, while above his voice I could hear the chatter of conversation in the office with telephones ringing in the background amid shouted instructions from time to time. After talking to me for twenty-five minutes or so Mr Lindsey asked me to complete an employment application form for which, as I returned it to him, he complimented me on the handwriting. It all seemed so like being at school except for the excited hubbub behind us, the shouts and the ringing of telephones.

The Chief Clerk then almost apologetically told me that I would start as the office boy and was therefore expected to do a number of simple tasks such as collecting the outgoing mail at night, making sure it was stamped and taken to the Post Office, escorting the cashier – who was an old lady – to and from the bank every day, and generally fetching and carrying stationery and other articles for the clerical staff. Since I had no template of work in my mind, there was nothing to match this against and I simply nodded in acquiescence. Mr Lindsey told me that I 'had the job' and that he was sure that before long there would be another office boy appointed, when I could move on to more responsible clerical work. The wage would be two pounds, two shillings and sixpence per week, less the obligatory national insurance stamp, and it would be paid in cash every Friday night. He said he was pleased to see me, that he would now show me out so that he could explain the process for 'clocking in' and 'clocking out', and that I was required to be present from 8.50a.m. until 5.30p.m. Monday to Friday, with one hour for lunch and no other breaks except as demanded by nature, as well as on alternate Saturday mornings from 8.50a.m. until 12.10p.m. to average the expected forty hours per week over a two-week period.

He showed me downstairs and introduced me to the modern clocking-in system, which was a large wall clock under which there was a box-like base with a handle on the left-hand side; when pulled it opened a slot just big enough to write a signature only on the paper roll exposed, from which I gathered it was clearly a major benefit to be right-handed. The clock automatically printed the time at which the lever had been pulled and the slot opened and, as I soon learned, one of the cashier's key tasks was to examine this daily to see at what time people came and left, and if punctuality didn't fall within prescribed limits to refer the matter to the Chief Clerk. Indeed, a large ledger was kept in which she wrote carefully in red ink each day the number of minutes individuals arrived late or departed early, and the aggregate for each employee – excluding of course the Chief Clerk and the mythical figure of the District Manager, whose status seemed to be something close to the deity and to whom I was not introduced that afternoon.

I returned home to be greeted enthusiastically by Ma, who was delighted when I gave her the news and promptly told me that while the shirt, school tie and grey trousers would suffice, I simply couldn't go to work in a blazer and the school shoes would have to be replaced by something smarter. Other than that, I was fit and ready to start work at 8.50a.m. on the Tuesday after the Bank Holiday, 8 August 1949. Childhood was at an end. Now I was to be given a national insurance number, I would begin to pay income tax, to pay Ma a formal 'board and lodgings' allowance, and I would therefore become a fully paid-up member of the working classes. In eighteen months' time I would be called up to join some branch of His Majesty's Forces for two years of National Service, but I would not be allowed to vote.

I was not staying on at school, in fact not staying anywhere; I was drifting, carried along by a stream of seemingly inevitable, predestined activity that felt neither good nor bad.

35

WORK . . .

The Saturday of the 1949 August Bank Holiday weekend was spent shopping with Ma to complete my outfit to her satisfaction, so that I would appear for my first day's serious work 'looking the part' once again. In pursuit of this objective I had acquired a blue and white Harris tweed sports jacket – or so the salesman told us, although there was no label inside to confirm this – together with a pair of thick, crepe-soled, brown shoes of which Ma did not wholly approve but which seemed to me to be both fashionable and suitable for the purpose. After all the 'part' I was to 'look' was that of an office boy.

It's true that when I presented myself for my first day's work, remembering as I walked through customer reception to pull the handle on the time clock immediately and sign my name carefully, grateful I was not left-handed, that I appeared more sportingly dressed than most of the other staff – but then they were hardly 'the epitome of sartorial elegance', an expression I had acquired from Pop and which seemed appropriate at the time. If the first morning dragged with endless introductions, always to older people – always addressed as 'Mr', 'Miss' or 'Mrs'– and a barrage of requests and instructions about what I was required to do: bringing tea, distributing the morning mail, collecting the carefully opened envelopes to see which could be reused and generally finding my feet, a long, slow day ultimately ended satisfyingly. However, the following month passed in a blur, as I became acquainted not only with my new colleagues but also with the layout and contents of the building, which was Dunlop's north-eastern distribution depot and district office. The depot consisted of a large warehouse, which stored every size of tyre for any vehicle from a wheelbarrow to an earthmover, with a host of related accessories ranging from individual tyre pressure gauges to the latest wheel-balancing equipment. There was also a service garage, where tyres under complaint were inspected or service was provided for privileged special customers such as a local Le Mans competitor, and where two ageing delivery vans were housed every night. The origins of the building, which lay behind the Haymarket in the city centre and within the precincts of King's College, Durham University, were immediately obvious from this layout. What now served as the district office of this international market leader had been a hayloft above a stable where horses had been kept, and the rest of the premises had been devoted to storing and carting goods in horse-drawn delivery vans. The pitched roof of the hayloft had been re-covered to make it weatherproof, but its simple construction still allowed airborne dirt from city-centre traffic to filter slowly through it overnight; this deposited a visible film of dust on papers, desks, floors and furniture, requiring the daily attention of the elderly lady cleaner.

Most of the space in the hayloft was devoted to a general office, with the remainder given over to a few private offices created by the erection of simple wooden partitions; only the District Manager's office had frosted glass windows to shield him and his commercially sensitive activities from the gaze of the endless traffic of staff along the corridors – although it did little to prevent his booming voice from being heard almost anywhere in the depot. The cashier's office on the opposite side of the corridor had a permanently locked door, with only a small hatch above the office boy's desk to receive cash which had been paid over the counter for the occasional retail transaction. Most conversations took place through the hatch; more importantly, it allowed money to be drawn daily for petty-cash purchases such as petrol for the delivery vans and, even more crucially, the handing out of weekly pay packets every

Friday afternoon. Every single cash transaction was signed for by the recipient, having already had an authorising signature. The sums involved were thought to be so vital to the well-being of this international giant that the Chief Clerk checked and balanced the cash on a daily basis, before it was again locked in an enormous steel safe to which only three people knew the combination.

The only other staff to have separate offices were those whose seniority or job function demanded it: the telephonist and the two secretaries, to safeguard confidentiality of communications, and of course the Chief Clerk. At one end of the office there was a locked cupboard in which all the stationery including pencils, note pads, blank invoice-cum-despatch notes and even carbon papers were stored securely; the key to this treasure trove was kept by the senior of the two section leaders.

A strict hierarchy ruled, with the District Manager, Mr Nesbit, being the overlord of all of the activities within the geographic area for which he was responsible. In a most military manner that included the most northerly English counties immediately below the Scottish border, which were tidily numbered 1 (Northumberland), 2 (the centre of Newcastle), 3 (Durham), and 4 (Cumberland and Westmorland). The Chief Clerk was next in seniority and was responsible functionally only for the administration of the sales force, but executively for all the warehouse and administrative activities, and the staff who conducted them, within the depot. He exercised his authority directly through two section heads in the office, a storekeeper and a service manager; the latter, as the technical specialist, managed the complaints function and the service garage. This waterfall of authority, with minimal delegation, was more complex than but in essence not much different from school; the section leaders were senior to the service manager but didn't exercise any authority over him; all three were senior to the storekeeper but did not exercise any direct executive authority over him either. Similarly the cashier was responsible directly to the Chief Clerk, even though neither she nor the role were thought more responsible, and nor was either better paid, than any other clerk over twenty-one, which this cashier certainly was; yet she was privy to a bank of confidential files detailing how much every weekly paid employee received, their age and personal history. Only the section leaders, the service manager and the storekeeper, who were paid monthly by cheque, escaped her scrutiny. There was one other senior group in the hierarchy: the four salesmen, who responded directly to the District Manager. Each of them was assigned a sales district, was allocated that very rare, precious asset, a fully expensed car, and they nominally worked from home, although they were frequently in the office on Mondays or Fridays for meetings, instructions or that boss-versus-subordinate exchange of views known as 'a bollocking' – at first incomprehensible to me, later routine.

Then of course there were the women, including the cashier Mrs Watson; she was an elderly lady, a widowed grandmother with 'a weak chest' and symptoms similar to my own, whose choice of daily medication, 'Liquafruta' – a garlic-based proprietary medicine – combined with cod-liver-oil capsules provided more security than the locks on the doors or the narrow aperture through which words, documents, and cash passed without the need for her to unlock the cash-office door. The others were Mary, the sad, long-faced telephonist who suffered from a permanent cold and was married to a prison officer, and the two unattached secretaries who were physically, temperamentally, and socially poles apart but who focused their common and mutually conflicting affection on Cyril Robinson, one of the two section leaders. Rita, the secretary who serviced the District Manager and the Chief Clerk in an administrative sense, was thin, prim, tall, flat-chested, red-haired, bespectacled and dressed in tweeds with sensible shoes. Patricia, who looked after the two section leaders but found Cyril's work more interesting than Charlie's, was short, blonde, with a figure, face and pouting glossy lips closely resembling those of the new film starlet Diana Dors; her lack of inches was compensated by stilt-like high heels on her strapped sandals, requiring the utmost skill to retain her balance while producing the most amazing movements beneath her fashionable clothes as she walked.

It was clear that the cashier, the telephonist and the two secretaries were filling 'women only' jobs and that every other job in the office was 'men only', and they were an even more disparate bunch than the four women. The Chief Clerk was a quiet, thoughtful, orderly, married man who, because of various disabilities – primarily that he was prematurely deaf and wore a hearing aid – had been excused war service. As his senior job required, he dressed conventionally and always wore a hat to the office; his one minor self-indulgence appeared to be that he smoked a pipe, sometimes in his office and always on arriving or leaving. He lived in Gosforth, a respectable, middle-class district, and travelled to work by bus, because despite his acknowledged competence and senior status he was not provided with a company car as were the salesmen; that was a minor source of visible and frequently articulated irritation. However, soon after my arrival he acquired a large, old, pre-war saloon car, the restoration of which, including its respraying, became a principal activity for the garage fitter when he was not required on company business – a fact now remarked upon sarcastically, if reciprocally, by the salesmen. The car soon became Mr Lindsey's principal leisure activity at weekends, using the extensive facilities of the Dunlop garage which clearly were superior to those he had at home. He walked with a curious, flat-footed, shuffling action, exaggerated by the wide bottoms on his suit trousers; we had many opportunities to observe it as apart from his deafness he was believed to have some kind of bowel disorder, requiring him to visit the locked executive lavatory immediately outside the general office with more than normal frequency. One of the lessons I soon learned was that in a small community like this, everyone made it their business to know everyone else's business, rather like the neighbours of whom my mother so disapproved who 'lived in each other's pockets'; therefore any habit as minor as going to the lavatory rather more frequently than others might expect was going to lead inevitably to some collective debate as to why.

The two section leaders fulfilled their senior role by remaining somewhat distant from the other members of staff, but since Charlie Blasdale had been on active service with the RAF in the Far East flying Beaufighter aircraft, his style of both submitting to higher authority and exercising his own was more liberal than Cyril's. Cyril had the pleasant, smiling appearance of an easy-going companion, while in reality he more often exhibited the telltale signs of a nervous, obsessive, middle-aged bachelor who still lived with his mother and who really had no need to work for a living. His spare time was spent competing in cross-country motorbike trials, on which he expended a substantial amount of money; but that made him an extremely desirable companion in the eyes of the two secretaries, to whom he responded in an even-handed way despite the tensions this egalitarian approach engendered. His combined expenditure still did not prevent him from being one of the first people most of us had ever known after the war who ordered, and was able to obtain, a brand-new motorcar – an achievement in itself given their limited availability, and a further irritation to Mr Lindsey.

Two senior clerks were a bridge between the section leaders and the younger members of staff: Doug Gomersall, a tall Yorkshireman of 6 foot 3 inches with a dishevelled appearance, contrasting with Maurice Nicholson who was a neat, pencil-slim, recently demobbed 'pukka' ex-RAF chap, demonstrated by his Flying Officer Kite moustache and his RAF Association tie. His carefully adopted style was probably intended to convey the image of the archetypal fighter pilot of Battle of Britain days, which he certainly hadn't been, and neither had he flown any aircraft anywhere: whereas Charlie, who had seen 'shot and shell' on active service, had the looks and behaviour of someone as far removed from the archetypal flying hero as possible.

Yet the real characters were in the lower reaches of the organisation, in the warehouse and despatch areas, which equated with 'below stairs' in domestic service and were entered physically via a vertical, spiral, metal staircase from our office in the hayloft to their stables below – a route

I was to travel thousands of times at rapidly increasing speeds, since most of the journeys were to take despatch documentation for an urgently awaited delivery. Albert Reavley, the chief storekeeper, made it clear with an unsmiling face on my first appearance just how seriously he took any activity in any area over which he had control, and that there must be no 'tomfoolery or larking about'. Since he was 6 feet 6 inches tall and built like a barn door, with his simian ancestry immediately discernible in his long arms and gait, this statement brooked no argument. He always spoke thoughtfully, unsmilingly and brusquely. His deputy, John Clelland, was another giant but an amiable one, although the real fun was to be had with the younger members of the team. They were all married or about to be, in their twenties, and determined to stretch the constraints of the job as much as they could without risking the ultimate penalty of the sack. Geoff Fulthorpe, Alan Forbes and Tommy Thirlwell were always ready, when things were quiet, to make a crude football from some old tyre wrappings and paper, bind it with tape and have a scratch game of three or four a side in the packing room, where the sliding doors could be closed to give an early warning of the approach of Albert the storekeeper. They had all learned how to skive effectively in His Majesty's armed forces. Better still was to be buttonholed by little, chubby Frank Keeley, a curious rural anachronism with the burr and rosy cheeks of the countryman, who was the despatch clerk with authority over the two regular van drivers. He had a cap permanently on his head and wore a blue, bib-fronted boiler suit into which his hands, one often clutching a lit pipe, would be thrust when he chatted to anyone who would listen while recounting tales about the two van drivers. Bill Pollard was the oldest man in the warehouse and the senior van driver, who knew the city like the back of his hand and although he often affected to be serious and unsmiling, he was a good-natured, easy-going man. The other van driver, Peter Rush, was known to us universally as 'Stan', in the odd way this community had of renaming people; he lived in Tynemouth and had married a widow of some substantial financial means. He was as well known for his readiness to indulge in hyperbole about his activities as he was for mangling the English language in their recapitulation. He kept a small, motorised dinghy at Tynemouth, inspiring him to appear at work every day and to drive his van not wearing the regulation Dunlop-badged cap, but in a seafaring skipper's yachting cap. He had been dubbed, in addition to his *nom de guerre* of Stan, the 'Duke of Tynemouth' – a scarcely veiled jibe at his boasts of personal wealth. His daily verbal gaffes had me inwardly convulsed while like everyone else I kept a very straight face as he described his wife wearing a 'cortege of flowers' at a ball, at his sighting of 'an optical seclusion' or at the 'disinterrogation' of a van's windscreen.

George Parker, the service mechanic, wore light green overalls emblazoned with the Dunlop badge, a mark of his specialist skills and to present the right company image in his customer contact; he was proud of his position and was happy to work alone, if only because unlike anyone else he frequently received gratuities for the work he did. Apart from the uniformed van drivers, the green-overalled fitter and the despatch clerk's blue, bib-fronted boiler suit, everyone else below stairs wore the customary, knee-length, brown dustcoat.

I had approached daily work without trepidation or expectation, unchanged by the first trying day of seeking to become familiar with strange people and surroundings before the real task of learning about the activities of the business could begin, when I was confronted with a very threatening situation – or at least that's the way I felt about it at the time. I had returned early from lunch on my second day, taken as usual at home and necessitating a physically demanding bicycle round trip to 5 Havelock Street and back to the depot, all within the allotted one hour. Having entered the office I was aware that, as often happened over the lunch period, only one person was on duty, and soon after my return a second, unmanned telephone started to ring while Doug was engaged in a conversation with a customer on another telephone. Since I had not been told I was to answer telephones, as my prescribed duties were those of an office boy, I merely went about my business and ignored the constant burr-burr-burr: but I was soon made aware by the agitated semaphore waving of arms that Doug expected me to pick up the ringing telephone and answer it. I had never answered a telephone in my life before and had only ever picked one up in one of the few local red public kiosks just to hear the curious purring sound, described in the kiosk as the dialling tone and, more in hope than expectation, to press button 'B' lest a previous user had been unable to connect and had forgotten to reclaim the money inserted. Occasionally this produced a windfall for us, usually twopence, which was soon spent on sweets, lucky dips or a packet of two 'Wild Woodbines'.

I stood staring at the black, bakelite telephone with its circular, silver, dialling disc while listening to its persistent cry to be answered. Doug put his hand over the mouthpiece of his phone and shouted to me, 'Pick the bloody thing up', which I did with trembling hands in a state of near-panic and heard a customer announce himself – I had no idea what our customer's names or businesses were – as he proceeded to enquire whether or not we had a '300–19', which I later discovered was a motorcycle tyre. I stammered 'What did you say?' He repeated his request and I simply put my hand over the mouthpiece, rather as my older colleague had done, waiting for him to finish his call, but he replicated my action like a monkey in a zoo by putting his hand over the other mouthpiece again and yelling with obvious agitation, 'Deal with it, for God's sake.' I can't remember what the outcome was, but it clearly wasn't very satisfactory for the customer, as I had heard his request for a 300–19 as being '300 for the time being', which made no more sense to my more senior colleague or indeed to the customer when I repeated it to him than it had done to me. After this embarrassing, nerve-racking experience I realised that the terrors of the telephone, the carrier of disembodied voices, had to be conquered, and I set about trying to master the art of listening to what people had to say in a variety of voices, accents and dialects of random grammatical accuracy while making notes at the same time.

In a personal, self-critical review of what I had done and what I should have done, I was conscious of a discomfort bordering on blushing shame at being the only person in the office who didn't handle the telephone with great eagerness, although I believed that I was probably more intelligent than any of them. For the first time in my life I was not being introduced to and learning about new things at the same time as my peer group; I was at a serious disadvantage in lacking their knowledge and skills and I had to tackle this strange technology to which I'd had no previous exposure at all – a gap every bit as obvious as the social gulf I had felt in my later years at grammar school.

About a month later, when I had made excellent progress in using the telephone – although it still was not one of my favourite activities – and I had mastered all of the simple yet unnecessarily convoluted paperwork processes within the office, and when I felt really comfortable in attempting any job I was asked, expected or invited to do, Mr Lindsey, whom I was beginning to admire increasingly for his calm management of the staff and the depot routines, called me into his office. He told me that Mr Nesbit, the District Manager, whom I had seen but not been introduced to and who hadn't once deigned to speak to me on his occasional forays through the office to the executive lavatory, had a task he wanted me to do for him. Mr Lindsey said that given my Matriculation result in mathematics this shouldn't be a problem, but he offered no more evidence or advice other than to say that later that same afternoon Mr Nesbit would call for me, which he did at about 3.30p.m., his customary hour for returning to the depot after he had been out for a very important business meeting over lunch with one of his principal customers. As usual he announced his arrival, unseen from where I sat, as he marched from the staircase the short distance along the corridor to his office, passing the secretary's office where he would open the door and call in 'Miss Jeffries'; that would be followed by the creak of the spring closure mechanism on his door and seconds later by the prim Miss Jeffries, with her notebook and pencil, creating the same creaking noise. I sat and waited expectantly until Miss Jeffries approached me, smiled her thin-lipped smile, and said, 'Mr Nesbit would like to see you now.' I stood on the coco mat outside his door and knocked gently until his voice boomed 'Come in', and as I entered I felt in a moment of déjà vu that this was like entering the headmaster's study of St Cuthbert's, except that it was by no means as grand. There were no red-buttoned leather settees or armchairs, there was no coal fire burning with dancing flames, while underfoot there was an apology for a carpet square in the middle of the familiar sea of brown linoleum. There was an impressive large desk, yet not as magnificent as that of Monsignor Canon Cunningham. It was similarly impeccably maintained, its polished wood gleaming, neat with orderly piles of paper on the leather desktop, while in the corner of the office behind Mr Nesbit was a mahogany coat-and-hat stand with a clothes brush and a hairbrush hanging from two of the prongs, and his dark blue, double-breasted suit jacket hung symmetrically on a wooden hanger, with a billowing white handkerchief in the top pocket. I moved my eyes to see Mr Nesbit staring at me, even more red-faced than usual, eyes bulging, wearing an impossibly brilliant white shirt over which dark blue braces vanished below the line of the desk, while the air was heavy with the unmistakable aromas of alcohol and cigarette smoke. The instant impression was that this was the inestimable 'Toad of Toad Hall' in residence, about to be at his most vulgar extreme. This was a happy thought, because it prepared me for what was a very curious, one-sided conversation. There was no introduction, no greeting; he simply told me: 'Cassidy, I want you to do some calculations for me. How long have you been here?'

'Five weeks and a day,' I replied with great, if unnecessary precision. Before I could enlarge upon this he hurried on. 'You'll know then that not all the tyres that go out of here are sold, because we provide some on a contract to the major bus users and charge them a rental for their use. We provide a stock of tyres which we hold on their premises; we fit them, remove them, change them, repair them and for this service we charge a rate per tyre.'

I wondered if I should say this sounds a bit like 'hire purchase', which might have added to my knowledge of this financial instrument, but happily I kept my counsel.

For the second time he was about to get my degree of knowledge hopelessly wrong, as he continued, 'You'll know, of course, all the major operators with whom we deal. The biggest is Newcastle Corporation Transport' [I longed to tell him that my father was a senior, invaluable member of this organisation and had been for a long time, but there was no opportunity to interject as he carried remorselessly on] 'and of course Sunderland Corporation Transport and the other major undertakings, with of course the rural bus operators and long-distance coaches such as United, Venture Transport and many of the larger private operators.'

He paused and stared at me, probably noticing my eyes blank with incomprehension as I nodded, making a mental note to find out more, a lot more, as soon as I left.

'Because the bus companies vary in size we charge different rates. For instance, at Newcastle City Transport say the rate is 0.05125 pence per mile. Now, prices need to be varied from time to time to take account of costs increasing: not just the cost of the tyres but the people we provide as well, and of course we need to understand how much turnover will be generated. I want you to take these examples, tell me what the new rates would be if they were increased by say 1 per cent, 2.5 per cent and some other interim stages and by taking this schedule of the mileages typically run in a year by the different companies, tell me how much the income would be estimated to be at present and at each particular new level. You can do that, can't you?'

I said meekly, 'Yes.'

He then said, 'That's all.'

It seemed to me it wasn't all, because there were two important pieces of information missing. The first had already formed in my mind because being so fresh from school, this was no different from being asked to calculate how quickly a bath with a capacity of 'y' would fill if the water was flowing at 'x' gallons per second through two taps to the bath – always assuming, of course, that the person filling the bath had put in the plug in the first place. The second, rather more pragmatically, was when I was expected to return with the figure.

I asked the first question: 'To be able to calculate the amount of money that you will get . . .'

He interrupted: 'Turnover the company will receive.'

'Yes, sir,' I said, 'I need to know how many wheels there are on each bus, don't I? Could you tell me?' I asked hesitantly.

'Doesn't make any difference,' he said.

I thought I would store this for guidance elsewhere.

'When would you like this to be done, sir?'

'Soon as possible,' he said, and with that simple timescale, said 'That's all.'

'Thank you, sir,' I said.

I considered walking backwards from the presence of this great man, as Robin Hood had done when he realised he was in the company of Richard the Lionheart, but remembered just in time that this was Mr Toad, so I turned round and walked out of his modest room, which seemed such an ill match for this large, self-important presence. I knew that three of my new colleagues 'below stairs' were employed as relief tyre fitters on these mileage contracts, to cover for holidays or sickness absence by the full-time fitters, and so I flew down the spiral stairs to ask them a series of questions about the differences in the bus fleets, the average number of tyres for each bus model and whether they had any idea of total mileages per annum. They were a mine of useful information, because of course they did the work, as they explained patiently that most of the buses in the Newcastle Corporation fleet were of a certain type with a fixed number of tyres per vehicle of the same size. Inevitably the fleet changed over time and had more than one model in operation, but they gave me a very good approximation of the number of types of each vehicle. On the other hand they explained that the composition of the fleets in most of the others differed, not only from Newcastle but from each other, and after an intensive, thirty-minute briefing I had a very good idea of the nature of the fleets. They also modified some of Mr Nesbit's ideas of the estimated mileage each fleet would be running in a year. I knew of course that while the number of tyres had no influence on the cost per tyre, the number of miles run in aggregate would make a significant difference to the aggregate turnover; reverting to school maths yet again it was possible to start with the answer Mr Nesbit wanted and work back to the rate per tyre/mile to achieve it, a variation of the common school examination question about vehicles where distance over time equals average speed.

Armed with this information I returned to my desk and began these calculations, to a sixth-decimal-place accuracy, while my three informants in the warehouse returned to their daily task of finishing *The Times* crossword, puzzled more by my breathless quest for information than the cryptic clues. By the time I had finished my sums which, since I didn't possess and couldn't use a slide rule, were all achieved by long multiplication and division, most people had left the premises, because prompt departure was the habit of everybody in the building except the designated locker-up. On the basis of this week's rota that was Albert Reavely the storekeeper, and he was enquiring when I would be leaving. I left with my sheaf of handwritten calculations which I checked at home that night, rechecking them once more before converting them to a neat set of tables. I drew one for each bus operator, with the horizontal axis showing the rate per mile per tyre at each 0.25 per cent rate increment, and the vertical axis showing the total number of fleet miles run, derived from the calculated averages of the tyres per bus multiplied by the fleet miles. This provided an impressive, yet simple portrayal of the escalating turnover that would result dependent on increased mileage due to an increasing population, additional buses, or new routes combined with increased mileage rates.

When I had finished I was pleased, believing it was a good piece of work, almost as good as my 'Atticeo' cricket records; I was still excited after I returned to the office the next morning and anxiously awaited the sound of Mr Nesbit's footsteps. I had already checked with Miss Jeffries that he would be in that morning; it was his normal habit to appear between 9.30 and 10.00a.m., clearly having already been to see one of his prized customers en route from his home on the coast near Whitley Bay to the office, and then it was his normal routine to deliver his car to George Parker. The garage fitter was required to clean the already gleaming vehicle while Mr Nesbit, in his elegant, if generously cut, dark blue suit, white shirt and silk tie, retreated to his office for a short while before he left at about midday for another one of his important client meetings – or earlier if that client was further away in the wilds of Northumberland, County Durham or Cumberland.

As soon as I heard the heavy footsteps and the creaking door I began to rehearse a well-prepared speech about how I had approached the task he had set me. Just as I'd made up my mind to go to the coco-matting starting line, having heard no one else go in before me, I was summoned to take some urgently required despatch documentation to the chief storekeeper, which I did at the double. I was frustrated to find no sign of Albert the Giant and was forced to hunt high and low for him before I eventually located him preparing for a stock recount in one corner of the warehouse. I gave him the documentation and hurried as fast as I could back to my desk to recompose myself, ready to re-engage with Mr Nesbit. I picked up the papers, looked at them again, stood on the coco matting, tapped lightly on the door and responded to the booming 'Come in.' To my pleasant surprise not only was I looking at the red face and bulging eyes, behind thick spectacles, of 'Mr Toad' but alongside him sat Mr Lindsey, wearing his usual, mildly sardonic but nevertheless pleasant half-smile.

'I've finished those figures for you, sir,' I said.

'Good,' he replied. 'Let me see them.'

I walked up with the impressive sheaf of calculations with my stated assumptions for each of ten vehicle fleets, complete with an individual graph and an overview, summarised in another graph showing the rates taken from each of the individual sheets which supported it. He looked at them, turning the sheets, and then suddenly pointed a beautifully manicured thick, pink, stubby finger at one of the numbers.

'That's wrong,' he said.

I was about to say 'No, it's not', when my school experience strangled the words and I simply replied, 'I don't think so; I've checked it twice.'

He looked at me witheringly. 'It's wrong.'

He picked up the sheaf, thrust it into my hand and said, 'Go away and check them again.'

'Yes, sir,' I said, humiliated and embarrassed and saying critically to myself as I left, 'How could I be so stupid, how could I do that in front of Mr Lindsey?' I retrieved my rough working sheets to recheck the point at which my calculations had gone wrong, marvelling as I did at the rapier-like mind that had instantaneously spotted the error in a mass of detail.

The man whom I thought had just demonstrated that he was the overlord of all this activity because his perception was so acute, who was so bright as to see in an instant that a calculation I had painstakingly checked and rechecked was incorrect, had in fact himself made an error – but how could I tell him? How could I explain that my numbers were correct after all? But there was nothing else for it, so I wearily gathered up the papers and once again stood in trepidation on the coco matting as I tapped the door yet again, fearing the worst and wondering how I was going to handle this. I was pretty certain that the threat of physical violence which hung over me when I went to the headmaster's study would be absent, but there might be worse to face in this case.

I responded to the familiar booming 'Come in', and began 'I've checked those numbers . . .', but I got no further, for he took them from me and said 'That's okay.' As I looked perplexed he repeated, 'That's okay; that's all', put the papers down on his desk, and I left. What did it all mean? I felt obliged to go to my mentor as I now saw him, Mr Lindsey, saying 'I've taken those figures back to Mr Nesbit and they were correct.'

'Were they?' he said, with the half-smile.

'Yes,' said I.

'Good,' said he.

After a morning's reflection I realised in a defining moment that I had learned something of critical importance, and however similar the circumstances appeared to be to those that prevailed at school, work was very different. For the first time in my life an adult with power over me had asked me to undertake a task in which the quality of the result had not given him pleasure – not even at the demonstration of learning by the pupil; but worse still, that junior's work had in some peculiar, unimaginable way threatened the older, more powerful man. He had been brusque but businesslike on his own, yet when I had returned with an impressive piece of work beyond the original requirements and within the timescale set, he had been offended. Why? Was it that another senior colleague had seen that work was somebody else's? By producing the figures and extending the range of outcomes as I had done, I had challenged some of his own assumptions, because unknown to him I had gone to a source which he, from his great height, could not tap: that of the tyre fitters. I determined there and then that whatever I did would be of the same quality, done with the same care and dedication, but I would make it clear that I regarded my work as good as anybody else's and probably better. This was going to be the way in which I would push my learning forward, demonstrate my capacity for work, to the extent that any job, no matter what it was, could be quite safely allocated to me. I knew that in this I would have an ally, albeit perhaps sometimes a silent one, in Mr Lindsey.

I was pursuing parallel forms of development at Dunlop. On the one hand I was exploring the world of work – or at least the Dunlop view of that world; since it was the only work that I had known, apart from delivering newspapers or picking potatoes with POWs, there was no other benchmark against which to measure it. On the other hand I was developing personally in ways which I'd had very limited opportunities to do previously, benefiting from friendships and relationships with people who were neither neighbours nor schoolmates. There was still an element of choice in this – to be passive or positive – but it was a wider, freer society with more ideas, more options and much more varied subjects of conversation. At Dunlop, as at home, I was aware that I was a junior member, but at work there was little evidence of the protective, benevolent guidance which was ever present at home.

36

. . . AND PLAY

Within a few weeks of having started my new life, while I was still absorbing all its complexities and struggling to integrate with this strange community, I learned of my extremely good Matriculation results. I registered for exactly the same course as Vincent had pursued between 1944 and 1946, to be undertaken at exactly the same place, the former Rutherford Grammar School premises in Bath Lane; and at work I was promoted to the position of Junior Clerk following the appointment of a new office boy, Albert Milbourne – who looked and behaved much as my close and long-standing literary companion, William Brown. Within a few more months Alan Maguire had returned from his National Service stint and yet another young man, Norman Atkinson – immediately nicknamed 'Gloops' – had been recruited as office boy.

Although a number of other youngsters – some with previous business experience and others, as I had once been, school leavers – joined the company over the next year, either to replace those departing for National Service or more often now to cope with the growth of a business rebuilding as wartime shortages and problems began to ease, it was this quartet – myself, Albert, Alan and Norman – who became the closest of companions. We also formed the core of a highly competent office team and provided a source of amusement for many others, but principally ourselves.

These three were to satisfy one of my own personal objectives: that of having fun, preferably with good companions, while doing a good job of work. After all, this had been our *raison d'etre* at home, as it had been in my newspaper round and throughout my school years, when I never found any conflict between working hard, learning from my efforts and yet simultaneously having a lot of fun doing it. However, both at home and at school, having fun was an explicitly acceptable, seemingly necessary part of the process to which most teachers subscribed, and it was not limited to the formal periods for sport or to subjects such as music. There was a noticeable difference in the workplace, though, where having fun was equated with not taking the job seriously, thereby forcing most people to respond by telling jokes or making humorous asides in a hushed whisper out of the boss's earshot, or by ending any frivolous conversation abruptly if a figure of authority even appeared in the general office. In consequence it meant that lunch hours became more precious, and we sought to pack them with a variety of diversionary entertainments.

The great Dunlop company's policies set the tone for this quasi-monastic atmosphere, but it was combined with a splash of Victorian benefaction: it sought to modify this by a concession to offset the tedium of daily working life through the medium of an officially organised, annual depot outing. It was held in June or July; the depot was 'closed for business' for a day and everyone, from the District Manager to the office boy, embarked by coach for a 'day out' at the company's expense. We travelled to some resort where lunch and tea were provided and where fraternising among management and staff, men and women, was allowed – rather as I had experienced during the war when potato picking in the fields of Blagden Hall with prisoners of war and local residents.

Since I had joined Dunlop in August I had missed the 1949 outing but could look forward to the 1950 trip, which I did with no more enthusiasm than I had to the Poor Children's Holiday Association trip to South Shields in 1938. In any case, this was never going to satisfy the daily needs of a quartet of high–spirited, active youngsters, who were bright enough, and collectively sufficiently streetwise, to challenge old attitudes. We soon learned, of course, that our shared passion was football, but since we had ample, long-established opportunities to play that in our own neighbourhoods at whatever level seemed appropriate, there was never any serious suggestion of forming a works football club. We did all enjoy the occasional impromptu 'kick abouts' on the car park, though, or the even more primitive games in the packing room, and we always had the opportunity to watch a rampagingly successful Newcastle United periodically at St James' Park. Cricket needed equipment, or funds to acquire it which we didn't have, but that still left scope for us to play cards; we quickly developed a formal, regular card school in our lunch hour, when a variety of games were played. These ranged from three-card brag, with its frenetic gambling, through 'pontoon' to whist and then to solo whist, which emerged to survive as the favourite and became our mainstay for a long time, particularly during the winter months. In the lunch hour we began to seek out quiet spots in the office, sometimes breaking every rule in the book to achieve our objectives — such as acquiring by unfair means the key to the locked stationery cupboard, so that we could enjoy the privacy needed to play diligently through the whole of the lunch hour while ignoring any unanswered telephone calls. The whereabouts of our card school were ultimately discovered, leading not only to a public rebuke by an angry Charlie, but also to a determination on our part to find an alternative venue that was even more secure — as uncrackable to those in authority as the wartime Enigma code had been.

Tyres in the warehouse were stacked in 12-foot-high, double-sided racks and, apart from the gigantic Albert Reavely and John Clelland, average-sized men required stepladders to enable them to reach tyres in the highest rows. Similarly, but even less accessibly, boxed inner tubes for tyres were stored on large shelves to a similar height. These shelves were also double-sided and were like the pigeonholes we used to sort incoming and outgoing mail, only on a Brobdingnagian scale. Our inventiveness led us to realise that we could use the specially made stepladders permanently located in this part of the warehouse to gain access to the top level of shelves, where behind a wall of large tube boxes we could create a makeshift, circular card table from a tyre display insert. There we could play our game in the peace and quiet of the warehouse at lunchtime, totally unseen, yet because of the stone floors we would be instantly alerted by audible footsteps if someone was approaching; then we would tone down our conversation or make a swift exit down the stepladder. This worked until we made the error of forgetting that stock counts were conducted on a monthly basis, always by the Chief Clerk accompanied by the Chief Storekeeper, when every single item in the warehouse, no matter how small, was counted and reconciled with a manually updated stock record. When discrepancies arose after a stock count had taken place, stock differences, as they were known, had to be resolved or confirmed by a physical recount. The first recourse when differences arose would be to ask the Stock Recording Clerk to check his postings to the stock record sheets after which, if the difference remained, the stock was recounted taking due account of any transactions that had occurred in the meantime.

One afternoon, some fifteen minutes after our lunch hour should have ended, we heard footsteps approaching; we remained silent, but to our horror the footsteps seemed to stop immediately below us. We were stalled in the middle of our game, having missed the opportunity to make our escape, and clearly a recount was to take place somewhere very close to us. Mr Lindsey's voice was unmistakable, as was Albert Reavely's, but worse still the ladder we had propped against the outer edge of the shelf on which we sat creaked in a way that told us it was Albert Reavely's heavy body that was hauling itself up. There could be only one conclusion; the only level out of his reach was the uppermost shelf on which we sat, momentarily frozen, and since it must be inner tubes which were to be recounted he would be obliged to get to the top – possibly even to climb into our gigantic pigeonhole to ensure he counted every item accurately. We held our breath and waited as first the dark hair on the top of his head appeared, then the spectacles on Mr Reavely's ruddy face; when he saw our strained, staring faces it turned almost purple as his veins dilated and his jaw dropped, while we waited for revelation and retribution. He counted the tubes deliberately, shouted the required number down to Mr Lindsey as he descended slowly, the ladder was removed, their steps retraced and their voices faded until we clambered down in silence and hurried back separately and embarrassedly to our desks.

Later, the giant Albert spoke to each of us individually, introducing me to being on the receiving end of one of his growling bollockings with the clear message that if we wanted 'to bugger about' we should do so elsewhere – 'but not in my warehouse again or else!' We humbly accepted the well-deserved rebuke and were grateful that the Chief Storekeeper, who was one of the trusted top team, had not exposed our presence – probably because he was following the unwritten working-man's code to protect his own, in which we as juniors were included, so as not to be thought to be 'sucking up to the gaffer'.

It seemed our card games were destined to lose some of their thrill by being constrained by unswerving conformity to the designated lunch hour, when Alan was promoted unexpectedly to become Stock Record Clerk – without any increase of pay, of course, but with the priceless benefit of inheriting the Stock Recorder's 'private' office. In this role the jobholder's need for concentration provided us with a legitimate opportunity to close the door, shielding us from passing eyes, while the large table needed to display and post goods movements to the stock sheets made a perfect card table. We were in business again and all Alan had to do was to accumulate a bank of credits by his performance in this new role to protect us from the consequences of accidental exposure. It was the perfect challenge.

At the same time the layers of childlike innocence that I had carried from a Catholic family upbringing and a Catholic grammar-school education were peeled away increasingly rapidly. Sex, politics, religion and sport probably accounted for 99 per cent of the conversations in the depot, whether upstairs or downstairs, and although the sports chat was dominated by the growing success of Newcastle United there was also cricket to discuss, now that the County Championship was in full flow. That was accompanied by visits from other international touring sides such as India, New Zealand, South Africa and the West Indies, offering some prospect of success after the third successive series defeat at the hands of Australia. Boxing was popular and a constant topic of conversation because of the succession of British heroes who became serious world-title contenders, like Bruce Woodcock, Freddie Mills and best of all Randolph Turpin, who beat the great American middleweight Sugar Ray Robinson to become world champion. This and every other major contest were broadcast live, with commentaries by Raymond Glendenning accompanied by inter-round summaries by Barrington Dalby, and had us glued to our wireless sets at home. Debate raged in the packing room for weeks before any big match; money was demanded to back up unlikely predictions and the post-mortem analysis was frequently as acrimonious as the pre-match speculation was lengthy. What I enjoyed most was the way older men trotted out sporting history in fondly remembered detail, providing an educational introduction to pre-war national heroes like Jimmy Wilde, Benny Lynch and Tommy Farr as well as to American giants like Joe Louis, Gene Tunney and Jack Dempsey.

The other major sporting topic of everyday conversation was horseracing. It differed from other sports like football, cricket or boxing, where the interest lay in the sport itself, in that with racing the main attraction lay in the opportunity it offered for gambling, with the inherent if remote prospect for most working men of a large windfall win to break the tedium of everyday financial constraints. Rather like our lunchtime card games, it also offered the vicarious thrill associated with being an illegal activity which had to be carried out under cover to avoid the watchful eye of the law. This was not new to me; Ma had introduced me to it many years before, creating an interest in picking winners begun by my first-ever selection, Hypericum, having won The Oaks in 1946 at 14–1, despite having thrown its jockey through the tapes before the race had even started. My successful 'penny each way' bet, made with the bookies' runner in a nearby back lane, had been under the heavily disguised alias of 'Denis X', but my interest thereafter had been dormant except for the occasional big race flutter, funded again by Ma when she needed me to take her complicated 'three cross doubles and each way treble' sixpenny bet to the bookie. Now, however, I had a common interest with my new companions, of whom Norman was the knowledgeable 'horsey' expert, as we developed a system to bet regularly, although in pitifully small amounts, with each of us taking turns to make the selections and Norman seeking out the haunts of the local bookie to place our collective bets and recover any winnings.

The divisive effect of age differences shrank, finally to vanish in 1951 as I turned eighteen and was not only able but expected to join unaccompanied in adult conversations freely in a pub; it was in this largely, sometimes exclusively male company that conversation, debate and heated argument raged over what were thought to be the principal concerns of the day. I was no stranger to the appeal of saloon bars as a debating chamber, having been introduced by Pop to one of his favourite haunts, the 'Bodega', after Benediction on the Sunday following my sixteenth birthday. I was still at school, but as an acknowledgement of my growing maturity and having bought me a beer of my choice, he said simply, if inaccurately, 'There, now I know you drink. Treat it with care, don't abuse it and it will be a good friend for you, and at least you'll know that I'll know when you have been drinking.' But like my horserace betting, that had largely been an exception – apart from occasional visits to the 'Westfield' or the 'Blue Man' for special family occasions – until my new way of life as a working man demanded that I conformed by joining pub gatherings, occasionally after work on a

Friday evening and more frequently, if more briefly, on Saturday lunchtimes after our half-day's work.

I was well read in politics because of the interest developed during my daily newspaper delivery rounds and I had continued to take an active interest in them long after the newspaper boy's satchel had been set aside. I was familiar with religion, having been involved in challenging debates throughout my childhood that had only strengthened my firmly held view of the infallibility of the Catholic Church's Christian dogma; but sex was still a closed book and my attempts to understand it had thus far resulted only in further confusion. Just as I was to learn much more about this subject, unsought but never avoided, so too was I to learn that in practice politics extended to the workplace in ways far removed from my narrow view that this subject was bounded by what Mr Churchill, Mr Attlee and the major political parties did. Day after day I became involved in, or eavesdropped on, conversations and debates about leaders or those who were led, listened to thoughts that were as enquiring and open to persuasion as my own, while hearing others that were as heated in their insistence of a personal perspective as any prejudices I had ever heard aired. On such occasions these confrontations were frequently followed by a volley of bad language or a waving of arms, or after drink in the pub an all-too-obvious breach, even if only temporary, in friendly relations.

But conversations about sex tended to take a very different pattern. Somehow this was a matter that only the younger, unmarried adults talked about openly, except for Cyril; he, by virtue of being a section leader and a bachelor hotly pursued by the only two women in the depot who were eligible and available, was above this topic of conversation and remained silent on the subject. Interestingly both 'les girls' were the subject of intense speculation about their relative merits, the descriptions of most of which I didn't understand anyway – although it didn't take a Freud to realise what expressions like 'She's a goer' really meant. Rita seemed an unlikely sex bomb, but echoes of homespun philosophy such

as 'You can't tell a book by its cover' suggested that she might be the
more satisfying partner of the two. 'Not a chance,' I thought. Similarly
the two men who appeared least likely to be able to boast of serial sexual
exploits, George Lyons and Alan Charlton, always talked about them in
prospect as weekends drew near and in retrospect on Monday mornings.
Physically neither suggested that they were capable either of their
claimed irresistibility by the opposite sex, or of indulging in the
multitude of picaresque adventures about which they talked and of
which even Don Juan would have been proud. Alan, an ex-sailor whose
short stature, of about 5 feet 3 inches, and crushed features I had seen
first when I attended my initial interview at Dunlop, spoke loudly and
bawdily about his many conquests in graphic detail; they had even the
most experienced men crying 'Enough', but curiously no one had ever
seen him with a woman. Neither indeed had they seen George Lyons, a
gangly, bespectacled, bow-legged, lively personality who worked in the
service department and whose exploits were always with married women
– 'No one ever misses a slice off a cut cake' – and centred on one of his
local pubs, 'The Trap' at Coxlodge, allegedly frequented by hordes of
attractive, sexually liberated, married women 'longing for it'. There was
little doubt that both knew well the saloon-bar vocabulary of the male
predator, but there was more evidence of a fantasising Walter Mitty than
there was of Clark Gable in their proclaimed ability to attract women
'like bees to a honeypot'.

I realised that the colourfully ridiculous tale can be as good a source of
learning as textbook accuracy if you know the difference, and slowly my
knowledge and vocabulary of this delicate subject increased; it was too
delicate to be referred to at home but too important to be ignored at
work, and I concluded that some practical learning had to be considered.

Novels, of course, continued to provide some stimulating insight into
the pleasures and pitfalls of female company. I had gathered from my
eldest brother Alan's muttered reaction when he started reading my
library editions of Dennis Wheatley's latest books, which contained some

lurid details of Gregory Salust's exploitive peccadilloes, that when he said these books were 'too old for you' he really meant they were sexually interesting. Vincent's more liberal attitude remained, but his habit of reading *Lilliput* had ceased – probably because he now had a serious relationship and was edging towards marriage. Sydney was ahead of me in the practical exploration of female charms, as I had become aware at the 'Essoldo' while I was still at school, when the lights went up on one occasion to reveal him with Joannie and Mary, two young neighbourhood girls, on the carpeted floor under the double seats in the back row. Once at work I came to the conclusion, more by accident than design, that I should adopt a two-pronged, adult approach to this matter and, mindful of the potential pitfalls, play away rather than on my home pitch around Havelock Street, engaging with some of my old school and more recent work colleagues in this pursuit.

In a period of reflective conversation over a cup of hot Bovril at work one cold winter's afternoon, Albert and I decided to go on Friday night to the Palace Theatre in the Haymarket, very close to where we worked, to see Jane, the cartoon pin-up of the *Daily Mirror* made famous in wartime, with the express intention of learning more about 'the real thing' in the flesh in adult company. Although we toyed with the prospect of staying in town enjoying other male pursuits until the variety theatre opened its doors at 7.30p.m., we were both obliged first to go our own opposite ways home to deposit the bulk of the weekly pay packet with our respective waiting mothers. The performance was a disappointment, although our fellow voyeurs in the vertiginous upper reaches of the 'gods' were not, as we collectively suffered a seemingly interminable succession of jugglers, off-key singers, and heavily thighed dancers accompanied by a sparse, frequently discordant band misnamed 'The Palace Orchestra'; but eventually the compère welcomed 'the world-famous, the armed services' favourite pin-up, Britain's secret weapon, JANE', with a loud roll of drums. The stage curtains parted and there on a circular dais stood the naked beauty, holding a large, ostrich-feathered fan over her principal asset, the other hand thrust 'Statue of Liberty' style aloft, giving me my first reunion with naked female parts since Mary's tit was exposed so many years before. But any joy to be derived from Jane's ample display was distracted by the pulling open of a dozen or more dirty raincoats as old men whipped out spyglasses, binoculars or hankies, the latter to wipe their steamed-up spectacles as they drooled, cackled and muttered in hopeless lust. The curtains closed and reopened several times to reveal the spotlighted Jane in a series of fixed, unmoving poses – as demanded by the Lord Chamberlain – each of which was greeted by polite applause from the orchestra stalls and dress circle, contrasting with the grunting, half-laughing, gurgling sounds of lustful appreciation around us. Then the curtain came down for the last time, the theatre lights went up and the spyglasses were smuggled back into the inner pockets of dirty raincoats, as their owners looked furtively around. It had been an entertaining, informative evening, but not quite in the way we had hoped.

Shortly after this educational experience I found myself being persuaded to attend a dance in a church hall, the principal arguments in favour being that it was cheap and certainly affordable, which the popular Oxford Galleries or the upper-crust Old Assembly Rooms were not; it was an appropriate place to learn how to 'ballroom dance', and there was an excess of unattached, young girls anxious to practise their various skills. There were some disadvantages – primarily that there would be a healthy sprinkling of older men and women dancing, some of whom would be the parents of the young dancers.

My former schoolfriend George Allan, who was an extremely good-looking lad with the easy charm and confidence born of being an only child of wealthy, adoring parents, introduced me to the idea, and also to the next Saturday evening 'hop'; given his ability to attract friends of either sex it made for a happy entrée to a new pleasure, although without my even venturing onto the dance floor. Nevertheless I spotted those dances I could cope with easily, like the Bradford Barn Dance, the Veleta and the Gay Gordons, whereas I knew I would need to practise seriously before the quickstep, foxtrot and waltz could be attempted, and the tango was definitely out of the question in the short term. In addition there was the old, recurring problem of suitable attire: or more accurately footwear, because my thick, crepe-soled shoes, still the most fashionable accessory in my limited wardrobe, refused to glide over the French-chalk-dusted church-hall floor when I surreptitiously tried this out, as the dancing was in progress and the lights were dimmed.

But within a month I had solved both problems and had experienced the assorted pleasures of dancing partners. They effortlessly taught me the steps by example; some of them held me close enough to increase rapidly my appreciation of the female body, some of their physical assets had developed faster than their ability to control their desires, and there were those older women who pulled me to their steel-corseted frames as they pushed me in a goose-step parody of a barn dance. But of more practical value I had met a growing number of girls who, contrary to my first expectations, were proving to be excellent company as well as skilful dancing partners, and if life wasn't a continuous social whirl I was already expanding my admittedly narrow range of leisure activities. Above all it took me out of the male-dominated worlds I had known at home and school, propelled by the need to know more about girls if I was ever going to be able to understand those adult conversations at work before playing a full part in them.

Soon plans began to be released for the annual outing, and this new topic of conversation began to dominate the debating lists as the chosen date drew near. There was great excitement when we all gathered, slightly earlier than our usual start time, on the day of the outing, with everyone in their best clothes. The warehouse staff managed to look both the best dressed and the strangest in their unfamiliar clothing. It was a warm, sunny morning and the luxury coach, which was to take thirty-five of us to Keswick in the Lake District, was already parked with the door invitingly open and a smartly dressed driver standing at ease at the foot of the entrance. Everyone milled around waiting for permission to board and instructions as to where we would be allowed to sit, which for newcomers like me was an important yet missing piece of information. The open door to the depot told us that some, including Mr Lindsey, were inside attending to last-minute business matters, while the absence of Mr Nesbit's shining black saloon was seen as a testament to his dedication to his principal customers, rather than a criticism of his timekeeping; when he arrived later it was as a passenger in Bobby Jackson the salesman's car, in the interests of public safety for the return journey. Gradually little knots of like-minded individuals gathered, mostly talking animatedly about what was to come and benefiting from the experience of those who had made similar trips; it all seemed to presage a much better day than the only other bus trip I had been on, with the PCHA in 1938, although this one did share the common attractive ingredient of being free of charge.

After an early problem that required George the garage fitter to change out of his finery and into overalls to fit and balance some racing tyres we were loaded, avoiding the front seats required by the overlords, George rejoined us, the door to the depot was slammed and the 'Closed for Depot Outing' sign was hung on the outside of the folding metal grille as it was padlocked. It soon became obvious that the critical decision was not whom to sit with but whom to avoid, as a good deal of jockeying for position went on, rather like a game of draughts. The comely Patricia, in her highest heels and most revealing dress, evidenced displeasure at Cyril's reluctance to sit with her, for while she smiled sweetly at the leering Bobby Wells, who sat readily alongside her, she fixed a gimlet-like eye on Rita to ensure she gained no immediate advantage. There was some enforced jollity introduced by the three sales reps, who clearly were under instruction to so do with welcome promises to 'buy you a drink when we get there for all you've done for me', and after a short stop for morning coffee which allowed more changes of immediate travelling companions, we arrived on a lovely summer's lunchtime at a breathtakingly beautiful hotel in Keswick. There we decanted, made our way to the public bar and began to extract the promised free drinks.

The day passed in a memorable flash of intense, liberated enjoyment as new groups formed, some to drink and chat, some to play dominoes or cards for substantial stakes, some to wander in the hotel grounds, and one or two others – of whom Cyril and Pat were the least obvious – to find more private corners as befitted the more intimate nature of their intended activity. Some became noisily cheerful, others lugubriously rued the decision to play dominoes for such high stakes, some reminisced fondly of pre-war days and of 'those that are gone', while the older, non-drinking fraternity hoped that 'they don't forget to tell us when dinner's ready'. Mrs Watson talked quietly and grandly about her lieutenant-commander son-in-law as she demurely ordered a 'B & B' – a potentially lethal cocktail of brandy and Benedictine – before a gong sounded and we all made our way up a grand, wide staircase to a dazzling dining room with white tablecloths, silver cutlery, sparkling crystal and vases of fresh flowers. While what seemed an army of waitresses stood by silver trays waiting to serve me, jugs of beer were brought, glasses of water served, bread offered, as whispered hints circulated the table of which cutlery to use first. 'Toad' gave a benevolent if rather restrained message of thanks for our efforts, and enjoined us to remember the company's generosity in response to our loyal service past, present and to come. And so the day continued: back to dominoes and beer after lunch for some, fresh air and recovery for others – and near disaster for at least one. Old Joe Andrews, the West Coast salesman, strayed into a bull's paddock and when faced by the snorting beast made his escape over a barbed-wire fence, ripping his trousers in the most embarrassingly revealing of places in this surprisingly athletic act of self-defence. I gleaned these facts when I overheard him explaining that the reason he had bought a large bag of cakes at a local shop, carried in clasped hands behind his back, was to cover the damage and limit the risk of unintentional exposure.

The trip home in the dimly lit bus was enlivened by rousing community singing, mainly of old music-hall songs and a scattering of more soulful romantic wartime songs. There was an occasional lapse by some into the vulgarity of what I was told were 'rugby songs', bringing sly smiles to the female faces and lewd cackles from those who had overindulged, while Norman Lindsey (I was now secretly on first-name terms) made full use of his deafness to avoid potential conflict.

I had never been in a hotel before, never been waited on before and could now see what great possibilities might lie ahead – well summed up by the inscribed message on one of the stained-glass windows in the bar in which I and most others had spent much of the day: 'Toil is sweet but pleasure's sweeter.'

37

THE DEPOT INSPECTOR CALLS

During the winter of 1949/50 the 'chest' problems I had suffered in my last year at school began to re-emerge, not that they had ever gone away entirely in the first place. There was no reason why they should have, since the conditions in which we lived were unchanged – a combination of postwar austerity, ever-present constraints on spending, the same domestic environment of coal fires, damp, chilly rooms apart from the kitchen, together with the constant presence of animals whose contribution to my problems neither I nor anyone else fully recognised at the time. What may well have contributed significantly also to the decline in my health was my now-regular attendance most evenings at night school in the old Rutherford College in Bath Lane, where after the walk to and from home on dark, late-autumn evenings following a day's work, the unheated premises, the bare stone floors and the ever-present smell of gas from the gaslights had an incrementally adverse effect. During the worst of these attacks I was badly affected by prolonged bouts of coughing which were physically draining, and I had to abandon my normal practice of walking or cycling to and from Dunlop to travel by trolleybus. However, except for one or two days' absence when the attacks were at their worst, theoretically ameliorated by Dr Taylor's brown-and-cream-layered universal panacea, I managed to cope, although frequently making alarming wheezing noises resembling those of badly played bagpipes. The symptoms persisted throughout the summer of 1950 and from time to time became even worse – obviously, yet to me mystifyingly, related to the fact that I was now playing cricket seriously for a club side at junior level; regularly after an evening match I would wake up during the night fighting for my breath and in an extremely distressed condition.

Through the following winter of 1950/1 this condition caused me – at my mother's direction and following doctor's advice – to give up my attendance at night school, because of the unhealthy combination of my condition with the unsatisfactory environment there; although there was no significant improvement as a result, neither was there any further deterioration. But as my eighteenth birthday drew near in February 1951, so did my impending National Service call-up; I was summoned to attend a medical board, the outcome of which in my present state was entirely predictable – although apparently not to the appointed doctor, who rather than rejecting me as 'unfit for service' deferred me. Thereafter I was required to attend a series of medicals, with the same predictably depressing outcome, every three months. Deferment was in the belief that the symptoms would clear up quickly, which always seemed improbable, while retaining me on the active list – thus ensuring that His Majesty's government would not have to pay a pension if, through overzealousness, the medical board had accepted me. I referred to my state as 'dejected', a category not recognised by His Majesty's armed forces but that in my view lay somewhere between deferment and rejection, because it had an inhibiting effect on my career progression with Dunlop – although I recognised His Majesty's government's wisdom in reserving first option on my services if they should yet need me to counteract the worldwide spread of communism or the growing nuclear threat.

Having heard tales of time wasted on meaningless duties from many of those who had served in the armed forces during the war, or on National Service afterwards, I wasn't particularly concerned about the forgone 'development experience'; yet in a more important way it was another blow to my developing self-confidence. Of course I had always known I was small, slight and not particularly strong, but if I was ultimately to be told I was 'unfit' for any kind of duty, that raised spectres of a short, unfulfilled life.

In reality, however, this was not the first time fate and I had clashed and it was unlikely to be the last; if anything it simply reinforced my view that Dunlop, which I had entered in a genuine belief that I would be there for a reasonably short time before completing National Service and then going on to university afterwards, now looked more likely to provide a golden opportunity for a longer-term career. I had made a good start by using my reliable, well-developed memory and my excellent if truncated education, so that I could now carry out any of the basic administrative routines efficiently and had already suggested – it seemed to some rather precociously – a number of improvements to procedures that I found tortuous, tedious, time-consuming and above all, pointless. I saw very little difference in my dissatisfaction with these office routines from that I had experienced with the newsagent's planning of my delivery rounds, although here I could not introduce improvements covertly as I had done previously with Mr Hannah's schedules. The need to suggest change, explain the reasons for it and the ensuing delay or disinterest by most of my seniors – 'yours not to reason why, yours but to do and die' – created a determination to persuade, even if it was preceded by long periods of frustration. Yet throughout this the apparently reserved, quiet, deaf-yet-listening Mr Lindsey never discouraged my puppy-like enthusiasm and I had willing allies in the card-school quartet; we developed as an informal systems and procedures review panel while we played our hands of solo whist.

I had obtained rapid promotion, by Dunlop standards, by being given a variety of increasingly complex jobs, even if that was without pay increases. Those were geared rigidly to an age scale, irrespective of what duties we had or how well they were carried out, until we achieved the maximum basic wage at the age of twenty-one. After that further wage progressions would be due entirely to the merit of individual performance, or more realistically the whim of the person who determined the increases, unless promotion was presented by a pair of empty 'dead man's shoes'.

The core function of the depot was to receive tyres and accessories from Dunlop factories and to issue them to customers. No selling was involved because supplies still fell short of demand, a continuing hangover from the war years. The stock represented a precious asset for the business and had to be carefully accounted for by the administrative routines controlling the issue of tyres, geared to the basic invoice/despatch document. This was a simple, four-part set that, despite its critical importance, was prepared by hand after inserting a metal plate into a prenumbered pad, interleaving three sheets of carbon paper, and using only an indelible pencil writing details of the customer's name, address, and account number, as well as the quantity and description of the goods being sent. Of the four-part set the top copy was batched daily in sequence and sent to the UK headquarters in Birmingham for an invoice to be raised; the second copy was used by the Stock Recording Clerk to maintain an accurate record of stock; the third copy was used by the warehouse to 'pick' and despatch the goods, after which it was returned to be 'married up' with the second copy by the Stock Recording Clerk; and the fourth copy went to the customer with the goods.

A complex set of subsidiary routines had been constructed and implemented uniformly throughout Dunlop worldwide to ensure that the company was paid in full for any goods sold and that all stock was held securely until that happened. To achieve that every task was supervised or subsequently checked, every alteration to documentation required three authorising signatures, while physical stock counts were made repeatedly and compared with the appropriate paper-based record.

Precisely the same rigid, interlocking process was applied to the payment of wages and the purchase of goods or services locally where these were not provided by the Central Purchasing or Stationery Departments at Fort Dunlop, Birmingham. Pitifully small amounts of cash, stocks of pencils and carbon papers were subject to the same controls, scrutiny and checks. The value was irrelevant: large- or small-value items or services were not distinguished, only right or wrong; either everything was fully accounted for or it was not. If it was not, whatever it was, a tyre, a penny or a toilet roll, it had to be found or its reason for being missing established.

These principles were identical to those which had governed the creation of the greatest empire in history and the provisioning of countless British armies, including those in which Private 1988 Cassidy had fought a century earlier.

The control from the all-powerful centre was stifling and the marginal freedom to act which was allowed was accompanied by excessive controls that inhibited most people, particularly those in authority, from any innovation or risk taking. It was a situation which all young men had encountered before, irrespective of their job or position, and the question was not if but when they would conform to the established rules. Finally, to guarantee absolute adherence to laid-down rules and an unwavering ideological subscription to the wisdom of those who governed us, there were the itinerant depot inspectors, whose purpose in life was to hunt out errors of omission and commission by errant employees, weak managers and deviants. Everyone held them in awe and dreaded their unannounced arrival.

That was the climate in which we, the young, solo–playing, rule-challenging gang of four, found ourselves repeatedly discussing what were essentially minor changes and improvements to, or elimination of, systems that irked and delayed us. We knew that those like Charlie who had experienced the dangers of active service were even more reluctant than we were to conform unquestioningly, but there was little joy and even less prospect of promotion or better pay if they didn't. Nevertheless, after one particularly bad day we determined to speak up and confront Charlie with a proposition. We had debated and agreed it over our lunchtime card game, which unhappily coincided with one of Mrs Watson the cashier's periodic bouts of illness, as a result of which she had to go home sick. Normally when she was due to be absent, as at holiday times, she prepared the outline wages sheets in advance, omitting only weekly variables such as overtime payments or sickness absence deductions, but on this occasion there had been no time to do so. Charlie the Section Leader, who was expected to deputise when Mrs Watson was away, although he made little secret of his dislike for doing so, was called in to discuss this with Mr Lindsey in the glass-fronted box which passed as the Chief Clerk's office. There was a loud, heated debate, which most of us in the general office found little difficulty in following, in which Charlie clearly articulated his reluctance to do so on this occasion; using the forceful approach he had developed as a squadron leader in the RAF, he seemed unprepared to be persuaded or coerced, a stance he emphasised when all of us heard the ringing term 'Bullshit' above the angry debate. There were red faces and more mutterings before ultimately Charlie, in high dudgeon, emerged looking extremely displeased, so it was with a lack of political acumen or sense of timing that Alan Maguire and I made our approach to discuss our scheme to improve the accuracy of the documentation going to the warehouse. We believed it would be beneficial to all concerned but it required Charlie's consent; it was with some surprise and dismay that we saw his red face, with pulsating veins on his forehead, looking at us as he said briefly and vehemently, 'Piss off.'

We retired crestfallen, yet within twenty-four hours the world had changed as first Alan was called in to the Chief Clerk's office, to be told that he was going to be appointed Stock Recording Clerk – which would certainly enable us to reopen the previous day's debate with Charlie; and then I was told that I would be required on this occasion to deputise for Mrs Watson in the preparation of the weekly wages sheets. From the briefing it seemed, however, that the importance of accuracy in the calculation of overtime and tax deductions was subordinate to the need not to discuss with anyone what individuals were paid – although I could have told Mr Lindsey that a collective debate took place most Fridays in the packing room when pay packets were opened and examined in great detail, and that there were no secrets between people on broadly equal pay. The gravity of the task I was undertaking was emphasised by the close supervision I was to have when I was actually calculating tax due, although I knew that I could do this mechanical task comfortably and allow anyone to check whatever they wanted, whenever they wanted to, afterwards. Once again my simple gifts of clear handwriting, a good memory and absolute concentration enabled me to present a completed payroll with which no one could have found fault, while I gained by understanding for the first time the way in which tax tables were computed and how simple cross-balancing of columns of figures could guarantee a perfectly accurate result. Even better, there was fun to be derived from deciphering the scribbled signatures on the time-clock rolls, even if recording in red ink the minutes lost in the time book was tedious, and this task enabled me to study closely the handwriting of the Chief Storekeeper and the Section Leaders. It was soon to come in very useful in learning how to forge their initials, required when errors had been made by me, or my closest companions, even before a docket had been released to the stores. True, it was forgery — but it was forgery done with good intent to avoid a tedious and time-consuming, irrelevant procedure.

As Deputy Cashier I now began to visit the post office regularly, with an obligatory escort, to purchase the National Insurance stamps required for the week's payroll before affixing them by mouth and hand to individual record cards; and I went regularly to the bank in one of the delivery vans on Fridays, when I was drawing the wages cheque to prepare the weekly pay packet.

Pay days always began and ended excitingly, as first there was the trip in the van holding the cheque I'd written carefully, which had been signed by both the District Manager and the Chief Clerk as required by the rules, before presenting it to the teller at Lloyds Bank in Grey Street. The bank was in an elegant, Georgian building in the most graceful street in Newcastle, and the teller had been chosen no doubt to match the quality of the surroundings. A man in his early fifties, he was always perfectly groomed, frequently in an elegant, grey, Prince of Wales check suit, and in summer he always wore a silver rose clip in his buttonholed left lapel in which was a small rose, freshly cut daily. The cheque would be accompanied by my calculation from the payroll of the number of £5 notes, £1 notes, ten-shilling notes, and the amount of silver and copper coins required to complete the pay packets; all of these were then meticulously and slowly counted out for me before being placed in the green drawstring bag I carried. I never once addressed the teller by name in all my visits, nor did he deign to speak to me, but rather he observed me with a slightly wrinkled nose or puckered eyebrow above his carefully clipped moustache; on other occasions, when I accompanied Mrs Watson in the subordinate role of escort, I noted that she always had a warmer reception. My return to the cashier's office would be followed by re-sorting the cash into the required individual amounts and agreeing the balance before inserting it into the pay envelopes I had pre-written, which listed on the outside the calculation of the gross and net amount with details of the additions and deductions, in effect duplicating the payroll sheet. In my view this was a wholly unnecessary duplication, but bearing in mind Charlie's dismissive 'Piss off' it was only much later that I was able to encourage the introduction of a pay slip, which was a perforated duplicate copy of the payroll sheet prepared at the same time.

Charlie was happy because he had escaped the tedium of having to spend some hours concentrating on boring figures with the possibility of a tedious search if, as usually happened, they didn't balance first time; Mr Lindsey was happy because his protégé had performed skilfully a task that was viewed as important and confidential; and I was happy to have found a job that was much more interesting than the daily routine of preparing sales dockets. When Mrs Watson recovered and returned, I assumed gradually the unofficial role of Deputy Cashier.

As a result of this duty I now found myself alternating with Mrs Watson on Saturday mornings, which always required a visit to the bank to lodge any cheques received that day or the substantial amounts of cash from retail transactions which had been conducted on Friday afternoon, after the pay-day visit to the bank had been made. Since Saturday was also a day on which I paid a brief visit to the local pub en route to my Saturday afternoon cricket in the summer, and since the visit to the bank was paid for from petty cash, this became a more pleasant way of spending a large part of the mandatory three hours and twenty minutes' working time. One Saturday, having pocketed the bus fare but walked slowly to the bank, and after depositing the cash and being uplifted by the sight of the splendidly attired teller, I realised as I left that I would have to hurry back to the depot, using the fare on the return journey, otherwise the depot would be locked or at best I would keep somebody waiting which would seriously displease them. I was still thinking about the impending cricket match when I stepped off the bus close to the Haymarket, and at first I didn't notice that virtually everyone was passing me in the opposite direction, or that they seemed more excitable and were hurrying more than usual. It was only when I got to the top of Northumberland Street and was about to cross the road that I realised I was alone in an area normally crowded with people; lumbering towards me were three enormous, brown bears with chains dangling from their legs. At first I thought it was one of the King's College student 'rag' activities, but realised as they got nearer that this was serious. Fortunately the bears were hampered in their movements by their chains, while a pursuing uniformed man cracked a large whip as he struggled vainly to regain control. I decided that discretion was the better part of valour as I fled, and it was only later I found out that the bears, which were part of an act due to perform at the Palace Theatre, were being paraded around the city centre as a promotional gimmick when they had decided to take matters into their own hands – or paws – and have some enjoyment, rather as I had done on my visit to the bank.

Curiously this incident occurred very close to another and bore a startling resemblance to it. At home we had all experienced the irritation of being pursued by Roger the dog after leaving home for work; he was always reluctant to return home, irrespective of the anger or scorn heaped upon him. On this particular morning I happened to turn and saw Roger surreptitiously shadowing me as I approached the bus stop on the corner of Elswick Row and Elswick Road, outside Beysen's, the cake shop. I instructed him to 'Go home' in a loud voice and with a pointed finger; he retreated round the corner as I stood looking in the direction of the bus, but out of the corner of my eye I saw him reappear in his usual manner on these occasions with bent legs, drooped ears and tail, in a grovelling crawl. I told him several times to 'Go home', each more angry than the previous since there was still no sign of the bus: but he only lay prostrate on the pavement with his head flat to the ground, his ears collapsed and his eyes uplifted in the pleading manner with which we were all so familiar – when suddenly he rose, turned and ran swiftly back in the direction of the house. As I was pondering on my successful tactics in causing this remarkable change of mind on his part, I turned to see a large bull snorting, steaming and dripping saliva, running along the middle of Elswick Road; only then did I notice the absence of people and traffic. It was too late and too dangerous to try to make my escape as Roger had done, so I flattened myself as best I could against the lamppost and watched the mad beast charge past. The bull had escaped from the pens outside the abattoir on Scotswood Road, had attacked and scattered people and vehicles, behaviour with which Roger was no doubt extremely familiar because of his reputation for foraging around the abattoir regularly; it also explained how he had picked up the signals long before I did and had made his escape. The bull unfortunately didn't and, as the *Evening Chronicle* informed us later that day, had been cornered and shot somewhere in Fenham. Meanwhile I, having survived these potentially fatal encounters with wild animals, now learned when I reached work, late and still shaken, that the Depot Inspectors had arrived.

The Depot Inspectors were talked about in hushed terms and their image so soon after the end of the war was very similar to that of the

Gestapo or any other secret police force – broadly that of unlistening brutes who swept in unannounced to examine documents and look for errors. This caused dark stories to circulate freely about people having left the company in disgrace after their visits, particularly those who were working in the cashier's office or the stock recording office, where errors or dubious actions might lead to a loss of cash or goods. While their visits were never pre-announced, there was unlikely to be more than a two-year gap between them and once there they would stay for several weeks, during which no individual or document would escape their scrutiny and no error, no matter how trivial, would remain uninvestigated. When I met them I realised quickly that the image I had conjured up of Gestapo-like figures could not have been more accurate.

John Varley, the Chief Depot Inspector, was a small, stooping man with a skull-like face above hunched shoulders, who moved by pivoting his whole body from side to side. He wore steel-rimmed glasses and had a habit of constantly licking his lips when talking to you, with his head tilted slightly and a faint mocking smile on his lips, as if anticipating some fatal error on your part. He was accompanied by a Mr Abrahams, a middle-aged man yet younger than Mr Varley, who wore a bland expression and was clearly the accomplice, with a deliberately disarming slowness of thought and speech but whom you knew was equally deadly. Having arrived at 9a.m. and presented their credentials to the Chief Clerk, they wasted no time in small talk but immediately set about their business, with their first two points of call being – predictably – the cashier's office and the stock recording clerk's office. There they completed an immediate check of cash to strike a balance, followed by a physical stock count in the warehouse, and from these two important datum points proceeded to work outwards and backwards to the last time they had visited. It was a mammoth task, which always ensured the visit lasted several weeks; as each batch of documents was checked in the most excruciating detail to ascertain, for instance, that every single invoice set had been accounted for, they affixed their scrutineer's stamp with a little brass cylinder held by a chain from their waistcoats. When pressed downwards against the document it would rotate a hidden seal to imprint their initials, which they completed by hand with the date of the check. Their questions were unsmiling and objective; they avoided conversation other than to say 'Good morning' when they arrived and 'Good evening' when they left. Their eyes appeared to be everywhere and there was a genuine sense of disquiet among the staff, although the Newcastle depot need not have worried because their standards were known to be high – a tribute to the grip that Mr Lindsey exercised on the activities and the rigidity of the systems. They observed the writing of dockets and the answering of telephone calls, but they were much more concerned with the factual accuracy of what was done. They inspected the timekeeping records of individuals and their absence records, they rechecked income tax calculations, and even checked whether or not the black and red signals in the card index of customers accounts were updated immediately. In their eyes effort counted for little; absolute adherence was all.

When the physical stock count was compared with the stock records there were, unusually, a substantial number of discrepancies. At the time the Stock Recording Clerk was a newly appointed, tall, young Scotsman, a very presentable, well-spoken and polite young man whom we had all been made aware had been identified for promotion as a future salesman – a matter that gave us a certain amount of irritation, because his qualifications seemed only to be what we'd overheard Mr Nesbit describe as his 'imposing appearance', rather than his brainpower. He seemed to us to be 'as dim as a Toc H lamp', a description we'd heard Frank Keely use. Given the physical stature of three of us in the quartet, we were not prepared to acknowledge that what we lacked in height was not more than compensated by our superior brainpower, but the prospect of this tall, polite, but dim young man being rewarded with a brand-new, fully expensed motorcar seemed to us to be a rather spiteful act. It was because of his impending promotion to a newly created role of Sales Trainee that he was being grounded in the mechanics of the business, and it was for that reason that he had been appointed recently to the job of Stock Recording Clerk. We knew that he would not have been Mr Lindsey's choice, but nevertheless it had happened; and now when the stock count had been taken by the inspectors a substantial number of errors had been revealed. Of course there was always the possibility that the losses were real, that there was some malpractice or theft from the stores – perhaps because the store staff had lost their usual meticulous attention to detail. Neither seemed likely, and in the ensuing investigation it was revealed that all the many discrepancies had been caused by inaccurate posting of transactions to the stock record. While initially we were pleased that justice seemed likely to prevail, our smugness was premature, because the clerical shambles did nothing to diminish his promotion prospects; while in the process of determining that it was his carelessness that was responsible, the inspectors pored over alterations to documents. My heart missed a beat, realising that my own harmless and well-intentioned forgeries of signatures on alterations might be revealed and bring about my downfall.

There was also a serious debate between the Depot Inspectors and the Chief Clerk about the wisdom of allowing me, at 'such a tender age', to compile the payroll and in the process exercise 'primary control over the cash' in the absence of the cashier; but eventually the cadaverous Mr Varley and his smiling, monosyllabic assistant Mr Abrahams were satisfied and left, bequeathing me a lexicon of new and previously unfamiliar terms such as 'the dangers of collusion', 'compensating errors' and 'heavily disguised defalcation'. This visit confirmed Dunlop's obsessive belief that every single penny invested in assets or paid out in cash for services had to be accounted for exactly, whatever the cost in so doing, while by contrast what their investigations revealed was that appointments were often decided on a subjective basis that had no logic if viewed against past results.

Shortly afterwards Ken, the salesman-in-waiting, was quietly removed from the post of Stock Recording Clerk while I, retaining my duties as

Deputy Cashier, was told I had been selected to attend a week-long course for management trainees at Fort Dunlop, during which I would be accommodated at the Arden Hotel in New Street, Birmingham. We were to travel there on the Sunday, present ourselves at Fort Dunlop at 8.30 on the Monday morning, and the course would finish on the following Friday afternoon. This was to be yet another first, because I had neither been to Birmingham nor stayed in a hotel before. It's true that I had been to London to watch Newcastle United play in a Cup Final, but that was to stay with friends working in the Civil Service who were lodged in dormitories in a youth hostel in Balham – conditions not dissimilar to Havelock Street. This was to be much grander. The other trainees, all aged between eighteen and twenty-five, were also lodged in the Arden or its sister hotel the Cobden; we travelled together by tram from Steelhouse Lane to the Dunlop factory on Tyburn Road, Erdington, after a walk through the postwar reconstruction of Birmingham, which resembled one huge building site. Fort Dunlop, the UK Tyre Group's headquarters, was a huge complex covering 275 acres in an area that was the heart of the booming British motor industry, surrounded by familiar names such as Pressed Steel, Fisher Ludlow, SU Carburettors and dozens of others. There were 20,000 people who worked on the Dunlop site alone, and as we disembarked from the rattling tram to walk down the spur road to the commercial offices of Fort Dunlop it was like being in a crowd leaving a football match which your team had lost very heavily, since most people looked as grim and miserable as the weather or the noisy, smelly atmosphere.

But we trainees had no negative feelings, and after a hesitant request for directions to the uniformed commissionaire, with his sergeant-major bearing, black, patent-leather cross belt and swagger stick, we found ourselves in the bare training-course assembly room. A few hesitant introductions were made among the newly met participants, who had come from all over Scotland, Wales, Northern Ireland, London and the Midlands. We were of different sizes, shapes, religions, with different accents and varying interests or expectations – of which mine were probably as low as any other. I was there because I was there, I had no idea what was going to be required of me and I had no real expectations for the outcome.

Shortly after 8.45 in walked a stooping, balding, moustachioed gentleman smoking a cigarette, who in a languid, chain-smoking style talked to us monotonously in an upper-crust voice about the course content in which we were going to immerse ourselves for the week. The principal aim was to be to add an overview of the great Dunlop empire at home and abroad to the basic knowledge we had gained at depot level, with particular, but not exclusive, emphasis on the major product group – tyres. He spoke to us in the manner of a country vicar, albeit in a badly attended rural church, and he seemed even more disinterested in us than he was in the course which was to follow. Nevertheless he continued, chain smoking and drawling absent-mindedly, until shortly before 9.30 when he announced that we were to be joined by the Sales Director, Mr R.C. Hiam, and two of his senior lieutenants, Mr Denis Hays and Mr Gilbert H. Way; as he finished this explanation the door opened and in walked three impeccably groomed, seriously important-looking men, whom I described to my mother afterwards as being so crisp in their appearance that 'It looked as though they had been carried from their homes to the training room wrapped in cellophane.' I had thought Mr Nesbit was perfectly and expensively groomed, but these three were in a different league – not a wrinkle or a crease in their suits, not a hair out of place on their heads, not a furrow on their suntanned brows, not a speck on the virginal white cuff that appeared beneath the sleeve of their uniform, dark blue suits, while the gold cufflinks and the gold watches they wore gleamed. They seemed relaxed as they produced shining, slim, gold cigarette cases from their inner pockets, synchronously tapped the cigarettes on the outside of the cases, while the leader smiled a welcome to us as he lit up and began to speak easily, warmly and reassuringly with a mix of light humour and serious messages. His companions sought a little too hard to impress as they added their comments in a choreographed way that sounded stilted by comparison. They all looked, acted and dressed in a similar style, but Bob Hiam was different. I had seen and recognised the 'gold standard' among leaders, despite my inexperience. I was impressed by him, much more than I had been by having my own hotel room and free use of a bathroom with toilet. Over the next twenty-four hours I learned from my conversations with my course companions that they were a motley crew, who in the main had neither my intelligence nor knowledge of the business; many had precious little humour, and by Tuesday night I wondered if most of them had been selected in the first place on similar criteria to my colleague Ken. But there were one or two with flickerings of talent, prime among whom was a young man in his early twenties from Hazel Grove in Stockport, who worked at Manchester depot. He was as bright as a button, with a cheeky sense of quick-witted humour, but seemingly disinterested in working too hard; nevertheless, he was a good companion. He was knowledgeable about the business but was not really very interested by it.

We had been briefed that the visit would include a tour of the factory, the largest of its kind in Europe, as well as some of the commercial office departments related most closely to our work at the depots. Nothing had prepared me for the factory environment, and after a day spent observing and understanding the processes, I was left with an indelible loathing for the appalling conditions in which people were required to work – at best distressingly uncomfortable, and at worst dangerous. From the mill, where long rolls of latex fresh from Malayan rubber plantations were torn and noisily masticated by giant, heated calender rollers until it was sufficiently pliable for the filthy carbon-black powder to be fed to it in suffocating clouds in stifling heat, to the end of the dirty, sweaty, smelly, choking process in the deafeningly noisy mould shop, where the vulcanised, red-hot tyres were prised from the individual moulds, it seemed to me like hell on earth. If this bore any resemblance to conditions at Vickers Armstrong, and it surely did, no wonder Alan had volunteered to risk death in the skies during the war and had railed against returning to the factory floor afterwards.

The following day was little better, although it was cleaner and less dangerous, with the benefit of showing us how our efforts in producing accurate, handwritten sales dockets assisted a huge army of female operators – some young, some very old – to produce invoices, statements and sales statistics to fill the Dunlop coffers and better inform the great minds who ran this worldwide empire. Yet it was the memories – of the soulless atmosphere, of the isolation of the individual, of the voiceless but noisy air filled with the clack of Powers Samas machines and the clatter of long carriages being returned on the Burroughs machines – that remained. No wonder Roma, like Alan, had been glad to escape, after eight years of a similar but perhaps less intensively depressing environment at Vickers, for marriage in 1943.

On Monday we had been given a programme which seemed at the time to indicate how important we were because on our last night we were to dine in the 'visitors' dining room', with waitress service and extremely good food, and were to be entertained by a visit to the Hippodrome theatre, to be followed by a valedictory address by Mr R.C. Hiam at lunch on the final day. In the meantime, late on the Tuesday afternoon as we were returning to our hotel by tram after the thought-provoking factory tour, the lad from Hazel Grove and I decided we should have an evening out together on Wednesday night, for which he said he would make some enquiries about possible venues, and we agreed to meet up later that evening for a beer.

I thought as I tapped on his bedroom door at about eight o'clock that I heard voices followed by a shouted 'Wait', and a few moments later he opened the door while completing his dressing, although it struck me that he was in a rather dishevelled and distracted state. He said, 'I'll be with you in a few minutes', and as I started to follow him he put his hand out to stop me, laughed, and winking pointed to the bed, where the maid who had served us at breakfast that morning was lying naked with an almost embarrassed look on her face while managing to cover some but by no means all of herself. He went back into his room, picked up his jacket, blew her a kiss, threw something into the waste-paper bin and left, with me closing the door behind him. I felt that my progress with the opposite sex was clearly lacking something, because he seemed to be taking events at a pace that I considered impossible, but it later transpired that he had at least used some of his time with the naked maid to establish an entertaining venue for Wednesday night. It was to be the 'Barton Arms' in Aston, about halfway between our hotel and Fort Dunlop; a drink at the pub was to precede a striptease show at the Hippodrome next door, and to complete the package the smitten maid was to meet him there, not with a friend, and I was expected to return to the hotel alone – déjà vu all over again.

On Thursday night things returned to normal as we enjoyed our chaperoned visit to the variety theatre – from which 'Mr Hazel Grove' absented himself for other pleasures – followed on the final day by lunch in yet another executive dining room. There we were treated to a farewell which was encouraging and optimistic, mixed with a dash of fondness, by Mr Hiam, who in the process established himself firmly as my benchmark for public speaking and visible leadership and to whose remarks, by default or popular demand, I was obliged to respond. I had journeyed to Birmingham feeling I might have 'arrived' and that Dunlop could be the only possible career for me – unsurprisingly in the circumstances, because it was only through Dunlop's generosity that I had been exposed to experiences which I knew neither my father nor any others I knew had ever had access to, and in the process I was setting my own expectations. I had started work at Dunlop knowing nothing about business or working relationships, or of eating out or speaking up, or of restaurants or hotels or other cities: and not a lot about social graces or the opposite sex.

However, while the benefits derived from the opportunities to learn from or about previously unknown, inaccessible people, places and protocol fed my increasingly optimistic view of the future, all this was put sharply and disappointingly into perspective by learning at the very end of our visit that we were a very much lower caste of trainee. There was a higher level, a university graduate cadre, who were simultaneously but separately being groomed over a longer course, in a better hotel, for stardom in the imperial outreaches of the Dunlop globe, while I and the others like me were to be at best the foot soldiers. That, allied to the chilling prospect that failure for me would end the prospect of breaking out of the cycle of working-class life, to be condemned to work on the shop floor of a Dunlop tyre factory or a Vickers machine shop or the marginally better but still depressing mass office conditions of either, made me think very carefully and realistically about my prospects. Was it back to great-grandfather again, who had served twenty years in the colours, admittedly without wounds but without promotion either, and whose only stroke of good fortune appeared to have been winning the Bangalore Sweepstake or ill gains from the sacking of Delhi after the mutiny? Was my life in business going to be a rerun of his but without the booty? Well, we would have to see about that.

I left, as did the others, with pledges to keep in touch, while the memory of the smooth, suave, charismatic personality of Bob Hiam drove out even the image of the coquettish, naked maid who had succumbed so readily to the easy and freely offered charms of the young man from Hazel Grove – from whom I never heard again.

38

THE KING IS DEAD . . .

A
s the end of 1951 approached, the dismantling by events of
the old domestic order of a once-unified household headed
by Ma and Pop, in almost absolute control, was increasingly
evident. This order had survived for over thirty years with
very few changes, other than Roma's departure after her marriage in
1943 and the lengthy though temporary absences of Alan and Vincent on
active service, and there had been short-term additions to the household
in the shape of Alan's late first wife May, her sister Peggy even more
briefly and a series of paying lodgers who were either servicemen or
civilians. Throughout this long period we had lived happily within a
minimal household budget constantly under strain, financed principally
from Pop's wages as an employee of Newcastle Corporation Transport
and in the shadow of war – enduring it, preparing for it or recovering
from it. Each time the gross domestic income had swelled, our temporary
bubble of affluence had burst soon afterwards and we had returned
quickly to our normal state of poverty. Nevertheless there had been
moments of great promise during 1951, prime among which was
Newcastle winning the FA Cup in convincing style for the first time
since I was born. There should have been one also from the much-
trumpeted Festival of Britain on London's South Bank, although its
appeal barely reached beyond the Home Counties; while yet another war,
this time in Korea, came to an end. As if to prove every silver lining has
a cloud, Churchill's return to power in October came after Ernie Bevin,
on whose knee I had been dangled as a baby, died; the king had an

operation for lung cancer; and Randolph Turpin lost his world middleweight crown to Sugar Ray Robinson in a rematch. The BBC, meanwhile, thought the time ripe to re-establish pre-war order rather than perpetuate wartime camaraderie, with its policy statement that in future there would be 'no regional accents and no women announcers' for news bulletins. Some things just didn't change – a view underscored when a Mass Observation Poll confirmed that Mrs Average Housewife worked fifteen hours per day: knowledge that Ma for one didn't need to have corroborated.

The two principal supporting contributors to the household budget emphasised the march of time by moving on and out after their marriages. Alan remarried a local girl, Agnes Charlton, whom he had met in the newsagent's shop where I had been and Sydney still was employed as a paperboy, while Vincent was due in late December to marry a schoolteacher, Joan Britton, from an allegedly wealthy family. Alan was still struggling to come to terms with his work on the shop floor of Vickers Armstrong, far removed from the glamour and vicarious pleasures of being a much-feted member of an elite bomber squadron; his seething frustration often boiled over in bouts of ill temper which his dedicated pursuit of his ancillary role as a daring goalkeeper in departmental works sides at Vickers helped to alleviate. However, before he remarried he gave up the unequal struggle with his inner self and followed Pop onto the buses, initially as a conductor – a sad reminder of how difficult it was to change the pattern of a working-class inheritance without educational success.

Meanwhile, Vincent was pursuing his own erratic, undulating course, having successfully overcome the first two educational hurdles of the scholarship and school-certificate examinations, been refused at the officers' training 'water jump', then sadly fallen at the university final examinations; but, maintaining the horseracing analogy, he had remounted before falling finally and irretrievably at the second attempt. Sadly but predictably all this was traceable back to his absences from school many years before, during Ma's illness, when he had assumed the role of daily carer-in-chief and more specifically washerwoman to the family. He had at this stage lost crucial time when his fifth-form classmates were being introduced to calculus, a deficiency he never remedied, while his painful, self-torturing attempts to understand the incomprehensible had only drawn forth further scorn when the female lecturer had pleaded with him, 'Please, please, Mr Cassidy, move to the back of the lecture theatre; your baffled look is putting me off.' Things didn't improve thereafter either, owing principally to his selfless support for Ma when he joined Richardson's Leather Works in order to secure immediate income; this work experience, together with his voluntarily taken Intermediate B.Sc. studies, automatically removed any choice of degree course from him when he became entitled to a National Serviceman's Grant to undertake a degree programme. He knew in 1947 what he hadn't known in 1945 when he was conscripted – that English Language and Literature was the only sensible course to pursue; but he didn't and couldn't pursue it, and so with great sadness he left university to job-hunt again. Although he avoided the trap of automatically going back to Richardson's by his decision to join the international giant Procter & Gamble, or more prosaically its Newcastle base of Thomas Hedley & Co., as a research laboratory assistant, the portents were not good. Within two years he was to marry, and once again the household finances would take their predictably regressive step. Joan, the young, university-educated schoolteacher from a 'better class background', must have known what potentially lay in store for her when she was brought home to meet the family at 5 Havelock Street. First Ma stopped being busy in her unending cycle of chores, then Pop emerged from the scullery in his usual semi-undressed state to meet her, while I lounged nonchalantly reading and wheezing on the chaise longue with the thick book substitute for a broken caster, and Sydney lay sprawled under the kitchen table composing a fan-mail letter to his movie hero of the moment, Humphrey Bogart.

Roma's potential escape through education had been prematurely ended due solely to the fact she was a girl and our collective financial need overrode any personal ambitions, with Ma insisting she obtained 'suitable' paid work sooner rather than later; while Alan's prospects had been terminally damaged by his failure to pass the scholarship examination. Although Vincent had done better than either, his university education had ended prematurely – but even that promised much better career prospects than might otherwise have been the case.

Rex, meanwhile, was studying and working with his usual diligence although unfortunately, because of his apprentice status, he was not able to contribute to the family budget. When he left the grammar school in July 1947 he had, on the advice of the Youth Employment Bureau and as was expected and indeed required, taken gainful employment while waiting for his school certificate results. His job was Junior Clerk at the local offices of the PAC, the government's Public Assistance Committee, which provided financial relief for the unemployed and their dependants; their very attendance was a reminder, if any was needed, of the hardships of being unemployed, while the dingy premises of the PAC made sure they did not expect too much by way of relief. Happy though Rex was at the PAC under the tutelage of Miss Thwaite, he quietly nurtured a deep conviction that he would achieve his personal agenda – which included self-esteem, public recognition and wealth – by pursuing his interest in some branch of science. These were seeds planted initially by Vincent's creation of a home laboratory, further nurtured in his grammar-school studies, and fertilised by Pop's only sister Auntie Minnie, who as Rex's godmother had subsequently taken him literally to her ample bosom. He was undoubtedly an attractive child, exceptional in a noisy household by being extremely quiet; it was said, no doubt with a touch of hyperbole, that he hadn't spoken for the first three years of his life. He had an appealing face topped by a mass of Shirley Temple-like curls; these attributes had combined to cause Auntie Minnie to seek permission, usually readily granted, to take Rex out on occasions and regularly if not frequently to have him stay overnight with her in her flat in Strickland Street. There she lavished affection on him as he became a willing respondent to her invitations, which he unsurprisingly loved, no doubt just as he found sleeping with her in the only bed in her flat an experience that was both physically and emotionally comforting.

However, it was during these early days that Auntie Minnie implanted the seeds of some of his ambitions by her constant references to her eldest brother, JP, to whom she was very close. He was the one who had achieved a wealthy and privileged lifestyle, owning a large residence in a desirable area of north London and having a half-share in a partnership owning a pharmacy in Great Portland Street, in which he practised. This was the ultimate determinant of Rex's career choice, as his leaving grammar school in 1947 coincided with the final preparations by the postwar Labour government for the creation of a National Health Service in 1948. These two steps converged to create the new opportunity with Timothy Whites & Taylors; anticipating the need for more dispensing pharmacists to cope with the expected demand for free medicine, they advertised for young school leavers with a good academic record to undertake a formal apprenticeship in pharmacy, where qualification could be achieved only by a combination of study and work experience. In a moment of inspiration Rex realised that he could with one step escape from the dinginess and drudgery of the PAC, follow in JP's footsteps without the need for unattainable financial support, and all that was needed was for him to achieve the required Matriculation standard in the school certificate. Without a moment's hesitation he used the office telephone to contact the grammar school, spoke to Canon Cunningham who, even though the results had not then been formally announced, immediately checked and confirmed to Rex that he had the required number of distinctions and credits to entitle him to Matriculation status. Rex knew immediately that he could take a major step and almost had one foot on the ladder to success.

A sequence of events swiftly followed in which he replied to the advertisement and was accompanied by an impeccably groomed Pop to meet Mr Davis, the Regional Manager; the two men clearly got on extremely well together, the apprenticeship documents were formally signed and sealed, and Rex was launched on a five-year course of study. At the end of 1951 it was approaching its conclusion, as he would be required to satisfy the examiners that he should be admitted to membership of the Pharmaceutical Society of Great Britain in the following year. He knew also, of course, that once he had taken his finals, win or lose, his deferred National Service would be activated and by the time he was demobbed any financial support from him for the family would be for an extremely limited period.

My health, still a matter for concern, had caused my educational continuity to be disrupted; my 'dejected' deferment offered no promise of an early resolution, while my modest yet welcome contribution to domestic finances eased at least some pressures. Sydney had now left St Aloysius' school, which Alan had attended before him, and after a short, unhappy stint in a local solicitor's practice as an office boy had decided to look for employment with more attractive prospects. He was due to visit the same Youth Employment Bureau most of us had been to some years before, but chose a lunchtime to ask Pop where Ellison Place was – the bureau's location – how to get there and roughly how much time the journey would take him. Pop was at home because he was working a late shift, while I had returned from Dunlop for lunch on a non-solo-playing day; as I was settling down to my meal – a standard in Ma's low-cost repertoire of liver on this occasion, so overcooked it closely resembled one of Mr Atwell's leather shoe soles – Sydney asked his questions. Pop's reaction to this simple request suggested that his liver was not in the best condition either. 'You don't know what? Where Ellison Place is? When I was your age I knew the name of every street in Newcastle', after which he gave a loud snort of contempt for what he obviously saw as culpable ignorance. Sydney, however, had demonstrated many times before that he was his father's son, with his father's prickly temperament, and as such was able to return fire with equally predictable salvoes.

'Yes,' he said scathingly, 'but your father was obviously a bloody sight more intelligent than mine is', and with that he glared menacingly at Pop, who produced a passable impersonation of a man unintentionally treading on very hot coals. His face simultaneously turned the colour of a Victoria plum and as his brain raced to connect to his mechanically moving, soundless lips, Ma stepped in to pacify him and with a barely concealed smile gently chide Sydney about swearing. Sydney went along, got the job and started work in the packing room of the Co-operative Wholesale Society Ltd in Waterloo Street.

Early in 1952, on a typically cold, inhospitable day, I reached my nineteenth birthday, just as the world was about to change for ever; a week later, on 7 February, the nation was informed that the king had died 'peacefully in his sleep at Sandringham'. Thus ended a reign that had begun in turmoil following the death of his father and the abdication of his brother, with the imposition of the burden of sovereignty on a shy man afflicted with a stammer; he had lived his early years in the belief that some of his physical shortcomings would be shielded by the semi-anonymity that he would have been afforded as brother to the king and that would have enabled him and his wife to live the normal, comfortable life of wealthy aristocrats. He had accepted this burden without complaint, at least publicly; he had remained steadfastly in London during the wartime blitz, where he formed a partnership with the 'old warrior', my hero Winston Churchill, who as a loyal and respectful subject had personified with the king the unity of the British people – at least to me as a reverential schoolboy. Now the king, the third in my lifetime, was dead and the nation mourned.

Our new sovereign was to be the Princess Elizabeth who, as the nation was informed, was now cancelling her intended visit to Australia and New Zealand, as her father had been obliged to do the previous year because of his failing health, to return home from Kenya as queen, while the due process began to establish the date of the coronation.

In the meantime it seemed Britain would recover from this shock and go on much as it had done in the previous nineteen years of my life, with occasional flashes of parochial enjoyment outnumbered by events which demonstrated there would be little change in the next nineteen years either. On a rare high note in May I watched Newcastle United beat Arsenal 1–0 at Wembley in the Cup Final, the first time in over sixty years that a club had won the Cup twice running; while the Iron Curtain, a term which Winston Churchill had coined in 1946, fell across Europe as the Cold War became colder. In addition the Middle East and Africa became global tinderboxes threatening to ignite even more wars, as revolution overthrew King Farouk in Egypt, a Harrow schoolboy called Prince Hussein succeeded his father as king of Jordan after his father's assassination in Jerusalem, and Britain, already demolishing the empire, was faced with a serious Mau Mau uprising in Kenya. America had moved up a gear by testing H-bombs as Britain was testing atomic bombs abroad, while on government orders formal Civil Defence organisations and routines had been established at all workplaces to respond to a potential Russian nuclear strike. At Dunlop I had been appointed a member of the official Civil Defence team, for which I was to receive 'an annual honorarium of five pounds'; I had been trained to deal with nuclear fallout and reintroduced to the beneficial properties of the stirrup pump and a bucket of sand if attacked. As the same Britain struggled to maintain old disciplines at home, Derek Bentley was hanged for the murder of a policeman carried out by his sixteen-year-old accomplice Christopher Craig, who escaped the noose; the last London tram was retired; a new Agatha Christie play, *The Mousetrap*, opened; and nearly seven years after the end of the war food was still rigidly rationed.

All of which seemed pretty much to mirror the experience of the Cassidy family. Pop reached sixty years of age and was now within sight of his own mandatory retirement date – still in the same job he'd taken in 1919 as Roma was being born; she, meanwhile, was pregnant with her fourth child, due before the end of 1952. Alan had a daughter who was baptised Barbara; Vincent, who had married Joan in December 1951, was making steady if unspectacular progress in his job and since Joan was working they could now afford to move to their own self-contained flat in a large Victorian house not far away from Havelock Street in Park Road – a marked improvement from the rooms that they rented from a widow living in the same house. The manner of their moving also emphasised how little things had changed, because like our own house move in 1940 a man with a hand-barrow completed it in one trip. The man this time was Freddie Scholar, a local rag-and-bone merchant, who in his rare respectable periods doubled as an odd-job man and handled the removal without the skills that I had observed so many years earlier when Uncle Sam had moved us to Havelock Street. Vincent and Joan's prized possession – one of not very many – was a large, mirror-fronted wardrobe, which was extremely heavy and which overhung the barrow at the front and sides, while Park Road where their new flat was located was an extremely steep street running from Elswick Road down towards the Tyne. Observing the dangers of this while walking alongside the barrow, more as guide and guardian than helper, Vincent remarked to Freddie Scholar that he should be very careful given the steepness of the incline thinking, much more self-interestedly on this occasion, about the security and well-being of his few possessions than he was about Freddie Scholar. It soon became apparent that his warning was well merited, if unheeded, for suddenly the barrow began to accelerate as Vincent, now breaking into a trot, enquired urgently what Freddie could do to apply a brake if the barrow looked like running out of control. The by-now-breathless Freddie, running at full tilt said 'Do this', and immediately turned the barrow into the high kerb; the result was that although the barrow did indeed stop dead in its tracks, the wardrobe did not and was precipitately shot, fortunately on its back, across the pavement to be arrested finally by the garden wall opposite. Apart from the fact that the wardrobe door never closed properly again no great damage was sustained, while the move had been carried out extremely economically.

Rex was having at the time his own flirtations with disaster; he had sat his qualifying examination in Edinburgh, only to be 'referred' in one of the set subjects by a narrow margin. Both because of the quality of his performance overall and the need to enlarge the qualified pharmacist population to meet the now alarmingly rising demand, he was allowed to resit the subject, again in Edinburgh, a few weeks later. There was no mistake this time and before he left Edinburgh he was duly announced as having qualified as a Member of the Pharmaceutical Society of Great Britain; given that he had both completed successfully the academic papers and the required number of hours' practical dispensing of medicines under qualified pharmaceutical supervision, he was entitled to practise immediately. For a few short weeks he did so as a locum pharmacist, on a handsome income compared to his previously modest apprenticeship wage, with immediate benefit to the family; since this was the first of what were to be many subsequent successes for the family, it was greeted appropriately with the ecstatic approval it deserved. With the money he gave Ma from his first month's salary the old kitchen range in Havelock Street, which Pop had spent so many hours black leading, was ripped out and a new, modern, marble fireplace was substituted. After the second month he bought Ma a wristwatch at Marks & Spencer – the first she had ever owned, which she wore until the day she died – and after this short, heady period he was enlisted as a member of Her Majesty's armed forces.

I continued quietly consolidating my reputation as a thoughtful clerk at Dunlop, as well as enjoying myself playing cricket with a minor league club and wrestling with the consequences on my promising career of continued deferment from National Service. Sydney steadily established his value at the CWS and was promoted from wrapping parcels to train in their footwear department, while looking forward to his National Service the following year.

The Cassidy family needed some reassurance that it might yet fulfil its early promise, if not repay fully the time and effort Ma and Pop had invested in shaping us; any appraisal of progress, internal or external, at this time would have concluded at best 'can do better' or at worst, 'lacks promise'.

In a minor announcement in December, the time-bomb exploded which had been ticking away since the end of the 1914–18 war and which was to trigger fundamental changes in the attitudes and structure of society, the upstairs-and-downstairs culture, in relationships between the 'haves' and the 'have nots', the managers and the managed, the wealthy and the poor: but few people at the time would have recognised its potential impact or have guessed the enormity of its consequences. It was disguised in the announcement, on 8 December 1952, that the queen had given her permission to allow the coronation ceremony to be televised. The immediate consequence was that those who could afford it began acquiring a television set in readiness for the following June, while those who couldn't made arrangements to watch others' televisions. Without that decision – coming as it did at a time when growing affluence had already been catalysed by the first postwar Labour government – and without the introduction of the low-cost package holiday, which itself derived from increased affluence and universal television ownership, it is doubtful that society could have changed so radically or in such a short space of time.

Yet had social attitudes not changed so dramatically, the outcome for the Cassidy family and for hundreds of thousands of other working-class families would have been very different. It is simply inconceivable that if the old order hadn't given way to a 'new society', Alan would ultimately have become a works manager, Vincent would have become a personnel director in a pharmaceutical business, Rex would have become a director with a major Swiss pharmaceutical company and lived most of his life in Switzerland, or that Sydney would have been so successful in the footwear industry at home and abroad.

After many trials and tribulations, and only as I turned forty, I was appointed a company director and went on to become the chairman or a director of a number of public companies. The first occurred long after my father's death, and as my mother was dying.

Had they still been alive, I think he would have derived most pleasure from the fact that I was for a time chairman of Boddingtons of Manchester and Newcastle United, interests so close to his own; whereas Ma would probably have been more pleased at my public stance on corporate governance issues, irrespective of the personal discomfort or cost. Both would have enjoyed hearing about the lives of the great and good that I met.

Neither needed to have seen or experienced financial benefits from our progress to say 'This is my son . . .', 'This is my daughter . . .' or 'These are my children' with any more pride than they had done in childhood.

In the end the prayers, the efforts, the hopes, the endless hours spent educating and developing their children, achieved the required result as far as Barbara and Henry Edward Cassidy were concerned. Sadly, he knew little of it and enjoyed the fruits of it less than she did, while she saw only the beginning of its flowering. Yet without the death of the king and the dawn of a new Elizabethan age, who knows whether anything would have changed? After all, there had been no good reason for society to have behaved as it did; it was simply 'the way things were'.